H

THE
Mushroom
Book

THE
Mushroom
Book

THOMAS LÆSSØE

GARY LINCOFF   ANNA DEL CONTE

Photography by
NEIL FLETCHER

A DK PUBLISHING BOOK

Visit us on the worldwide web at
http:// www.dk.com

PROJECT EDITOR Bella Pringle
US EDITOR Mary Sutherland
PROJECT ART EDITOR Sharon Moore
DESIGN ASSISTANT Murdo Culver
MANAGING EDITOR Mary-Clare Jerram
MANAGING ART EDITOR Amanda Lunn

**ILLUSTRATION RESEARCH AND
COMMISSION BY** Mustafa Sami

PRODUCTION CONTROLLER Alison Jones

US CONSULTANT Gary Lincoff

First American Edition, 1996
2 4 6 8 10 9 7 5 3 1

Published in the United States by DK Publishing, Inc.
95 Madison Avenue, New York, New York 10016
Copyright © 1996 Dorling Kindersley Limited, London
Text copyright © 1996 Thomas Læssøe

Library of Congress Cataloging-in-Publication Data

Læssøe, Thomas.
    The mushroom book / by Thomas Læssøe ; with recipes by Anna Del
Conte. — 1st American ed.
    p.   cm.
    Includes index.
    ISBN 0–7894–1073–7
    1. Mushrooms—Identification. 2. Mushrooms, Edible—Identification.
3. Mushrooms—Pictorial works. 4. Mushrooms, Edible—Pictorial works.
5. Cookery (Mushrooms) I. Del Conte, Anna. II. Title.
QK617.L245 1996   96-10835
589.2'22—dc20   CIP

> **Publisher's Note**
> If in any doubt about the edibility of a
> species do not cook or eat it.

Computer page make-up by Sharon Rudd and
Sharon Moore, Dorling Kindersley, Great Britain

Text film output by R&B Creative Services,
Great Britain

Reproduced by Colourscan, Singapore

Printed and bound in Italy by A Mondadori, Verona

CONTENTS

INTRODUCTION

FIELD GUIDE TO
WILD MUSHROOMS

ASCOMYCOTA

COOKING WITH WILD MUSHROOMS

WHAT IS A FUNGUS?

FUNGI ARE A diverse group of organisms and microorganisms that are classified within their own kingdom because they are neither plant nor animal. Unlike plants that photosynthesize, fungi draw their nutrition from decaying organic matter, or from living plants and animals. Many play a key role in the natural cycle as decomposers, returning nutrients to the soil. For humans, some fungi have great medicinal or culinary value, while others are considered destructive.

FUNGAL ACTIVITY

Fungi cannot produce their own energy so they either have to find other organisms to act as host, or they have to digest dead organic matter. Sometimes the host relationship can be mutually beneficial – for example, the so-called mycorrhizal fungi, tap into living tree roots in order to gain access to carbohydrates. In return, the fungus provides the plant with minerals. Sometimes the relationship can be parasitic. Mushrooms, like mildews and rusts, thrive as parasites on living plants, harming the plants but not killing them. In other cases, the parasitic fungus kills the host but persists in the dead matter. Fungal activity has a great impact on our lives. It is responsible for the damage caused to wood and other building material by dry rot, while its beneficial action has been used, for example, to produce enzymes for detergents, antibiotics such as penicillin, flavors for cheeses, bread that rises, and to convert sugar to alcohol.

PENICILLIN
Species within the genus Penicillium *produce flavors for blue and white cheeses, such as gorgonzola, and provide antibiotics, such as penicillin.*

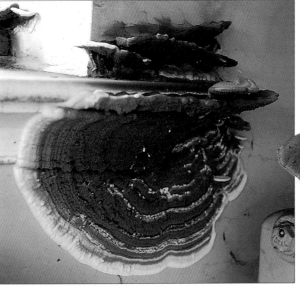

DRY ROT FUNGUS
A widespread fungus that thrives in buildings where it can spread for many yards, leaving the infected wood weak. The fruitbodies of the fungus alone, may reach 20in (50cm).

RED-GILLED CORT
Cortinarius semisanguineus, *with its uniformly reddish brown fruitbodies and striking blood-red gills, is an excellent source of bright red fabric dye. Along with other closely related species of wild fungi, it is mainly used to color wool.*

LIFE CYCLE OF A MUSHROOM

It is important to realize that the mushrooms you see growing in parks, woodland, and on roadsides are only the fruiting bodies of a higher fungus. Their function is to spread spores to enable the fungus to establish new colonies. Below the soil, inside the wood, or in other organic substrates is the main body of the fungus, consisting of threads called *hyphae*, which form a branching web collectively known as the *mycelium*. The mycelium spreads throughout the chosen substrate, absorbing nutrients. It may continue to grow for many years within the substrate but when environmental conditions are right, fruitbodies are likely to appear on the surface. Each fruitbody contains thousands of spores, and if one lands in a suitable site, it will germinate and grow to form a new mycelium.

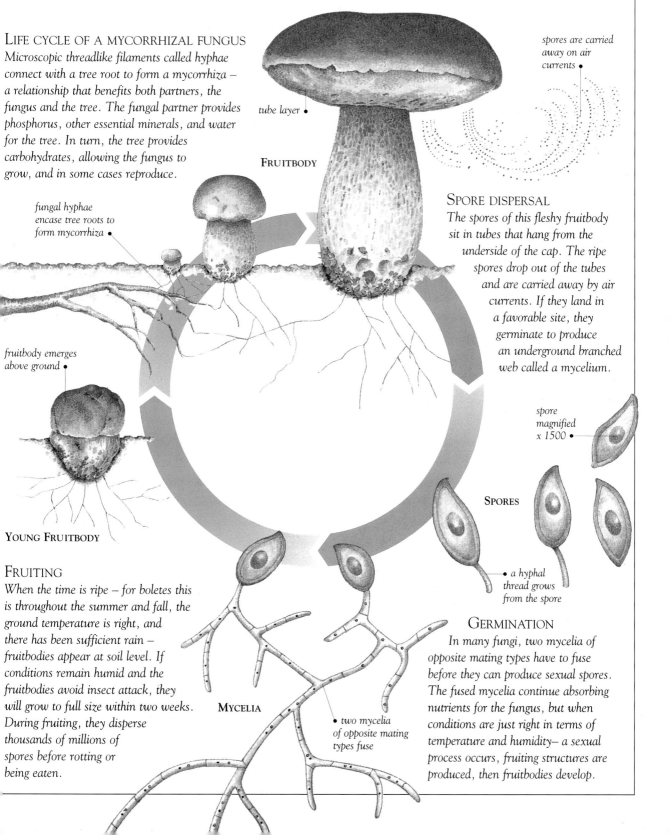

LIFE CYCLE OF A MYCORRHIZAL FUNGUS
Microscopic threadlike filaments called hyphae connect with a tree root to form a mycorrhiza – a relationship that benefits both partners, the fungus and the tree. The fungal partner provides phosphorus, other essential minerals, and water for the tree. In turn, the tree provides carbohydrates, allowing the fungus to grow, and in some cases reproduce.

fungal hyphae encase tree roots to form mycorrhiza ●

fruitbody emerges above ground ●

YOUNG FRUITBODY

FRUITING
When the time is ripe – for boletes this is throughout the summer and fall, the ground temperature is right, and there has been sufficient rain – fruitbodies appear at soil level. If conditions remain humid and the fruitbodies avoid insect attack, they will grow to full size within two weeks. During fruiting, they disperse thousands of millions of spores before rotting or being eaten.

tube layer ●

FRUITBODY

MYCELIA

● two mycelia of opposite mating types fuse

spores are carried away on air currents ●

SPORE DISPERSAL
The spores of this fleshy fruitbody sit in tubes that hang from the underside of the cap. The ripe spores drop out of the tubes and are carried away by air currents. If they land in a favorable site, they germinate to produce an underground branched web called a mycelium.

spore magnified x 1500 ●

SPORES

● a hyphal thread grows from the spore

GERMINATION
In many fungi, two mycelia of opposite mating types have to fuse before they can produce sexual spores. The fused mycelia continue absorbing nutrients for the fungus, but when conditions are just right in terms of temperature and humidity– a sexual process occurs, fruiting structures are produced, then fruitbodies develop.

FEATURES OF FRUITBODIES

MUSHROOMS HAVE DIFFERENT strategies for spreading spores. Most have an active mechanism that propels the spores into air currents, but a small number of fungi rely on passive methods, where the fruitbody or spore mass can be dispersed by animals, flies, or rain. The structure of the spore-producing surface also varies: some fungi simply have smooth fertile surfaces, while others have complex gills, spines, or pores to maximize the number of spores that can be held within a small surface area.

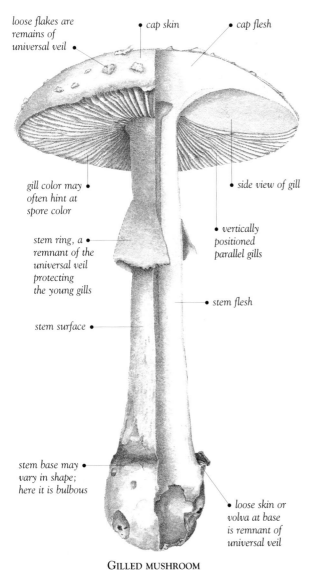

loose flakes are remains of universal veil •

• cap skin

• cap flesh

gill color may often hint at spore color •

• side view of gill

stem ring, a • remnant of the universal veil protecting the young gills

• vertically positioned parallel gills

stem surface •

• stem flesh

stem base may • vary in shape; here it is bulbous

• loose skin or volva at base is remnant of universal veil

GILLED MUSHROOM

FRUITBODY ANATOMY

Fruitbodies serve one purpose: reproduction. Their anatomy has evolved to create the most effective structures. In *Amanita* species (*see above*), the stem lifts the spore-producing tissue in the gills high above ground so that spores can be carried away on air currents. A veil protects developing young fruitbodies. In maturity, veil remnants can be seen as scales on the cap or as loose stem skin.

SPORE DISPERSAL FEATURES

Gills, tubes, and spines, although different spore-producing structures, have surfaces covered in *hymenium* – masses of closely packed fertile cells called *basidia* (*see p.43*). In some cases, the fertile cells are interspersed with sterile cells. The main function of sterile cells is not well understood but in *Coprinus* species (*see pp.146–147*), the sterile cells protrude from each gill edge to prevent the crowded gills from sticking together. When the spores reach maturity, a very precise and delicate mechanism actively propels the spores out of the fruitbody. They reach a position midway between two gills or are propelled to the center of a tube cavity. Gravity then allows the spores to fall down until they are completely free of the gills or the tubes. The turbulent airflow along the ground picks up the spores and carries them away. Most land in unsuitable places, but millions of spores are produced to increase the probability of some landing in favorable sites and germinating.

GILL ALIGNMENT

To propel the spores into the air currents, the gills or tubes have to be positioned vertically. If not, the spores are unable to drop out as they are released and then become stuck on the gills or tube walls. When this vertical alignment is altered, a fruitbody will try to adjust to the new position. When picked and lying in the basket, short-lived fruitbodies, such as the *Mycena* species (*shown here*), reposition cap and gills by altering the stem position. If the cap has been successfully realigned, there will be a spore deposit in the collecting basket on your return home.

stem changes position so that the cap and gills are vertical •

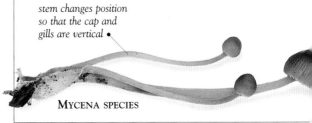

MYCENA SPECIES

FRUITBODY SHAPES

Fungal fruitbodies exhibit a bizarre variety of forms, but all support the spore-producing tissue – the *hymenium*. This tissue may be exposed on the upper or lower surface as in cup-shaped and gilled fungi (*see opposite*), or concealed within the fruitbody as in puffballs and truffles (*see p.34*). Fruitbodies that rely on passive dispersal, such as nest-shaped fungi, use their shape to best advantage. The force created by a splash of rainwater landing in the nest is enough to propel the "eggs," which contain the spores, out.

BALL-SHAPED
Hymenium often formed internally; spores are passively dispersed.

CUP-SHAPED
Hymenium lines inner/upper side of cup; spores are forcibly discharged.

NEST-SHAPED
"Eggs" with an internal hymenium are propelled by raindrops.

LOBED
Hymenium on surface of lobes; spores are actively discharged.

BRACKET-SHAPED
Hymenium lines tubes on underside of bracket; spores are actively discharged.

SKIN/CRUSTLIKE
Hymenium covers most of surface; spores are actively discharged.

CORAL-SHAPED
Hymenium covers most of surface, spores are actively discharged.

CLUB-SHAPED
Hymenium either covers surface or is situated in immersed flasks; spores are actively discharged.

TRUMPET-SHAPED
Hymenium on smooth to wrinkled, pale grayish outer side; spores are actively discharged.

PESTLE/PEAR-SHAPED
Hymenium formed within closed structure; spores are passively dispersed.

PHALLIC-SHAPED
Hymenium formed in egglike structures; slimy spore-mass is dispersed by flies.

STAR-SHAPED
Hymenium formed in closed structure that splits; spores are passively dispersed.

CAPS, STEMS, & GILLS

TO IDENTIFY A MUSHROOM correctly, mycologists use a number of terms to describe its physical characteristics. The shape and texture of the upper- and underside of the fruitbody, the appearance of the stem and how it is attached to the substrate, and how the gills are joined to the stem are all keys to identification. This visual glossary illustrates the precise terms used by mycologists to describe these features.

CAP FEATURES

Often, a cap raised on a stem is the first feature of a fruitbody to attract your attention when out foraying. There are four obvious cap features to be aware of: color, shape, surface appearance, and surface texture – whether dry, sticky, glutinous, or somewhere in between.

CONVEX
Cap shape somewhere in between flat and semiglobose

CONICAL
Cap tapers to a central point creating a tall shape

FUNNEL-SHAPED
Depressed center of cap

UMBONATE
Raised boss in center of cap

FOLDED
Brain- or honeycomb-like

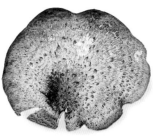

LOOSE SCALES
Removable veil scales

SCALY
Scales part of cap skin

GROOVED MARGIN
Distinct grooves present

RADIALLY STRIATE
*Striations represent gills s...
through thin-fleshed ca...*

CONCENTRIC ZONES
Zoned due to irregular growth

SHAGGY
Long, fibrous scales

STICKY
Cap skin in gelatinous matter

INROLLED MARGIN
Cap margin overlaps gills

STEM FEATURES

Once you have studied the cap, examine the size and shape of the stem, if there is one. Other features, such as the presence or absence of a ring, a volva, or a veil – visible as fine threads – are important. Also touch the stem to see if it is dry or sticky, and cut it in half to observe if it is solid, hollow, or chambered.

TAPERED TO BASE
Stem gradually narrows to base

CLAVATE
Swollen club-shaped base

ROOTING
Stem base roots in soil

STEM & RING
Stem and ring both present on stem

EQUAL
All gills are full length

VARYING LENGTHS
Gills of irregular lengths

FORKED
Gills split in two toward margin

GILL FEATURES

Fruitbodies with caps or brackets have spore-producing tissue on the underside. The tissue can be arranged on gills, spines, in a tube layer – the openings of which can be seen as pores – or it can be smooth. It is crucial to examine the underside. Many fungi look like gilled mushrooms when viewed from above, but when you turn them over you may find spines, pores, or a smooth layer instead of gills. To tell gilled fungi apart, examine how the gills radiate from where the cap is attached to the stem.

CROWDED
Gills are close together

WIDELY SPACED
Gills are far apart

JOINED TO COLLAR
Short, widely spaced gills

RADIATING
Gills radiate from cap margin

SPINES
More or less pointed spines cover underside

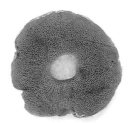

PORES
Underside covered in tubes with pore openings

MAZELIKE PORES
Underside with woody, branching plates, covered in hymenium

GILL SECTIONS

Small details, such as the way gills are attached to the stem or are free of the stem, are very important clues when trying to tell gilled species of mushrooms apart. Sometimes all the species within a genus have exactly the same type of gill attachment.

ADNATE
Broadly attached

ADNEXED
Narrowly attached

NOTCHED
Gills are indented

FREE
Not joined to stem

DECURRENT
Gills run some way down stem

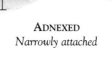

SINUATE NOTCHED
Gills are curved and notched

SPORE COLOR & FRUITBODY SIZE

ON ARRIVING HOME *from a foray, it is a good idea to take the spore deposit of any unidentified fungi. This enables you to establish the spore colors, helping to place your finds within their genera (see Identification Key pp.14–21). Fruitbody size, although less reliable, can also aid identification. Here we demonstrate how to accurately measure the dimensions of caps, stems, gills, and bracket fungi.*

STEP 1 △
Carefully position the fresh cap on two-tone paper. Place a drop of water on the top and cover with a glass bowl.

STEP 2 ▷
Leave the cap overnight. Gently lift off the glass and cap to reveal the deposit.

SPORE COLOR

For true spore color you need to obtain a thick spore deposit; you should observe the deposit in natural light. The color of the spores can be categorized as follows: pinkish to red, ocher to clay, rust-brown, purple-brown, black, white to cream. There are some exceptions to these color categories as a few gilled fungi, such as *Chlorophyllum molybdites* (see p.139) produce green spores. Spore color varies only a little within a genus, and in some cases, *Agaricus* species all produce chocolate-black spores.

TAKING A SPORE DEPOSIT

Select a fresh specimen; dried-out specimens do not deposit spores. Then using a sharp knife, remove the cap. Place the cap gill-side down on white or black paper (black paper will show up pale spores). If you are not sure whether the spores are pale or dark, place the cap half on white paper and half on dark paper. The best spore deposits are obtained if the cap and paper are under glass. Place a drop of water on the cap before covering it. Leave the cap for several hours or overnight – the longer you leave it the thicker the spore deposit. On inspection, the print left by the spores on the paper will mirror the spaces that exist between the gills.

PINKISH TO RED

OCHER TO CLAY

RUST-BROWN

PURPLE-BROWN

BLACK

WHITE TO CREAM

MEASURING FRUITBODIES

Although fruitbodies vary a great deal in size due to environmental factors, the quality of the chosen substrate, and other elements, size is still an important identification feature. Gilled mushrooms and most bracket fungi are fairly easy to measure (*see right*) with a ruler or tape measure. It is much more difficult, and less important, to measure spreading species such as *Coniophora* (*see p.58*) and *Stereum* (*see p.57*), whose skinlike fruitbodies grow along the length of a substrate.

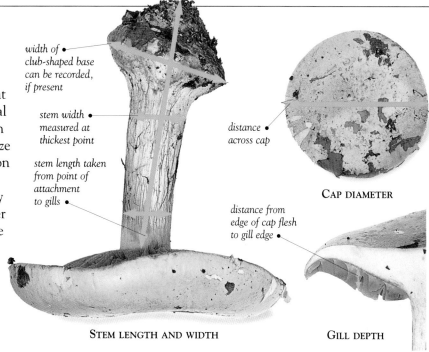

width of club-shaped base can be recorded, if present

stem width measured at thickest point

stem length taken from point of attachment to gills

STEM LENGTH AND WIDTH

distance across cap

CAP DIAMETER

distance from edge of cap flesh to gill edge

GILL DEPTH

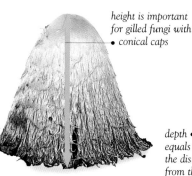

height is important for gilled fungi with conical caps

CAP HEIGHT

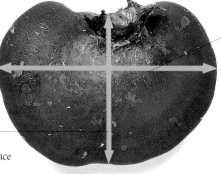

depth equals the distance from the substrate

BRACKET DEPTH AND WIDTH

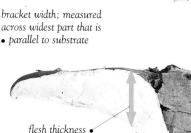

bracket width; measured across widest part that is parallel to substrate

flesh thickness in cross-section

BRACKET THICKNESS

FORAYING EQUIPMENT

Whether collecting fungi purely for identification or for eating (*see p.228*), take a basket, an airtight container, a knife, a notepad and pencils, or a camera with a macro lens. Sketch the fungus *in situ* or take a photograph of it to record transitory features, such as stem milk. You may find a hand lens (x 10 magnification) useful for studying small details, and take tweezers to handle delicate fungi. Ultimately, an avid amateur will need a microscope to study minute features, such as spore shape. To assess the smell of a fungus – a good clue to identity – place the fruitbody inside the container to concentrate the scent, then lift the lid slightly and sniff. If you are experienced enough to recognize the handful of deadly poisonous species, use taste, but remember, tasting is not the same as eating. Chew a small piece on the tip of the tongue, and note whether it is bitter or mild, then spit it out.

TWEEZERS

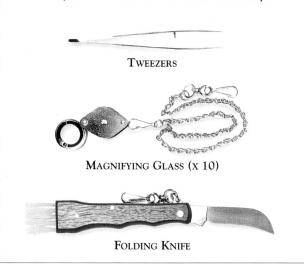

MAGNIFYING GLASS (x 10)

FOLDING KNIFE

NOTEBOOK

CAMERA

FOLDING BASKET

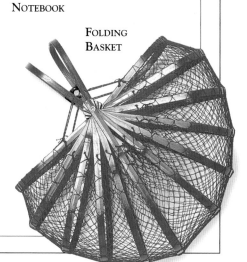

IDENTIFICATION KEY

TO IDENTIFY A MUSHROOM answer the questions below, then follow the key until you arrive at a page reference. Turn to the appropriate page within the Field Guide to Wild Mushrooms (see pp.22–225) and compare your fungus with the descriptions. The asterisk denotes species that appear in more than one place in the key.

WHAT SHAPE IS IT?

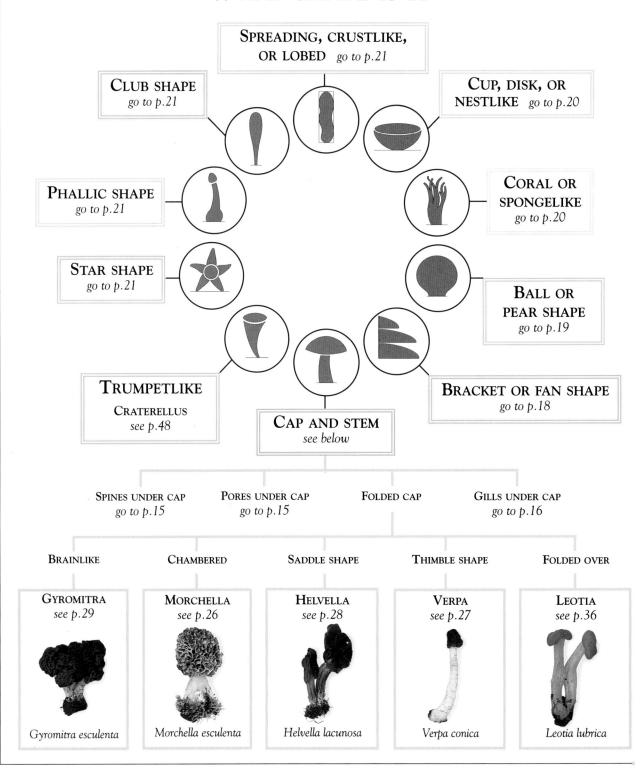

SPREADING, CRUSTLIKE, OR LOBED *go to p.21*

CLUB SHAPE *go to p.21*

CUP, DISK, OR NESTLIKE *go to p.20*

PHALLIC SHAPE *go to p.21*

CORAL OR SPONGELIKE *go to p.20*

STAR SHAPE *go to p.21*

BALL OR PEAR SHAPE *go to p.19*

TRUMPETLIKE
CRATERELLUS
see p.48

CAP AND STEM *see below*

BRACKET OR FAN SHAPE *go to p.18*

SPINES UNDER CAP *go to p.15* PORES UNDER CAP *go to p.15* FOLDED CAP GILLS UNDER CAP *go to p.16*

BRAINLIKE CHAMBERED SADDLE SHAPE THIMBLE SHAPE FOLDED OVER

GYROMITRA *see p.29*

MORCHELLA *see p.26*

HELVELLA *see p.28*

VERPA *see p.27*

LEOTIA *see p.36*

Gyromitra esculenta *Morchella esculenta* *Helvella lacunosa* *Verpa conica* *Leotia lubrica*

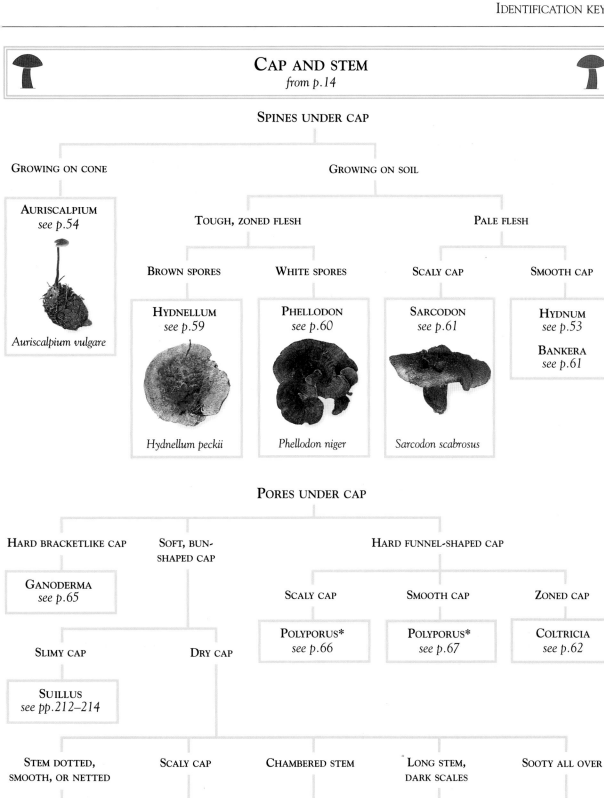

CAP AND STEM
from p.14

SPINES UNDER CAP

GROWING ON CONE

AURISCALPIUM
see p.54

Auriscalpium vulgare

GROWING ON SOIL

TOUGH, ZONED FLESH

BROWN SPORES

HYDNELLUM
see p.59

Hydnellum peckii

WHITE SPORES

PHELLODON
see p.60

Phellodon niger

PALE FLESH

SCALY CAP

SARCODON
see p.61

Sarcodon scabrosus

SMOOTH CAP

HYDNUM
see p.53

BANKERA
see p.61

PORES UNDER CAP

HARD BRACKETLIKE CAP

GANODERMA
see p.65

SOFT, BUN-SHAPED CAP

SLIMY CAP

SUILLUS
see pp.212–214

DRY CAP

STEM DOTTED, SMOOTH, OR NETTED

BOLETUS
see pp.202–208

CHALCIPORUS
see p.208

TYLOPILUS
see p.215

SCALY CAP

STROBILOMYCES
see p.215

Strobilomyces strobilaceus

CHAMBERED STEM

GYROPORUS
see p.209

Gyroporus castaneus

LONG STEM, DARK SCALES

LECCINUM
see pp.210–211

Leccinum scabrum

SOOTY ALL OVER

PORPHYRELLUS
see p.215

HARD FUNNEL-SHAPED CAP

SCALY CAP

POLYPORUS*
see p.66

SMOOTH CAP

POLYPORUS*
see p.67

ZONED CAP

COLTRICIA
see p.62

CAP AND STEM
from p.14

GILLS UNDER CAP

EQUAL GILLS AND/OR CRUMBLY FLESH

VARYING GILLS AND FIBRILLOSE FLESH

WITH MILK INSIDE

WITHOUT MILK INSIDE

WHITE SPORE DEPOSIT
go to p.17

GREEN SPORES

LACTARIUS
see pp.189–198

RUSSULA
see pp.180–188

CHLOROPHYLLUM
see p.139

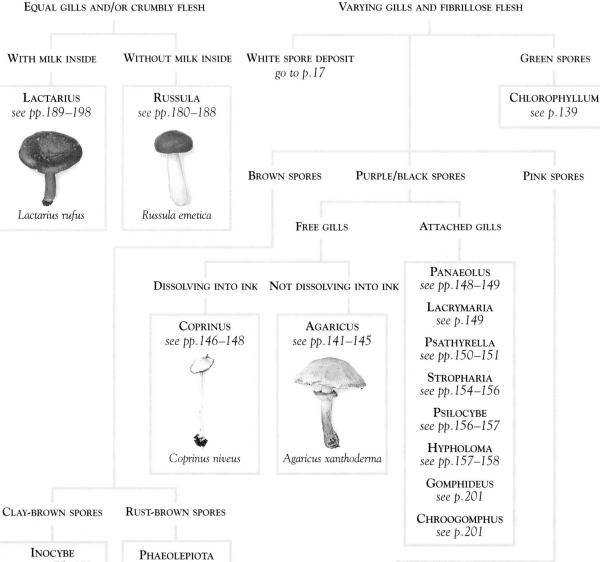

Lactarius rufus

Russula emetica

BROWN SPORES   **PURPLE/BLACK SPORES**   **PINK SPORES**

FREE GILLS   **ATTACHED GILLS**

DISSOLVING INTO INK   **NOT DISSOLVING INTO INK**

PANAEOLUS
see pp.148–149

LACRYMARIA
see p.149

PSATHYRELLA
see pp.150–151

COPRINUS
see pp.146–148

AGARICUS
see pp.141–145

STROPHARIA
see pp.154–156

PSILOCYBE
see pp.156–157

HYPHOLOMA
see pp.157–158

GOMPHIDEUS
see p.201

CHROOGOMPHUS
see p.201

Coprinus niveus

Agaricus xanthoderma

CLAY-BROWN SPORES   **RUST-BROWN SPORES**

INOCYBE
see pp.175–179

PHAEOLEPIOTA
see p.121

CONOCYBE
see p.153

PHOLIOTA
see pp.159–161

GALERINA
see pp.163–164

Inocybe rimosa

AGROCYBE
see pp.152–153

HEBELOMA
see pp.174–175

PAXILLUS
see p.199

KUEHNEROMYCES
see p.164

GYMNOPILUS
see pp.164–165

CORTINARIUS
see pp.165–173

ROZITES
see p.179

ATTACHED GILLS   **FREE GILLS**

WITH SAC   **WITHOUT SAC**

LEPISTA
see pp.90–91

MACROCYSTIDIA
see p.110

CLITOPILUS
see p.123

ENTOLOMA
see pp.123–126

VOLVARIELLA
see p.127

PLUTEUS
see pp.128–129

Volvariella bombycina

Pluteus cervinus

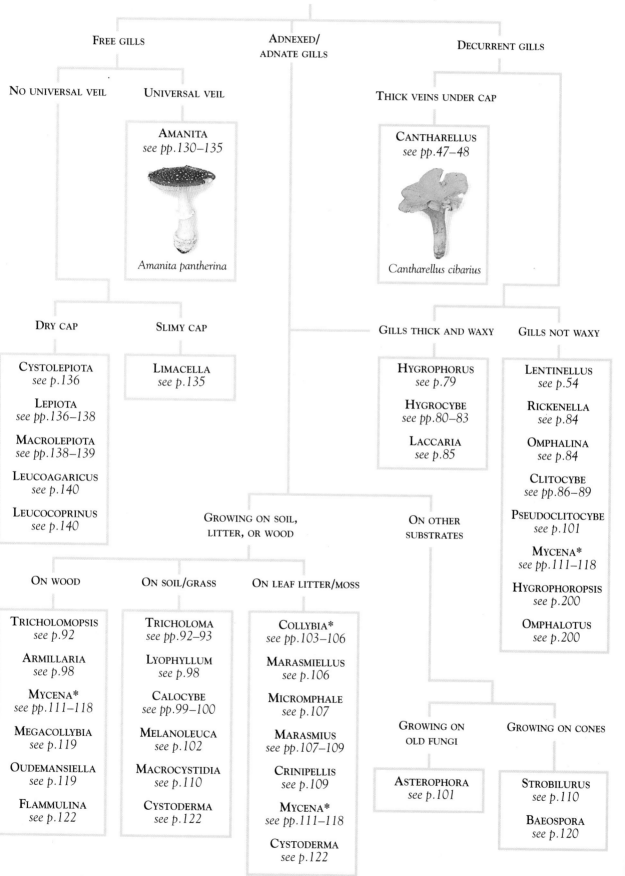

CAP AND STEM
from p.16

WHITE SPORE DEPOSIT (GILLS UNDER CAP)

FREE GILLS

NO UNIVERSAL VEIL

UNIVERSAL VEIL

AMANITA
see pp.130–135

Amanita pantherina

DRY CAP

CYSTOLEPIOTA
see p.136

LEPIOTA
see pp.136–138

MACROLEPIOTA
see pp.138–139

LEUCOAGARICUS
see p.140

LEUCOCOPRINUS
see p.140

SLIMY CAP

LIMACELLA
see p.135

ADNEXED/ADNATE GILLS

GROWING ON SOIL, LITTER, OR WOOD

ON WOOD

TRICHOLOMOPSIS
see p.92

ARMILLARIA
see p.98

MYCENA*
see pp.111–118

MEGACOLLYBIA
see p.119

OUDEMANSIELLA
see p.119

FLAMMULINA
see p.122

ON SOIL/GRASS

TRICHOLOMA
see pp.92–93

LYOPHYLLUM
see p.98

CALOCYBE
see pp.99–100

MELANOLEUCA
see p.102

MACROCYSTIDIA
see p.110

CYSTODERMA
see p.122

ON LEAF LITTER/MOSS

COLLYBIA*
see pp.103–106

MARASMIELLUS
see p.106

MICROMPHALE
see p.107

MARASMIUS
see pp.107–109

CRINIPELLIS
see p.109

MYCENA*
see pp.111–118

CYSTODERMA
see p.122

ON OTHER SUBSTRATES

GROWING ON OLD FUNGI

ASTEROPHORA
see p.101

GROWING ON CONES

STROBILURUS
see p.110

BAEOSPORA
see p.120

DECURRENT GILLS

THICK VEINS UNDER CAP

CANTHARELLUS
see pp.47–48

Cantharellus cibarius

GILLS THICK AND WAXY

HYGROPHORUS
see p.79

HYGROCYBE
see pp.80–83

LACCARIA
see p.85

GILLS NOT WAXY

LENTINELLUS
see p.54

RICKENELLA
see p.84

OMPHALINA
see p.84

CLITOCYBE
see pp.86–89

PSEUDOCLITOCYBE
see p.101

MYCENA*
see pp.111–118

HYGROPHOROPSIS
see p.200

OMPHALOTUS
see p.200

BRACKET OR FAN SHAPE
from p.14

WRINKLED UNDERSIDE

UNDERSIDE SMOOTH OR HAIRY

UNDERSIDE WITH PORES

NORMAL/SPLIT GILLS *go to p.19*

UNDERSIDE WITH SPINES *go to p.19*

PHLEBIA
see p.57

STEREUM*
see pp.56–57

NORMAL PORES

MAZELIKE PORES

Phlebia tremellosa

AURICULARIA
see p.44

THELEPHORA
see p.59

Stereum hirsutum

CHONDROSTEREUM
see p.56

HYMENOCHAETE
see p.62

DAEDALEA
see p.76

DAEDALEOPSIS
see p.77

LENZITES
see p.77

TONGUELIKE

DEPRESSED, SCALY

SHELF, HOOF-SHAPED

CLUMPED

STACKED

FISTULINA
see p.64

POLYPORUS*
see pp.66–68

LAETIPORUS
see p.69

TRAMETES
see pp.73–74

Fistulina hepatica

Polyporus squamosus

Laetiporus sulphureus

GRIFOLA
see p.69

MERIPILUS
see p.70

Trametes versicolor

INONOTUS
see p.63

BJERKANDERA
see p.72

TRICHAPTUM
see p.72

LACQUERED SURFACE, BROWN SPORES

SOFT, PALE FLESH

TOUGH TO WOODY, WHITE TO PALE FLESH

TOUGH TO WOODY, DARK BROWN FLESH

GANODERMA
see p.65

PIPTOPORUS
see p.68

TYROMYCES
see p.70

HAPALOPILUS
see p.71

TRICHAPTUM
see p.72

TRAMETES
see p.74

HETEROBASIDION
see p.75

FOMITOPSIS
see p.76

FOMES
see p.76

PHELLINUS
see p.63

INONOTUS
see p.63

PHAEOLUS
see p.71

PYCNOPORUS
see p.74

GLOEOPHYLLUM
see p.75

Ganoderma applanatum

BRACKET OR FAN SHAPE
from p.18

NORMAL GILLS ON UNDERSIDE

WHITE TO PURPLE SPORES

PLEUROTUS
see p.78

Pleurotus ostreatus

PANELLUS
see p.121

BROWN SPORES

CREPIDOTUS
see p.162

Crepidotus mollis

SPLIT GILLS ON UNDERSIDE

SCHIZOPHYLLUM
see p.64

Schizophyllum commune

SPINES ON UNDERSIDE

FLESH FIRM

CREOLOPHUS
see p.55

Creolophus cirrhatus

JELLYLIKE

PSEUDOHYDNUM
see p.46

Pseudohydnum gelatinosum

BALL OR PEAR SHAPE
from p.14

UNDERGROUND

TUBER
see p.34

ON SOIL

SOFT AND WHITE

LYCOPERDON*
see pp.223–224

ON WOOD

HARD AND DARK

SMALL AND PIMPLED

HYPOXYLON
see p.41

LARGE/ZONED INSIDE

DALDINIA
see p.41

RED AND CAGELIKE

CLATHRUS
see p.217

Clathrus ruber

THICK-SKINNED/ BLACK INSIDE

SCLERODERMA
see p.225

THIN-SKINNED (PUFFBALL)

HUGE

CALVATIA*
see p.222

Calvatia gigantea

OPENING IRREGULAR

CALVATIA*
see p.221

Calvatia excipuliformis

HOLE OPENING AT TOP

IN WOODLAND LITTER

LYCOPERDON*
see pp.223–224

IN GRASSY AREAS

VASCELLUM
see p.221

BOVISTA
see p.223

CORAL OR SPONGELIKE
from p.14

JELLYLIKE	ANTLERED	SPONGELIKE	DENSELY BRANCHED	WITH SPINES

CALOCERA
see p.46

CLAVULINOPSIS*
see p.49

SPARASSIS
see p.51

CLAVULINA
see p.51

RAMARIA
see pp.52–53

HERICIUM
see p.55

Calocera viscosa

Clavulinopsis corniculata

Sparassis crispa

Hericium coralloides

CUP, DISK, OR NESTLIKE
from p.14

CUP WITH EGGS	CUP OR DISK SHAPE WITHOUT EGGS	EAR SHAPE

CYATHUS
see p.218

Cyathus striatus

CRUCIBULUM
see p.218

GROWS ON WOOD

GROWS PARTIALLY
UNDERGROUND

SEPULTARIA
see p.32

Sepultaria arenicola

GROWS ON SOIL
OR STRAW

LONG-STEMMED

DUMONTIA
see p.39

Dumontia tuberosa

OTIDEA
see p.31

AURICULARIA
see p.43

SHORT OR NO STEM

DISCIOTIS
see p.27

PEZIZA
see pp.30–31

TARZETTA
see p.32

ALEURIA
see p.33

GELATINOUS FLESH

NEOBULGARIA
see p.36

Neobulgaria pura

BULGARIA
see p.37

ASCOCORYNE
see p.37

FIRM FLESH

SCARLET, WITH STEM

SARCOSCYPHA
see p.29

Sarcoscypha austriaca

NO STEM, RED, AND
WITH HAIRS

SCUTELLINIA
see p.33

Scutellinia scutellata

SMALL AND BALD

BISPORELLA
see p.38

CHLOROCIBORIA
see p.38

RUTSTROEMIA
see p.39

SPREADING, CRUSTLIKE, OR LOBED
from p.14

PORES OR TEETH	WRINKLED	WARTY	SMOOTH/CRACKED	LOBED/GELATINOUS
SCHIZOPORA *see p.72*	SERPULA *see p.38*	CONIOPHORA *see p.58*	STEREUM* *see pp.56–57*	TREMELLA *see pp.44–45*

Coniophora puteana

Stereum rugosum

Tremella mesenterica

EXIDIA
see p.45

CLUB SHAPE
from p.14

PIMPLED SURFACE

ON TRUFFLES/LARVAE	ON WOOD
CORDYCEPS *see p.42*	XYLARIA *see p.40*

Cordyceps militaris

Xylaria hypoxylon

SMOOTH SURFACE

DULL BROWN TO BLACK	WHITE/YELLOW/ ORANGE	ON SCLEROTIUM
TRICHOGLOSSUM *see p.35* GEOGLOSSUM *see p.35* CLAVARIADELPHUS *see p.50* MACROTYPHULA *see p.50*	MITRULA *see p.35* CLAVULINOPSIS* *see p.49* CLAVARIA *see p.49*	TYPHULA *see p.50*

Typhula erythropus

PHALLIC SHAPE
from p.14

WHITE STEM	ORANGE STEM
PHALLUS *see p.216*	MUTINUS *see p.216*

Phallus impudicus

Mutinus caninus

STAR SHAPE
from p.14

RED WITH RAYS	DULL, WITH INNER BALL
CLATHRUS *see p.217*	GEASTRUM *see pp.219–220* ASTRAEUS *see p.225*

Clathrus archeri

FIELD GUIDE TO WILD MUSHROOMS

Equip yourself with a few basic tools, such as a fold-away knife and an open-weave basket, and follow this species-by-species guide to collecting and identifying wild mushrooms. Information on habitat, fruiting, size, and range will enable you to pinpoint the true identity of your mushroom finds, and help you to assess their edibility.

HOW THIS CHAPTER WORKS

IN THIS CHAPTER *on identifying mushrooms species we have taken two divisions of the fungal kingdom, the* Ascomycota *and the* Basidiomycota, *where the fungi known as mushrooms and toadstools belong. The species are arranged in a sequence that reflects how mycologists believe they are interrelated. With more than fifty thousand known species in these two divisions, it would be impossible to feature them all here. This North American edition is based on the premise that mushrooms, primarily described and photographed in Europe, can be used to identify North American collections.*

202 ◆ FIELD GUIDE TO WILD MUSHROOMS

- scientific family name
- scientific class name
- description of family's characteristics
- photographs show typical example of a species, color variations, and stages of growth
- scientific species name
- species' common name

BOLETACEAE

CLASS: *Homobasidiomycetes*

Fungi commonly referred to as boletes do not all belong to the *Boletaceae*. A few are classified in the family *Gomphidiaceae* (see p.211) and the *Strobilomyceteaceae* (see p.215). Boletes are soft-fleshed fungi with pores rather than gills. Some species turn blue, black, or red when cut. Nearly all *Boletus* species form mycorrhiza with trees. Oak and pine woods are the best places to look for edible species. A few boletes are poisonous.

smooth, slightly greasy feel to surface of cap

pale or dark brown cap is bun-shaped, with skin slightly overhanging

BOLETUS AEREUS

Bronzy Bolete

This bolete can look very similar to *B. edulis* (see right). However, its cap is often a darker dull chestnut color, with a fine, velvety surface texture somewhat like the cap skin of *B. aestivalis* (see p.203). The stem is also darker brown, often with a brownish to rust-colored net. As the stem is nearly as thick as the cap diameter, the fruitbody has a squat, almost rounded shape, and its white flesh does not change color when cut. It is a very high quality edible, mainly enjoyed by those living in central to southern Europe since this species of bolete is rare in other parts of the world.

tubes are easily loosened and sinuate

SIDE VIEW

- species' distinguishing features and noteworthy characteristics

- typical color of spore deposit
- typical size of mature fruitbody
- environment in which fungus is commonly found
- notes on world distribution

■ SPORE DEPOSIT Brownish olive.
■ SIZE Cap 7–15cm, up to 30cm (w); stem 6–10cm (h) x 4–8cm (w).
■ HABITAT Mycorrhizal with mature deciduous trees, often oak or beech.
■ RANGE Widespread in north temperate zones; reported from California.

white stem flesh may be maggoty or stained yellow by a parasite

SECTION

BOLETUS EDULIS

King Bolete

One of the most sought-after of all edible mushrooms, this species is closely related to several other similar and equally edible boletes. (see pp.236–237 for recipes). Good markers include the pale net pattern on the upper stem and the yellowish to olive pores.

flesh white

SECTION

■ SPORE DEPOSIT Olive-brown.
■ SIZE Cap 10–25cm, down to 5cm (w); stem 10–20cm (h) x 3–10cm (w).
■ HABITAT In moss-rich woodland, where it forms mycorrhiza with conifer trees, primarily Norway spruce.
■ RANGE As a complex, widespread and common in north temperate zones.

pores are white to yellow, fine, and rounded

- photograph of fruitbody as it grows in chosen habitat

■ FRUITING Singly, a few together, or in troops. Summer–autumn.

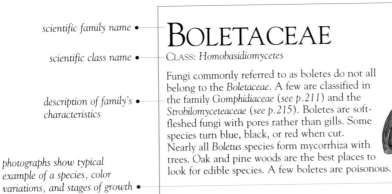

UNDERSIDE

■ FRUITING Singly or in troops on well-drained soil. Summer–autumn.

- description of fruiting season
- underside view revealing pores, spines, gills, or smooth surface
- habit: typical substrate and how fruitbodies grow – for example, singly or in troops

EDIBLE OR POISONOUS?

A symbol appears next to the species common name when its fruitbody is edible or poisonous. The absence of a symbol indicates that the fruitbody is not sufficiently tasty, or too small to be considered edible; or that its edibility is unknown. Remember, however, that there are no hard and fast rules to edibility. Old and young people, for example, can be allergic to the proteins found in wild fungi. Note that the chef's hat in brackets identifies mushrooms that are edible, but these should be approached with caution. They may cause gastric upsets if not cooked thoroughly – blanched or sautéed before consumption (*see Cooking with Wild Mushrooms pp.228–235*).

DEADLY POISONOUS   POISONOUS

CAN BE EDIBLE   EDIBLE   CHOICE

---

degree of edibility (see above)

size of fruitbody in relation to a man's hand (see below right)

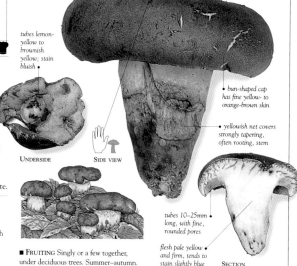

BOLETUS APPENDICULATUS

Spindle-stemmed Bolete

The most striking feature of this fleshy *Boletus* species is its vivid lemon-yellow tubes. It also has a similarly colored net over the stem, which is usually wider in the middle, tapering sharply toward the base. This stem base is often found to be rooting. A fine felt covers the golden reddish brown cap skin, and both the tubes and the flesh stain slightly bluish. It is a quality edible, distinguishable from *B. radicans*, which has a paler cap and bitter taste.

tubes lemon-yellow to brownish yellow; stain bluish

bun-shaped cap has fine yellow- to orange-brown skin

yellowish net covers strongly tapering, often rooting, stem

UNDERSIDE   SIDE VIEW

■ SPORE DEPOSIT Olive-brown.
■ SIZE Cap 8–20cm (w); stem 7–15cm (h) x 2.5–6cm (w).
■ HABITAT In woods, mycorrhizal with deciduous trees such as oaks.
■ RANGE Widespread in southern Europe; reported from California.

■ FRUITING Singly or a few together, under deciduous trees. Summer–autumn.

tubes 10–25mm long, with fine, rounded pores

flesh pale yellow and firm, tends to stain slightly blue

SECTION

---

warm orange-brown cap skin tends to overhang

cap surface is dry and dull, often with fine cracks

white net covers pale brown, barrel-shaped stem

SIDE VIEW

tubes 10–15mm long and sinuate

white firm flesh is attacked by maggots

SECTION

cross-section of fruitbody shows gill attachment, and whether the flesh is solid, chambered, or hollow

BOLETUS AESTIVALIS

Summer Bolete

This species is very similar to *B. edulis* (*see opposite*), but the cap skin cracks and is a paler color. The stem net is more pronounced and extensive. *B. aestivalis* tends to occur some weeks before the main flush of *B. edulis* and *B. aereus* (*see opposite*), but in some areas fruits alongside *B. luridiformis* (*see p.204*).

■ SPORE DEPOSIT Olive-brown.
■ SIZE Cap 7–15cm, up to 25cm (w); stem 6–15cm (h) x 2–5cm (w).
■ HABITAT Woods, mycorrhizal with deciduous trees, such as beech and oak.
■ RANGE Widespread in north temperate zones; not reliably reported in N. A.

■ FRUITING In troops or a few together, under deciduous trees. Summer–autumn.

BOLETUS PINOPHILUS

Pinewood King Bolete

Another *B. edulis* look-alike (*see opposite*), but with a much richer brown cap and stem. Also the net extends farther down the stem. As its common name suggests, this excellent edible is exclusively found with pine trees, on sandy soil.

■ SPORE DEPOSIT Olive-brown.
■ SIZE Cap 10–20cm, up to 25cm (w); stem 10–15cm, up to 20cm (h) x 4–8cm, up to 10cm (w).
■ HABITAT In woods, mycorrhizal with pine trees, on sandy soils.
■ RANGE Widespread in Europe and other north temperate zones.

■ FRUITING Singly or a few together, on sandy soil. Summer–autumn.

FRUITBODY SIZE

The species featured in this section vary in dimension, ranging from the size of a football to that of a pin head. This makes it impossible to display them in proportion to one another. A hand and mushroom symbol appears with most of the entries, providing an at-a-glance guide that compares the average size of a fruitbody with a man's hand (8in/20cm long).

Below 6mm   100-150mm

6-12mm   150-200mm

12-25mm   200-300mm

25-50mm   300-400mm

50-100mm   400-800mm

ASCOMYCOTA

An amazingly diverse selection of large and small fungi belong to the subdivision of the fungal kingdom known as Ascomycota. They are identified by the presence of a spore-bearing structure called an ascus. The ascus is typically cylindrical and usually contains eight spores that can be discharged from the ascus top. This group contains edibles such as morels and true truffles. Many of the fungi have cup or disk-shaped fruitbodies and others have flask-shaped structures. Family division within the Ascomycota is partly determined by the method of spore dispersal and the color of spores.

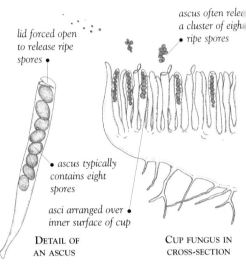

lid forced open to release ripe spores •

ascus often relec a cluster of eigh
• ripe spores

• ascus typically contains eight spores

asci arranged over • inner surface of cup

DETAIL OF AN ASCUS

CUP FUNGUS IN CROSS-SECTION

MORCHELLACEAE

CLASS: *Discomycetes*

Morels are among the best known mushrooms: they are regarded as one of the top ten edibles (*see p.239 for recipe*), their fruitbodies are easy to identify, and they appear in spring. In Europe and North America these species are picked on a commercial scale. Morels favor limestone areas and occur where the soil has been disturbed. They produce mass fruitings after forest fires.

irregular ridges and • pits in ovoid head

young caps are • darker in color than mature ones

• hollow interior

• meal surface

SECTION

grows on moss • and soil

SIDE VIEW

MORCHELLA ESCULENTA

Common Morel

A distinctive species with a ridged honeycomb-like head. M. *esculenta* varies considerably in shape and size. More common is the Black Morel (M. *elata* complex), which has black radial ribs. Be careful not to confuse M. *esculenta* with the poisonous *Gyromitra esculenta* (*see p.29*), which has a more brainlike head.

■ **SPORE DEPOSIT** Cream to pale brown.
■ **SIZE** Cap 5–20cm (h); stem 5–12cm (h) x 2–10cm (w).
■ **HABITAT** Under dead elms, old apple trees, poplars, tulip poplars, and pine.
■ **RANGE** Almost worldwide but less common in northern regions.

■ **FRUITING** Singly or in troops, often hidden among herbs and grass. Spring.

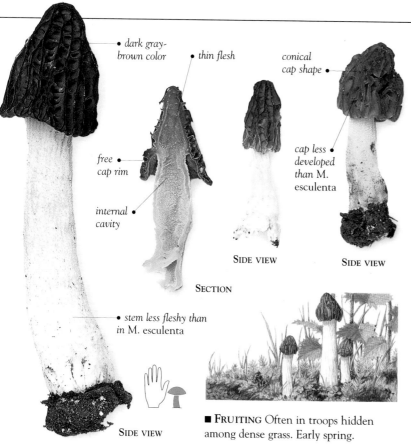

dark gray-
brown color •

• thin flesh

conical
cap shape •

free •
cap rim

internal •
cavity

cap less
developed
than M.
esculenta

SIDE VIEW

SIDE VIEW

SECTION

• stem less fleshy than
in M. esculenta

SIDE VIEW

■ **FRUITING** Often in troops hidden
among dense grass. Early spring.

MORCHELLA SEMILIBERA

Half-free Morel

A smaller species than M. esculenta
(see opposite) with a less developed
cap that has a free edge. Although
M. semilibera tastes similar to
M. esculenta, it is not such a choice
edible because it is less fleshy.
Typically, its fruiting season lasts
longer than that of M. esculenta.
M. semilibera can be confused with
Verpa species (see below) but in
contrast to M. semilibera, these have
small caps, which are attached only
to the top of the stem.

■ **SPORE DEPOSIT** Cream.
■ **SIZE** Cap 1–4cm (h);
stem 3–10cm (h) x 1–2cm (w).
■ **HABITAT** Open woodland areas, along
paths in damp places, on rich soil.
■ **RANGE** Widespread in eastern North
America and the Pacific Northwest.

VERPA CONICA

Thimble Cap

Verpa species can be distinguished
from Morchella species by examining
the cap; Verpa species are attached
only at the top of the stem. Verpa
conica varies in shape but the cap
surface is almost smooth, unlike
the related V. bohemica, which has
a wrinkled cap. In both species,
the stem is long compared with
the height of the cap. Although
recommended in Europe, instances
of stomach cramps and incoordination
have been reported in North America.

■ **SPORE DEPOSIT** Cream.
■ **SIZE** Cap 2–4cm (h);
stem 3–10cm (h) x 0.5–1.5cm (w).
■ **HABITAT** In limestone areas especially
under old apple trees.
■ **RANGE** Widespread in north
temperate zones, locally fairly common,
rare in cold regions.

■ **FRUITING** In troops among leaf litter,
usually in undergrowth. Spring.

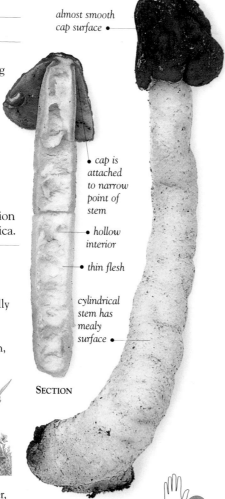

almost smooth
cap surface •

• cap is
attached
to narrow
point of
stem

• hollow
interior

• thin flesh

cylindrical
stem has
mealy
surface •

SECTION

SIDE VIEW

DISCIOTIS VENOSA

Cuplike Morel

Although this species resembles one
of the large Peziza species (see p.30),
it is a true member of the
Morchellaceae. Its cup shape flattens
and may become convex with age.
It can easily be identified by its
chlorinelike smell, very brittle
flesh, and strongly reduced stem.
Although esteemed as an edible in
Europe, it is hard to identify readily
in North America, and little or
nothing is known about the edibility
of its look-alikes.

■ **SPORE DEPOSIT** Cream.
■ **SIZE** Cup 4–10cm (w).
■ **HABITAT** On nutrient-rich soil
in parks and forests.
■ **RANGE** Widespread but uncommon.

■ **FRUITING** Singly or in troops, often
on bare soil. Spring–early summer.

HELVELLACEAE

CLASS: *Discomycetes*

A family with several species that superficially resemble *Morchella* species (*see p.26*), but differ microscopically and in their chemical makeup. The fruitbodies of most species appear in autumn, although a number can be found in spring, most notably those in the *Gyromitra esculenta* complex. Some species are toxic, and deaths are reported from *Gyromitra esculenta*, which also contains a potent carcinogen.

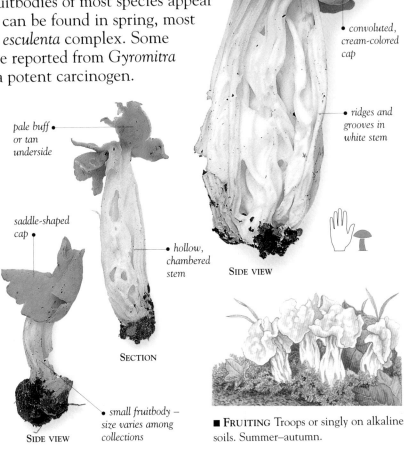

• convoluted, cream-colored cap

• ridges and grooves in white stem

SIDE VIEW

HELVELLA CRISPA

Common White Saddle

A species that is easily identified by the furrowed stem, saddle-shaped cap, and pale, creamy coloring. It varies in size but is typically a large species. This and other *Helvella* species often occur with species of *Peziza* (*see p.30*) and *Inocybe* (*see p.176*). Although listed as edible in some guides, it has been shown to contain the carcinogen monomethylhydrazine.

■ **SPORE DEPOSIT** White.
■ **SIZE** Cap 2–6cm (w); stem 3–12cm (h) x 0.5–2.5cm (w).
■ **HABITAT** On soil in deciduous or conifer forests.
■ **RANGE** Widespread and common in most north temperate regions.

pale buff or tan underside •

saddle-shaped cap •

• hollow, chambered stem

SECTION

• small fruitbody – size varies among collections

SIDE VIEW

■ **FRUITING** Troops or singly on alkaline soils. Summer–autumn.

---

cap saddle-shaped or convoluted with several lobes •

lobes are gray to blackish gray with paler undersides •

stem is chambered inside •

SECTION

• stem is shades of gray and deeply grooved

SIDE VIEW

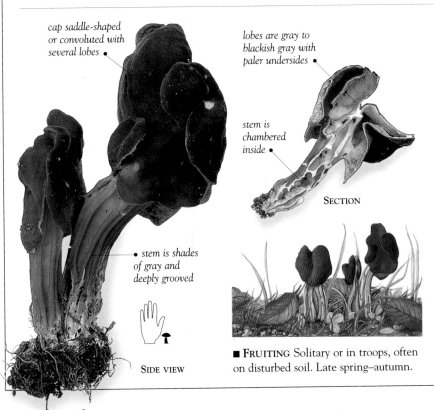

■ **FRUITING** Solitary or in troops, often on disturbed soil. Late spring–autumn.

HELVELLA LACUNOSA

Common Gray Saddle

This is perhaps the most common of *Helvella* species but it is not edible and should be treated with caution. It is extremely variable in size, shape, and color, although it is always a shade of gray and has either a saddle-shaped cap or a convoluted cap with lobes. Like *H. crispa* (*see above*), the stem has distinct grooves.

■ **SPORE DEPOSIT** White.
■ **SIZE** Cap 1–5cm (w); stem 2–8cm (h) x 0.5–1.5cm (w).
■ **HABITAT** On alkaline soils and gravel; occurs in forests and more open areas.
■ **RANGE** Widespread in temperate and alpine zones of both the northern and southern hemispheres.

GYROMITRA ESCULENTA

False Morel ☠

This species has a dark brown, brainlike cap with a chambered interior. It is carried on a short white stem. The appearance of fruitbodies in spring among conifers makes this poisonous fungus easy to identify. In parts of Europe this fungus is eaten after careful drying, which removes toxins. Similar, often larger and more vivid orange-brown species occur, and can be common in North America.

- **SPORE DEPOSIT** White.
- **SIZE** Cap 5–15cm (w); stem 1–5cm (h) x 2–4cm (w).
- **HABITAT** Close to conifers, often pine, on sandy soil or wood chips.
- **RANGE** Widespread in north temperate zones; locally common.

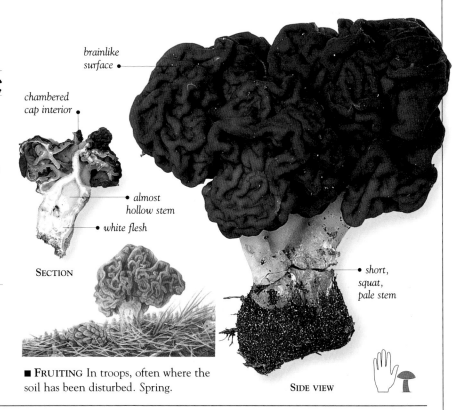

brainlike surface

chambered cap interior

almost hollow stem

white flesh

SECTION

short, squat, pale stem

- **FRUITING** In troops, often where the soil has been disturbed. Spring.

SIDE VIEW

SARCOSOMATACEAE

CLASS: *Discomycetes*

These predominantly brightly colored, wood-inhabiting cup-fungi are mainly tropical, but a few characteristic species occur in temperate climates. Many have firm flesh and long-lasting fruitbodies that appear either in winter or spring. The genus shown here is sometimes placed in its own family, because unlike other members of the *Sarcosomataceae*, it does not store large amounts of water in its fruitbodies.

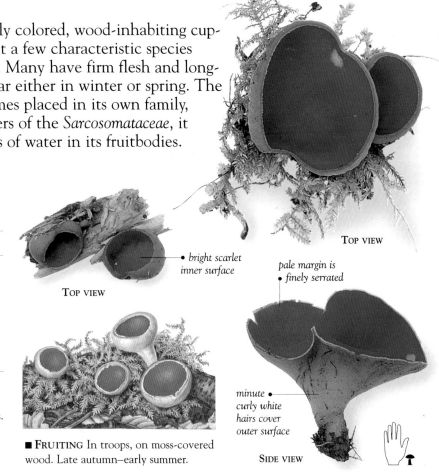

often found on mossy trunks

TOP VIEW

SARCOSCYPHA AUSTRIACA

Curly-haired Elf Cup

This species is bright scarlet with tiny corkscrewlike hairs on the outside of the cup. By contrast, the very similar-looking *S. coccinea* has straight hairs. Four additional species of *Sarcoscypha* occur but have more localized distributions.

- **SPORE DEPOSIT** White.
- **SIZE** Cup 1–8cm (w); stem 2cm (h).
- **HABITAT** On wood in deciduous areas.
- **RANGE** Widespread throughout Europe and probably other parts of the north temperate zone.

bright scarlet inner surface

TOP VIEW

pale margin is finely serrated

minute curly white hairs cover outer surface

SIDE VIEW

- **FRUITING** In troops, on moss-covered wood. Late autumn–early summer.

PEZIZACEAE

CLASS: *Discomycetes*

Many of the familiar cup-fungi are found in this family, the most well-known belonging to the genus *Peziza*. The species are all cup-shaped. Colors vary from yellow or brown to lilac or blue. Most cup-fungi discharge a visible cloud of spores from microscopic sacs.

liver-brown inner surface

TOP VIEW

cup expands and darkens with age

granular, reddish brown outer surface

TOP VIEW

irregular cup margin

SIDE VIEW

stemless cup sits on soil

PEZIZA BADIA

Olive-brown Cup

One of the typically brown-colored *Peziza* species, *Peziza badia* can only be positively identified under the microscope. It is liver-brown in color but as it matures, the inside of the cup-shaped fruitbody turns a darker shade of olive-brown. Large and paler brown species can be found on rotten trunks.

- **SPORE DEPOSIT** White.
- **SIZE** Cup 1.5–7cm (w).
- **HABITAT** On acid soil by paths in conifer stands or on banks of ditches in boggy areas close to birch trees.
- **RANGE** Widespread and common in north temperate zones.

■ **FRUITING** Troops and small clusters on sandy soils. Summer–autumn.

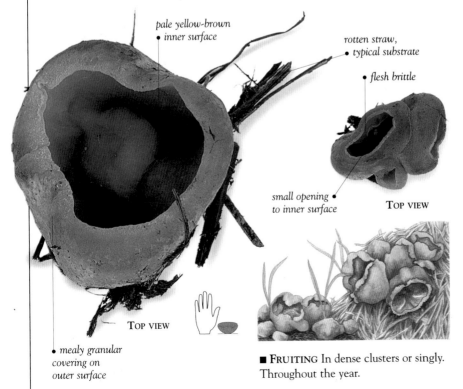

pale yellow-brown inner surface

rotten straw, typical substrate

flesh brittle

small opening to inner surface

TOP VIEW

TOP VIEW

mealy granular covering on outer surface

■ **FRUITING** In dense clusters or singly. Throughout the year.

PEZIZA VESICULOSA

Bladder Cup

Tightly rolled edges with a curved margin create the distinctive bladderlike shape of this fungus. It has a small opening for spore release and, unlike other *Peziza* species, it hardly expands with age. The outer surface is pale buff, and it is among the most thick-fleshed in the genus. It is often found growing alongside cup-fungi and agarics (fungi with gills), on nutrient-rich substrates.

- **SPORE DEPOSIT** White.
- **SIZE** Cup 3–10cm up to 15cm (w) x up to 4cm (h).
- **HABITAT** In parks, gardens, around farmhouses; on composted manure and mulch in flower beds, and rotting straw.
- **RANGE** Widespread and common in north temperate zones.

PEZIZA SUCCOSA

Yellow-milk Cup

A similar appearance to other *Peziza* species with its cup shape and olive-brown coloring. The flesh color, however, is the key identification feature: when cut with a knife, it gradually turns yellow and exudes a milky yellow juice. With age, the cup becomes irregular in shape.

■ **SPORE DEPOSIT** White.
■ **SIZE** Cup 0.5–5cm (w).
■ **HABITAT** On clay-rich soils, along roadsides in deciduous areas, often alongside *Helvella* and *Inocybe* species.
■ **RANGE** Widespread and common in Europe and also found in east and central North America.

a fairly pale specimen, usually darker

margin more or less even

almost smooth outer side

flesh stains yellow after breaking

TOP VIEW

FRAGMENT

TOP VIEW

cup expands with age

■ **FRUITING** Solitary or in troops. Summer–autumn.

OTIDEACEAE

CLASS: *Discomycetes*

A large family consisting of many soil-inhabiting species. They either have typical cup-shaped fruitbodies or ear-shaped fruitbodies with a slit down one side. Some of the cup-shaped forms are brightly colored and have dark hairs at the margin or on the entire outer surface. Family characteristics mainly lie in the spore-sac structure; the spores are released by a puffing action.

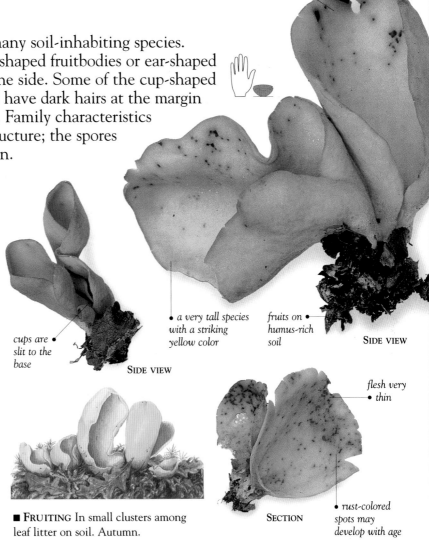

inner and outer surface smooth

OTIDEA ONOTICA

Lemon Peel Fungus

A spectacular lemon to yellow, rosy orange cup-fungus, which is earlike in shape. It is a representative of a fairly difficult genus of cup-fungi but this particular species can be readily identified. *Otidea* species are said to be edible but cannot be recommended. The smaller and browner species, *Otidea leporina*, is mainly found in needle beds in conifer forests.

■ **SPORE DEPOSIT** White.
■ **SIZE** Fruitbody 1–3cm (w) x 3–10cm (h).
■ **HABITAT** On the ground in conifer woods, but the fungus is not strictly associated with any host.
■ **RANGE** Widespread but with scattered occurrence in north temperate zones.

cups are slit to the base

a very tall species with a striking yellow color

fruits on humus-rich soil

SIDE VIEW

SIDE VIEW

flesh very thin

■ **FRUITING** In small clusters among leaf litter on soil. Autumn.

SECTION

rust-colored spots may develop with age

finely toothed cup margin

SECTION

short stem

outer surface has granular covering

light buff interior

wine-goblet shaped even when mature

SIDE VIEW

grayish cream spore-producing layer inside cup

often grows on bare soil

TOP VIEW

■ FRUITING In small groups mostly on bare soil. Summer–autumn.

TARZETTA CUPULARIS

Dentate Elf Cup

This species belongs to a small genus of closely related species, where size is a major distinguishing feature. *Tarzetta cupularis* lies in the middle of the range, *T. caninus* having the largest cup at 5cm in diameter. Both species are wine-goblet shaped even when mature, and the cup margin has small, triangular teeth. The degree of stem development and microscopic features also help determine the species. All members of the genus occur on rich calcareous or clay soils in parks and forests.

■ SPORE DEPOSIT White.
■ SIZE Cup 0.5–1.5cm (w) x 0.5–2.5cm (h).
■ HABITAT On clay or calcareous soil in parks and conifer forests.
■ RANGE Widespread and common in north temperate zones.

GEOPORA ARENICOLA

Sandy Earth-cup

Geopora arenicola produces fairly large cup-shaped fruitbodies with a hairy brown outer surface. Inside the cup the tiny flask-fungus parasite *Melanospora brevirostris* can sometimes be found. Earth-cups have also been placed in the genus *Sepultaria*. It is difficult to distinguish many species in this genus. The spores of *G. arenicola*, however, are comparatively large. All *Sepultaria* species are sunk in the soil and some never produce more than a tiny opening from which they disperse spores. When very mature some fruitbodies may split in a starlike pattern and can thus be more easily located. *Humaria hemisphaerica* is very similar but develops on the soil surface.

■ SPORE DEPOSIT White.
■ SIZE Cup 0.5–2cm (w).
■ HABITAT Buried beneath gravel or sand along roads or in gravel pits.
■ RANGE Widespread and common in Europe, but easily overlooked. Found in northeastern US and California.

smooth interior

TOP VIEW

cup splits open to release spores

old, excavated specimen

TOP VIEW

cup buried in mossy, sandy soil

TOP VIEW

cup often splits in lobes with age

fruitbody can be mistaken for insect burrow

■ FRUITING Troops break through gravel or sand. Summer–autumn.

TOP VIEW

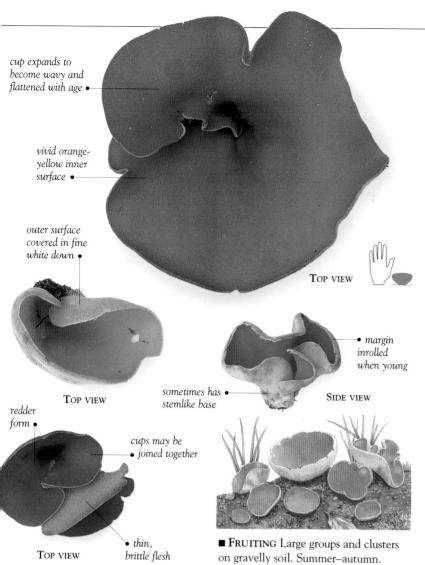

cup expands to become wavy and flattened with age •

vivid orange-yellow inner surface •

outer surface covered in fine white down •

TOP VIEW

TOP VIEW

sometimes has • stemlike base

• margin inrolled when young

SIDE VIEW

redder form •

cups may be • joined together

• thin, brittle flesh

TOP VIEW

■ **FRUITING** Large groups and clusters on gravelly soil. Summer–autumn.

ALEURIA AURANTIA

Orange Peel Fungus

One of the most attractive and common of the cup-fungi. Well-developed specimens are easy to distinguish from other species in the family although a smaller reddish orange species, *Melastiza chateri*, may cause confusion. It grows on similar sites, where a number of *Scutellinia* species (*see below*) can also be found. In contrast to the almost smooth *Aleuria aurantia*, *Melastiza chateri* can be identified by the very short brownish hairs at the margin of the cup. Found mostly throughout Europe, but does not occur in North America. Although occasionally eaten, *Aleuria aurantia* mainly serves a decorative rather than a culinary purpose; it must be cooked because it is toxic when raw.

■ **SPORE DEPOSIT** White.
■ **SIZE** Cup 2–10cm (w); occasionally cups less than 0.5cm and large specimens broader than 15cm.
■ **HABITAT** Disturbed sites, such as on dirt roads, and on new lawns.
■ **RANGE** Widespread and common in European north temperate zones.

SCUTELLINIA SCUTELLATA

Common Eyelash Cup

A common, highly distinctive fungus that grows on rotten wood. Other species in the genus favor damp soil. *Scutellinia scutellata* has very conspicuous long-haired "eyelashes" at the cup margin. The vivid orange-red color is due to the presence of carotene, also present in a range of other orange-colored fungi. The spore shape and spore ornamentation, seen under the microscope, offer the best clues for identification in this difficult genus.

■ **SPORE DEPOSIT** White.
■ **SIZE** Cup 0.5–1cm (w).
■ **HABITAT** On wet wood throughout forested areas. Also common among willow trees and in bogs and other marshy places.
■ **RANGE** Widespread and common in the north temperate zones.

grows on wet rotten wood substrate •

• typically in dense swarms

TOP VIEW

black hairs project • inward when immature

• black hairs project outward when cup is fully mature

TOP VIEW

bright • orange-red inner surface

TOP VIEW

■ **FRUITING** In dense swarms on rotten wood. Late spring–winter.

TUBERACEAE

CLASS: *Discomycetes*

Fungi that develop underground fruitbodies are collectively known as truffles, and none can compare in economic importance with the edible tuber truffles. The very distinct smell and taste have always attracted mankind and other animals, and today a handful of species are among the most expensive foods. Truffles, unlike most other fungi, do not have the mechanism for violent spore discharge. They rely on animals, such as pigs and squirrels, to transport fruitbodies. North America has more than 200 kinds of underground tuberlike fungi, and even a few species of true truffles.

TUBER AESTIVUM

Summer Truffle

The least expensive of the true edible tubers, *Tuber aestivum* occurs over most of Europe in association with the roots of deciduous trees. Like its relatives, it has a distinct but rather faint aroma. Flies attracted to *Tuber* species help collectors pinpoint truffle sites.

- ■ **SPORE COLOR** Yellow-brown.
- ■ **SIZE** Fruitbody 2–5cm (w).
- ■ **HABITAT** Found among roots of beech and birch trees.
- ■ **RANGE** Europe, to southern Scandinavia.

pyramidal • black warts on surface

SIDE VIEW

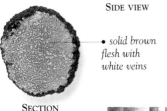

• solid brown flesh with white veins

SECTION

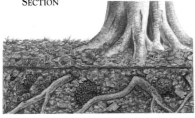

- ■ **FRUITING** Singly below soil level among tree roots. Summer.

TUBER MAGNATUM

White Truffle

A specialty from the Piemonte region of Italy, *Tuber magnatum* has a spicy odor and flavor. Attempts to cultivate by inoculating suitable host roots are being carried out on a large scale and may cause prices to drop in the near future.

- ■ **SPORE COLOR** Brown.
- ■ **SIZE** Fruitbody 2–8cm (w).
- ■ **HABITAT** Buried in calcareous soil among roots of oak, but also found under poplars and willows.
- ■ **RANGE** Piemonte region of northwestern Italy.

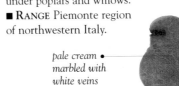

pale cream • marbled with white veins

SECTION

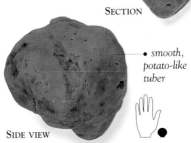

• smooth, potato-like tuber

SIDE VIEW

- ■ **FRUITING** Singly, buried among tree roots. Autumn–winter.

TUBER MELANOSPORUM

Perigord Truffle

This is the royal truffle of France, named after the Perigord district. This truffle is traditionally collected by skilled pickers employing trained dogs or pigs. It is a warmth-loving species, confined to southern France, Italy, and Spain where the annual yield is about 330 tons. *Tuber melanosporum* is now commercially available as inoculated seedlings. *Tuber brumale* is a similar species that occurs farther north, reaching the British Isles. Other edible *Tuber* species occur in North America.

- ■ **SPORE COLOR** Dark brown.
- ■ **SIZE** Fruitbody 2–7cm (w).
- ■ **HABITAT** Occurs under species of Mediterranean oaks and other host trees on calcareous, red Mediterranean soils.
- ■ **RANGE** Confined to southern Europe.

coal black surface •

SIDE VIEW

• rough rind made up of hundreds of polygonal warts

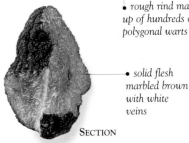

• solid flesh marbled brown with white veins

SECTION

- ■ **FRUITING** Singly, buried among tree roots. Late autumn–early spring.

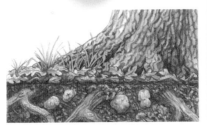

GEOGLOSSACEAE

CLASS: *Discomycetes*

Earth-tongues and their allies have fruitbodies elongated into club-shaped structures, lifting the spore-producing part above ground. In North America most species are associated with, and often prefer, a forest habitat, while some species prefer boggy areas. They are small, often brightly colored mushrooms found growing on plant stems.

GEOGLOSSUM FALLAX

Scaly Earth-tongue

The genus *Geoglossum* is similar in appearance to *Trichoglossum* but the species have no hairs covering the fruitbodies. Most fruitbodies are black, but *Geoglossum fallax* is dark brown and has a scaly pattern on the upper part of the stem. Many species of earth-tongue are now threatened as a result of habitat loss; pastureland is slowly being abandoned, and fertilizers are added to improve arable yields. Planting of conifers on marginal lands only adds to the problem.

- **SPORE DEPOSIT** Dark brown.
- **SIZE** Club 3–7cm (h) x 0.3–0.7cm (w).
- **HABITAT** On soil in woods.
- **RANGE** Widespread and quite common throughout Europe and eastern North America although easily overlooked.

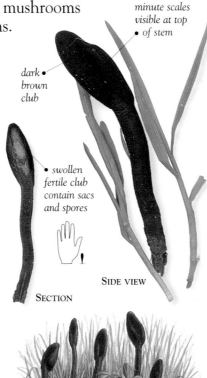

minute scales visible at top of stem

dark brown club

swollen fertile club contain sacs and spores

SECTION

SIDE VIEW

- **FRUITING** Small groups in moss, or hidden in tall grass. Autumn.

TRICHOGLOSSUM HIRSUTUM

Shaggy Earth-tongue

The hallmark of the *Trichoglossum* species is the bristly hairs that project from the flesh over the entire club-shaped fruitbody. The swollen area of the club holds the microscopic asci containing long, multiseptate spores. The head of the club is normally slightly compressed, and it often varies greatly in shape and size.

- **SPORE DEPOSIT** Dark brown.
- **SIZE** Club 3–12cm (h) x 0.3–1cm (w).
- **HABITAT** On rotting wood in moss and in wet woods.
- **RANGE** Widespread throughout the north temperate zones.

- **FRUITING** Troops in grass, leaf litter, or moss. Late summer–autumn.

MITRULA PALUDOSA

Bog Beacon

This attractive fungus, with a glistening orange head and white stem, is a complex of species that can only be differentiated microscopically. Its spores are colorless, and the flesh is smooth. A range of similar fungi, found in drier habitats, are placed in the *Leotiaceae* (*see p.36*).

- **SPORE DEPOSIT** White.
- **SIZE** Club 2–5cm (h) x 0.2–1cm (w).
- **HABITAT** Stagnant, unpolluted water.
- **RANGE** North temperate zones; prefers northern areas and higher altitudes.

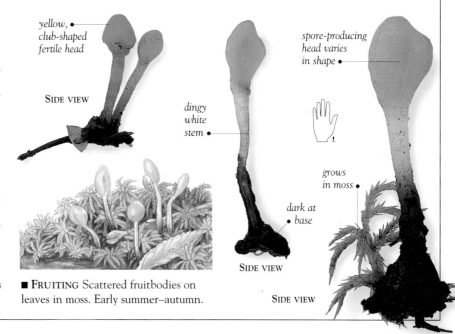

yellow, club-shaped fertile head

SIDE VIEW

dingy white stem

spore-producing head varies in shape

grows in moss

dark at base

SIDE VIEW

SIDE VIEW

- **FRUITING** Scattered fruitbodies on leaves in moss. Early summer–autumn.

LEOTIACEAE

CLASS: *Discomycetes*

Leotiaceae, until recently classified as *Helotiaceae*, contains a wealth of tiny, mostly disk-shaped fungi with spores borne in asci – with a small ring within the tip. Many species are firm-fleshed, almost rubbery in texture. Some species have fruitbodies that are well hidden among tall grass or in thick leaf litter; others have much showier fruitbodies arranged in swarms on rotten wood.

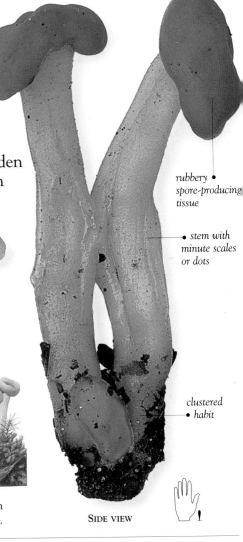

- *rubbery spore-producing tissue*
- *stem with minute scales or dots*
- *clustered habit*

SIDE VIEW

LEOTIA LUBRICA

Jelly Babies

A delightfully named fungus with small pestle-shaped, rubbery fruitbodies. The spore-producing tissue is situated on the convex head. *Leotia lubrica* can develop a blackish green hue as a result of a fungal infection, but even healthy specimens can turn olive in color when mature.

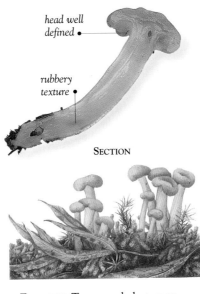

- *head well defined*
- *rubbery texture*

SECTION

- ■ **SPORE DEPOSIT** White.
- ■ **SIZE** Club 2–5cm (h) x 0.3–1cm (w).
- ■ **HABITAT** Damp woods among leaf litter and moss.
- ■ **RANGE** Widespread and common in most of the north temperate zone.

■ **FRUITING** Troops and clusters on damp soil, among mosses. Autumn.

- *disk-shaped flat top*
- *spore-producing tissue*

TOP VIEW

- *fruitbody is pale pink and translucent*
- *rubbery texture*

SIDE VIEW

■ **FRUITING** In clusters on fresh bark of fallen beech. Late autumn.

NEOBULGARIA PURA

Beech Jelly-disk

Newly emerged, fresh specimens of *Neobulgaria pura* are very firm and rubbery but later, after exposure to the weather, they will eventually collapse and become much thinner and less attractive. Still, they will persist from autumn into winter. The margin is finely toothed, and the spore-producing top surface is virtually flat. In habit and habitat, it is similar to *Bulgaria inquinans*, but it is much paler and softer.

- ■ **SPORE DEPOSIT** White.
- ■ **SIZE** Disks 0.5–3cm (w) x 1cm thick.
- ■ **HABITAT** Occurs on the relatively fresh bark of fallen beech trunks and branches, often next to *Hypoxylon fragiforme* (see p.41).
- ■ **RANGE** North temperate zones; in most areas where beech occurs.

BULGARIA INQUINANS

Black Jelly Drops

An unusual feature in *Bulgaria inquinans* is the jet black spores, in this case very conspicuous, and not usually encountered in the family. When touched, fingers become smudged by a layer of black spores that have collected on top of the licorice-like fruitbodies; the surrounding bark may be black with ejected spores. Of the eight spores formed within each ascus, however, only the top four develop the dark coloring. The staining property of the spores has been used for dyeing wool. In their natural habitat, the disks may appear blue, not black, due to their reflective qualities.

- **SPORE DEPOSIT** Jet black.
- **SIZE** Disk 0.5–4cm (w) x 1cm thick.
- **HABITAT** On recently fallen beech or oak trunks, and always on the bark, mostly on the upper surface.
- **RANGE** Widespread and common where host trees occur in north temperate zones.

fertile disk is black and smooth

fruitbodies are rubbery and firm in texture

surface of disks covered in ejected black spores

SECTION

TOP VIEW

black spores collect on nearby bark

grows on bark from beech or oak

TOP VIEW

scurfy brown exterior

SIDE VIEW

■ **FRUITING** In swarms, on fresh bark of fallen tree trunks. Autumn–winter.

ASCOCORYNE CYLICHNIUM

Large Purple-drop

The most obvious feature of this fungus and its near relatives is the reddish purple, gelatinous, cup-shaped fruitbodies. They are similar to but much thinner than *Bulgaria inquinans* and are also found in woods. Both bark and exposed wood serve as substrates. *Ascocoryne cylichnium* is distinguished from *Ascocoryne sarcoides* by its broader disks and longer spores. Also, *A. sarcoides*, unlike *A. cylichnium*, forms a distinct brainlike imperfect state, where asexual spores are produced. Several other smaller species occur in the northern hemisphere.

- **SPORE DEPOSIT** White.
- **SIZE** Disk 0.5–2cm (w) x 0.2–0.4cm thick.
- **HABITAT** On a wide range of deciduous trees.
- **RANGE** Widespread and fairly common in the north temperate zones.

rubbery texture

smooth upper and lower surface

distinct reddish purple disks

SIDE VIEW

short stalk attached to substrate

grows on wood or bark

TOP VIEW

■ **FRUITING** In swarms on tree stumps and branches. Autumn–winter.

brainlike gelatinous flesh

IMPERFECT STATE OF *ASCOCORYNE SARCOIDES*

CHLOROCIBORIA AERUGINASCENS

Green Stain

This species produces a blue-green stain inside its woody substrate. The tough, disk-shaped fruitbodies are a similar blue-green color but are less commonly seen. Some related species, especially *Chlorociboria aeruginosa* may also produce a green stain in fallen or stored wood. Spore size is a key feature in distinguishing the separate species.

- **SPORE DEPOSIT** White.
- **SIZE** Disk 0.2–1cm (w) x 0.1cm thick.
- **HABITAT** Deciduous woods, often on a fallen oak or hazel log.
- **RANGE** Widespread and fairly common in north temperate zones.

- **FRUITING** Scattered or clustered on dead wood. All year.

disk-shaped fruitbody

disk raised on short stem

SIDE VIEW

margin sometimes wavy, irregular

underside of disk lighter in color

surface of wood may be unstained

SIDE VIEW

smooth margin

verdigris color

TOP VIEW

fruitbodies scattered on stained wood

TOP VIEW

infected wood used to make decorative veneers

STAINED WOOD

wood stained blue-green by fungal activity

dense swarm of disks on deciduous trees

typically grows on bare deciduous trees

TOP VIEW

disks may have an irregular outline and rusty spots

TOP VIEW

smooth surface to fruitbody

nail-head shaped

TOP VIEW   **SIDE VIEW**

- **FRUITING** In swarms on fallen bare wood. Autumn–early winter.

BISPORELLA CITRINA

Lemon Disk

The clustered habit and vivid yellow color of this tiny species mean that you can see it from a surprising distance in a woodland landscape. Although it has a typical form and occurs in a characteristic habitat, it could be mistaken for a number of other yellow, closely related cup-fungi. Some of these species differ only microscopically, or in having the disk-shaped fruitbody raised on a stem. Some species of *Bisporella* occur alongside their blackish imperfect states, others occur on old *Xylaria* species (see p.40).

- **SPORE DEPOSIT** White.
- **SIZE** Disk 0.1–0.3cm (w); less than 1mm thick.
- **HABITAT** Bare, deciduous trees; often on beech and oak.
- **RANGE** Widespread and very common throughout north temperate zones.

SCLEROTINIACEAE

CLASS: *Discomycetes*

Members of this family develop *sclerotia* – solid masses of fungal tissue protected by a hard black rind – that survive from one season to the next, eventually giving rise to mostly long-stemmed, cup- or disk-shaped fruitbodies. Most species attack living plant tissue and can severely damage crops, such as apple trees and canola. The fruitbodies are often brown and the stems are blackened toward the base.

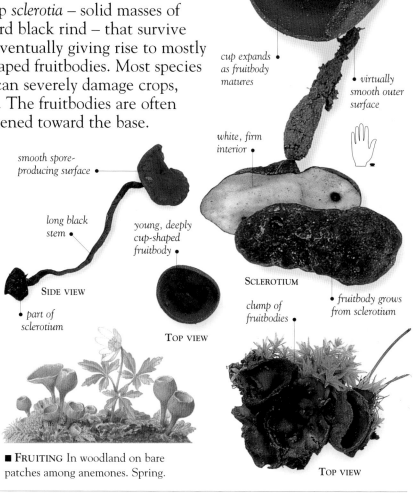

- cup expands as fruitbody matures
- virtually smooth outer surface
- white, firm interior
- smooth spore-producing surface
- long black stem
- young, deeply cup-shaped fruitbody
- **SCLEROTIUM**
- clump of fruitbodies
- fruitbody grows from sclerotium
- part of sclerotium
- **SIDE VIEW**
- **TOP VIEW**
- **TOP VIEW**

DUMONTINIA TUBEROSA

Tuber Cup

The cup-shaped chestnut-brown fruitbody grows up out of an elongated black sclerotium, formed underground. This species has perhaps the largest fruitbodies of the family.

- ■ **SPORE DEPOSIT** White.
- ■ **SIZE** Cup 0.5–3cm (w); stem 2–10cm (h); sclerotia 1.5–4cm long.
- ■ **HABITAT** Parasitic on wood anemones in Europe. On ground in US.
- ■ **RANGE** Widespread and local to common in some areas of Europe and North America.

■ **FRUITING** In woodland on bare patches among anemones. Spring.

- navel-like center
- attached by short stalk to oak branch
- **SIDE VIEW**
- cup-shape flattens with age
- **TOP VIEW**

RUTSTROEMIA FIRMA

Brown Oak-disk

A species that forms no true sclerotium but shares other characteristics with the rest of the family, favoring one specific host genus, in this case oak trees. The wood turns black from the fungal activity. It is smaller than *Dumontinia tuberosa* (*see above*), but it is still one of the larger species of *Sclerotiniaceae*. In eastern US, the common species is *Rutstroemia* (*Ciboria*) *macrospora*, which is smaller, short-stemmed, and grayish.

- ■ **SPORE DEPOSIT** White.
- ■ **SIZE** Disk 0.5–1.5cm (w); stem 0.2–1cm long.
- ■ **HABITAT** On fallen oak branches.
- ■ **RANGE** Widespread in Europe.

- occurs in groups on discolored wood
- fine wrinkles on underside of disk
- **TOP VIEW**
- **UNDERSIDE**

■ **FRUITING** Singly or in small groups on oak branches. Autumn.

Xylariaceae

Class: *Pyrenomycetes*

Flask fungi, the common name for the *Pyrenomycetes*, are so called because asci and spores develop within tiny flask-shaped organs. In the *Xylariaceae*, the numerous species mostly produce composite fruitbodies containing a number of flasks within firm flesh. Spores are ejected by force and are typically very dark. You can often see the spores with the naked eye as a dark, sooty smudge on the tree bark.

• fertile upper part

black flasks • embedded in white flesh

Sexual state   dark brown • furry stem   Section

Xylaria hypoxylon

Carbon Antlers

A very conspicuous species, *Xylaria hypoxylon* has striking white, antler-shaped fructifications that stand out on stumps in deciduous wood. By late autumn the mature fruitbody appears coal-black and less branched. In section the flesh is white like in most species of *Xylaria*.

■ **Spore Deposit** Black.
■ **Size** Fruitbody 1–6cm (h) x 0.2–0.5cm (w).
■ **Habitat** Deciduous trees especially on stumps in parks and forest.
■ **Range** Widespread and common throughout north temperate zones.

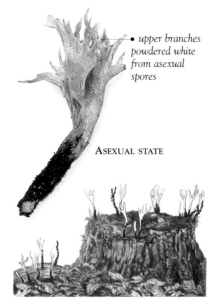

• upper branches powdered white from asexual spores

Asexual state

■ **Fruiting** In small groups on tree stumps. All year.

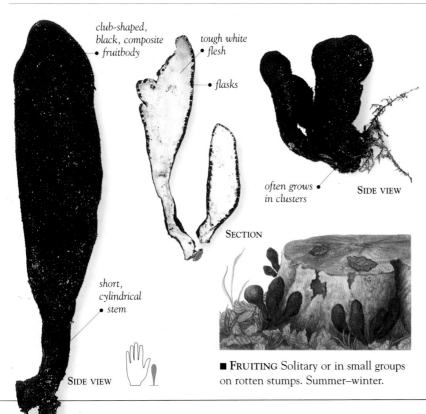

club-shaped, black, composite • fruitbody

tough white • flesh

• flasks

often grows • in clusters   **Side view**

Section

short, cylindrical • stem

Side view

■ **Fruiting** Solitary or in small groups on rotten stumps. Summer–winter.

Xylaria polymorpha

Dead Man's Fingers

Although confined to a shadowy existence at soil level, this is a well-known fungus. It typically grows in small, dense clusters and the clubs have rounded tips. In section, the flesh is thick. In north temperate regions another common species, *Xylaria longipes*, is similar in size, but its fingers are slender and smaller. It is generally confined to dead sycamore wood.

■ **Spore Deposit** Black.
■ **Size** Club 3–10cm (h) x 1–4cm (w).
■ **Habitat** In woods and parks; attached to wood of beech and maple; often at soil level.
■ **Range** Widespread, and rather common, in north temperate zones.

DALDINIA CONCENTRICA

Cramp Balls

This stands out among the flask fungi, being very large and zoned in dark and light bands inside the composite fruitbodies. The flasks (perithecia) are arranged in a layer just beneath the rusty brown surface, with their mouths opening to the surface in order to make a passage for the forcibly ejected black spores. The composite fruitbodies persist for a long time. The surface eventually turns black, and they become crumbly in texture.

- **SPORE DEPOSIT** Black.
- **SIZE** Fruitbody 2–10cm (w).
- **HABITAT** Mostly found on still standing dead or dying trunks of ash, and also on birch and a range of other deciduous trees in parks and forests, especially following fire damage.
- **RANGE** Widespread in north temperate zones, common in some regions of North America and Europe.

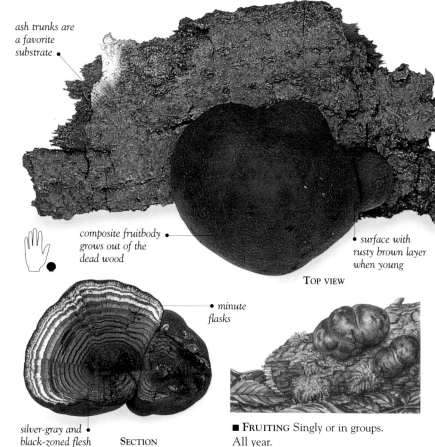

ash trunks are a favorite substrate

composite fruitbody grows out of the dead wood

surface with rusty brown layer when young

TOP VIEW

minute flasks

silver-gray and black-zoned flesh **SECTION**

- **FRUITING** Singly or in groups. All year.

overmature composite fruitbodies turn black

SIDE VIEW

composite hemispherical fruitbodies

DETACHED FRUITBODIES

FRAGMENTS

surface surrounded by blackish spores

dead beech bark darkened by deposited spores

TOP VIEW

HYPOXYLON FRAGIFORME

Beech Wood-wart

A wood- and bark-degrading species. The composite fruitbodies range from pink through brick red to black, when overmature. A nearly identical species, *H. howeianum*, occurs on other deciduous trees. A flat, spreading, reddish brown species, *H. rubiginosum* is also common. On hazel and alder a purple species, *H. fuscum*, occurs.

- **SPORE DEPOSIT** Black.
- **SIZE** Fruitbody 0.5–3cm (w).
- **HABITAT** In forests; on bark of freshly fallen beech trees.
- **RANGE** Widespread and common wherever beech occurs in north temperate zones.

- **FRUITING** Troops on the bark of beech trees. All year.

CLAVICIPITACEAE

CLASS: *Pyrenomycetes*

Members of this family are either feared crop parasites or feed on insects. The ergot-producing *Claviceps purpurea* is infamous for causing death in medieval times when it infested grain used in making bread. Typically, the flasks – the organ in which the asci and spores develop – are borne within composite fruitbodies and, as a rule, are supported on long stems.

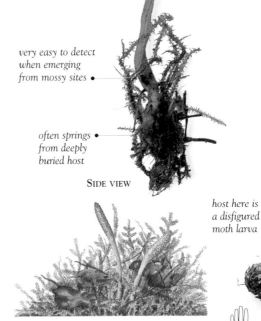

flasks break through swollen head creating • pimply surface

smooth lower part of club • without flasks

CORDYCEPS MILITARIS

Orange Caterpillar Fungus

A parasite whose mycelium, after killing the host, replaces the inside of moth larvae or pupae. In time, an orange-red composite fruitbody emerges. On the upper region of the club, the flasks can be seen as protruding spikes. *Cordyceps* species are primarily of tropical and sub-tropical distribution; they parasitize insects and trufflelike fungi.

■ **SPORE DEPOSIT** White.
■ **SIZE** Club 2–5cm (h) x 0.3–0.8cm (w).
■ **HABITAT** On dead moth larvae and pupae, either in forests or grassland.
■ **RANGE** Widespread in the north temperate regions.

very easy to detect when emerging from mossy sites •

often springs from deeply buried host

SIDE VIEW

host here is a disfigured moth larva •

■ **FRUITING** Singly or in small groups from pupae or larvae. Summer–autumn.

SIDE VIEW

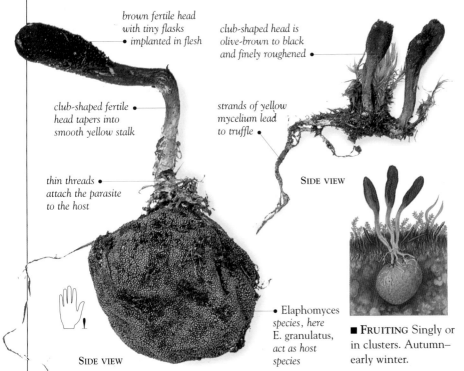

brown fertile head with tiny flasks • implanted in flesh

club-shaped head is olive-brown to black and finely roughened •

club-shaped fertile • head tapers into smooth yellow stalk

strands of yellow mycelium lead to truffle •

thin threads • attach the parasite to the host

SIDE VIEW

• Elaphomyces species, here E. granulatus, act as host species

■ **FRUITING** Singly or in clusters. Autumn–early winter.

SIDE VIEW

CORDYCEPS OPHIOGLOSSOIDES

Slender Truffle-club

A group of *Cordyceps* species have evolved to become parasites on *Elaphomyces*, a genus of underground ascomycete fungi. *C. ophioglossoides* attaches itself to the underground fruitbody of the host with yellow threads. *C. capitata* can also occur on the same host.

■ **SPORE DEPOSIT** White.
■ **SIZE** Club (fertile part) 1–3cm (h) x 0.5–1cm (w); stem including rooting part up to 10cm long.
■ **HABITAT** Emerges from *Elaphomyces muricatus* or *E. granulatus* in both conifer and deciduous woods.
■ **RANGE** Widespread and locally common in north temperate zones.

BASIDIOMYCOTA

This division of the fungal kingdom contains many fungi that superfically bear no resemblance to one another – gilled mushrooms and puffballs belong here as do jelly fungi, coral-shaped fungi, toothed fungi, bracket, and crust fungi – but under the microscope their similarity becomes clear. They all produce spores on microscopic, typically club-shaped structures known as basidia, where one sexual spore sits at the tip of each of four outgrowths called sterigmata.

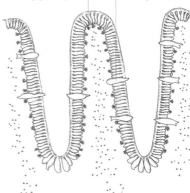

hymenium – closely packed fertile cells covering gill surface

sterile cells (cystidia) are often present among basidia

one spore is born at the tip of each sterigma

clamps are a key feature of basidiomycetes

STRUCTURE OF BASIDIA

CROSS-SECTION OF GILLS

spores fall between gills and are wind dispersed

AURICULARIACEAE

CLASS: HETEROBASIDIOMYCETES

This family belongs with the jelly fungi, which can be partly identified by the gelatinous nature of the flesh. Under the microscope, the spore-bearing structure appears elongated – each segment giving rise to a spore. The spore-producing tissue is situated on the underside of the fruitbodies – it is smooth or wrinkled. *Auriculariaceae* is a mixed group, and so classification is constantly under review.

AURICULARIA AURICULA-JUDAE

Wood Ear

The distinctive ear-shaped fruitbody is gelatinous when fresh but hardens when dry. The tan-brown outer surface is covered in downy hairs, and the inner surface is wrinkled. Although considered bland in the West, it is eaten in the Chinese diet, dried or boiled with rice, and is prized for its medicinal value.

- ■ **SPORE DEPOSIT** White.
- ■ **SIZE** Fruitbody 2–10cm (w).
- ■ **HABITAT** A complex of species found on both deciduous and coniferous wood.
- ■ **RANGE** Widespread in warmer parts of the north temperate zones.

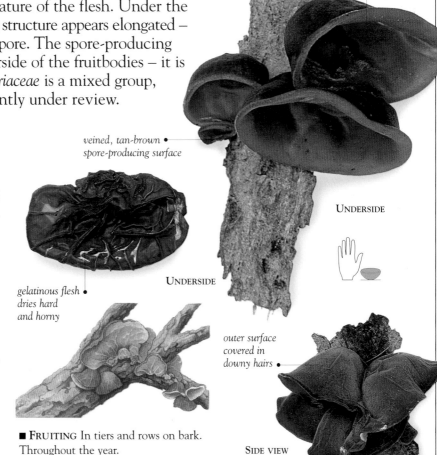

ear-shaped fruitbody

veined, tan-brown spore-producing surface

UNDERSIDE

gelatinous flesh dries hard and horny

UNDERSIDE

outer surface covered in downy hairs

- ■ **FRUITING** In tiers and rows on bark. Throughout the year.

SIDE VIEW

AURICULARIA MESENTERICA

Tripe Fungus

This species has attractive marked zonation on the top surface due to fine, velvety hairs. At first glance, it appears to be a bracket fungus, but when handled, it can be identified by its rubbery, gelatinous flesh. It is rare or absent in all but the southernmost part of the United States. Although considered edible, it is not worthwhile.

■ **SPORE DEPOSIT** White.
■ **SIZE** Bracket 4–15cm (w) x 1–5cm deep and 0.2–0.5cm thick.
■ **HABITAT** On deciduous wood. Where there is dead elm, it can be abundant alongside other elmwood fungi.
■ **RANGE** Widespread in Europe but somewhat local; southern North America, rare in the US.

upperside of bracket has velvety zoned covering

TOP VIEW

green color due to algae

flesh is rubbery and jellylike in texture

wrinkled and veined spore-producing surface

UNDERSIDE

■ **FRUITING** Tiers of brackets on wood. Throughout the year.

TREMELLACEAE

CLASS: *Heterobasiomycetes*

A more closely defined family, now that it has been found that all true members are parasitic on other wood-inhabiting fungi. Most species can dry out into inconspicuous skinlike structures, which rehydrate in wet weather. The fruitbodies can thus persist for months. The basidia are split lengthwise. Here the family is treated in a broad sense.

brown coloratio

TOP VIEW

flesh very gelatinous

fruitbody strongly folded, brainlike

TREMELLA FOLIACEA

Leafy Brain Fungus

A brown species, easy to identify by its strongly folded and highly gelatinous fruitbodies attached to tree bark. It is a parasite but its range of hosts is unknown. *Ascotremella faginea*, a strongly folded gelatinous *Discomycete*, may resemble *T. foliacea*.

■ **SPORE DEPOSIT** White.
■ **SIZE** Fruitbody 4–12cm (w).
■ **HABITAT** Parasitic on deciduous trees, but also pine in parks and woods.
■ **RANGE** Widespread in north temperate zones.

dried-up fruitbody can be reconstituted by rainwater.

DRY SPECIMEN

■ **FRUITING** Clumps on dead branches, or on fallen trunks. Autumn–winter.

TREMELLA MESENTERICA

Yellow Brain Fungus

The striking, almost transparent yellow color of this jelly fungus makes it easy to see on dark autumn days. In dry weather the fruitbody shrivels up, but it becomes rehydrated in moist conditions. A common North American look-alike is *Dacrymyces palmatus* (*see p.46*), which occurs on conifer logs and has a distinct white mycelial attachment to the wood. It has tuning fork-shaped basidia.

■ **SPORE DEPOSIT** White.
■ **SIZE** Confluent fruitbody 1–6cm long.
■ **HABITAT** Parasitic on *Corticiaceae* found within deciduous branches; often in piles of brushwood.
■ **RANGE** Widespread and common in north temperate zones.

fruitbody sits on bark of deciduous branch

TOP VIEW

soft, flabby gelatinous lobes

white form or color lost in prolonged wet spell

dried-out, brittle flesh

dark orange fruitbody revives in wet weather

DRY SPECIMEN

■ **FRUITING** Singly, breaking out from within bark. Mostly late autumn–winter.

---

black surface with brainlike folds

spreading fruitbodies often fuse together

TOP VIEW

fruitbodies appear on bark-clad or bare dead deciduous wood

EXIDIA GLANDULOSA

Black Brain Fungus

This species looks like tar and is firmer and less gelatinous to touch than *Tremella mesenterica* (*see above*). *Exidia* and *Tremella* species are in fact not closely related, but here they have been kept together for identification purposes. The yellowish brown to brown *Exidia recisa*, also found on deciduous wood, can often resemble a small *Auricularia auricula-judae* (*see p.43*). *E. truncata* occurs mainly on oak.

■ **SPORE DEPOSIT** White.
■ **SIZE** Fruitbodies often 2–10cm long.
■ **HABITAT** In forests; bare and bark-clad dead wood of deciduous trees.
■ **RANGE** Widespread and common in north temperate zones.

TOP VIEW

surface becomes more folded and wrinkled with age

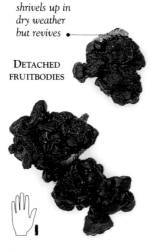

shrivels up in dry weather but revives

DETACHED FRUITBODIES

■ **FRUITING** Confluent fruitbodies form on bark and wood. Late autumn–winter.

PSEUDOHYDNUM GELATINOSUM

Toothed Jelly

Although it resembles a member of the *Hydnaceae* (*see p.53*), this unique and unmistakable species is classified with an entirely different group. The flesh is gelatinous, and the cap is more or less semicircular, with a slightly rough or downy surface. The spore-producing underside is covered with pale spines. The short, fat stem is often attached at the side of the cap. The cap varies in color from almost white to dark gray-brown. Although edible, it is not worthwhile.

- ■ **SPORE DEPOSIT** White.
- ■ **SIZE** Cap 1–8cm (w); stem 0.5–3cm (h).
- ■ **HABITAT** On rotting conifer wood; rarely found on well-rotten deciduous stumps or fallen branches.
- ■ **RANGE** Widespread in the north temperate zone. Also occurs in warmer regions throughout North America.

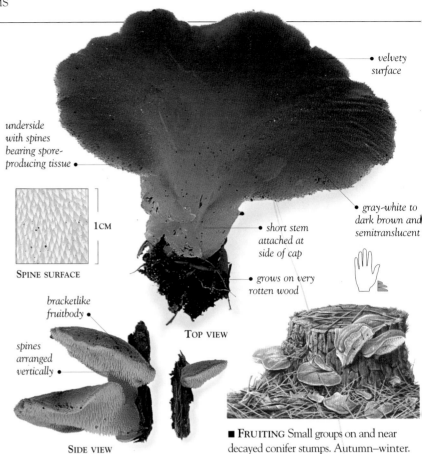

underside with spines bearing spore-producing tissue

1CM

SPINE SURFACE

• *velvety surface*

• *gray-white to dark brown and semitranslucent*

• *short stem attached at side of cap*

• *grows on very rotten wood*

TOP VIEW

bracketlike fruitbody •

spines arranged vertically •

SIDE VIEW

■ **FRUITING** Small groups on and near decayed conifer stumps. Autumn–winter.

DACRYMYCETACEAE

CLASS: *Heterobasidiomycetes*

A family with unique tuning fork-shaped basidia, on which the spores are borne. The mostly orange fruitbodies have a gelatinous to rubbery texture. Typical shapes include club- and antler-shaped in *Calocera*, and trumpet-shaped as in *Tremiscus helvelloides*. The very common species *Dacrymyces palmatus* has tiny cushion-shaped gelatinous fruitbodies. All can degrade woody substrates.

CALOCERA VISCOSA

Jelly Antler

Unlike the similarly shaped coral and club-fungi (*see pp.49–53*), this jelly fungus grows only on the rotten wood of conifer trees and is tough and rubbery in texture. There are a few other smaller species of *Calocera*, the most common being *C. cornea*, which is much smaller, has unbranched to rarely forked clubs, and grows on the twigs and branches of deciduous woods.

- ■ **SPORE DEPOSIT** White.
- ■ **SIZE** Fruitbody 3–10cm (h).
- ■ **HABITAT** On decayed conifer wood.
- ■ **RANGE** Widespread and common in north temperate zones.

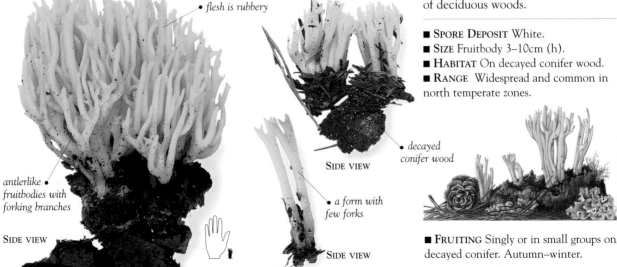

• *flesh is rubbery*

antlerlike • *fruitbodies with forking branches*

SIDE VIEW

SIDE VIEW

• *a form with few forks*

SIDE VIEW

• *decayed conifer wood*

■ **FRUITING** Singly or in small groups on decayed conifer. Autumn–winter.

CANTHARELLACEAE

CLASS: *Homobasidiomycetes*

The flavors of *Cantharellus* and its allies are among the most desirable of all edible fungi, and wild-picked species are exported worldwide. *Cantharellus* are shaped somewhat like species of *Clitocybe* (*see p.86*) but the underside of the cap bears thick veins, characteristically forked, rather than true gills, and some species are virtually smooth underneath. *C. cibarius* is solid and firm-fleshed, while *C. tubaeformis* and *Craterellus cornucopioides* are hollow. *Cantharellaceae* develop more than four spores on their basidia. All species are mycorrhizal with trees.

CANTHARELLUS CIBARIUS

Common Chanterelle

This species varies widely in color, but is often yellow with a hint of red. All forms smell similar to dried apricots and are very good edibles (*see p.244 for recipe*). *C. cibarius* has its main season in summer, but its harvest can be ruined by low rainfall. *Hygrophoropsis aurantiaca* (*see p.200*) looks similar and is harmless, while *Omphalotus olearius* (*see p.200*) is a poisonous look-alike.

- **SPORE DEPOSIT** Pale cream.
- **SIZE** Cap 2–12cm (w); stem 2–10cm (h) x 0.4–1.5cm (w).
- **HABITAT** With spruce and pine, but also with deciduous trees, such as oak.
- **RANGE** Widespread in cold and warm temperate regions of the northern hemisphere; very common to rare.

CANTHARELLUS LUTESCENS

Golden Chanterelle

This is a *Cantharellus* species that occurs in woodland with alkaline soils. The yellow-brown cap is more or less funnel-shaped. The stem is hollow and the flesh rather thin. The spore-producing layer on the underside of the cap is almost smooth and paler than the veins found in *C. tubaeformis*, which has gill-like ridges. In this respect it resembles species of *Craterellus* (*see p.48*). Like most other *Cantharellus* species, it is a delicious edible (*see p.244 for recipes*).

- **SPORE DEPOSIT** Pale cream.
- **SIZE** Cap 2–7cm (w); stem 3–7cm (h) x 0.3–0.8cm (w).
- **HABITAT** In damp, moss-rich, calcareous woodland; mycorrhizal.
- **RANGE** Widespread but rather local, in temperate and warm temperate regions of Europe and Asia.

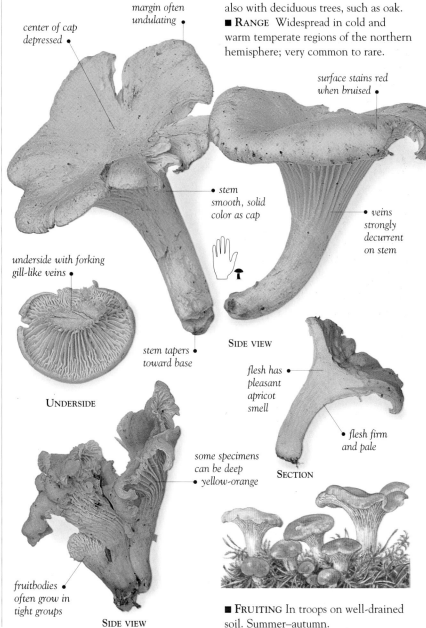

margin often undulating

center of cap depressed

surface stains red when bruised

stem smooth, solid color as cap

veins strongly decurrent on stem

underside with forking gill-like veins

UNDERSIDE

stem tapers toward base

SIDE VIEW

flesh has pleasant apricot smell

flesh firm and pale

SECTION

some specimens can be deep yellow-orange

fruitbodies often grow in tight groups

SIDE VIEW

- **FRUITING** In troops among moss in damp forests. From early autumn.

- **FRUITING** In troops on well-drained soil. Summer–autumn.

CANTHARELLUS TUBAEFORMIS

Trumpet Chanterelle

Its dull coloring and ability to blend in with its background make *C. tubaeformis* difficult to find. Less fleshy than *C. cibarius* (*see p.47*), it normally grows in such profusion that large quantities can be gathered in the fall for drying or to eat freshly cooked (*see p.244 for recipe*).

- **SPORE DEPOSIT** White.
- **SIZE** Cap 1–6cm (w); stem 3–8cm (h) x 0.3–0.8cm (w).
- **HABITAT** Commonly found on well-rotten logs in mossy, wet conifer woods.
- **RANGE** Widespread in temperate northern hemisphere; northern North America.

- **FRUITING** Large troops among moss in woods. Autumn–winter.

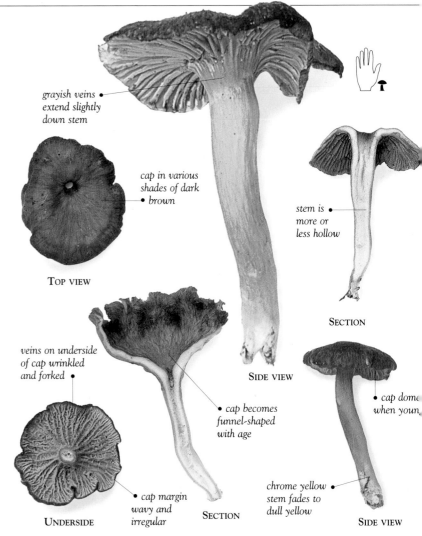

grayish veins extend slightly down stem

cap in various shades of dark • brown

TOP VIEW

stem is • more or less hollow

SECTION

veins on underside of cap wrinkled and forked •

• cap becomes funnel-shaped with age

SIDE VIEW

• cap dome when young

UNDERSIDE

• cap margin wavy and irregular

SECTION

chrome yellow • stem fades to dull yellow

SIDE VIEW

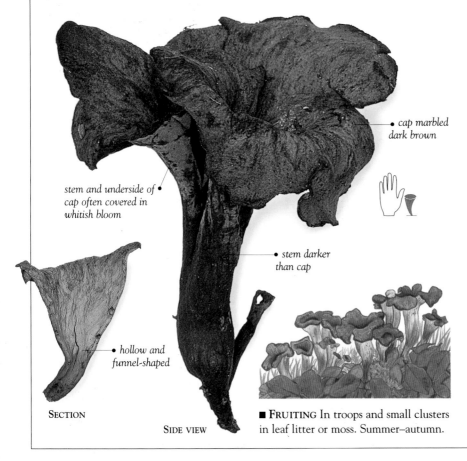

• cap marbled dark brown

stem and underside of • cap often covered in whitish bloom

• stem darker than cap

• hollow and funnel-shaped

SECTION

SIDE VIEW

- **FRUITING** In troops and small clusters in leaf litter or moss. Summer–autumn.

CRATERELLUS CORNUCOPIOIDES

Horn of Plenty

Despite the German and French names, both of which mean "death trumpet," this is a culinary delight with a mild and pleasant taste well suited to fish dishes (*see p.243 for recipe*). Like *Cantharellus tubaeformis* (*see above*), its dark coloring makes it difficult to see in its habitat. But when spotted it occurs en masse, so a basketful can be picked from a small area. A look-alike North American species, *C. fallax*, is even more fragrant.

- **SPORE DEPOSIT** White.
- **SIZE** Cap 3–10cm (w); stem 1–2cm (w)
- **HABITAT** On fairly rich and often calcareous soil in deciduous woods but also associated with conifers.
- **RANGE** Widespread in temperate northern hemisphere; abundant in some areas, almost absent in others.

CLAVARIACEAE

CLASS: *Homobasidiomycetes*

Members of this family are either shaped like simple clubs or are branched. Though many species are yellow, this colorful family also includes striking purple, rose, and pure white representatives. Several species occur in grass nearby *Entoloma* species (*see p.123*), *Trichoglossum*, or *Geoglossum* (*see p.35*), or especially with *Hygrocybe* (*see pp.80–83*).

CLAVULINOPSIS HELVOLA

Yellow Spindles

One of many simple club-shaped species with a yellow coloration. This species can only be correctly identified by examining the spores under the microscope. The spores have prominent warts, unlike the smooth spores of other species in the genus. *C. luteoalba* and *C. laeticolor* are similar species. *C. luteoalba* is apricot-colored and has a musty smell, in contrast to the odorless *C. helvola* and *C. laeticolor*.

■ SPORE DEPOSIT White.
■ SIZE Club 3–7cm (h) x 0.2–0.4cm (w).
■ HABITAT Moss-rich meadows, mature lawns, and some wooded habitats.
■ RANGE Widespread in temperate regions including the Far East; common in Europe and northeastern North America.

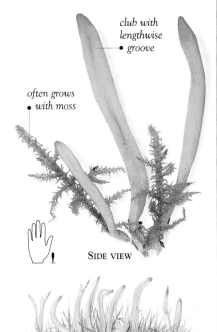

club with lengthwise groove

often grows with moss

SIDE VIEW

■ FRUITING Solitary or in small groups in moss or grass. Autumn.

CLAVARIA VERMICULARIS

White Spindles

This fragile species almost always grows in tufts, distinguishing it from *C. fragilis*, which tends to produce individual clubs. When *C. vermicularis* dries out, the tips of the clubs often stain yellow or tan.

■ SPORE DEPOSIT White.
■ SIZE Club 3–10cm (h) x 0.2–0.4cm (w).
■ HABITAT Densely clustered in grassy areas and damp woods; on soil.
■ RANGE Widespread in temperate and warm temperate regions; Quebec to North Carolina, Pacific Northwest to California.

■ FRUITING Mostly in tufts often deep in moss and grass. Autumn.

CLAVULINOPSIS CORNICULATA

Antler Coral

Typically antler-shaped, but varying in color from sulfur-yellow to orange or tan. The base is white and has a feltlike surface. The flesh has a mealy smell. It is one of the more common *Clavulinopsis* species.

■ SPORE DEPOSIT White.
■ SIZE Fruitbody 2–8cm (h).
■ HABITAT On the ground in conifer forests; also reported in moss and deciduous woods.
■ RANGE Widespread in temperate regions and often one of the more commonly found club-fungi.

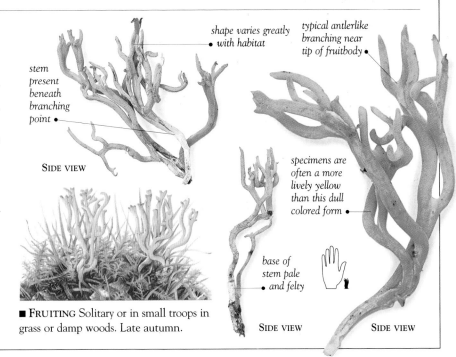

shape varies greatly with habitat

typical antlerlike branching near tip of fruitbody

stem present beneath branching point

SIDE VIEW

specimens are often a more lively yellow than this dull colored form

base of stem pale and felty

SIDE VIEW

SIDE VIEW

■ FRUITING Solitary or in small troops in grass or damp woods. Late autumn.

MACROTYPHULA FISTULOSA

Pipe Club

Although often overlooked because it blends in with the forest floor, this hollow-stalked coral is unmistakable when found. *Macrotyphula fistulosa* has a slender club-shaped fruitbody and looks hollow like a leaf stalk. It has yellow to tawny coloring. A European twisted form, sometimes considered an independent species, *M. contorta* is less easy to identify. The closely related *M. juncea* is thinner and grows on leaf litter and in damp woods.

■ **SPORE DEPOSIT** White.
■ **SIZE** Club 5–20cm (h) x 0.2–0.8cm (w).
■ **HABITAT** In forests buried among damp leaf litter, especially on beech.
■ **RANGE** Widespread in north temperate regions and subarctic areas; across northern North America.

■ **FRUITING** Singly on decaying sticks in leaf litter. Late autumn.

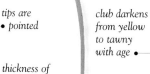

tips are
• pointed

thickness of club varies considerably •

club darkens from yellow to tawny with age •

slightly twisted form •

SIDE VIEW

SIDE VIEW

• deciduous substrate

club tapers • toward base

SIDE VIEW

SIDE VIEW

CLAVARIADELPHUS PISTILLARIS

Giant Club

An impressively sized club-fungus with a lemon flush on young fruitbodies but becoming dull tan with age. When bruised it darkens. The flesh is bitter to taste. The similar but flat-topped fairy club, *C. truncatus* occurs in conifer woods, is ocher-spored, and is both sweet to taste and a good edible.

■ **SPORE DEPOSIT** White.
■ **SIZE** Club 10–20cm (h) x 2–6cm (w).
■ **HABITAT** Calcareous woodland, often with beech; on soil.
■ **RANGE** Widespread in north temperate regions; eastern North America and West Coast.

■ **FRUITING** In troops among leaf litter in woodland. Autumn.

---

smooth white
• surface

fertile head cylindrical or club-shaped •

sclerotium brown and lens-shaped; • white inside

stem red at bottom, with fine hairs •

SIDE VIEW

sclerotium attached • to substrate

• satin white fertile head

fruitbody contains white spores •

several sclerotia can be attached to same leaf • stalk

SIDE VIEW

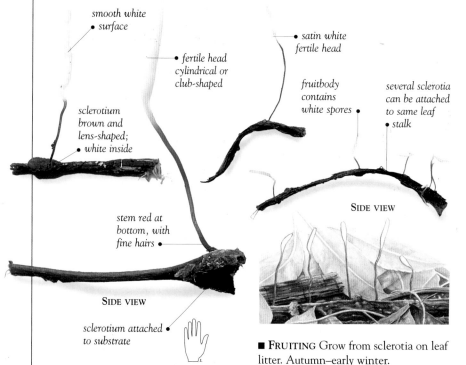

■ **FRUITING** Grow from sclerotia on leaf litter. Autumn–early winter.

TYPHULA ERYTHROPUS

Red-stemmed Tuber Club

Typhula species are tiny and because of this they are often overlooked. They mostly occur late in autumn and develop from small over-wintered resting bodies called sclerotia. These are often attached to a specific substrate, such as bracken or sedges, depending on the species. A number of *Typhula* species can cause severe damage to crops, such as grass and clover.

■ **SPORE DEPOSIT** White.
■ **SIZE** Club 0.5–3cm (h) x 0.1–0.2cm (w).
■ **HABITAT** On leaf ribs and stalks, in damp deciduous woods.
■ **RANGE** Widespread in north temperate zones; common in Europe and eastern North America.

CLAVULINACEAE

CLASS: *Homobasidiomycetes*

Members of this very small family have relatively large basidia, each usually bearing only two spores on strongly curved, hornlike sterigmata (*see p.43*). Most species have branched coral-shaped fruitbodies similar to the *Clavariaceae* (*see p.49*) or the *Ramariaceae* (*see p.52*).

tips fringed
• or crested

often associated
• with moss

typical •
whitish
form

• base with thick
more or less
fused branches

grows on
damp soil •

SIDE VIEW

SIDE VIEW

CLAVULINA CRISTATA

Crested Coral Fungus

This familiar woodland fungus varies greatly in shape and color, but the toothlike, crested tips of the branches make the species distinctive. White and gray forms exist but can hardly be distinguished from one another since intermediate shades occur.

- **SPORE DEPOSIT** White.
- **SIZE** Fruitbody 2–6cm (h).
- **HABITAT** Damp situations in forests and on roadside shoulders.
- **RANGE** Widespread in northern temperate zones.

- **FRUITING** Solitary or in small groups on damp soil. Summer–early winter.

SPARASSIDACEAE

CLASS: *Homobasidiomycetes*

Cauliflower fungi constitute a very small but highly distinctive-looking family with huge, fleshy fruitbodies consisting of a multitude of lobes. All species are associated with dead wood. *Sparassidaceae* have lobes with the spore-producing layer on one side only.

SECTION • branched
internal
structure

strongly folded
fruitbody is difficult
but worthwhile
to clean •

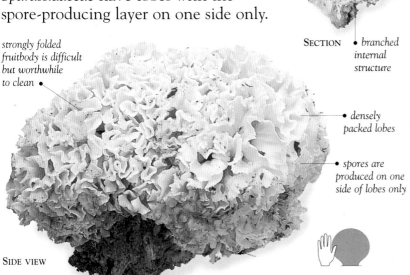

• densely
packed lobes

• spores are
produced on one
side of lobes only

SIDE VIEW

SPARASSIS CRISPA

Cauliflower Fungus

The pleasant taste and impressive size make *Sparassis crispa* a very popular edible and easily identifiable fungus. An equally good species, *S. herbstii*, lacks the long rooting stalk, has thicker lobes, and prefers oak woods. *Sparassis crispa* causes a brown rot in lumber.

- **SPORE DEPOSIT** White.
- **SIZE** Fruitbody 10–40cm (w).
- **HABITAT** On and around conifer stumps and logs.
- **RANGE** Widespread in north temperate zones; eastern North American and West Coast.

- **FRUITING** Mostly solitary at the base of trunks or stumps. Late summer–autumn.

RAMARIACEAE

CLASS: *Homobasidiomycetes*

All the many species of *Ramaria* are highly branched. Seen under the microscope, their spores are pale yellow to dark ocher, with warty, ridged, or spiny walls. Since the edible species tend to be rare and some members are poisonous, these highly attractive fungi are best avoided.

RAMARIA BOTRYTIS

Pink-tipped Coral Fungus

This typically fleshy member of the genus is identifiable by its pink tips and dense branching pattern. It is massive and fleshy, the flesh being firm with a pleasant fruity taste but is not recommended; the fairly similar but more colorful orange-pink *R. formosa* is poisonous. Since many species are rare and poorly understood, it is not easy to identify these splendid *Ramaria* species.

- **SPORE DEPOSIT** Ocher.
- **SIZE** Fruitbody 7–15cm (h).
- **HABITAT** On the ground under conifers, especially spruce and fir.
- **RANGE** Widespread in north temperate and warm temperate zones; local to rather rare.

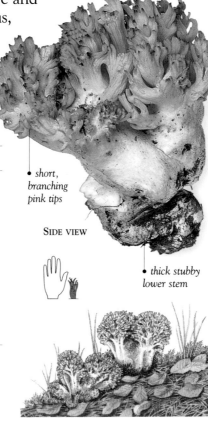

- *short, branching pink tips*

SIDE VIEW

- *thick stubby lower stem*

■ **FRUITING** Solitary or in rings or lines among moss and leaves. Autumn.

RAMARIA SANGUINEA

Red-spotted Coral Fungus

The wide range of more or less vivid yellow or orange species of *Ramaria* can be very difficult to identify, and there has been a great deal of confusion in field guides. *R. sanguinea* can usually be recognized by the red spots that develop on the surface of the lower stem with age or when bruised. The flesh has a mild taste. *R. langentii* is larger and does not develop red spots.

- **SPORE DEPOSIT** Ocher.
- **SIZE** Fruitbody 8–15cm (h).
- **HABITAT** Occurs on alkaline soil among conifers, like pines, or with deciduous trees, like beech.
- **RANGE** Widespread in Europe, and elsewhere in the north temperate zone; eastern North America.

■ **FRUITING** In rings or lines, but also solitary, on forest soil. Autumn.

RAMARIA ABIETINA

Greening Coral Fungus

Among the small and less fleshy *Ramaria* species, this is the easiest to identify, since it stains verdigris all over with age. *R. apiculata* also has green coloring, but this is limited to the branch tips. It also grows on conifers and is larger. *R. eumorpha* and *R. myceliosa*, among others, are similar but do not stain green.

- **SPORE DEPOSIT** Ocher.
- **SIZE** Fruitbody 3–8cm (h).
- **HABITAT** On thick needle beds under conifers, especially spruce.
- **RANGE** Widespread throughout conifer forests of North America.

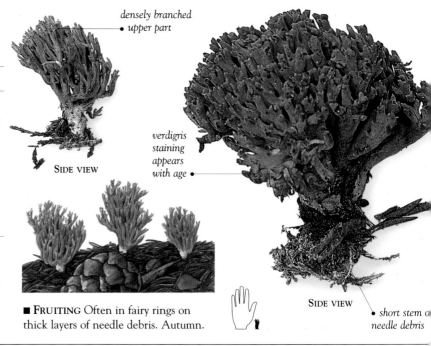

- *densely branched upper part*

SIDE VIEW

verdigris staining appears with age

SIDE VIEW

- *short stem on needle debris*

■ **FRUITING** Often in fairy rings on thick layers of needle debris. Autumn.

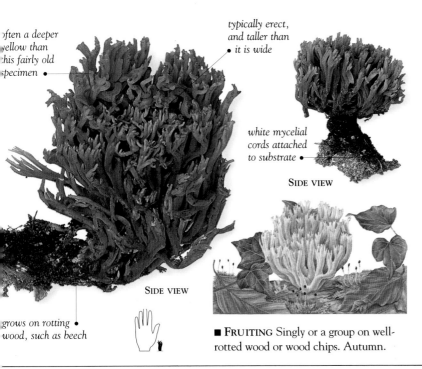

often a deeper yellow than this fairly old specimen

typically erect, and taller than it is wide

white mycelial cords attached to substrate

SIDE VIEW

SIDE VIEW

grows on rotting wood, such as beech

■ **FRUITING** Singly or a group on well-rotted wood or wood chips. Autumn.

RAMARIA STRICTA
Straight Coral Fungus

Habitat is one of the best clues for identifying *Ramaria stricta*. The fruitbody is attached directly, or by white cords, to rotten wood. This branching fungus is tipped with pale yellow, and the flesh is stained brownish. The taste is typically distinctively bitter. Shape and size vary greatly. Large compact forms can be found on sawdust or wood chips.

■ **SPORE DEPOSIT** Ocher.
■ **SIZE** Fruitbody 4–12cm (h).
■ **HABITAT** Usually appears from half-buried deciduous wood, often beech, but also on conifer wood.
■ **RANGE** Widespread in north temperate zones; mostly common.

HYDNACEAE
CLASS: *Homobasidiomycetes*

This is a small family of fungi with spines or teeth acting as the support for the spore-producing organs, the basidia, on the underside of the cap. The spores are smooth and translucent when seen under a microscope. All species of *Hydnaceae* form mycorrhizal associations with certain trees.

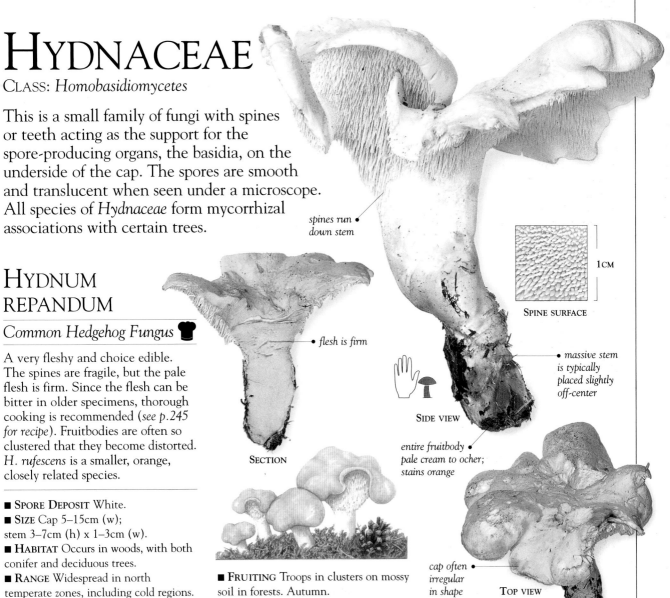

spines run down stem

1CM

SPINE SURFACE

HYDNUM REPANDUM

Common Hedgehog Fungus

A very fleshy and choice edible. The spines are fragile, but the pale flesh is firm. Since the flesh can be bitter in older specimens, thorough cooking is recommended (*see p.245 for recipe*). Fruitbodies are often so clustered that they become distorted. *H. rufescens* is a smaller, orange, closely related species.

■ **SPORE DEPOSIT** White.
■ **SIZE** Cap 5–15cm (w); stem 3–7cm (h) x 1–3cm (w).
■ **HABITAT** Occurs in woods, with both conifer and deciduous trees.
■ **RANGE** Widespread in north temperate zones, including cold regions.

flesh is firm

SECTION

SIDE VIEW

massive stem is typically placed slightly off-center

entire fruitbody pale cream to ocher; stains orange

■ **FRUITING** Troops in clusters on mossy soil in forests. Autumn.

cap often irregular in shape

TOP VIEW

AURISCALPIACEAE

CLASS: *Homobasidiomycetes*

This is a small family whose species either inhabit conifer cones or deciduous and conifer trees. They are decomposers and therefore beneficial to the ecosystem since they break down rotting material, such as cones and tree stumps, into nutrients for trees and plants. Above the family level these fungi are considered to belong with the bigger and more fleshy *Creolophus* and *Hericium* species (*see opposite*). The spores, borne on basidia, are formed either on spines underneath a cap or on gill-like structures. Species of *Lentinellus* are sometimes assigned to their own family.

LENTINELLUS COCHLEATUS

Cockle-shell Fungus

The clustered, more or less cockle-shaped, fruitbodies and gills with serrated edges are distinguishing features. Some forms have a strong, pleasant anise smell, while others are odorless. The cap surface is smooth, unlike that of several relatives. The flesh is rather bitter and not really worth eating. Species of *Lentinus* can seem very similar in appearance but differ in spore characters under the microscope. *Lentinula edodes*, the well-known shiitake mushroom, although similar in appearance, is related to the true agarics – gilled mushrooms in the *Tricholomataceae* (*see p.84*).

- **SPORE COLOR** White.
- **SIZE** Cap 2–6cm (w); stem 2–5cm (h) x 0.8–1.5cm (w).
- **HABITAT** Stumps of deciduous trees.
- **RANGE** Widespread in north temperate zones; locally common.

- **FRUITING** Layered clusters on rotting deciduous trees. Late summer–autumn.

AURISCALPIUM VULGARE

Pinecone Tooth

One of the most distinctive fungi, this grows directly out of buried, decaying cones in needle litter. The stem is attached to one side of the furry kidney-shaped cap, which has long spines hanging from the underside. Its coloring makes it difficult to spot in needle litter, despite being very common.

- **SPORE DEPOSIT** White.
- **SIZE** Cap 0.5–2cm (w); stem 3–10cm (h) x 0.2–0.3cm (w).
- **HABITAT** On cones in mature forests and ornamental plantings.
- **RANGE** Widespread in north temperate zones following distribution of pine, spruce, and Douglas fir.

- **FRUITING** Singly or in pairs from well-rotted cones. Throughout the year.

margin pale

stem attached at side of cap

stem darker than cap

stem with brown felty covering

SIDE VIEW

stem attached by felty mycelium

TOP VIEW

kidney-shaped cap covered with fine hairs

grayish spines hang vertically on underside

UNDERSIDE

SIDE VIEW

HERICIACEAE

CLASS: *Homobasidiomycetes*

Most members of this family are big, fleshy, and decay wood. They all have basidia and spores borne on hanging, vertical spines. Look for fruitbodies in mature forests where the natural cycle of growth and decay proceeds without interference. Most of the species are edible, but you should avoid picking them since they are fairly rare and a delightful sight for others to enjoy. Take a pair of binoculars because species such as *H. erinaceum* can grow high up in old trees.

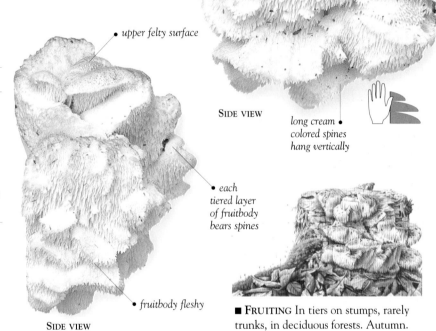

cream-colored irregular layers of brackets with spines underneath

upper felty surface

SIDE VIEW

long cream colored spines hang vertically

CREOLOPHUS CIRRHATUS

Layered Tooth-fungus

Creolophus is a very small genus, closely related and similar to the genus *Hericium*. *C. cirrhatus* resembles a layered fleshy bracket or polypore (*see p.66*), but instead, this species has spines developing on the underside. The upper surface is also warty or spiny.

each tiered layer of fruitbody bears spines

- ■ **SPORE DEPOSIT** White.
- ■ **SIZE** Bracket 10–20cm (w) x 10cm deep x up to 10cm thick.
- ■ **HABITAT** In woods, on stumps of deciduous trees.
- ■ **RANGE** Reported in Colorado but probably widespread.

fruitbody fleshy

SIDE VIEW

■ **FRUITING** In tiers on stumps, rarely trunks, in deciduous forests. Autumn.

HERICIUM CORALLOIDES

Coral Tooth-fungus

This striking species complex grows along fallen trunks and on standing trees. The spines appear to come from all over, but are in fact found on branches originating from a common point. Cooked young fruitbodies have the taste and texture of crabmeat.

multibranched coral-like fruitbody with long hanging spines

FRAGMENT

old specimens are dirty yellow

cream flesh

long whitish spines clearly seen in section

SECTION

■ **FRUITING** Solitary or along large dead trunks. Late summer–late autumn.

- ■ **SPORE DEPOSIT** White.
- ■ **SIZE** Bracket 10–40cm (w) x 5–20cm deep x 10–30cm thick.
- ■ **HABITAT** On fallen or standing dead deciduous trees, but similar species sometimes found on conifers.
- ■ **RANGE** Widespread in north temperate zones; locally fairly common.

CORTICIACEAE

CLASS: *Homobasidiomycetes*

Members of this group of fungi tend to be very simple, often forming a white film on wood and bark. Only under the microscope do their distinctive features come to light. Among the hundreds of species, however, some do have striking features that make field identification reliable. *Stereum* species are normally placed in the family *Stereaceae*; they have been included here for convenience.

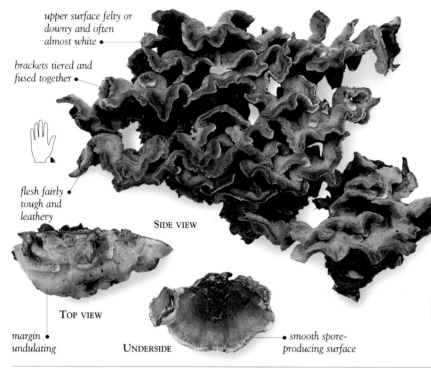

upper surface felty or downy and often almost white •

brackets tiered and fused together •

flesh fairly tough and leathery

SIDE VIEW

TOP VIEW

margin undulating

UNDERSIDE

• smooth spore-producing surface

CHONDROSTEREUM PURPUREUM

Silver Leaf Fungus

The purple color on young fruitbodies, together with the multitude of tiers and rows that this fungus creates, makes it easy to identify. It causes silver-leaf disease on cherry and plum tree species. The wood eventually develops a white rot. The flesh is waxy and gelatinous in contrast to the true *Stereum* species. In dry conditions it is hornlike in texture. Unlike *Stereum* species, the spores do not react with iodine reagents (no blue color develops).

- **SPORE DEPOSIT** White.
- **SIZE** Confluent brackets 2–5cm (w).
- **HABITAT** On the wood of many deciduous trees, which it attacks while they are still alive and healthy.
- **RANGE** Widespread in north temperate zones; common in most regions.

- **FRUITING** In tiers on bark and wood of deciduous trees. Most of the year.

STEREUM RUGOSUM

Furrowed Parchment Fungus

This abundant forest fungus can be spotted from a distance as a thick, rather featureless, grayish skin on dead standing trunks. Red lines will soon appear if you scrape the surface. The same is true of *S. sanguinolentum*, but this occurs on conifer bark and develops brackets.

- **SPORE DEPOSIT** White.
- **SIZE** Spread 1–6cm across.
- **HABITAT** On deciduous trees, often standing dead trunks, frequent on species such as hazel, birch, and alder.
- **RANGE** Widespread and common in Europe; occurs in eastern North America and in a wider area in north temperate zones.

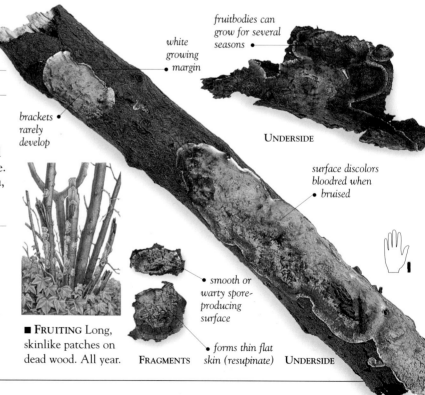

brackets rarely develop

white growing margin

fruitbodies can grow for several seasons •

UNDERSIDE

surface discolors bloodred when bruised

- **FRUITING** Long, skinlike patches on dead wood. All year.

FRAGMENTS

• smooth or warty spore-producing surface

• forms thin flat skin (resupinate)

UNDERSIDE

STEREUM HIRSUTUM

Hairy Leather-bracket

A bright yellow to tan bracket with a smooth spore-bearing surface on the underside that often runs down the substrate. The cap is hairy, with indistinct zones in concentric circles. The flesh is thin but tough, and does not stain when bruised. *S. subtomentosum* has wider brackets and yellow-staining flesh.

■ **SPORE DEPOSIT** White.
■ **SIZE** Confluent brackets 2–6cm (w).
■ **HABITAT** Often on bark or the cut surface of stored hardwood trees, especially on oak, birch, and beech.
■ **RANGE** Widespread in cold and warm north temperate zones; common.

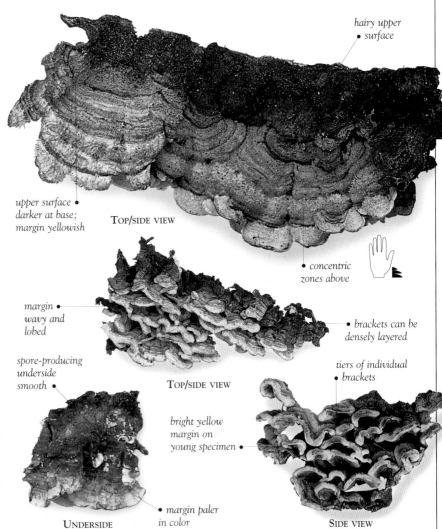

hairy upper surface

upper surface darker at base; margin yellowish

TOP/SIDE VIEW

concentric zones above

margin wavy and lobed

brackets can be densely layered

spore-producing underside smooth

TOP/SIDE VIEW

tiers of individual brackets

bright yellow margin on young specimen

UNDERSIDE

margin paler in color

SIDE VIEW

■ **FRUITING** Abundant on dead, felled, deciduous trees. All year.

---

flesh has jellylike texture

upper surface of bracket felty, almost white

TOP/SIDE VIEW

tiered semi-circular brackets with hairy margins

spore-producing surface veined

SIDE VIEW

orange to pink in color

UNDERSIDE

■ **FRUITING** In dense tiers on bark of deciduous stumps. Autumn–early winter.

PHLEBIA TREMELLOSA

Jelly Bracket

Exceptional among *Phlebia* species, *P. tremellosa* has well developed protruding brackets, although part of the spore-producing layer runs down the bark. The upper side is velvety, while the yellow to orange underside is covered with ridges and veins. The whole structure is soft and jellylike. The closely related *P. radiata* is common on similar substrates, but is bright orange and thinner, with neither caps nor brackets. The underside has radiating veins and wrinkles.

■ **SPORE DEPOSIT** White.
■ **SIZE** Confluent brackets 4–15cm (w).
■ **HABITAT** On the stumps of deciduous trees, such as birch and beech, and very rarely on conifers.
■ **RANGE** Widespread and common in north temperate zones.

CONIOPHORACEAE

CLASS: *Homobasidiomycetes*

The fungus species *Serpula lacrymans*, which is the cause of dry rot, is a member of the *Coniophoraceae*. Other members of the family may also affect wood in houses but normally without the serious problems that dry rot causes. All species resemble members of the *Corticiaceae*, but the spores are colored, and it has been shown that these fungi are in fact related to the *Paxillaceae* (*see* p.199).

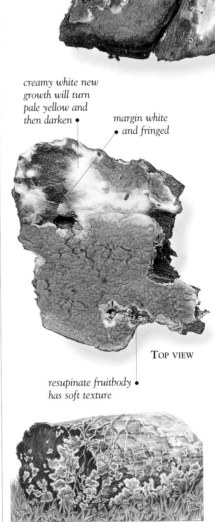

fruitbody flattened against substrate (resupinate)

causes a brown or wet rot

center stained brown by spores

TOP VIEW

spore-producing surface becomes rough and warty with age

SERPULA LACRIMANS

Dry Rot Fungus

A fungus to fear, since it can ruin construction lumber by causing a serious brown rot, leaving the wood without any strength. Its odor is musty and unpleasant. It thrives inside buildings with poor ventilation and has been found only in a few sites outdoors. The long, fanlike fruitbodies are closely flattened onto the surface and exude droplets. As well as the brown veined fruitbodies, the fungus also produces a copious white weft of mycelium.

- **SPORE DEPOSIT** Yellow to olive-brown.
- **SIZE** Fruitbody up to 50cm across.
- **HABITAT** Lumber, where it can move from wet to dry wood. Mortar or other alkaline substances neutralize the acids that it produces.
- **RANGE** Widespread and common in buildings; in the wild on east and west coasts of North America.

- **FRUITING** On wood and walls in houses. Throughout the year.

creamy white new growth will turn pale yellow and then darken

margin white and fringed

TOP VIEW

resupinate fruitbody has soft texture

- **FRUITING** Flat on planks and dead wood. All year but mainly in autumn.

CONIOPHORA PUTEANA

Cellar Fungus

As the name implies, cellars are a favorite site for this fungus, but it can occur in any part of a building that is damp. It is one of the chief causes of wet rot in buildings and is also frequent in forests, where it causes a brown rot. The adpressed (resupinate) fruitbodies, which are devoid of brackets or caps, can be over a meter long. They have a fringed white margin, and the central part of the fruitbody is yellow to olive-brown from maturing spores. The surface becomes wrinkly and warty with age. The fruitbody can be lifted away from the substrate, unlike most species in the *Corticiaceae*.

- **SPORE DEPOSIT** Yellow-brown.
- **SIZE** Fruitbody 5–100cm across.
- **HABITAT** On wet lumber indoors and on all types of wood outdoors.
- **RANGE** Widespread both in the wild and indoors, in north temperate zones.

THELEPHORACEAE

CLASS: *Homobasidiomycetes*

Members of this family vary greatly in the shape and in the construction of their fruitbodies. The simplest are resupinate – forming a thin skin over the substrate – while others are fan-shaped. The most complex have caps and stems. *Thelephoraceae* are often associated with trees, forming mycorrhizal associations.

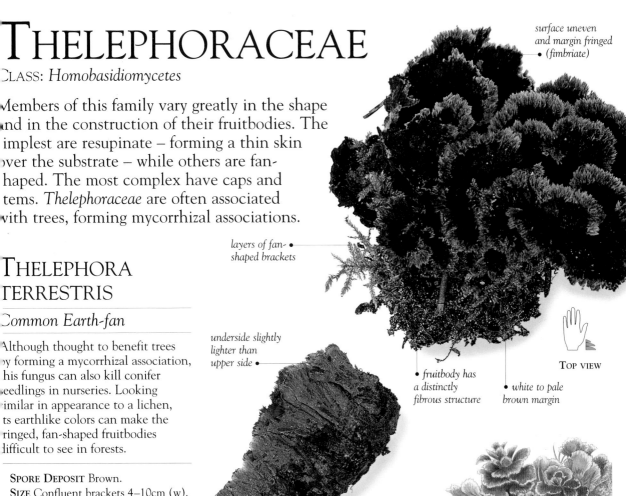

surface uneven and margin fringed • (fimbriate)

layers of fan-• shaped brackets

TOP VIEW

THELEPHORA TERRESTRIS

Common Earth-fan

Although thought to benefit trees by forming a mycorrhizal association, this fungus can also kill conifer seedlings in nurseries. Looking similar in appearance to a lichen, its earthlike colors can make the fringed, fan-shaped fruitbodies difficult to see in forests.

underside slightly lighter than upper side •

• fruitbody has a distinctly fibrous structure

• white to pale brown margin

SPORE DEPOSIT Brown.
SIZE Confluent brackets 4–10cm (w).
HABITAT On the ground, especially sandy soil in woods; pine stands, and often along horse paths and trails.
RANGE Widespread and common in north temperate zones.

• spore-producing surface is irregularly warty

UNDERSIDE

■ FRUITING Layered brackets on acid soil, or on old conifers. All year.

margin pale •

young specimens exude bloodred droplets •

spiny spore-bearing surface •

dark knobbly surface of • mature cap

SIDE VIEW

TOP VIEW

brown-zoned • tough flesh

spiny • underside

SECTION

■ FRUITING In small clusters, often deep in moss or lichens. Autumn.

HYDNELLUM PECKII

Bloody Tooth

Despite having a fleshy fruitbody with spines underneath, this is not a close relative of *Hydnum repandum* (see p.53). The flesh resembles cork in texture and has an extremely unpleasant taste and odor. The spores are also very different, being brown and warty. Young and growing fruitbodies of this species produce bloodred droplets.

■ SPORE DEPOSIT Brown.
■ SIZE Cap 3–7cm (w); stem 1–6cm (h) x 0.5–2cm (w); spines 3–4mm long.
■ HABITAT Associated with pine and spruce in native woods and planted areas, including sand dunes planted with pine.
■ RANGE Widespread but local in north temperate zones; Pacific NW.

PHELLODON NIGER

Black Tooth

The margin of this dark tooth fungus is distinctly pale blue in young specimens. Fruitbodies are often fused together, and the cap is flat or slightly depressed in the center. Spines on the underside are blue-gray at first, turning gray. *Phellodon melaleucus* is similar but thinner, paler, and less felty on the cap. Both species have the distinct smell of fenugreek, especially when dry. *Phellodon melaleucus* is found in nutrient-poor, acid forest land.

- **SPORE DEPOSIT** White.
- **SIZE** Cap 10cm (w); stem 5cm (h) x 2cm (w); spines up to 3mm long.
- **HABITAT** On calcareous soils in moss-rich conifer woods and pine stands. Often found in mixed deciduous woods.
- **RANGE** Widespread but local in north temperate zones.

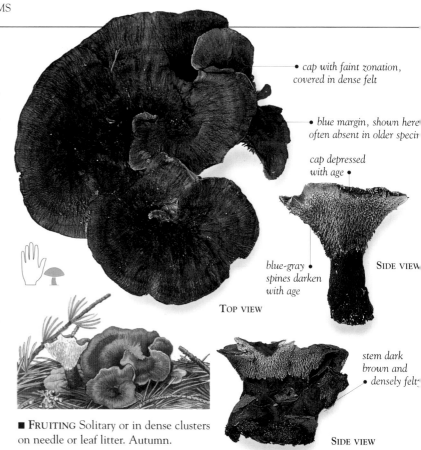

cap with faint zonation, covered in dense felt

blue margin, shown here often absent in older specimens

cap depressed with age

SIDE VIEW

blue-gray spines darken with age

TOP VIEW

stem dark brown and densely felt

SIDE VIEW

■ **FRUITING** Solitary or in dense clusters on needle or leaf litter. Autumn.

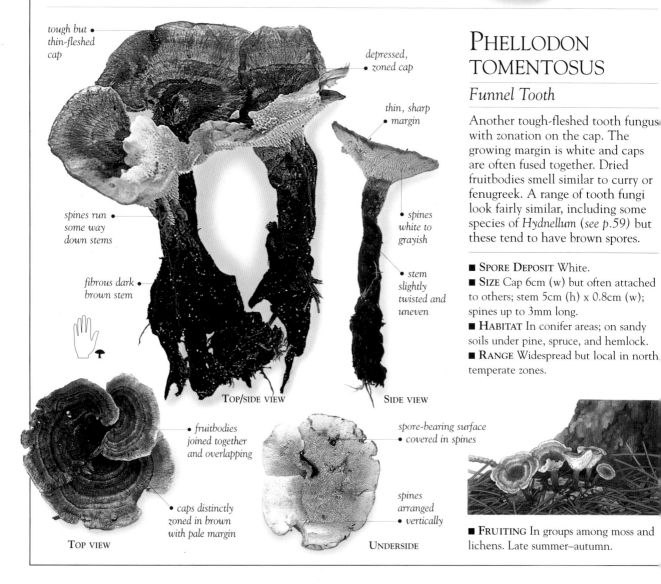

tough but thin-fleshed cap

depressed, zoned cap

thin, sharp margin

spines run some way down stems

fibrous dark brown stem

spines white to grayish

stem slightly twisted and uneven

TOP/SIDE VIEW

SIDE VIEW

PHELLODON TOMENTOSUS

Funnel Tooth

Another tough-fleshed tooth fungus with zonation on the cap. The growing margin is white and caps are often fused together. Dried fruitbodies smell similar to curry or fenugreek. A range of tooth fungi look fairly similar, including some species of *Hydnellum* (see p.59) but these tend to have brown spores.

- **SPORE DEPOSIT** White.
- **SIZE** Cap 6cm (w) but often attached to others; stem 5cm (h) x 0.8cm (w); spines up to 3mm long.
- **HABITAT** In conifer areas; on sandy soils under pine, spruce, and hemlock.
- **RANGE** Widespread but local in north temperate zones.

fruitbodies joined together and overlapping

caps distinctly zoned in brown with pale margin

TOP VIEW

spore-bearing surface covered in spines

spines arranged vertically

UNDERSIDE

■ **FRUITING** In groups among moss and lichens. Late summer–autumn.

SARCODON SCABROSUS

Blue-footed Scaly-tooth

Sarcodon species are large and fleshy, and some, such as S. scabrosus, have a distinctly scaly cap surface. The flesh has a more cheesy texture than the leathery or corklike Phellodon and Hydnellum species. S. scabrosus can be distinguished from the similar S. imbricatum by its olive to blackish stem base. S. scabrosus is bitter, but S. imbricatum is enjoyed by many people. There is a decline in the occurrence of these Sarcodon species throughout Europe and several have recently appeared on an endangered species list.

■ **SPORE DEPOSIT** Brown.
■ **SIZE** Cap 4–14cm (w); stem 3–8cm (h) x 1–3.5cm (w); spines up to 1cm long.
■ **HABITAT** Associated with trees in both deciduous and conifer woods.
■ **RANGE** Widespread but local to rare in north temperate zones.

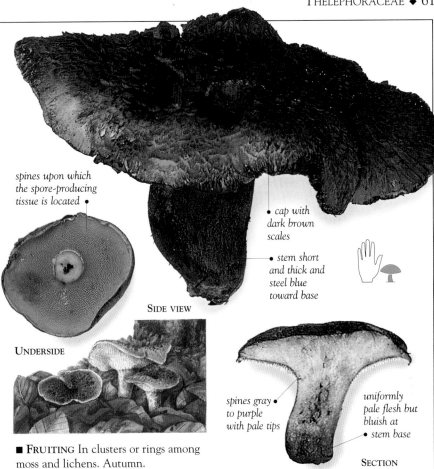

spines upon which the spore-producing tissue is located •

cap with dark brown scales

stem short and thick and steel blue toward base

SIDE VIEW

UNDERSIDE

■ **FRUITING** In clusters or rings among moss and lichens. Autumn.

spines gray to purple with pale tips

uniformly pale flesh but bluish at stem base

SECTION

BANKERA FULIGINEOALBA

Blushing Fenugreek-tooth

Bankera species tend to lift part of the substrate out of the ground when they emerge and, as a result, are often misshapen. They look more or less like Sarcodon species but have a white spore powder rather than a colored one. The relatively soft flesh of Bankera fuligineoalba turns slightly pink with age.

■ **SPORE DEPOSIT** White.
■ **SIZE** Cap 5–10cm (w); stem 2–6cm (h) x 1–3cm (w); spines up to 5mm long.
■ **HABITAT** In dry, sandy pine woods; forms mycorrhizal associations.
■ **RANGE** Widespread but local in north temperate zones.

mature cap reddish, shape variable

white zone toward the top of the stem

covered with long white to gray spines •

surface of stem brownish below

UNDERSIDE

SIDE VIEW

cap distinctly misshapen and often split in older specimens

cap flat at first, becoming centrally depressed with age

TOP VIEW

crowded whitish spines run down the stem

yellowish brown to pink flesh

SECTION

■ **FRUITING** Singly or in small clusters in sandy soil under pine trees. Autumn.

HYMENOCHAETACEAE

CLASS: *Homobasidiomycetes*

Members of this family vary widely. Some are polypores, while others have a smooth fertile layer. Some produce tough perennial brackets, but others are short-lived and may lie flat along logs or branches. These mushrooms are characterized by the presence of dark brown thick-walled hairs, called *setae*.

TOP VIEW

HYMENOCHAETE RUBIGINOSA

Rigid Leather Bracket

This common oakwood fungus almost blends in with its habitat but once seen, its abundance becomes apparent. The underside of each small bracket appears smooth, but a powerful hand lens reveals tiny rigid hairs all over the surface.

- **SPORE DEPOSIT** White.
- **SIZE** Bracket 1–6cm (w) x 1–4cm deep x about 0.1cm thick.
- **HABITAT** On heartwood of stumps or fallen branches of deciduous trees.
- **RANGE** Widespread in north temperate zones.

margin wavy and sometimes lobed •

surface brown at first, becoming very dark with age •

• dark brown zones on top of rigid bracket

underside covered with minute stiff • hairs

TOP VIEW

UNDERSIDE

• cocoa-brown color of fertile surface

TOP VIEW

• number of zones increases with age

■ **FRUITING** In crowded tiers on rotting heartwood. All year.

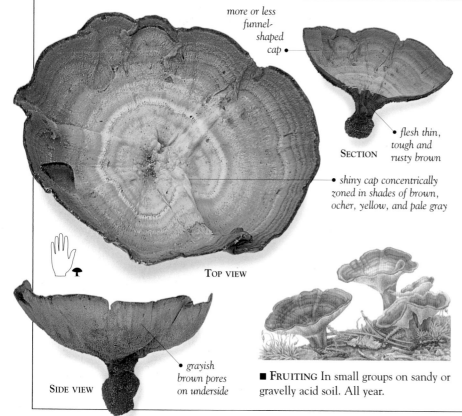

more or less funnel-shaped cap •

• flesh thin, tough and rusty brown

SECTION

• shiny cap concentrically zoned in shades of brown, ocher, yellow, and pale gray

TOP VIEW

SIDE VIEW

• grayish brown pores on underside

■ **FRUITING** In small groups on sandy or gravelly acid soil. All year.

COLTRICIA PERENNIS

Funnel Polypore

A highly unusual polypore, since it is bound to the soil rather than dead logs or standing trunks. Its golden brown colors are typical of many *Hymenochaetaceae*. The flesh is quite tough, and the tubes run down the felty stem. It resembles several tooth fungi from above, but a glance at the pored rather than spiny underside immediately reveals the difference.

- **SPORE DEPOSIT** Golden brown.
- **SIZE** Cap 2–10cm (w); stem 2–6cm (h) x 0.3–0.8cm (w); tubes approx 2mm long.
- **HABITAT** On the ground in conifer woods; fairly common on buried wood. Rarely found in deciduous forests.
- **RANGE** Widespread and rather common in north temperate zones.

INONOTUS RADIATUS

Alder Bracket

This polypore produces such large masses of brackets that it is very easy to locate. It is a bright yellow to orange-red color when young, but turns rust-brown with age. The pore surface reflects the light so that the color depends on the angle from which it is viewed. The flesh is tough. When growing on fallen trunks, the tube layer sometimes develops without brackets.

SPORE DEPOSIT Pale yellow-brown.
SIZE Bracket 3–8cm (w) x 1–3cm deep x up to 3cm thick.
HABITAT Parasitic, mostly on alder; also seen on birch, beech, and maple.
RANGE Widespread and common in north temperate zones.

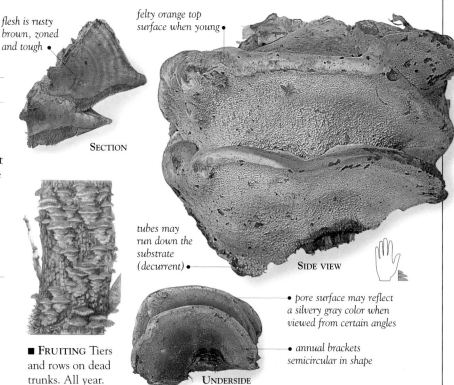

flesh is rusty brown, zoned and tough •

felty orange top surface when young •

SECTION

tubes may run down the substrate (decurrent) •

SIDE VIEW

• pore surface may reflect a silvery gray color when viewed from certain angles

• annual brackets semicircular in shape

UNDERSIDE

■ **FRUITING** Tiers and rows on dead trunks. All year.

PHELLINUS IGNIARIUS

Gray Fire Bracket

This bracket is extremely woody and can persist for many years on living host trees. With age, brackets may develop deep cracks in which moss and lichens gain a foothold. Mycologists often tend to disagree about how to delimit this species, and here *Phellinus igniarius* is considered in a broad sense.

■ **SPORE DEPOSIT** White.
■ **SIZE** Bracket 10–40cm (w) x 10–20cm deep x up to 20cm thick.
■ **HABITAT** Parasitic on a range of trees, commonly birch, aspen, willow, and apple, causing white rot.
RANGE Widespread and fairly common in north temperate zones.

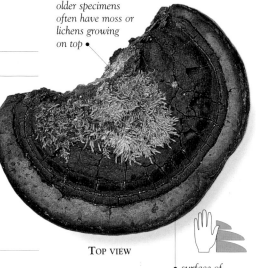

older specimens often have moss or lichens growing on top •

TOP VIEW

• surface of bracket gray to almost black, smooth or cracked to some degree

1CM

PORE SURFACE

pores are gray to • gray-brown

UNDERSIDE

■ **FRUITING** Singly or a few together on living trees. All year.

INONOTUS HISPIDUS

Shaggy Polypore

The thick-fleshed brackets have a shaggy surface. They are annual and fall off the tree each year. Young brackets are flame-orange colored, gradually turning brown.

■ **SPORE DEPOSIT** Yellowish brown.
■ **SIZE** Bracket 15–40cm (w) x 10–20cm deep x up to 10cm thick.
■ **HABITAT** Parasitic on deciduous trees and stumps, especially oak.
■ **RANGE** Widespread and common to rare in north temperate zones.

■ **FRUITING** Single or fused brackets on living trees. Summer–autumn.

FISTULINACEAE

CLASS: *Homobasidiomycetes*

This small family, with *Fistulina* as the only well-known genus, is truly memorable once seen. *Fistulina hepatica* is one of those fungi responsible for making old oaks hollow. Besides the striking tonguelike shape and color, the pore surface consists of individual, easily separable tubes, quite unlike the joined tubes in all other polypores (*see pp.62–63*).

bracket more or less tongue-shaped •

• veined flesh with bloodred juice

SECTION

short stem attached • at the side

TOP VIEW

■ FRUITING Singly on lower part of tree trunk. Late summer–autumn.

FISTULINA HEPATICA

Beefsteak Fungus

This fungus produces a tongue-shaped bracket, sometimes on a short stem. The upper surface is moist or sticky, and the spore-bearing underside consists of separable short tubes. The cut flesh has the appearance and the texture of beef or liver, hence its vernacular name, and even contains a red juice resembling blood. Although said by many to be an excellent edible, the texture and acidic taste of *Fistulina hepatica* leave much to be desired. The would-be gourmet could perhaps leave the fungus in the woods for other people to enjoy.

■ SPORE DEPOSIT White.
■ SIZE Bracket 10–25cm (w) x up to 20cm deep x up to 6cm thick; tubes 1–1.5cm long.
■ HABITAT Mature living oak trees in woods, parks, and open spaces.
■ RANGE Widespread but rather local in north temperate zones.

SCHIZOPHYLLACEAE

CLASS: *Homobasidiomycetes*

This small family, of nearly cosmopolitan distribution, is distinguished by its peculiar gill-like structures. Each "gill" is split, and the two parts curl inward to protect the spore-producing layer in dry conditions. Fungi with simpler ear-shaped fruitbodies like *Auricolariopsis* species may be related to *Schizophyllum*.

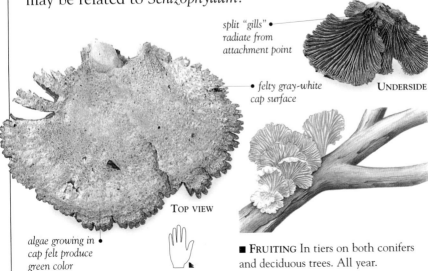

split "gills" • radiate from attachment point

• felty gray-white cap surface

UNDERSIDE

TOP VIEW

algae growing in • cap felt produce green color

■ FRUITING In tiers on both conifers and deciduous trees. All year.

SCHIZOPHYLLUM COMMUNE

Split-gill Fungus

This species is able to grow on wood that has been baked by the sun and dried out by the wind for most of the year. *Schizophyllum commune* has often been found on driftwood. It is very easy to cultivate on artificial substrates and will readily produce fruitbodies. These particular qualities have made it a popular subject for scientific research in such fields as genetics and anatomy. It has even been isolated from human feet and, in one case, scar tissue inside a person's mouth. Not a choice edible, but it has been reported as a food source among certain tribal people.

■ SPORE DEPOSIT White.
■ SIZE Fruitbody 5cm (w).
■ HABITAT On a wide range of deciduous wood substrates. Also found on straw bales, mostly in exposed sites.
■ RANGE Widespread and common in the north temperate zone but absent from northernmost areas.

GANODERMATACEAE

CLASS: *Homobasidiomycetes*

Most members of this family develop brackets with a more or less lacquered surface covered in a distinct clay-brown stain from ejected spores. The brackets of some species are highly decorative. Others grow for many years on living hosts, reaching impressive dimensions. They produce a white rot.

GANODERMA PFEIFFERI

Coppery Lacquer Bracket

This species is much easier to identify in winter than during the active growth period in spring through to autumn. The tube layer is protected by a thick, waxy yellow substance in the winter. The surface is covered with a copper-colored lacquer that can be melted with a flame. The smell is pleasant.

- **SPORE DEPOSIT** Brown.
- **SIZE** Bracket 20–50cm (w) x up to 25cm deep x up to 15cm thick; tube layer 10cm thick.
- **HABITAT** At the base of mature living beech trees, rarely other hosts, where it forms a white heart-rot.
- **RANGE** Widespread but local in middle and southern Europe.

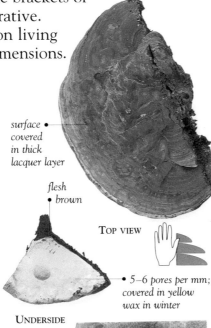

surface covered in thick lacquer layer

flesh brown

TOP VIEW

5–6 pores per mm; covered in yellow wax in winter

UNDERSIDE

- **FRUITING** Sprouting from ground level or a few meters up. All year.

GANODERMA LUCIDUM

Varnished Polypore

An annual species with a distinct lacquered stem supporting an oyster-shaped shiny red and purple-black bracket. Pores are whitish, and the tubes are brown. The flesh, although white at first, also turns brown. There are several closely related species, some of which grow on conifers. This species, also known as *Ling Chih*, is used for medicinal purposes in China and Japan.

- **SPORE DEPOSIT** Brown.
- **SIZE** Bracket 10–30cm (w) x 10–20cm deep x up to 3cm thick.
- **HABITAT** On deciduous trees, stumps, and logs.
- **RANGE** As a complex, including an eastern North American stemless form, widespread in north temperate zones.

- **FRUITING** Singly or in groups around stumps of deciduous trees. All year.

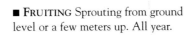

ivy enclosed by bracket

TOP VIEW

surface of bracket partly colored by thick spore deposit

cream-colored pores

UNDERSIDE

thin lacquer layer hardly visible in section

flesh dark brown, typically with pockets of white tissue

SECTION tubes

- **FRUITING** Low on stumps or standing dead, rarely living, trees. All year.

GANODERMA APPLANATUM

Artist's Fungus

The underside of this bracket can be used as a canvas, hence the name. Scratching the white surface with a sharp point produces a brown "artwork" that keeps well. It is similar to *G. australe*, which has a thicker, pale brownish crust.

- **SPORE DEPOSIT** Brown.
- **SIZE** Bracket 10–60cm (w) x up to 30cm deep x 2–8cm thick.
- **HABITAT** On stumps and trunks of dead or living trees, especially deciduous trees, like aspen. Also reported on conifers.
- **RANGE** Widespread and common in north temperate zones.

POLYPORACEAE

CLASS: *Homobasidiomycetes*

This family includes a rather mixed group of white-spored, soft- to woody-textured polypores. They are hoof- to bracket-shaped, or have caps and stems. The genus *Polyporus* is a close relative of the gill-bearing *Pleurotus* (see p.78) and *Lentinus*, but here, to make things simpler for identification, it is united with most other white-spored polypores. Other families that include pored fungi are *Hymenochaetaceae* (see p.62), *Fistulinaceae* (see p.64), and *Ganodermataceae* (see p.65). *Boletaceae* (see p.202) also have pores.

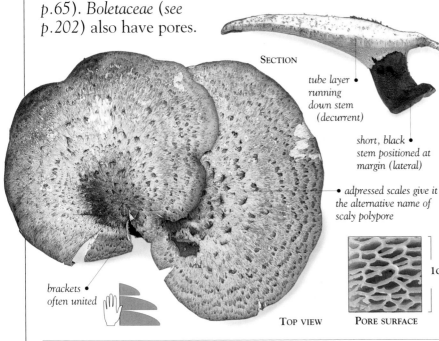

SECTION

tube layer running down stem (decurrent) •

short, black • stem positioned at margin (lateral)

• adpressed scales give it the alternative name of scaly polypore

brackets • often united

1CM

TOP VIEW

PORE SURFACE

POLYPORUS SQUAMOSUS

Dryad's Saddle

Early in the season this impressive and unmistakable polypore seems to explode out of half-dead trees or stumps. It grows large and then quickly disappears, being devoured by a multitude of insects, until only a dried-up "carcass" is left. This is then broken down by other fungi. Unlike most polypores, this species has fruitbodies that can be eaten; the taste resembles watermelon rind.

- ■ **SPORE DEPOSIT** White.
- ■ **SIZE** Bracket 10–60cm (w) x 10–30cm deep x up to 5cm thick; tube layer about 1cm thick.
- ■ **HABITAT** Parasitic on deciduous trees in woods, on street trees, and in parks.
- ■ **RANGE** Widespread and common in north temperate zones.

- ■ **FRUITING** Clusters or singly on deciduous trees. Late spring–summer.

POLYPORUS TUBERASTER

Tuberous Polypore

Known from ancient times in the Mediterranean where the sclerotia, weighing as much as 35lb (15kg), were collected, and the emerging fruitbodies were subsequently harvested and eaten. The central stem and raised cap scales separate it from *P. squamosus*. Small forms, without sclerotia, are often found. Although edible it is rather tough.

- ■ **SPORE DEPOSIT** White.
- ■ **SIZE** Cap 5–20cm (w); stem up to 8cm (h) x 1.5cm (w); tube layer up to 5mm thick.
- ■ **HABITAT** In deciduous trees, often on calcareous soils; causes wood decay.
- ■ **RANGE** Western North America in the aspen zone.

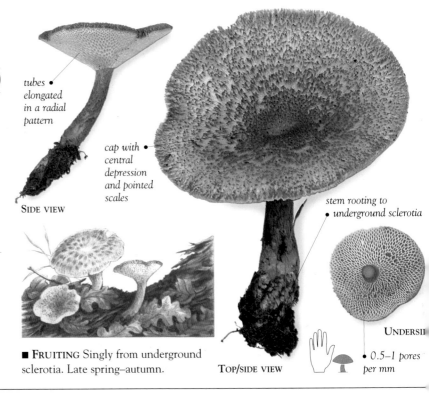

tubes • elongated in a radial pattern

cap with • central depression and pointed scales

SIDE VIEW

stem rooting to • underground sclerotia

UNDERSII

• 0.5–1 pores per mm

TOP/SIDE VIEW

- ■ **FRUITING** Singly from underground sclerotia. Late spring–autumn.

POLYPORUS BADIUS
Liver-brown Polypore

The best clue to the identification of this *Polyporus* species is the smooth and shiny funnel-shaped cap, pale gray-brown when young and then rich dark chestnut with a bright orange-brown margin. In wet weather, the cap is greasy. The edges of the cap can be thin and fragile in dry specimens. The short, gray-black stem is attached off center or at the margin, and the pores extend some way down it. The pores are circular and creamy white. *Polyporus melanopus*, a rarer but similar species, can be distinguished by the cap surface, which is felty and never shiny. It occurs on calcareous soil.

- ■ **SPORE DEPOSIT** White.
- ■ **SIZE** Cap 5–20cm (w); 2–4cm up to 8cm (h) x 0.5–2cm (w); tube layer 1mm thick.
- ■ **HABITAT** In damp woods, growing on a wide range of deciduous and conifer stumps and logs.
- ■ **RANGE** Widespread, local to common in north temperate zones.

tubes run • down the dark stem (decurrent)

•iny creamy white •ores turn yellowish •rown with age •

• smooth shiny surface turns dark

1CM

PORE SURFACE

TOP/SIDE VIEW

•rt stem •ced off center at margin   UNDERSIDE

■ **FRUITING** Singly or a few together on tree trunks. Late spring–autumn.

POLYPORUS VARIUS
Varied Polypore

The cap of this smooth-surfaced *Polyporus* species is a uniform golden-yellow to cinnamon color, contrasting with the off-center black stem. Tiny forms with a central stem are occasionally found.

- ■ **SPORE DEPOSIT** White.
- ■ **SIZE** Cap 3–12cm (w); stem up to 8cm (h) x 0.5–1.5cm (w); tube layer less than 1mm thick.
- ■ **HABITAT A** range of deciduous hosts, on stumps, branches, and logs.
- ■ **RANGE** Widespread and common in north temperate zones.

■ **FRUITING** A few together on dead or dying trees. Late spring–autumn.

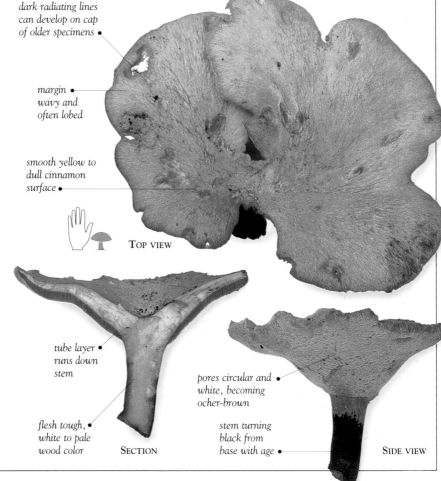

dark radiating lines can develop on cap of older specimens •

margin • wavy and often lobed

smooth yellow to dull cinnamon surface •

TOP VIEW

tube layer • runs down stem

flesh tough, • white to pale wood color   SECTION

pores circular and • white, becoming ocher-brown

stem turning black from base with age •   SIDE VIEW

POLYPORUS BRUMALIS

Winter Polypore

This familiar fungus does not develop fruitbodies until mid-autumn, and peaks in early winter. The tough agaric-like fruitbodies persist through winter but in Europe a similar species, *P. ciliatus*, takes over in spring. The pores of *P. brumalis* are distinctly larger, circular, and they elongate with age. Those of *P. ciliatus* can hardly be seen. Both species have a fringed margin when young and form a white rot. A range of other similar *Polyporus* species occur mainly in warmer climates.

- ■ **SPORE DEPOSIT** White.
- ■ **SIZE** Cap 3–8cm (w); stem 2–6cm (h) x up to 0.5cm (w); tube layer up to 2mm thick.
- ■ **HABITAT** In piles of brushwood and on dead, fallen deciduous branches or trees, especially birch.
- ■ **RANGE** Widespread and common in north temperate zones.

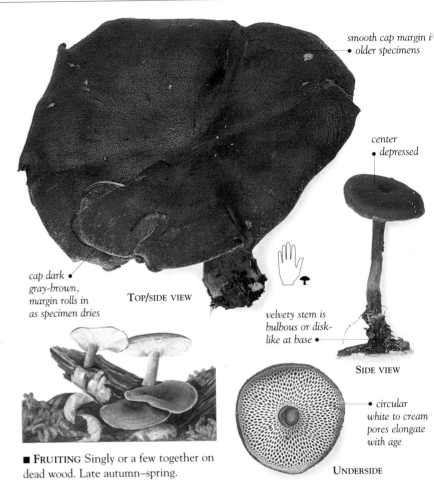

smooth cap margin i older specimens

center depressed

cap dark gray-brown, margin rolls in as specimen dries

TOP/SIDE VIEW

velvety stem is bulbous or disk-like at base

SIDE VIEW

circular white to cream pores elongate with age

UNDERSIDE

■ **FRUITING** Singly or a few together on dead wood. Late autumn–spring.

PIPTOPORUS BETULINUS

Birch Polypore

This annual species will be found in any forest where older birch trees are present. Attacked trees eventually die, but the polypore can continue fruiting on them for some time and can cause a brown rot in the wood. The gray-brown surface is skinlike in texture, and the flesh is soft but firm. (Surface is gray in North America.) It was once used both for sharpening razors and as a polishing agent in the watchmaking industry. The brackets are often attacked by the flask fungus *Hypocrea pulvinata* when on the tree, and by another flask fungus, the orange *Hypomyces aurantius*, once the tree or polypore has fallen.

- ■ **SPORE DEPOSIT** White.
- ■ **SIZE** Bracket 5–30cm (w) x 2–6cm thick; tube layer up to 1cm thick.
- ■ **HABITAT** In damp woods; parasitic on mostly older birch trees, which it eventually kills.
- ■ **RANGE** Widespread and common in north temperate zones.

semicircular bracket with no, or only a rudimentary, stem-like attachment

often swollen near attachment point

margin is rounded and smooth

TOP VIEW

smooth brown surface cracks to reveal white flesh

flesh pure white, relatively soft but fairly tough

SECTION

pore surface white in growing specimens, with 3–4 pores per mm tube layer

UNDERSIDE

■ **FRUITING** Few together on rotten, but standing, birch trunks. All year.

LAETIPORUS SULPHUREUS

Chicken-of-the-Woods

This splendid and easily identifiable *Laetiporus* species has an almost luminous quality. It breaks out of living trees in early summer and can quickly produce very large yellow fruitbodies. Excellent in stews when young, but developing a disagreeable odor when older. Causes digestive upsets if grown on *Eucalyptus*.

- **SPORE DEPOSIT** White.
- **SIZE** Brackets 10–50cm (w) x 10–30cm deep x 1–5cm thick; tube layer up to 5mm thick.
- **HABITAT** Common on deciduous trees in some regions, on conifers in others.
- **RANGE** Widespread and common in north temperate zones.

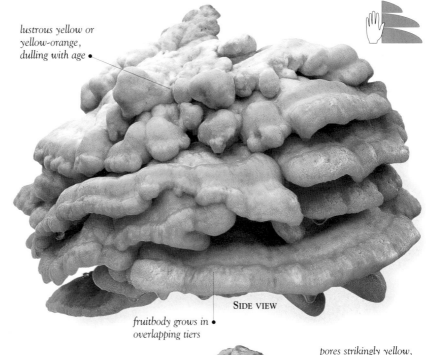

lustrous yellow or yellow-orange, dulling with age •

SIDE VIEW

fruitbody grows in • overlapping tiers

- **FRUITING** Mostly in tiers, often high up in living trees. From early summer.

flesh pale yellow with indistinct zonation •

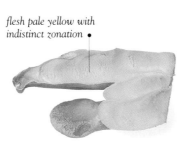

SECTION

pores strikingly yellow, • 3–5 per mm tube layer

soft • fruitbody turns crumbly and cheeselike with age

UNDERSIDE

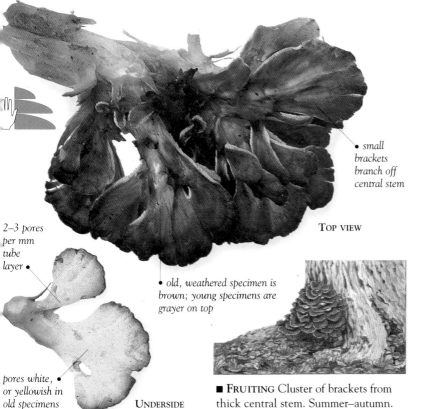

• small brackets branch off central stem

TOP VIEW

2–3 pores per mm tube layer •

• old, weathered specimen is brown; young specimens are grayer on top

pores white, • or yellowish in old specimens   **UNDERSIDE**

- **FRUITING** Cluster of brackets from thick central stem. Summer–autumn.

GRIFOLA FRONDOSA

Hen-of-the-Woods

Invariably found at the base of ancient oaks, within which it produces a white rot. It can resemble *Meripilus giganteus* (see p.71) but the brackets are smaller and grayer, and the pores do not stain gray when handled. It is a choice edible but only when young. *Polyporus umbellatus* also looks similar but each bracket has a central stem, and it is also a choice edible when young.

- **SPORE DEPOSIT** White.
- **SIZE** Confluent bracket up to 50cm (w); single bracket 2–6cm (w) x up to 7cm deep x 0.2–1cm thick; tube layer up to 5mm thick.
- **HABITAT** Base of living oaks in woods and parks; on some conifer stumps.
- **RANGE** Widespread but rather local in north temperate zones.

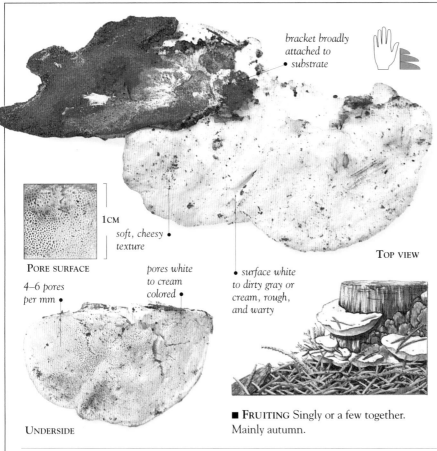

bracket broadly attached to • substrate

TOP VIEW

PORE SURFACE

1CM

soft, cheesy • texture

4–6 pores per mm •

pores white to cream colored •

• surface white to dirty gray or cream, rough, and warty

UNDERSIDE

■ FRUITING Singly or a few together. Mainly autumn.

TYROMYCES STIPTICUS

Bitter Bracket

One of the best indicators when attempting to identify this whitish, nondescript bracket fungus is its black-spotted white cap and its extremely bitter taste. Other white species are milder tasting, some bruise red, and others are confined to deciduous areas. *T. stipticus* is distinctly triangular in shape, and this can be seen clearly in section. In humid weather, the pores are known to exude a whitish liquid that dries to a cream color.

■ **SPORE DEPOSIT** White.
■ **SIZE** Bracket 5–12cm (w) x 3–7cm deep x up to 2.5cm thick.
■ **HABITAT** Causes a brown rot on dead wood of both conifers and deciduous stumps and logs.
■ **RANGE** A boreal species in eastern and western North America.

TYROMYCES CAESIUS

Blue-cheese Polypore

The brackets of *Tyromyces caesius* have a soft, spongy texture. The slightly felty surface is pale to dark blue; the pores are white or stained blue. There are about 3–6 pores per millimeter in the tube layer.

■ **SPORE DEPOSIT** White.
■ **SIZE** Bracket 3–8cm (w) x 2–5cm (h) x 1.5cm thick; tube layer up to 6mm thick.
■ **HABITAT** Mostly on conifer stumps but also on deciduous wood.
■ **RANGE** Widespread and common in north temperate zones.

■ **FRUITING** Singly or grouped on rotten conifer stumps or trunks. Autumn.

HAPALOPILUS NIDULANS

Purple Dye Polypore

This relatively soft species is uniformly cinnamon in color. It is famous for its brilliant purple color reaction with alkaline solutions and for producing the same color when used for dyeing wool. *Pycnoporus cinnabarinus* (see p.74) is tougher and a brighter cinnabar color.

■ **SPORE DEPOSIT** White.
■ **SIZE** Bracket 2–12cm (w) x 2–8cm deep x 1–4 cm thick; tube layer up to 1cm thick.
■ **HABITAT** On deciduous trees.
■ **RANGE** Widespread and common to local in north temperate zones.

■ **FRUITING** Singly, grouped, fused or in tiers, on dead wood. All year.

bracket broadly attached to substrate •

produces a white • rot in wood

TOP VIEW

surface downy • when young, becoming smooth

1CM

PORE SURFACE

all parts of this polypore are • reddish cinnamon

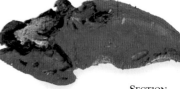

SECTION

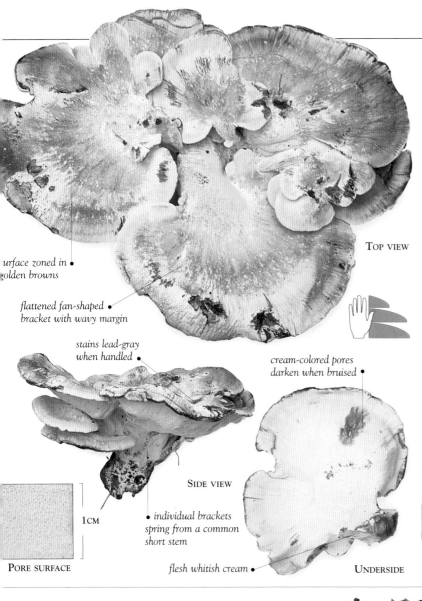

urface zoned in golden browns

flattened fan-shaped bracket with wavy margin

TOP VIEW

stains lead-gray when handled

cream-colored pores darken when bruised

SIDE VIEW

1CM

PORE SURFACE

individual brackets spring from a common short stem

flesh whitish cream

UNDERSIDE

MERIPILUS GIGANTEUS

Black-staining Polypore

This massive species is edible when very young. The whitish pores stain blackish when handled, as does the whole mushroom when cooked. It is easy to recognize by its overall size, densely layered brackets, golden brown coloring, and gray to blackish staining.

- **SPORE DEPOSIT** White.
- **SIZE** Fruitbody up to 80cm (w); each bracket 10–30cm (w) x 10–30cm deep x 1–3cm thick; tube layer up to 1cm thick.
- **HABITAT** Primarily on dying deciduous trees or stumps, causing a white rot.
- **RANGE** Eastern North America.

- **FRUITING** In dense tufts at the base of stumps or trunks. Autumn.

PHAEOLUS SCHWEINITZII

Pine Dye Polypore

This is an impressive polypore when actively growing. Each year the fruitbody arises from a more or less central stalk, and has a brilliant sulfur-yellow margin around concentric zones of rusty brown colors. Later in the year it turns a dirty brown color before it rots away. Young greenish yellow pores that turn dark brown when touched help identify this species. The flesh contains a pigment used to produce yarn dyes in many colors.

- **SPORE DEPOSIT** White.
- **SIZE** Bracket 15–30cm (w) x 1–3cm thick; tube layer up to 1cm thick.
- **HABITAT** Developing from underground roots, around conifers, especially pine and Douglas fir.
- **RANGE** Widespread and common in north temperate zones; worldwide.

old specimen, no longer growing, is fairly uniform dark brown

surface strongly felty or hairy

1CM

PORE SURFACE

TOP VIEW

young specimen turmeric yellow in color

SIDE VIEW

- **FRUITING** Mostly solitary on ground near trees or stumps. Summer–winter.

TRICHAPTUM ABIETINUS

Conifer Purple-pore

When it is present, this bracket fungus tends to be abundant. The purple color is only seen on the tube layer when young, or at the growing margin in more mature brackets. The pores are angular and may split with age. The brackets tend to be fused and arranged in tiers. The similar *T. biforme* grows on deciduous wood and differs in anatomical details. Other *Trichaptum* species found on conifers can be identified by the presence of white to brownish "teeth" or "gills" underneath.

- **SPORE DEPOSIT** White.
- **SIZE** Bracket 2–4cm (w) x 2cm deep x 0.2–0.3cm thick, but often fused.
- **HABITAT** On conifers and bark, a white rot producer; found throughout conifer forests of North America.
- **RANGE** Widespread and common in north temperate zones.

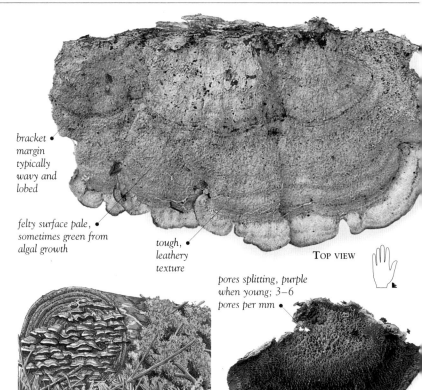

bracket • margin typically wavy and lobed

felty surface pale, sometimes green from algal growth

tough, • leathery texture

TOP VIEW

pores splitting, purple when young; 3–6 pores per mm

UNDERSIDE

- **FRUITING** In rows and tiers, often on stacked spruce lumber. All year.

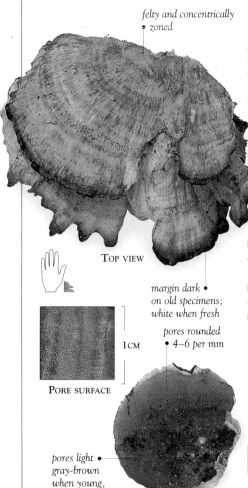

felty and concentrically • zoned

TOP VIEW

margin dark • on old specimens; white when fresh

pores rounded • 4–6 per mm

1CM

PORE SURFACE

pores light • gray-brown when young, then dark ash gray

UNDERSIDE

BJERKANDERA ADUSTA

Smoky Polypore

An abundant species wherever there is dead deciduous wood. The brackets are thin and easily told by their tiny ash-gray pores. In section, a thin dark layer is seen between the flesh and the tube layer. The less common *B. fumosum* is larger with paler pores.

- **SPORE DEPOSIT** White.
- **SIZE** Bracket 3–7cm (w) x 1–5cm deep x up to 8mm thick; tube layer up to 2mm thick.
- **HABITAT** In forests forms a white rot; especially common on aspen.
- **RANGE** Widespread and common in north temperate zones.

- **FRUITING** In rows or tiers on sides of stumps or dying hardwood trees. All year.

SCHIZOPORA PARADOXA

Deceiving Polypore

Despite being common, this polypore is usually missed by the average forager. It is resupinate but can have tiny protruding brackets when it grows on vertical substrates. The pores often resemble flattened teeth when inspected at close range.

- **SPORE DEPOSIT** White.
- **SIZE** Fruitbody 5–50cm long.
- **HABITAT** In woods, on decayed deciduous trees and stumps.
- **RANGE** Eastern and central North America; worldwide.

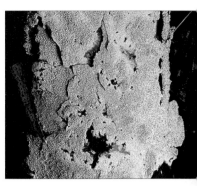

- **FRUITING** Skinlike patches on wood or bark. Throughout the year.

TRAMETES GIBBOSA

Beech Bracket

The inner, upper surface of this bracket is stained green by algal growth. It is a firm-fleshed species with elongated pores that form a fine maze. The fruitbodies are annual or perennial. *Trametes hirsuta* (*see below*) is a thinner, hairier species whose pores are grayer and less elongated.

- **SPORE DEPOSIT** White.
- **SIZE** Brackets 10–30 cm (w) x 5–20cm deep x 1–4 cm thick.
- **HABITAT** In forests, typically forms a white rot on beech.
- **RANGE** Widespread and common in north temperate zones; not reported for North America.

- **FRUITING** Singly or in tiers on top of stumps of deciduous wood. All year.

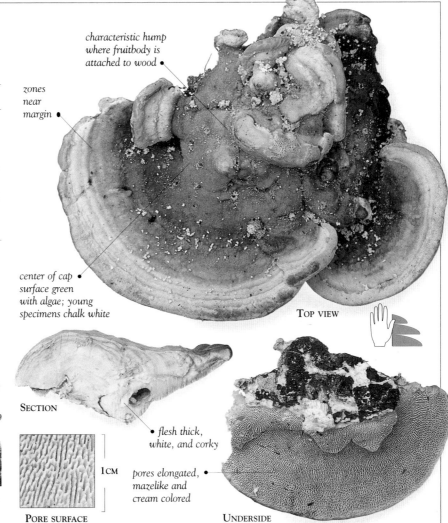

characteristic hump where fruitbody is attached to wood •

zones near margin •

TOP VIEW

• center of cap surface green with algae; young specimens chalk white

SECTION

• flesh thick, white, and corky

1CM

PORE SURFACE

pores elongated, mazelike and cream colored •

UNDERSIDE

TOP VIEW

• margin with short adpressed hairs

• stiff hairs on inner parts, often stained green by algae

angular pores • white, then turning grayish

UNDERSIDE

• 1–4 pores per mm tube layer

• rounder brackets found on top side of branches

TOP VIEW

- **FRUITING** In rows and tiers on deciduous trees. All year.

TRAMETES HIRSUTA

Hairy Bracket

The surface of *Trametes hirsuta* is covered in straight, stiff hairs, hence its common name. The hairs are more obvious on the inner parts of the bracket, as here. Near the growing margin, they tend to be more adpressed and silky. The bracket surface also has concentric zones of ridges and color variation but is primarily gray with a brown margin. The flesh is firm and tough. The annual fruitbodies are often found in exposed sites where foresters have been at work or where there has been storm damage.

- **SPORE DEPOSIT** White.
- **SIZE** Bracket 5–12cm (w) x 3–8cm deep x 0.3–1cm thick.
- **HABITAT** In forests, it produces a white rot on a range of deciduous trees.
- **RANGE** Widespread and fairly common in north temperate zones.

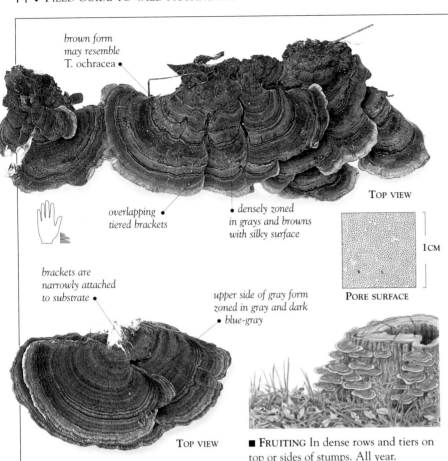

brown form may resemble T. ochracea

overlapping tiered brackets

densely zoned in grays and browns with silky surface

Top View

Pore Surface

1CM

brackets are narrowly attached to substrate

upper side of gray form zoned in gray and dark blue-gray

Top View

■ **Fruiting** In dense rows and tiers on top or sides of stumps. All year.

Trametes Versicolor

Turkey Tail

This species has thin, layered brackets with dark alternating zones. It is perhaps the most familiar bracket fungus. They are commonly used in dried flower decorations. The slightly thicker and browner *T. ochracea* is a more northern species, and it can be difficult to distinguish from *T. versicolor*. *T. versicolor*, however, is more flexible and has smaller pores. The fruitbodies in both species are annual but can sometimes develop further in spring, making positive identification difficult.

■ **Spore Deposit** White.
■ **Size** Bracket 2–7cm (w) x 1–5cm deep x 1–5mm thick; tube layer up to 3 mm thick.
■ **Habitat** Forms white rot on deciduous trees in woods, parks, and gardens.
■ **Range** Widespread and very common in north temperate zones.

Pycnoporus Cinnabarinus

Cinnabar Bracket

Its bright cinnabar color makes this bracket very easy to identify. The thinner *P. sanguineus* occurs in warmer climates and appears as if seared with a hot iron. Both species prefer exposed sunny sites and dry, sun-baked wood. The bracket becomes paler and smoother with age.

■ **Spore Deposit** White.
■ **Size** Bracket 3–10cm wide x 2–6cm deep x 0.5–2cm thick; 2–3 pores per mm tube layer.
■ **Habitat** Forming a white rot on deciduous woods in warm, sunny, exposed sites.
■ **Range** Widespread and common to rare in north temperate zones.

pores fine and rounded to elongated

Underside

entire fruitbody cinnabar in color

Side View

surface more or less smooth and slightly wrinkled when mature

fine silky hairs on surface disappear with age

mature specimens with thin, sharp margin

brackets on top of branches are round in shape

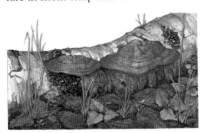

■ **Fruiting** Singly or a few together on dead trunks. All year.

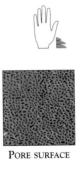

Pore Surface

1CM

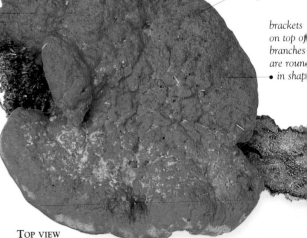

Top View

TOP VIEW

PORE SURFACE

1CM

older, inner areas are dark brown and felty

vivid golden yellow growing margin

vivid orange-yellow all over when young

TOP/SIDE VIEW

■ **FRUITING** Mostly irregular lumpy brackets on pine stumps. All year.

GLOEOPHYLLUM ODORATUM

Scented Bracket

This polypore is not edible or very decorative, but it has a pleasant smell, rather like a mixture of fennel and oranges. It develops cushion-shaped, slightly felty, perennial fruitbodies on top of conifer stumps. The growing margin is bright yellow to orange; older parts are almost black. G. *sepiarium* and G. *abietinum*, both widespread and common, have gill-like pores and typically occur on sun-baked conifers; the gray to dull brown G. *trabeum* grows mainly on construction lumber.

■ **SPORE DEPOSIT** White.
■ **SIZE** Bracket 5–20 cm wide x 5–20cm deep x 2–5cm thick; tube layer up to 1cm, rarely thicker.
■ **HABITAT** On conifer stumps, usually spruce; causes a brown rot.
■ **RANGE** Uncommon to rare in conifer forests of Rocky Mountains.

HETEROBASIDION ANNOSUM

Conifer-base Polypore

A most destructive species, at least in densely planted conifer stands, where it can spread underground and infect the root systems of neighboring healthy trees. It is often hard to identify, but usually has an irregular bracket shape and a corklike or crusty texture.

■ **SPORE DEPOSIT** White.
■ **SIZE** Bracket 5–25cm (w) x 3–15cm deep x 1–3cm thick; tube layer up to 1cm thick or more.
■ **HABITAT** On conifer stumps, dead trunks, or roots; rarely on deciduous wood.
■ **RANGE** Widespread and common in north temperate zones.

■ **FRUITING** Groups of brackets at the base of conifer stumps. All year.

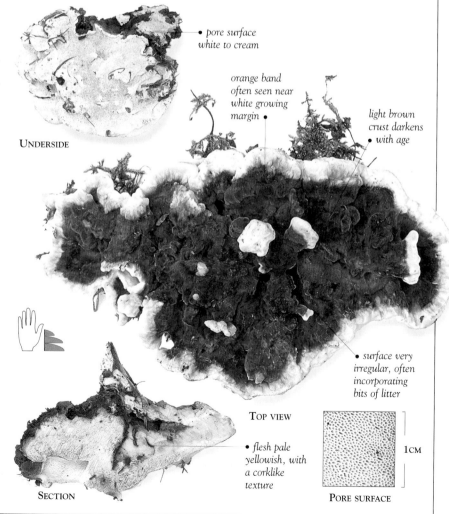

UNDERSIDE

pore surface white to cream

orange band often seen near white growing margin

light brown crust darkens with age

surface very irregular, often incorporating bits of litter

TOP VIEW

flesh pale yellowish, with a corklike texture

SECTION

PORE SURFACE

1CM

FOMES FOMENTARIUS

Tinder Fungus

This perennial polypore has been put to many uses in its time. Its use as tinder is well documented, but the flesh from large specimens was, and still is, used in the manufacturing of hats and other clothing. The pore surface is gray to gray-brown. This species exists in several different forms, depending on the host.

- **SPORE DEPOSIT** White.
- **SIZE** Brackets 5–30cm (w) x up to 25cm deep; annual tube layer 5mm thick.
- **HABITAT** A parasite on living deciduous trees, especially birch and alder; it will continue to fruit on fallen wood and forms a white rot.
- **RANGE** Widespread and often common in north temperate zones.

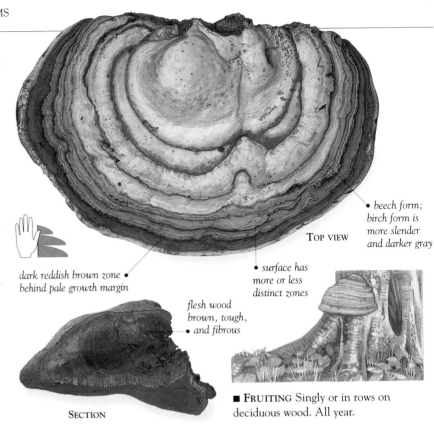

dark reddish brown zone behind pale growth margin •

TOP VIEW

• beech form; birch form is more slender and darker gray

• surface has more or less distinct zones

flesh wood brown, tough, • and fibrous

SECTION

- **FRUITING** Singly or in rows on deciduous wood. All year.

FOMITOPSIS PINICOLA

Red-belted Polypore

Similar to *Fomes fomentarius* (*see above*) but with bright yellow and red zones near the margin. The surface feels lacquered; it melts if heated with a match. The pores are yellow and the flesh pale and hard.

- **SPORE DEPOSIT** White.
- **SIZE** Bracket 10–40cm (w) x 5–25cm deep and up to 10cm thick.
- **HABITAT** On dead or dying wood; parasitic, causes brown rot.
- **RANGE** Widespread and common to locally absent in north temperate zones.

- **FRUITING** Singly or on top of each other on dead wood. All year.

DAEDALEA QUERCINA

Thick Mazegill

Although slightly flexible when fresh, this polypore is as hard as lumber when dry. Young pores near the growing margin are rounded but later develop into a maze of thick plates that radiate from the point of attachment. Other common polypores with mazelike pores (*see opposite*) are easy to distinguish; the brackets are thinner and, unlike *Daedalea quercina*, they do not occur on oak heartwood.

- **SPORE DEPOSIT** White.
- **SIZE** Bracket 10–30cm (w) x 5–20cm deep x 3–7cm thick.; pores 1–3cm thick.
- **HABITAT** In forest on oak and other deciduous trees; forms a brown rot.
- **RANGE** Widespread and fairly common in north temperate zones.

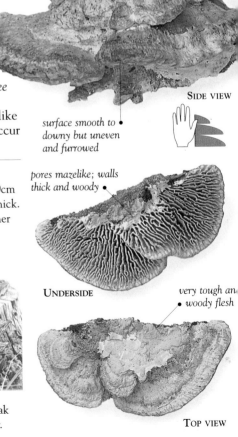

SIDE VIEW

surface smooth to • downy but uneven and furrowed

pores mazelike; walls thick and woody •

UNDERSIDE

very tough an • woody flesh

TOP VIEW

- **FRUITING** Mostly on stumps of oak and other deciduous wood. All year.

DAEDALEOPSIS CONFRAGOSA

Thin Mazegill

When fresh, the pale gray pores bruise red. The brackets are very thin, only thickening toward the base. The surface of the bracket is pale gray to yellowish when young, turning a dingy red-brown with age or developing zones in this color. The pore shape is variable, and can be rounded or mazelike in pattern.

- **SPORE DEPOSIT** White.
- **SIZE** Bracket 8–15cm (w) x 5–10cm deep x 0.5–4cm (even 6cm) thick.
- **HABITAT** On a wide range of deciduous trees in some areas; willows and birches being favorite substrates; forms a white rot.
- **RANGE** Widespread and rather common in north temperate zones.

- **FRUITING** In vertical rows on dead or dying wood. All year.

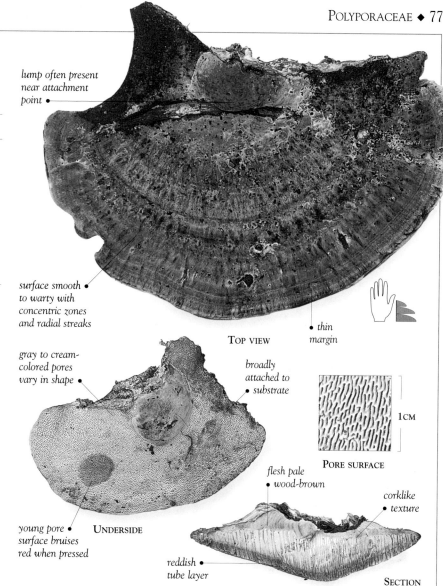

lump often present near attachment point

surface smooth to warty with concentric zones and radial streaks

TOP VIEW

thin margin

gray to cream-colored pores vary in shape

broadly attached to substrate

young pore surface bruises red when pressed

UNDERSIDE

flesh pale wood-brown

corklike texture

reddish tube layer

SECTION

1CM

PORE SURFACE

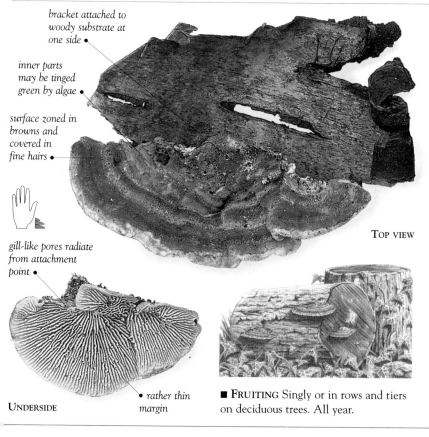

bracket attached to woody substrate at one side

inner parts may be tinged green by algae

surface zoned in browns and covered in fine hairs

TOP VIEW

gill-like pores radiate from attachment point

UNDERSIDE

rather thin margin

- **FRUITING** Singly or in rows and tiers on deciduous trees. All year.

LENZITES BETULINA

Gill Polypore

From above, this bracket fungus can be mistaken for various species of *Trametes* (see p.73) – to which the small *Lenzites* genus is closely related. The gill-like pores on the underside, however, are a more easily identifiable characteristic. The semicircular brackets, which often appear in groups, are leathery and covered in fine hairs.

- **SPORE DEPOSIT** White.
- **SIZE** Bracket 3–10 cm (w) x 1–5cm deep x 1–2cm thick.
- **HABITAT** Forms white rot on many kinds of deciduous wood or occasionally on conifers; it favors birch in some areas, oak or beech in others.
- **RANGE** Widespread and fairly common to locally rare in north temperate zones.

PLEUROTUS CORNUCOPIAE

Trumpet Oyster Mushroom

Here, the common name gives away a distinct mark – the trumpet-shaped cap. Other marks are the fairly central stem and decurrent gills that join together to form a net. The similar looking *P. pulmonarius* has simple gills and a less developed stem, and it fruits in summer. *P. dryinus* has veil fragments on the stem and cap.

- ■ **SPORE DEPOSIT** Pale lilac.
- ■ **SIZE** Cap 4–12cm (w); stem 1–5cm (h) x 0.5–2.5cm (w).
- ■ **HABITAT** Forms a white rot on deciduous trees; often prefers elm and has increased where Dutch elm disease has left abundant substrate.
- ■ **RANGE** Widespread but occurs mainly in southern regions of Europe; not reported in North America.

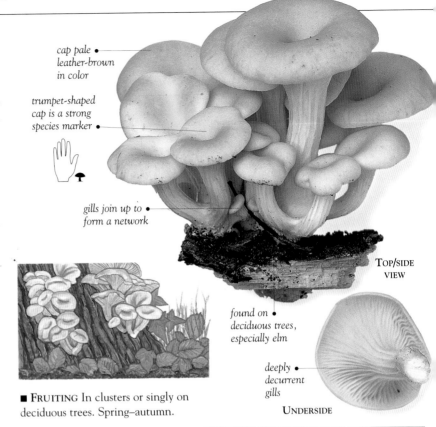

cap pale leather-brown in color

trumpet-shaped cap is a strong species marker

gills join up to form a network

found on deciduous trees, especially elm

deeply decurrent gills

TOP/SIDE VIEW

UNDERSIDE

■ **FRUITING** In clusters or singly on deciduous trees. Spring–autumn.

---

smooth cap more or less oyster-shaped

cap color ranges from brown to dark gray-blue

SIDE VIEW

stem positioned at cap margin; very short or absent

springs up in tiers or rows

UNDERSIDE

gills crowded, soft, and cream colored

SECTION

PLEUROTUS OSTREATUS

Common Oyster Mushroom 🍴

In Europe, the coloring ranges from cream to almost black; In North America, from cream to gray-brown. Its unique gray-lilac spore print color distinguishes it from other look-alikes. Another choice "oyster," *P. populinus*, is restricted to poplars. The complex is cultivated and can now be found in local markets.

- ■ **SPORE DEPOSIT** Pale dingy gray-lilac.
- ■ **SIZE** Cap 6–20cm (w); stem 0–5cm (h) x 1–2cm (w).
- ■ **HABITAT** On a wide range of deciduous trees; more rarely on conifers.
- ■ **RANGE** Widespread in northern temperate zones.

■ **FRUITING** In tiers and rows on dead or dying trees or logs. Autumn–winter.

PLEUROTUS ERYNGII

Umbel Oyster Mushroom 🍴

This choice edible does not occur in North America. In Europe, it is easily recognized by its peculiar habitat; it attaks the roots of various (umbellifer) carrot family plants. The cap tends to be pale, as in species such as *P. pulmonarius* and *P. cornucopiae* (see above), with a surface somewhat like fine suede.

- ■ **SPORE DEPOSIT** Whitish.
- ■ **SIZE** Cap 4–10cm (w); stem 0–4cm (h) x 1–2.5cm (w).
- ■ **HABITAT** Restricted to three different groups of umbelliferous plants, either in alpine meadows or coastal areas.
- ■ **RANGE** Widespread throughout central and southern Europe; not reported in North America.

■ **FRUITING** On the ground at the base of umbelifers. Summer–autumn.

HYGROPHORACEAE

CLASS: *Homobasidiomycetes*

Most members of the *Hygrophoraceae*, the wax-caps, tend to have thickish, waxy gills that range from adnexed to decurrent. There are two major groups. *Hygrophorus* species are mostly dull-colored and form mycorrhiza with trees, while the genus *Hygrocybe* (sometimes called meadow caps) occurs mainly in grassland and has many brightly colored members.

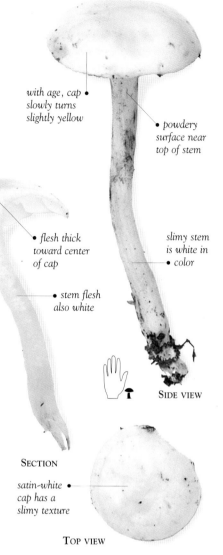

• *with age, cap slowly turns slightly yellow*

• *powdery surface near top of stem*

• *flesh thick toward center of cap*

• *stem flesh also white*

• *slimy stem is white in color*

SIDE VIEW

satin-white cap has a slimy texture •

TOP VIEW

HYGROPHORUS EBURNEUS

Satin Wax-cap

When found in wet weather, this aromatic but inedible species drips with slime from its sparkling white cap. This is the type of the genus *Hygrophorus*: the species on which the concept of the genus is based.

- **SPORE DEPOSIT** White.
- **SIZE** Cap 3–8cm (w); stem 4–10cm (h) x 0.5–1cm (w).
- **HABITAT** Mycorrhizal with beech, oak-pine woods, and eastern conifers.
- **RANGE** Widespread in northern temperate regions; reported in eastern North America and California.

• *gills white in color*

• *thick, waxy gills*

UNDERSIDE

SECTION

- **FRUITING** In small clusters, among leaf litter. Autumn–early winter.

brown to olive-brown cap has thick slime layer

gills are clearly decurrent •

distinctively pale yellow gills •

UNDERSIDE

• *top of stem not slimy*

yellowish stem also slimy •

TOP/SIDE VIEW

SIDE VIEW

- **FRUITING** In small groups among moss and lichens. Late autumn–early winter.

HYGROPHORUS HYPOTHEJUS

Herald of Winter

A late-fruiting species, identified by its association with pine trees, as well as by its yellow gills, and slimy cap and stem. The glutinous caps of many late fall mushrooms seem to help them survive the cold better than their dry-capped cousins. There are several other *Hygrophorus* species found with pine, but they can all be distinguished from this species by their different color.

- **SPORE DEPOSIT** White.
- **SIZE** Cap 3–5cm (w); stem 4–7cm (h) x 0.5–1cm (w).
- **HABITAT** Mycorrhizal with pine, preferring sandy soil; typically found following first spells of frost.
- **RANGE** Widespread in the north temperate zones, locally common.

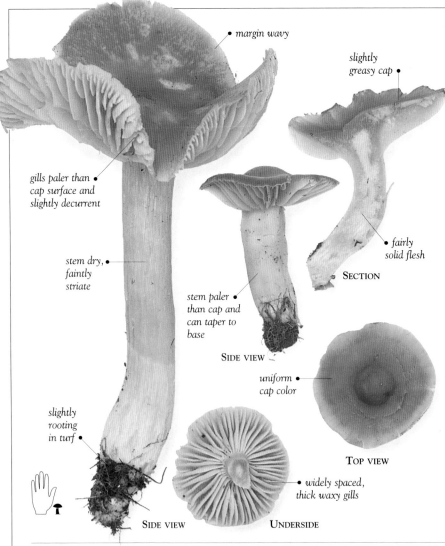

margin wavy

gills paler than cap surface and slightly decurrent

stem dry, faintly striate

stem paler than cap and can taper to base

SIDE VIEW

slightly rooting in turf

SIDE VIEW

slightly greasy cap

fairly solid flesh

SECTION

uniform cap color

TOP VIEW

widely spaced, thick waxy gills

UNDERSIDE

HYGROCYBE PRATENSIS

Buff Wax-cap

Hygrocybe species do not form strict associations with trees and are often found growing in wild, unimproved meadows. *H. pratensis* is fleshy and a fine edible. It is orange in color, and dry to slightly greasy on the cap. This species and *H. virginea* (see *below*) are often referred to the genus *Camarophyllus*.

- **SPORE DEPOSIT** White.
- **SIZE** Cap 2.5–6cm (w); stem 2.5–6cm (h) x 0.5–1.5cm (w).
- **HABITAT** In grassy areas, thickets, and dense forests; also in woods.
- **RANGE** Widespread and fairly common in north temperate zones.

- **FRUITING** In groups or rings in moss and grass. Autumn.

HYGROCYBE VIRGINEA

Snowy Wax-cap

A rather variable species, best identified by its color, decurrent thick gills, and the absence of any smell or slime. It is edible but not as good as *H. pratensis* (see above). *H. russocoriacea* is similar but has a strong smell of leather, although this scent has also been compared to sandalwood or pencil sharpenings. Minor anatomical details lead mycologists to place *H. virginea* in the genus *Camarophyllus*. Slimy capped specimens are usually referred to as *H. nivea*.

- **SPORE DEPOSIT** White.
- **SIZE** Cap 1.5–5cm (w); stem 2–7cm (h) x 0.3–1cm (w).
- **HABITAT** In open deciduous and coniferous woods.
- **RANGE** Widespread and common in eastern and northern North America, the Rockies, and northern California.

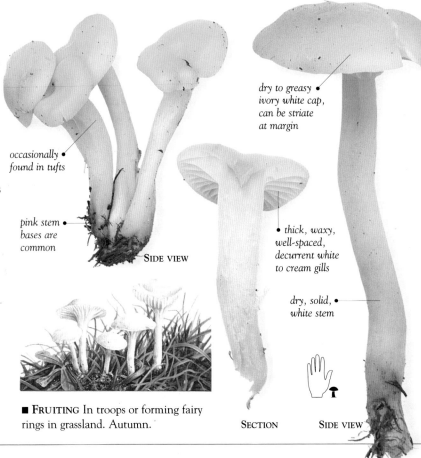

occasionally found in tufts

pink stem bases are common

SIDE VIEW

dry to greasy ivory white cap, can be striate at margin

thick, waxy, well-spaced, decurrent white to cream gills

dry, solid, white stem

SECTION   **SIDE VIEW**

- **FRUITING** In troops or forming fairy rings in grassland. Autumn.

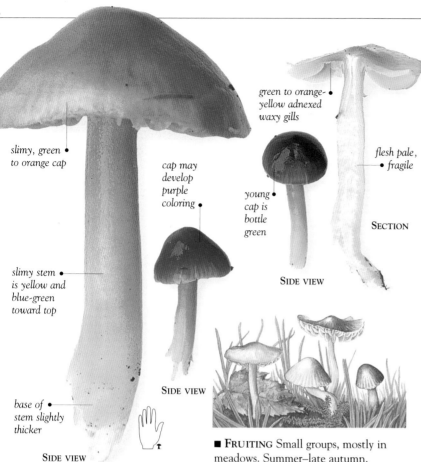

slimy, green to orange cap

cap may develop purple coloring

slimy stem is yellow and blue-green toward top

base of stem slightly thicker

SIDE VIEW

green to orange-yellow adnexed waxy gills

young cap is bottle green

SIDE VIEW

flesh pale, fragile

SECTION

SIDE VIEW

■ **FRUITING** Small groups, mostly in meadows. Summer–late autumn.

HYGROCYBE PSITTACINA

Parrot Wax-cap

This is one of the most spectacular of all wax-caps, but identification can be made difficult by the vast range of colors that specimens of different ages exhibit. When young, the caps are deep bottle green. Purple, orange, and yellow then appear, creating a range of colors similar to those displayed by an exotic parrot. The fruitbody has a slimy surface, especially when young, and is almost odorless.

■ **SPORE DEPOSIT** White.
■ **SIZE** Cap 1–4cm (w); stem 3–7cm (h) x 0.4–0.8cm (w).
■ **HABITAT** Along roadsides, but primarily in damp, rich soil in coniferous and deciduous woods often with *Geoglossum* and *Glavulinopsis* species.
■ **RANGE** Widespread and common in north temperate zones; common in eastern North America.

HYGROCYBE CALYPTRAEFORMIS

Pink Wax-cap

The fragile, elegant dusky pink fruitbodies are unmistakable. *H. citrinovirens* has a similar shape, but is yellow-green and orange. Other species include the yellow to orange *H. acutoconicus* and the bright red *H. cuspidatus*.

■ **SPORE DEPOSIT** White.
■ **SIZE** Cap 3–7cm (w); stem 5–10cm (h) x 0.5–1cm (w).
■ **HABITAT** In deep humus, in coniferous and mixed woods.
■ **RANGE** Widespread in Europe and eastern North America; also reported in coastal redwood forests in California.

■ **FRUITING** In small groups in grass and moss. Autumn.

mature cap opens out fully and splits radially

fleshy, well-spaced waxy pink gills

UNDERSIDE

pink colored cap

tightly closed conical cap of young specimen

SIDE VIEW

pinkish flush at top of stem

whitish pink stem is fragile and difficult to pull out of the substrate

SIDE VIEW

pale pink gills are narrowly attached

SECTION

HYGROCYBE CONICA

Blackening Wax-cap ☠

This is probably the *Hygrocybe* species with the broadest range of habitats. This, together with its wide variation in color, size, and shape have led some mycologists to propose a range of species and varieties. They all go black with age or when handled. *H. conica* has been reported to be slightly poisonous.

■ **SPORE DEPOSIT** White.
■ **SIZE** Cap 1–5cm, rarely up to 10cm (w); stem 2–10cm (h) x 0.4–1.5cm (h).
■ **HABITAT** In grassy areas, open woods, and deep woods.
■ **RANGE** Widespread and common in north temperate zones.

■ **FRUITING** In groups in a wide variety of grassy sites. Summer–late autumn.

- pale gray to red gills
- fruitbody turns black with age
- SECTION
- dry, fibrillose cap, more or less conical in shape
- yellow to red cap
- yellow to red stem
- stains black when handled
- SIDE VIEW
- longitudinally striated stem
- SIDE VIEW
- SIDE VIEW
- SIDE VIEW
- stem often paler at base
- TOP/SIDE VIEW

HYGROCYBE CHLOROPHANA

Golden Wax-cap

There are several common yellow species of *Hygrocybe*. This one is quite large, with narrowly attached gills and a convex cap that is slightly slimy. The cap becomes flattened with age and has a more or less striate margin. The stem is also sometimes slimy but has a powdery top. The fruitbody is fairly uniform in color, generally ranging from rich orange-yellow to pale yellow. *H. ceracea* is somewhat smaller and drier, with broadly attached or decurrent gills.

■ **SPORE DEPOSIT** White.
■ **SIZE** Cap 1.5–7 cm (w); stem 2.5–10cm (h) x 0.3–0.8cm (w).
■ **HABITAT** In grassy woodland areas and open woods.
■ **RANGE** Widespread and fairly common in eastern North America, Texas, and Pacific Northwest.

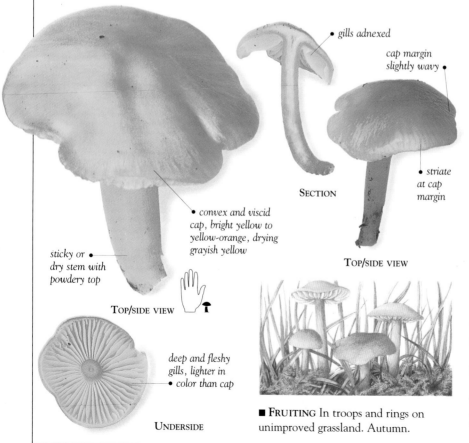

- gills adnexed
- cap margin slightly wavy
- SECTION
- striate at cap margin
- convex and viscid cap, bright yellow to yellow-orange, drying grayish yellow
- TOP/SIDE VIEW
- sticky or dry stem with powdery top
- TOP/SIDE VIEW
- deep and fleshy gills, lighter in color than cap
- UNDERSIDE

■ **FRUITING** In troops and rings on unimproved grassland. Autumn.

HYGROCYBE COCCINEA

Scarlet Wax-cap

This species of *Hygrocybe* is best distinguished from other red species by its slightly grainy cap surface, which is dry but becomes sticky in wet weather, and adnate gills. *H. punicea* (*see below*) and *H. splendidissima* are more fleshy and have adnexed gills. Small and more orange forms of *H. coccinea* can be more difficult to identify and need to be examined under the microscope. It is edible but not recommended.

- **SPORE DEPOSIT** White.
- **SIZE** Cap 1.5–6cm (w); stem 4–8cm (h) x 0.4–1cm (w).
- **HABITAT** In open deciduous and coniferous woods.
- **RANGE** Widespread and fairly common in eastern North America and California.

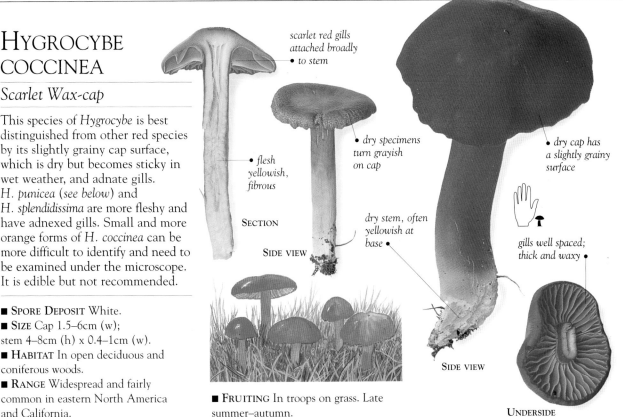

scarlet red gills attached broadly • to stem

• flesh yellowish, fibrous

SECTION

SIDE VIEW

• dry specimens turn grayish on cap

dry stem, often yellowish at base •

SIDE VIEW

• dry cap has a slightly grainy surface

gills well spaced; thick and waxy •

UNDERSIDE

- **FRUITING** In troops on grass. Late summer–autumn.

---

crimson red • cap darkens to gray with age

dry stem, • longitudinally fibrillose

SIDE VIEW

adnexed • gills

pale crimson to • orange gills

SECTION

UNDERSIDE

HYGROCYBE PUNICEA

Crimson Wax-cap

A large fleshy species with a slightly moist, dark red cap. The gills are narrowly attached. In contrast, *H. splendidissima* has a dry cap and a sweet, sickly smell. It is also a brighter vermilion red.

- **SPORE DEPOSIT** White.
- **SIZE** Cap 4–12cm (w); stem 5–12cm (h) x 0.5–2.5cm (w).
- **HABITAT** In open deciduous and coniferous woods. Usually found with other species of *Hygrocybe*, *Geoglossum*, and *Clavulinopsis* and in humus under coastal redwoods in California.
- **RANGE** Widespread but local in north temperate zones; eastern North America, the Pacific Northwest, and California.

- **FRUITING** In small groups or scattered over a wide area on grassland. Autumn.

HYGROCYBE MINIATA

Vermilion Wax-cap

One of several small species of *Hygrocybe* with dry caps densely covered in scales. They are difficult to tell apart without examining the spores under the microscope. The similar *H. helobia* prefers less acid conditions and smells of garlic.

- **SPORE DEPOSIT** White.
- **SIZE** Cap 1–3cm (w); stem 1–6cm (h) x 2–8mm (w).
- **HABITAT** In open deciduous or mixed woods in humus, on moss, and rotting logs; scattered on soil.
- **RANGE** Widespread in north temperate zones, widely distributed throughout North America.

- **FRUITING** In troops on unimproved, often acid, grassland. Summer–autumn.

TRICHOLOMATACEAE

CLASS: *Homobasidiomycetes*

This huge and unwieldy family consists mainly of white-spored, gilled fungi. There are difficulties in separating the family from the *Hygrophoraceae* (*see p.79*) on the one hand, and from *Cystoderma* (*see p.122*) and *Phaeolepiota* (*see p.121*) on the other. All sorts of lifestyles are represented in the family, but the majority decompose dead plant remains, including leaf litter and dead wood. One notable exception is the genus *Tricholoma* (*see p.92*) whose species form mycorrhizal associations with a range of host trees.

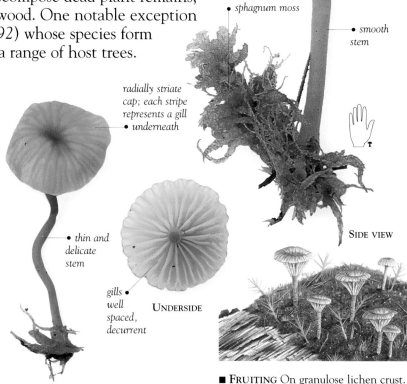

center of cap depressed •

small balls of algal-fungal cells are hidden in • sphagnum moss

• top of stem tinged violet-gray

• smooth stem

SIDE VIEW

OMPHALINA ERICETORUM

Turf Navel-cap

A small gilled mushroom that is also a lichen. In an unfavorable damp environment, the spores need an algal partner to form a colony.

■ SPORE DEPOSIT White.
■ SIZE Cap 0.5–1.5cm (w); stem 1–2cm (h) x 0.1–0.2cm (w).
■ HABITAT On acid soils among mosses, like sphagnum, and on rotten wood. Forms a lichen of small green balls, known as *Botrydina vulgaris*, with the green alga *Coccomyxa*.
■ RANGE Widespread in cooler regions of the north temperate zone.

radially striate cap; each stripe represents a gill • underneath

• thin and delicate stem

gills • well spaced, decurrent

UNDERSIDE

TOP/SIDE VIEW

■ FRUITING On granulose lichen crust. Summer–autumn.

RICKENELLA FIBULA

Orange Navel-cap

Species of *Rickenella* move from genus to genus but are nevertheless easy to recognize. They are tiny, have strongly decurrent gills, grow on moss, and have fine hairs all over – visible with a hand lens. There are two common species. *R. setipes* lacks the orange color of *R. fibula*, and has an almost black cap center and a very dark stem top.

■ SPORE DEPOSIT White.
■ SIZE Cap 0.3–1cm; stem 3–5cm (h) x 0.1–0.2cm thick.
■ HABITAT A typical lawn mushroom, but grows in a range of grassy situations where a host moss is available.
■ RANGE Eastern and southeastern North America and the Rockies.

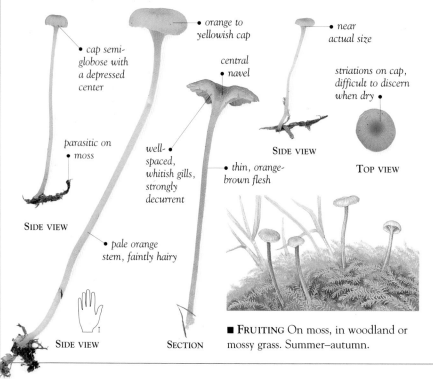

• orange to yellowish cap

• near actual size

• cap semi-globose with a depressed center

central • navel

striations on cap, difficult to discern when dry •

parasitic on • moss

well- • spaced, whitish gills, strongly decurrent

• thin, orange-brown flesh

SIDE VIEW

TOP VIEW

SIDE VIEW

• pale orange stem, faintly hairy

SIDE VIEW   SECTION

■ FRUITING On moss, in woodland or mossy grass. Summer–autumn.

LACCARIA AMETHYSTINA

Amethyst Deceiver

The beautiful amethyst colors of this *Laccaria* species are difficult to capture accurately on photographic film, but it is so common that it can easily be admired in its natural habitat. *L. amethystina* has globose spiny spores, and forms mycorrhizal associations with trees. Old specimens lose their color and can be difficult to tell from the reddish *Laccaria* species. The gills of all species are rather thick and well-spaced. *L. amethystina* is edible, but the fruitbody contains a high concentration of arsenic.

- **SPORE DEPOSIT** Pale violet to white.
- **SIZE** Cap 2–5cm (w); stem 3–7cm (h) x 0.4–0.8cm (w).
- **HABITAT** In association with a range of trees, especially oak and beech.
- **RANGE** Widespread and abundant; eastern North America.

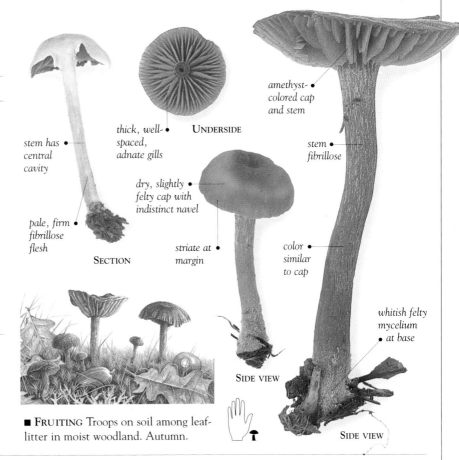

stem has central cavity

pale, firm fibrillose flesh

SECTION

thick, well-spaced, adnate gills

UNDERSIDE

dry, slightly felty cap with indistinct navel

striate at margin

amethyst-colored cap and stem

stem fibrillose

color similar to cap

whitish felty mycelium at base

SIDE VIEW

SIDE VIEW

- **FRUITING** Troops on soil among leaf-litter in moist woodland. Autumn.

---

cap slightly scaly or felty

pale form

TOP VIEW

dark form

TOP VIEW

old specimen becomes pale

thin-stemmed form

TOP/SIDE VIEW

UNDERSIDE

pink, well-spaced, thick gills

margin often serrated

dry cap, a shade of pink or reddish brown, drying paler

cap center slightly depressed

gills with decurrent tooth

strongly fibrillose and robust stem in this specimen

SIDE VIEW

SECTION

LACCARIA LACCATA

Common Deceiver

The vernacular name of this species derives from the extremely variable color of the fruitbodies. They can be found in a range of pink-browns but otherwise resemble *L. amethystina* (*see above*). *L. proxima* is bigger and has a more fibrillose stem, while *L. bicolor* has violet basal mycelium.

- **SPORE DEPOSIT** White.
- **SIZE** Cap 1–5cm (w); stem 2–6cm (h) x 0.2–0.6cm (w).
- **HABITAT** Mycorrhizal with trees in woods and parks; also in boggy places under willow trees; also under pine.
- **RANGE** Widespread and abundant in north temperate zones.

- **FRUITING** In troops, often on damp soil. Summer–early winter.

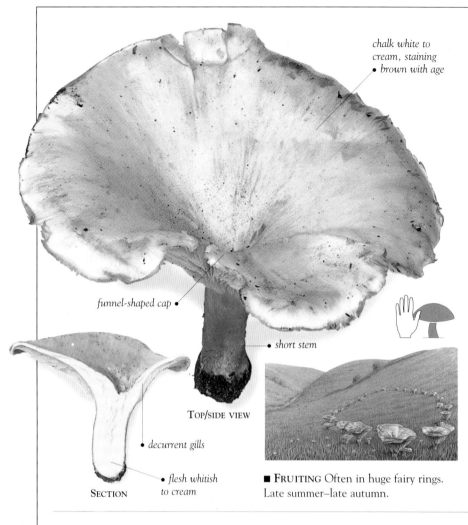

chalk white to
cream, staining
• brown with age

funnel-shaped cap •

• short stem

TOP/SIDE VIEW

• decurrent gills

SECTION

• flesh whitish
to cream

■ **FRUITING** Often in huge fairy rings.
Late summer–late autumn.

LEUCOPAXILLUS GIGANTEUS

Giant Funnel Cap

Size is definitely the most impressive
aspect of this species, which can
reach a diameter of up to 40cm.
The cap, stem, and gills are dingy
white to cream, and the stem is
shorter than that of the similar
Clitocybe geotropa (*see below*). The
cap is flat when young, but soon
becomes funnel-shaped. A technical
way to distinguish this genus from
Clitocybe is the blue-black reaction
of its spores in reagents containing
iodine. This fungus fruits in fairy
rings, the mycelia for which may
be hundreds of years old. Although
edible, it can cause gastric upsets.

■ **SPORE DEPOSIT** Whitish cream.
■ **SIZE** Cap 12–40cm (w);
stem 4–8cm (h) x 2–4cm (w).
■ **HABITAT** Mostly found on nutrient-
rich grassy areas, but also in parkland
and open woods in fairy rings.
■ **RANGE** Widespread in Europe,
eastern North America, and
Pacific Northwest.

CLITOCYBE GEOTROPA

Rickstone Funnel Cap

Among the *Clitocybe* species this is
a remarkably easy one to identify in
a genus otherwise ridden with
identification problems. The tall
stature and central umbo (raised
lump or boss) on the cap, together
with the pale leather brown colors
and a tendency to grow in fairy
rings, provide a combination of
distinctive features. In contrast,
Clitocybe nebularis (*see opposite*),
often found in similar habitats, is a
much grayer fungus with a typically
bun-shaped cap.

■ **SPORE DEPOSIT** White.
■ **SIZE** Cap 5–20cm (w);
stem 8–20cm (h) x 1–3cm (w).
■ **HABITAT** Mostly a forest species, and
in part of the range found mainly under
deciduous trees, but it also thrives in
certain types of conifer forests.
■ **RANGE** Widespread and common
in Europe, avoiding colder regions;
northern North America and Rockies.

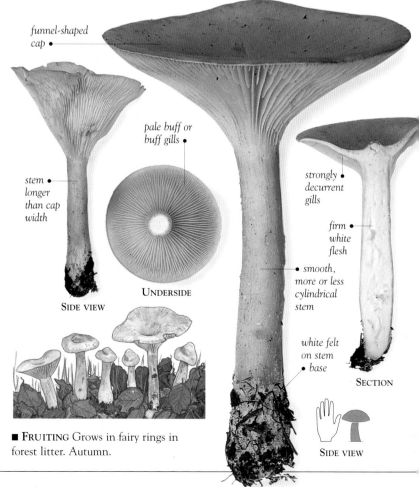

funnel-shaped
cap •

pale buff or
buff gills •

strongly •
decurrent
gills

firm •
white
flesh

• smooth,
more or less
cylindrical
stem

white felt
on stem
• base

SECTION

stem •
longer
than cap
width

UNDERSIDE

SIDE VIEW

SIDE VIEW

■ **FRUITING** Grows in fairy rings in
forest litter. Autumn.

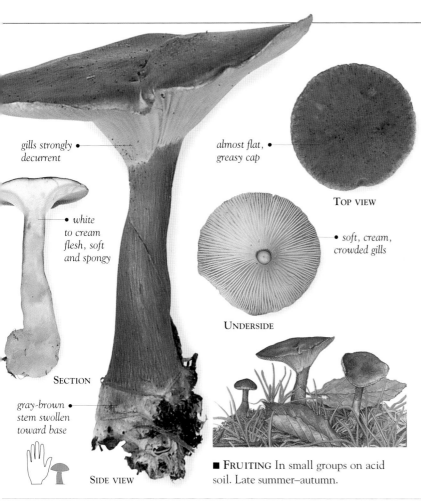

gills strongly • decurrent

almost flat, greasy cap

TOP VIEW

• white to cream flesh, soft and spongy

• soft, cream, crowded gills

UNDERSIDE

SECTION

gray-brown • stem swollen toward base

SIDE VIEW

■ **FRUITING** In small groups on acid soil. Late summer–autumn.

CLITOCYBE CLAVIPES
Club-footed Funnel Cap

The club-shaped stem, strongly swollen at the base and tapering toward the top, its fairly large size, and soft, cream-colored gills identify this species clearly. The cap surface has a greasy feel to it, and it often has a distinct pale margin. The entire fruitbody is soft and spongy, capable of holding a large amount of water. The flesh is white and it has a strong but sweet smell. It can cause transient illness, especially if alcohol is consumed.

■ **SPORE DEPOSIT** White.
■ **SIZE** Cap 4–8cm (w); stem 3–10cm (h) x up to 1.5cm (w) at the top and up to 3cm (w) at base.
■ **HABITAT** Mainly on humus-rich acid soil under conifers, especially white pine; also in deciduous forests where it typically grows under birch trees.
■ **RANGE** Widespread and mostly common in north temperate zones.

CLITOCYBE NEBULARIS
Clouded Funnel Cap

One of the most familiar European forest fungi, mostly found in fairy rings in mixed woodlands. It is fleshy and edible, but can cause stomach upsets, so it can not be recommended. It has a strong aromatic smell. The cap surface is finely felty and the smooth margin is inrolled. Note the similar but poisonous *Entoloma eulividum* (see p.124).

■ **SPORE DEPOSIT** Cream.
■ **SIZE** Cap 8–20cm (w); stem 5–10cm (h) x 1.5–4cm (w).
■ **HABITAT** On good soils in a range of woods and forests.
■ **RANGE** Widespread in north temperate zones; reported in Pacific Northwest.

■ **FRUITING** Mostly in fairy rings on leaf litter. Autumn–early winter.

sometimes seen with a parasitic species of Volvariella on top •

dark gray-brown to gray cap often has a whitish bloom •

• surface slightly felty to smooth

slightly • decurrent gills

TOP/SIDE VIEW

margin • inrolled

SECTION

base swollen, attached to • leaf litter

• crowded pale cream gills

UNDERSIDE

TOP/SIDE VIEW

CLITOCYBE GIBBA
Common Funnel Cap

A relatively easy species to identify, and although it is edible it is not recommended. It can be confused with several other fungi in the genus *Clitocybe* or with *Lepista flaccida (see p.90)* and *L. gilva*. The cap is a pale leather color, with a pinkish tinge, and is strongly depressed in the center. The gills are almost pure white and deeply decurrent.

■ **SPORE DEPOSIT** White to cream.
■ **SIZE** Cap 3–8cm (w); stem 2.5–6cm (h) x 0.5–1cm (w).
■ **HABITAT** Occurs on woodland litter in a very wide range of habitats, from lowland woodland to the alpine zone.
■ **RANGE** Widespread and common in north temperate zones.

■ **FRUITING** In troops on woodland litter. Late summer–autumn.

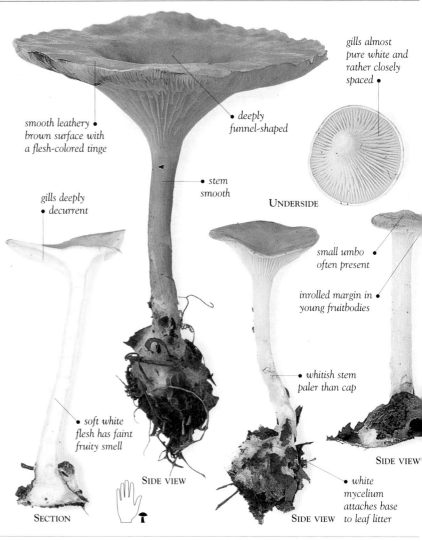

smooth leathery • brown surface with a flesh-colored tinge

gills deeply • decurrent

• deeply funnel-shaped

• stem smooth

gills almost pure white and rather closely spaced •

UNDERSIDE

small umbo often present •

inrolled margin in young fruitbodies •

• soft white flesh has faint fruity smell

SECTION

SIDE VIEW

• whitish stem paler than cap

SIDE VIEW

SIDE VIEW

• white mycelium attaches base to leaf litter

---

greenish blue; tinged brown as fruitbody ages

gills adnate to slightly decurrent •

margin • inrolled

SECTION

• flesh marbled and has strong anise smell

TOP/SIDE VIEW

cap convex or umbonate, sometimes • funnel-shaped

crowded gills paler than cap and stem •

stem base covered in fine • white hairs

UNDERSIDE

■ **FRUITING** In troops on woodland litter. Autumn.

CLITOCYBE ODORA
Fennel Funnel Cap

Apart from *C. odora*, there are a number of fragrant *Clitocybe* species with a strong anise or fennel smell. This one is unique in being blue-green all over, although a rare, totally white form also exists. As it matures, the cap turns gray or gray-brown. *C. odora* is also unusual within the genus in having gills that are barely decurrent. The other group of similar species, which includes *C. fragrans*, has leather-brown or white coloring and decurrent gills and, unlike *C. odora*, those species are not edible; they are often smaller.

■ **SPORE DEPOSIT** Dull pink.
■ **SIZE** Cap 3–6cm (w); stem 3–6cm (h) x 0.4–1cm (w).
■ **HABITAT** On woodland litter, with a preference for richer soils, in mixed woods or under conifers.
■ **RANGE** Widespread in north temperate zones.

CLITOCYBE METACHROA

Gray-brown Funnel Cap ☠

Commonly referred to as *C. dicolor*, this gray-brown fungus is now thought to be a form of *C. metachroa*. Small *Clitocybe* species such as this one are often very difficult to identify. *C. metachroa* can be told by its very indistinct smell, which is not yeasty, as in some look-alikes. It also has a cap that remains dark at the center with a striate margin and produces a white spore deposit. *C. vibecina* is very similar but has a strong, rancid, yeasty smell and taste, and occurs in both deciduous and coniferous woods.

- ■ **SPORE DEPOSIT** Whitish.
- ■ **SIZE** Cap 2.5–6cm (w); stem 3–6cm (h) x 0.3–0.7cm (w).
- ■ **HABITAT** In conifer woods, primarily pine, on litter
- ■ **RANGE** Widespread and common in Europe; across northern North America.

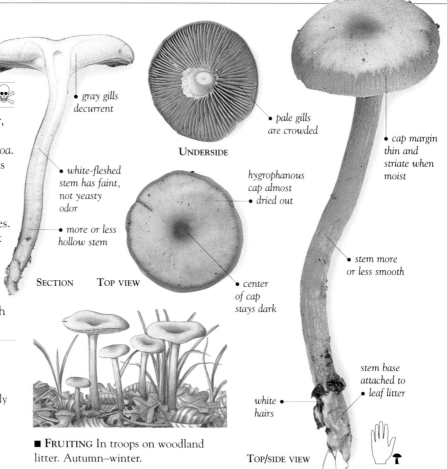

gray gills decurrent

pale gills are crowded

UNDERSIDE

white-fleshed stem has faint, not yeasty odor

more or less hollow stem

hygrophanous cap almost dried out

cap margin thin and striate when moist

SECTION **TOP VIEW**

center of cap stays dark

stem more or less smooth

stem base attached to leaf litter

white hairs

TOP/SIDE VIEW

- ■ **FRUITING** In troops on woodland litter. Autumn–winter.

thin, cracking surface layer

whitish to pale brown stem

cap often has dark spots in concentric rings

gills white to pale gray and decurrent

UNDERSIDE

TOP/SIDE VIEW

base attached firmly to grass turf

SIDE VIEW

cap has mealy surface and dries to a paler color

TOP VIEW

CLITOCYBE RIVULOSA

Sweating Mushroom ☠

This poisonous species is separated by some mycologists: *C. rivulosa* with more brownish colors (*as shown here*) and an almost pure white type, *C. dealbata*. They occur in grassy places and may be found with *Marasmius oreades* (*see p.108*). They are distinguished by the decurrent gills.

- ■ **SPORE DEPOSIT** White.
- ■ **SIZE** Cap 2–6cm (w); stem 1.5–4cm (h) x 0.3–0.6cm (w).
- ■ **HABITAT** In grassy areas including parks, lawns, and sports fields.
- ■ **RANGE** As a complex, widespread in north temperate zones.

- ■ **FRUITING** In grassy areas, often in fairy rings. Summer–autumn.

LEPISTA FLACCIDA

Tawny Funnel Cap

Species of *Lepista* can be similar to
Clitocybe species (*see p.86*), and
some resemble *Tricholoma* species
(*see p.94*). *Lepista* species are best
identified by microscopic features,
such as their rough-walled spores
and tinted spore prints. *L. flaccida*
has deeply decurrent gills and a
depressed cap center. It is fleshier
than *Clitocybe gibba* (*see p.88*), and
the spore deposit is darker.

- ■ **SPORE DEPOSIT** Cream.
- ■ **SIZE** Cap 4–12cm (w);
stem 3–7cm (h) x 0.5–1cm (w).
- ■ **HABITAT** On forest litter,
especially from conifers.
- ■ **RANGE** Widespread and common
in Europe; across northern
North America.

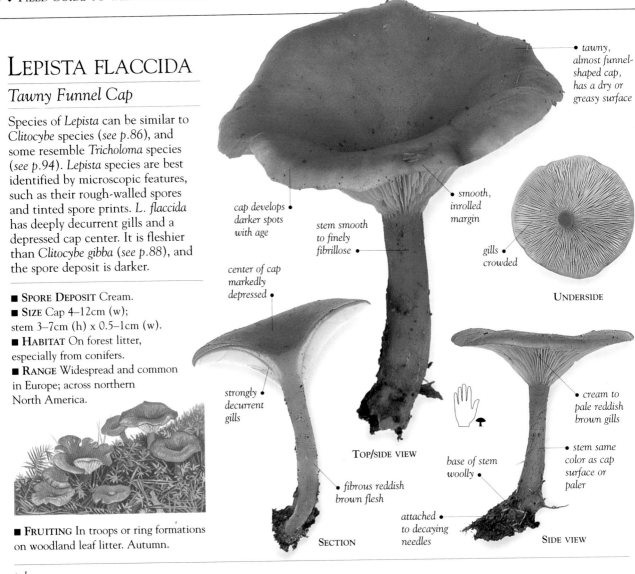

- **tawny,
almost funnel-
shaped cap,
has a dry or
greasy surface*

*cap develops •
darker spots
with age*

*stem smooth
to finely
fibrillose*

- *smooth,
inrolled
margin*

*gills •
crowded*

UNDERSIDE

*center of cap
markedly
depressed •*

*strongly •
decurrent
gills*

TOP/SIDE VIEW

- *cream to
pale reddish
brown gills*

- *stem same
color as cap
surface or
paler*

*base of stem
woolly •*

- *fibrous reddish
brown flesh*

*attached •
to decaying
needles*

SECTION

SIDE VIEW

■ **FRUITING** In troops or ring formations
on woodland leaf litter. Autumn.

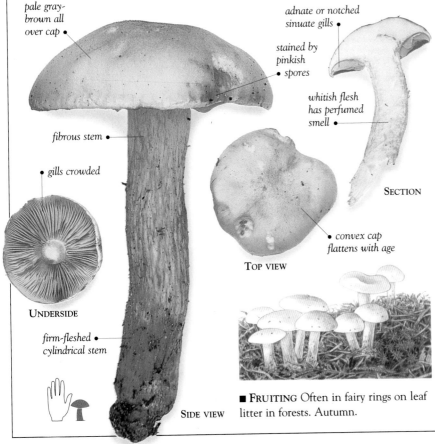

*pale gray-
brown all
over cap •*

fibrous stem •

- *gills crowded*

UNDERSIDE

*firm-fleshed •
cylindrical stem*

SIDE VIEW

*adnate or notched
sinuate gills •*

*stained by
pinkish
• spores*

*whitish flesh
has perfumed
smell •*

SECTION

- *convex cap
flattens with age*

TOP VIEW

■ **FRUITING** Often in fairy rings on leaf
litter in forests. Autumn.

LEPISTA IRINA

Strong-scented Blewit

In stature this species is very similar
to *L. nuda* and *L. personata* (*see
p.91*), but it is plain gray-brown all
over and has a much stronger
perfumed smell. The cap is convex,
becoming flattened with age, and
the cap margin is often wavy. The
stem has a fibrillose surface, and the
mature gills have a pinkish tinge.
Since several other species bear a
superficial resemblance to this
species, and it is known to cause
gastric upsets, it should not be
eaten. It sometimes occurs in mass
fruitings late in the season.

- ■ **SPORE DEPOSIT** Dingy pink.
- ■ **SIZE** Cap 5–15cm (w);
stem 5–10cm (h) x 1–2cm (w).
- ■ **HABITAT** Typically found on calcareous
soil where leaf litter has accumulated.
- ■ **RANGE** Widespread and common in
Europe; also found in northern North
America and Rockies.

LEPISTA NUDA

Wood Blewit

A popular and easy to identify edible, although care must be taken not to collect by mistake an *Entoloma*, a *Hebeloma*, or a *Cortinarius*. *L. nuda* is now cultivated on a commercial scale but is not yet widely available in shops. The cap tends to be a dingy violet-brown, while the gills are brighter violet. Most people find the smell and taste pleasant.

■ **SPORE DEPOSIT** Dingy pink.
■ **SIZE** Cap 5–20cm (w); stem 4–10cm (h) x 1.5–3cm (w).
■ **HABITAT** Nutrient-rich habitats, such as compost and thick forest litter.
■ **RANGE** Widespread and common in north temperate zones.

■ **FRUITING** In small groups and rings on rich soil or compost. Mainly autumn.

forms with more blue in cap are often found

• cap can be slightly hygrophanous

violet to violet-brown hues all • over fruitbody

stem surface fibrous •

UNDERSIDE

club-shaped base attached to leaf litter •

gills sinuate •

TOP/SIDE VIEW

SIDE VIEW

• firm flesh, marbled in lilac-blue tones

SECTION

• young cap is very dark and bun-shaped

SIDE VIEW

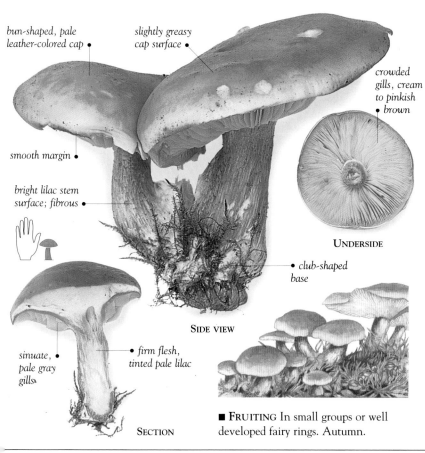

bun-shaped, pale leather-colored cap •

slightly greasy cap surface •

crowded gills, cream to pinkish • brown

smooth margin •

bright lilac stem surface; fibrous •

UNDERSIDE

• club-shaped base

SIDE VIEW

sinuate, pale gray gills•

• firm flesh, tinted pale lilac

SECTION

■ **FRUITING** In small groups or well developed fairy rings. Autumn.

LEPISTA PERSONATA

Blue Legs

Despite the common name of this fungus, the fibrous stem is not blue but a bright lilac. The cap is pale leather brown, and convex when young, flattening with age. The overall shape of the fruitbody tends to be more squat than that of *L. nuda* (*see above*), and it prefers more open habitats, although it can occur in calcareous forests. It is very fleshy and considered to be a high quality edible, but note caution as for *L. nuda* above.

■ **SPORE DEPOSIT** Dingy pink.
■ **SIZE** Cap 5–20cm (w); stem 3–7cm (h) x 1.5–4cm (w).
■ **HABITAT** Rich, calcareous soils, mostly in open grassy areas, road sides, and parks, but also on bare soil in calcareous forests.
■ **RANGE** Widespread and fairly common in Europe and North America.

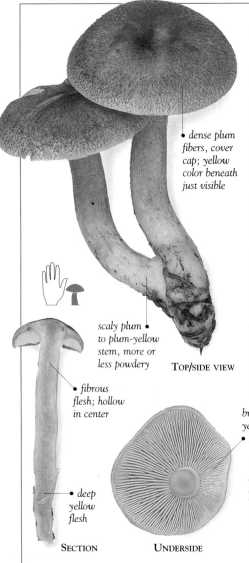

- dense plum fibers, cover cap; yellow color beneath just visible

scaly plum to plum-yellow stem, more or less powdery

TOP/SIDE VIEW

- fibrous flesh; hollow in center

- deep yellow flesh

SECTION

UNDERSIDE

TRICHOLOMOPSIS RUTILANS

Plums-and-custard

The beautiful plum-streaked cap and contrasting egg-yellow gills make this an attractive and instantly recognizable species. *T. decora*, often found in the same areas, lacks the red colors and has fine blackish hairs on the yellow cap. Unlike the similar mycorrhizal *Tricholoma* species, *Tricholomopsis rutilans* causes conifer decay.

- **SPORE DEPOSIT** White.
- **SIZE** Cap 5–10cm (w), occasionally wider; stem 4–10cm (h) x 1–2.5cm (w).
- **HABITAT** In woodlands and parks, confined to rotten conifers, usually with a preference for pine wood.
- **RANGE** Widespread and common in north temperate zones.

bright yellow gills

- **FRUITING** In small clusters on rotten wood. From late summer onward.

TRICHOLOMA PARDINUM

Poisonous Knight-cap ☠

A fleshy, very pale species with thin black scales in a concentric pattern. The white stem can have some dark scales. The flesh has a fresh mealy smell and flavor, but it is poisonous and can cause severe gastric upsets. Be careful since it looks similar to the edible *Tricholoma terreum* (see p.97).

- **SPORE DEPOSIT** White.
- **SIZE** Cap 4–15cm (w); stem 5–10cm (h) x 1.5–3cm (w).
- **HABITAT** Mycorrhizal with deciduous or conifer trees, in calcareous woodland.
- **RANGE** Primarily in the Pacific Northwest.

- **FRUITING** In troops in rich, calcareous woodland. Autumn.

TRICHOLOMA LASCIVUM

Oak Knight-cap ☠

A fungus that can be recognized by smell and habitat. It is a small to medium-sized *Tricholoma* species with a pale leather-colored cap and a strongly aromatic smell that some people find pleasant and others dislike. It is inedible and possibly poisonous. It can be confused with other pale *Tricholoma* species. *Tricholoma album* is paler and is found only beneath birches. *Calocybe gambosum* mostly occurs in spring.

- **SPORE DEPOSIT** White.
- **SIZE** Cap 4–8cm (w); stem 5–8cm (h) x 1–1.5cm (w).
- **HABITAT** In woods underneath oaks, beech, and hornbeam trees; it forms mycorrhizal associations.
- **RANGE** Widespread and common in Europe. Not reported in North America.

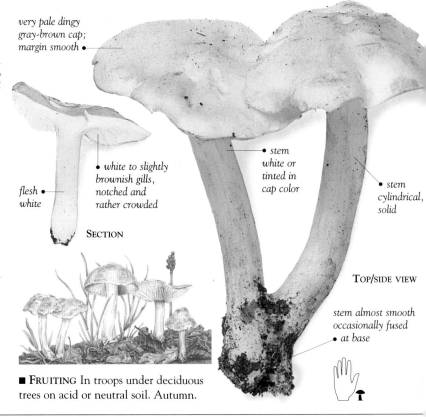

very pale dingy gray-brown cap; margin smooth

- white to slightly brownish gills, notched and rather crowded

flesh white

SECTION

- stem white or tinted in cap color

- stem cylindrical, solid

TOP/SIDE VIEW

stem almost smooth occasionally fused at base

- **FRUITING** In troops under deciduous trees on acid or neutral soil. Autumn.

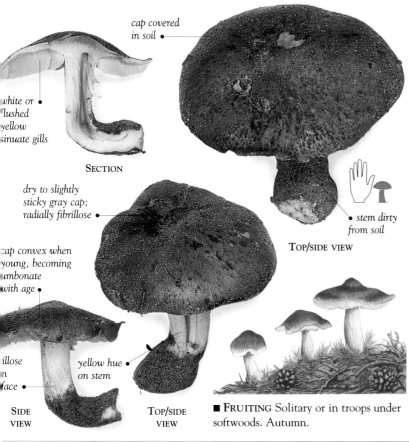

cap covered in soil •

white or flushed yellow sinuate gills •

SECTION

dry to slightly sticky gray cap; radially fibrillose •

cap convex when young, becoming umbonate with age •

illose n ace •

yellow hue on stem •

SIDE VIEW

TOP/SIDE VIEW

• stem dirty from soil

TOP/SIDE VIEW

■ **FRUITING** Solitary or in troops under softwoods. Autumn.

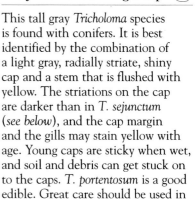

TRICHOLOMA PORTENTOSUM

Gray and Yellow Knight-cap

This tall gray *Tricholoma* species is found with conifers. It is best identified by the combination of a light gray, radially striate, shiny cap and a stem that is flushed with yellow. The striations on the cap are darker than in *T. sejunctum* (*see below*), and the cap margin and the gills may stain yellow with age. Young caps are sticky when wet, and soil and debris can get stuck on to the caps. *T. portentosum* is a good edible. Great care should be used in correct identification.

■ **SPORE DEPOSIT** White.
■ **SIZE** Cap 5–12cm (w); stem 5–10cm (h) x 1–3cm (w).
■ **HABITAT** Forms mycorrhiza with conifers, often on sandy soils.
■ **RANGE** Widespread and relatively common in north temperate zones.

TRICHOLOMA FLAVOVIRENS

Sandy Knight-cap

A yellow species with a sticky cap and yellow gills occurs in several forms. The robust form (*shown below*) is found in sand under pines. This is a good edible, but great care should be used in correct identification.

■ **SPORE DEPOSIT** White.
■ **SIZE** Cap 5–14cm (w); stem 5–10cm (h) x 1.5–2.5cm (w).
■ **HABITAT** Robust forms occur in sandy pine woods; slender forms under spruce.
■ **RANGE** Widespread and common in suitable habitats throughout north temperate zones.

■ **FRUITING** Troops in sand. Overwinters in California. Autumn–early winter.

TRICHOLOMA SEJUNCTUM

Deceiving Knight-cap

Similar to *T. portentosum* (*see above*), but with a green or brown cap. Although edible, it is best avoided since it can be confused with the poisonous *Amanita phalloides* (*see p.131*) if the sac and free gills of *A. phalloides* are overlooked. The beech form occurs on calcareous soils, but acidic soils are more usual.

■ **SPORE DEPOSIT** White.
■ **SIZE** Cap 5–10cm (w); stem 5–8cm (h) x 1–1.5cm (w).
■ **HABITAT** In woods or parks; forms mycorrhiza with deciduous trees such as beech and conifers.
■ **RANGE** Widespread in north temperate regions.

■ **FRUITING** Small groups or troops in woods. Autumn.

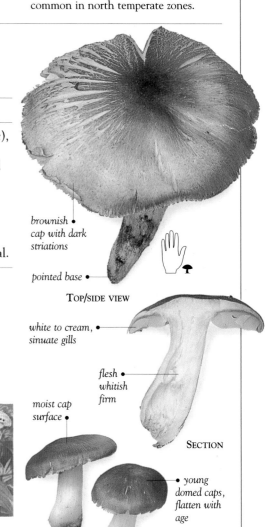

brownish • cap with dark striations

pointed base •

TOP/SIDE VIEW

white to cream, • sinuate gills

flesh • whitish firm

moist cap • surface

SECTION

• young domed caps, flatten with age

SIDE VIEW

TRICHOLOMA FULVUM

Birch Knight-cap

A tall *Tricholoma* species that is inedible and possibly poisonous. It is typically found near birch trees. The warm brown color of the fruitbody, together with yellowish flesh in the stem, are distinguishing features. As in other species of *Tricholoma*, the gills are sinuate and notched. The gills of *T. fulvum* are pale yellow, spotting with brownish marks when older. *T. albobrunneum* is similar but grows under conifers and lacks yellow flesh. *T. ustale* (*see below*) has pale flesh.

- **SPORE DEPOSIT** White.
- **SIZE** Cap 4–10cm (w); stem 7–15cm (h) x 1–2.5cm (w).
- **HABITAT** Forms mycorrhiza with species of birch and possibly with spruce.
- **RANGE** Widespread in north temperate zones. Range unknown in North America.

smooth, dry cap, can be greasy in wet weather

slight umbo in center of cap

sinuate notched gills, tinted yellow

yellow flesh has a bitter taste and mealy smell

yellow-brown stem

orange-brown cap with furrou margin

SECTION

TOP/SIDE VIEW

yellow gills become spotted brown with age

UNDERSIDE

- **FRUITING** In troops, mostly on damp ground under birches. Autumn.

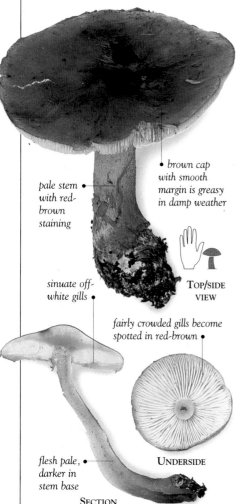

pale stem with red-brown staining

brown cap with smooth margin is greasy in damp weather

sinuate off-white gills

TOP/SIDE VIEW

fairly crowded gills become spotted in red-brown

flesh pale, darker in stem base

UNDERSIDE

SECTION

TRICHOLOMA USTALE

Burnt Knight-cap

Often associated with beech in richer deciduous woods, *T. ustale* lacks any unique identification features. The cap is greasy and the gills stain red-brown. The stem top lacks the distinct pale zone found in *T. ustaloides*. *T. populinum* is similar but occurs with poplar trees.

- **SPORE DEPOSIT** White.
- **SIZE** Cap 3–10cm (w); stem 4–10cm (h) x 0.5–2cm (w).
- **HABITAT** Forms mycorrhiza with beech, on neutral-calcareous soils.
- **RANGE** Widespread and common in Europe. Not reported in North America.

- **FRUITING** Solitary or in troops under deciduous trees, often beech. Autumn.

TRICHOLOMA AURANTIUM

Orange Knight-cap

The beautiful orange color, with white showing through on the stem, makes this one of the most attractive, but inedible, *Tricholoma* species. Depending on the weather, the cap may be sticky if wet or completely dry and almost velvety in texture.

- **SPORE DEPOSIT** White.
- **SIZE** Cap 5–15cm (w); stem 5–10cm (h) x 1–3cm (w).
- **HABITAT** Forms mycorrhiza with conifers, and more rarely with deciduous trees, such as aspen, on calcareous soils.
- **RANGE** Widely distributed in eastern North America and the Rockies.

- **FRUITING** In troops on alkaline soil. Autumn. Overwinters in California.

TRICHOLOMA SULPHUREUM

Gasworks Knight-cap ☠

A poisonous species that can be instantly recognized by its sulfur-yellow coloration and nauseating smell of gas, caused by a chemical compound called scatol. Some mycologists distinguish a smaller species, *T. bufonium*, which has a red-brown cap center and a similar smell.

■ **SPORE DEPOSIT** White.
■ **SIZE** Cap 2–8cm (w); stem 4–10cm (h) x 0.5–2cm (w).
■ **HABITAT** Forms mycorrhiza with deciduous and coniferous trees.
■ **RANGE** Widespread in north temperate zones.

■ **FRUITING** In troops, in deciduous and coniferous woods. Autumn.

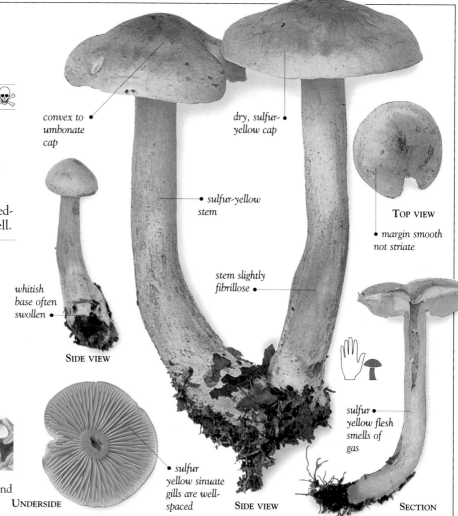

convex to umbonate cap

dry, sulfur-yellow cap

sulfur-yellow stem

TOP VIEW

margin smooth not striate

whitish base often swollen

SIDE VIEW

stem slightly fibrillose

sulfur yellow flesh smells of gas

sulfur yellow sinuate gills are well-spaced

UNDERSIDE

SIDE VIEW

SECTION

TRICHOLOMA SAPONACEUM

Soap-scented Knight-cap

This inedible species has often been divided into a number of varieties because it is extremely variable. All share the common characteristic of having a fleshy fruitbody that smells strongly of soap. Some forms have dark scales on the stem and the stem base is often pink. The gills range in color from cream to gray-green. Others stain more or less reddish, or have greenish colors. The cap is greasy in damp weather and lacks the striation of *T. portentosum* and *T. sejunctum* (see p.93).

■ **SPORE DEPOSIT** White.
■ **SIZE** Cap 4–10cm (w); stem 4–10cm (h) x 1–3cm (w).
■ **HABITAT** In woods forms mycorrhiza with deciduous trees, such as oak and beech, and also with conifers in a variety of soil types.
■ **RANGE** Across northern North America and the Rockies.

greasy cap in damp weather, becomes scaly when dry

pale gray or a darker gray-green but variable

smooth margin

TOP/SIDE VIEW

whitish flesh

sinuate, cream to pale gray-green gills, fairly well spaced

form with dark scales on stem

pink base

ECTION

SIDE VIEW

■ **FRUITING** Solitary or in troops in woodland. Autumn.

pale cap •
with brownish
adpressed
scales

yellow stained •
margin in old
specimens

convex to
• umbonate

whitish stem, •
more or less fibrillose

cylindrical
• stem

SIDE VIEW

TOP/SIDE VIEW

notched, •
sinuate gills

flesh •
fibrous

gills white •
to pale gray,
staining yellow

UNDERSIDE

pale flesh •
has a mealy or
cucumber scent

SECTION

TRICHOLOMA SCALPTURATUM

Yellow Staining Knight-cap

This brownish knight-cap belongs to a complex group of closely related species. It tends to be pale and fairly small, and older specimens stain yellow. Some mycologists separate a paler form as *T. argyraceum*. Although edible it cannot be recommended because of its similarity to the poisonous *T. pardinum* (see p.92).

■ **SPORE DEPOSIT** White.
■ **SIZE** Cap 2–8cm (w); stem 3–7cm (h) x 0.5–1cm (w).
■ **HABITAT** In woodland and parks, forms mycorrhiza, often with birch.
■ **RANGE** Widespread in Europe; range unknown in North America.

■ **FRUITING** Often in troops of several hundred fruitbodies. Autumn.

TRICHOLOMA SCIODES

Fleck-gill Knight-cap

This inedible sharp-tasting and gray-colored *Tricholoma* species can be recognized by the fairly acute umbo on the cap, and its black-spotted gills. It forms mycorrhiza with deciduous trees, mainly beech. *T. virgatum* is more silvery gray and conical and occurs in rich conifer forests. *T. orirubens* is darker and has blue and pink staining, especially at the base of the stem. This and *T. atrosquamosum* (see p.97) have more distinct hairlike cap scales.

■ **SPORE DEPOSIT** White.
■ **SIZE** Cap 4–8cm (w); stem 4–10cm (h) x 1–2cm (w).
■ **HABITAT** In forests forms mycorrhiza with deciduous trees, often with beech on good soil.
■ **RANGE** Widespread and common in Europe, except the boreal-arctic region; not reported in North America.

inrolled
• margin

UNDERSIDE

pale gray gills, with
dark-stained edge •

SIDE VIEW

umbonate cap, •
has dark adpressed
scales on an off-
white surface

pale stem with •
grayish hairlike
scales

more or less
cylindrical
• stem

pale •
fibrous
flesh

flesh smells earthy;
tastes mild, but
then burning hot •

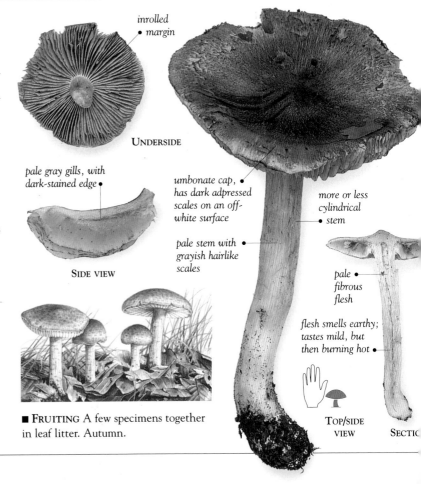

■ **FRUITING** A few specimens together in leaf litter. Autumn.

TOP/SIDE VIEW

SECTION

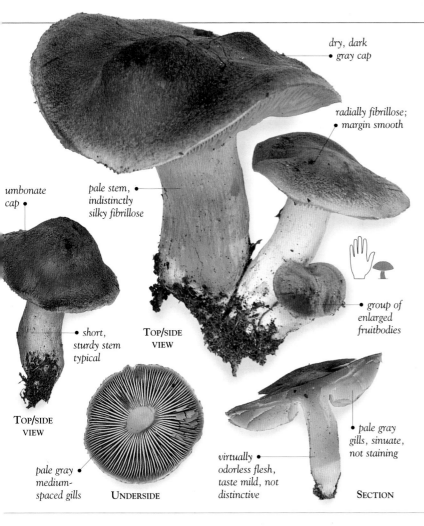

dry, dark
• gray cap

radially fibrillose;
• margin smooth

*umbonate
cap* •

pale stem, •
*indistinctly
silky fibrillose*

• *group of
enlarged
fruitbodies*

• *short,
sturdy stem
typical*

**TOP/SIDE
VIEW**

**TOP/SIDE
VIEW**

*pale gray
medium-
spaced gills* •

UNDERSIDE

virtually •
*odorless flesh,
taste mild, not
distinctive*

• *pale gray
gills, sinuate,
not staining*

SECTION

TRICHOLOMA TERREUM

Gray Knight-cap

As its scientific name suggests, *T. terreum* blends in almost perfectly with the soil surface. It has little smell, and the flesh is mild tasting. This is a good edible but be careful to avoid confusion with the poisonous *T. pardinum* (see p.92).

■ **SPORE DEPOSIT** White.
■ **SIZE** Cap 3–7cm (w); stem 2–5cm (h) x 0.5–1.5cm (w).
■ **HABITAT** With conifers on calcareous soil; mycorrhiza forming.
■ **RANGE** Northern North America.

■ **FRUITING** In troops on needle debris on rich soil. Autumn.

TRICHOLOMA ATROSQUAMOSUM

Dark-scaled Knight-cap

Dark coloring, black hairs on the stem, and a spicy smell mark this species, but it can be hard to identify. Be careful not to confuse this species with the poisonous *T. pardinum* (see p.92), which causes gastric upsets.

■ **SPORE DEPOSIT** White.
■ **SIZE** Cap 3–8cm (w); stem 4–8cm (h) x 0.5–1.5cm (w).
■ **HABITAT** On calcareous soil, forming mycorrhiza with both coniferous and deciduous wood.
■ **RANGE** Widespread but local in Europe; not reported in North America.

■ **FRUITING** Solitary or in small groups. Autumn–early winter.

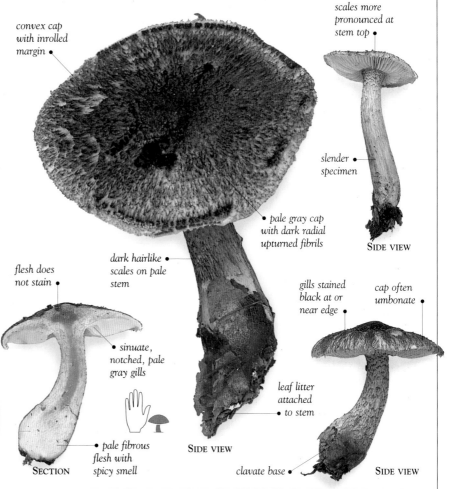

*convex cap
with inrolled
margin* •

*scales more
pronounced at
stem top* •

*slender
specimen*

SIDE VIEW

*flesh does
not stain* •

dark hairlike •
*scales on pale
stem*

• *pale gray cap
with dark radial
upturned fibrils*

• *sinuate,
notched, pale
gray gills*

*gills stained
black at or
near edge* •

*cap often
umbonate* •

*leaf litter
attached
• to stem*

• *pale fibrous
flesh with
spicy smell*

SECTION

SIDE VIEW

clavate base •

SIDE VIEW

ARMILLARIA CEPISTIPES

Honey Onion Mushroom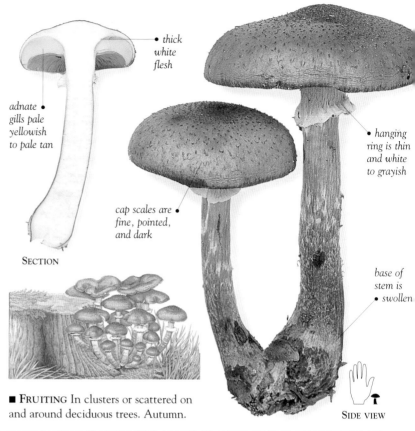

A range of similar fungi once grouped under the name A. *mellea* are now split into more than a dozen species. The true A. *mellea* is shown below. A. cepistipes, shown here, differs from A. *mellea* in stem shape; from the conifer-loving A. *ostoyae* in having finer cap scales and a thinner, white to grayish, stem ring; and from A. *gallica* by its black-centered young caps and a white stem ring. Take care when eating A. *cepistipes*; it can cause gastric upsets in some people.

- ■ **SPORE DEPOSIT** White.
- ■ **SIZE** Cap 3–12cm (w); stem 4–12cm (h) x 1–3cm (w).
- ■ **HABITAT** Mostly on dead or dying deciduous trees, but also on conifers.
- ■ **RANGE** Widespread and common in northern temperate zones; throughout Pacific Northwest.

thick white flesh

adnate gills pale yellowish to pale tan

SECTION

cap scales are fine, pointed, and dark

hanging ring is thin and white to grayish

base of stem is swollen

SIDE VIEW

- ■ **FRUITING** In clusters or scattered on and around deciduous trees. Autumn.

ARMILLARIA MELLEA

Honey Mushroom

The fungus illustrated below is now known as *Armillaria mellea* in the strict sense (*see above*). It has large yellowish fruitbodies and, unlike A. *cepistipes* (*see above*), the cap has sparse, pale scales, and the slender stem is long and pointed. It invariably grows in large clusters.

- ■ **SPORE DEPOSIT** White.
- ■ **SIZE** Cap 3–10cm (w); stem 8–20cm (h) x 1–2cm (w).
- ■ **HABITAT** In woodland, mainly with deciduous trees, often on fallen stumps.
- ■ **RANGE** Widespread in north temperate zones but local.

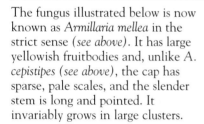

- ■ **FRUITING** Almost always found in dense tufts. Autumn.

LYOPHYLLUM CONNATUM

White Gray Gill ☠

To help identify this silky white *Lyophyllum* species, apply a drop of ferrous sulfate solution to the gills. The gills of this species will stain violet, whereas similar white *Clitocybe* species (*see pp.86–89*) do not. Still commonly known in North America as *Clitocybe dilatata*.

- ■ **SPORE DEPOSIT** White.
- ■ **SIZE** Cap 3–10cm (w); stem 5–12cm (h) x 0.5–1.5cm (w).
- ■ **HABITAT** Mostly on disturbed soil along roads and in woodland.
- ■ **RANGE** North temperate zones in Pacific Northwest and Rocky Mountains.

- ■ **FRUITING** In clusters or a few solitary fruitbodies on disturbed soil. Autumn.

LYOPHYLLUM PALUSTRE

Sphagnum Grayling

Whereas other fungus species associated with sphagnum moss usually have brown spores or decurrent gills, the inedible L. *palustre* has adnexed gills and white spores. The cap is thin-fleshed with striations to its center.

- ■ **SPORE DEPOSIT** White.
- ■ **SIZE** Cap 1–3cm (w); stem 4–8cm (h) x 0.1–0.3cm (w).
- ■ **HABITAT** Found only on sphagnum moss, which it kills, in boggy places.
- ■ **RANGE** Widespread throughout the north temperate zones; in eastern North American bogs.

- ■ **FRUITING** In troops or fairy rings, on sphagnum moss. Summer–autumn.

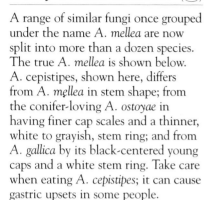

LYOPHYLLUM DECASTES

Fried Chicken Mushroom

Mycologists disagree on how to separate the fleshy *Lyophyllum* species. *L. decastes* forms clusters late in the season and prefers park and garden soils. Among several apparently closely related species, *L. fumosum* differs in having the stem fused into a trunklike base.

■ **SPORE DEPOSIT** White.
■ **SIZE** Cap 5–10cm (w); stem 4–10cm, up to 15cm (h) x 0.5–2.5cm (w).
■ **HABITAT** Not directly associated with trees; found mostly along woodland paths and in garden settings and parks.
■ **RANGE** Widespread and common throughout the north temperate zones.

■ **FRUITING** Found in dense clusters. Autumn, mostly late in the season.

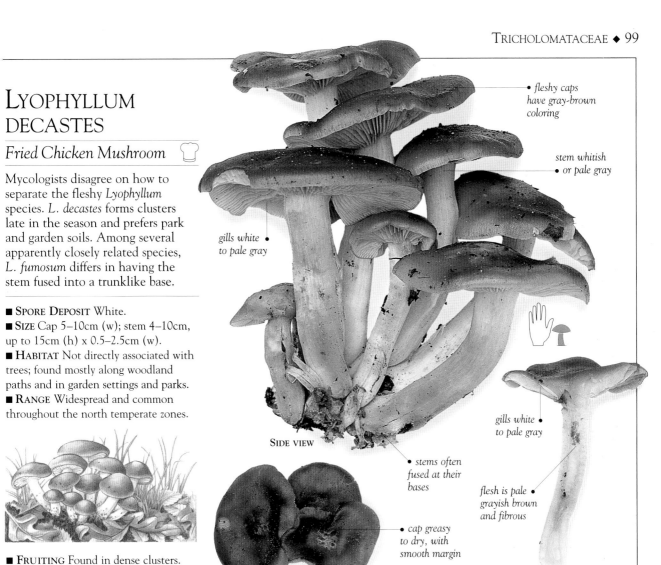

• *fleshy caps have gray-brown coloring*

stem whitish • *or pale gray*

gills white • *to pale gray*

SIDE VIEW

• *stems often fused at their bases*

• *cap greasy to dry, with smooth margin*

TOP VIEW

gills white • *to pale gray*

flesh is pale • *grayish brown and fibrous*

SECTION

---

very fleshy cap is cream-white and slightly greasy

margin of cap is smooth and • *slightly inturned*

surface of cream-white stem is smooth • *in texture*

adnexed gills are cream-white and crowded •

SIDE VIEW

• *flesh is whitish and firm*

SECTION

■ **FRUITING** In troops or fairy rings among grass or herbs. Spring–summer.

CALOCYBE GAMBOSA

St. George's Mushroom

In Europe, this familiar late spring fungus is a sought-after edible. It is very fleshy and usually has cream-white coloring, although a brownish form exists. The smell is very yeasty. It is included in this North American guide because it might occur here and be overlooked by those looking only for morels in the spring, or who only collect seriously later in the season. Other *Calocybe* species are smaller, more brightly colored fungi, and fruit in the autumn.

■ **SPORE DEPOSIT** Cream-white.
■ **SIZE** Cap 3–12cm (w); stem 2–7cm (h) x 1–2.5cm (w).
■ **HABITAT** Found on rich soil in grassland, calcareous woods, and quite often in gardens and parks.
■ **RANGE** Widespread and locally common in Europe and adjacent parts of Asia. Not reported in North America.

CALOCYBE CARNEA

Pink Fair-head

This species is typically associated with grass and can often be seen on lawns and in parks. The pink cap and stem contrast with its white gills. This often makes for easy identification, although it can be difficult to see in deep grass. Even though it is considered edible, it is not really worth eating due to its size. *Calocybe persicolor* may be the same species but is said to be duller and to have a hairy stem base.

- **SPORE DEPOSIT** Cream white.
- **SIZE** Cap 1–4cm (w); stem 2–4cm (h) x 0.3–0.8cm (w).
- **HABITAT** In lawns, grassy areas, and open woods. Also found in fertilized agricultural pastureland.
- **RANGE** Widespread in north temperate zones; rather uncommon.

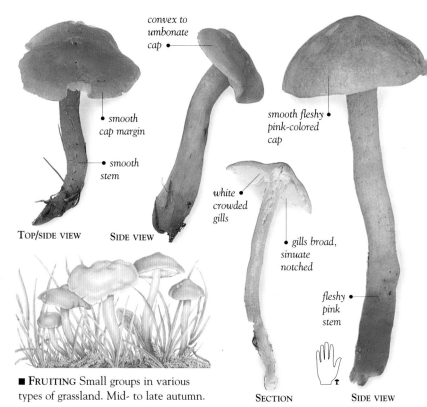

smooth cap margin

convex to umbonate cap

smooth stem

TOP/SIDE VIEW

SIDE VIEW

smooth fleshy pink-colored cap

white crowded gills

gills broad, sinuate notched

fleshy pink stem

SECTION

SIDE VIEW

- **FRUITING** Small groups in various types of grassland. Mid- to late autumn.

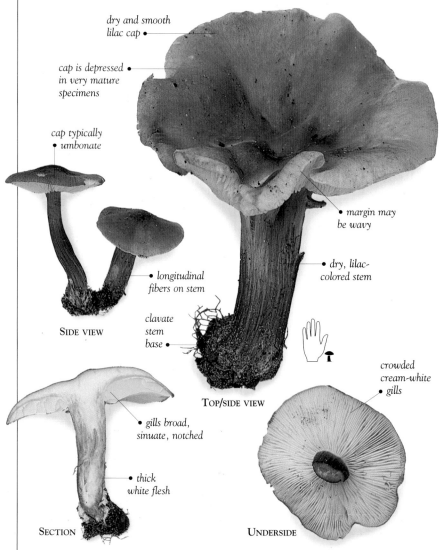

dry and smooth lilac cap

cap is depressed in very mature specimens

cap typically umbonate

longitudinal fibers on stem

SIDE VIEW

clavate stem base

margin may be wavy

dry, lilac-colored stem

TOP/SIDE VIEW

gills broad, sinuate, notched

thick white flesh

SECTION

crowded cream-white gills

UNDERSIDE

CALOCYBE IONIDES

Lilac Fair-head

This colorful *Calocybe* species is confined to rich soils in calcareous woods and riverplain forests. It is distinguished from *C. carnea* (*see above*) by its habitat and the lilac cap and stem. Its flesh has a mealy smell and flavor, but it is not a worthwhile edible. *C. obscurissima* is very similar but has a gray-brown color on cap and stem.

- **SPORE DEPOSIT** White.
- **SIZE** Cap 2–6cm (w); stem 3–5cm (h) x 0.4–1cm (w).
- **HABITAT** Found on rich soil in deciduous or mixed wood.
- **RANGE** Widespread in Rocky Mountains and Europe.

- **FRUITING** Small groups among leaf litter in woodland. Autumn.

ASTEROPHORA PARASITICA

Pick-a-back Toadstool

Asterophora species occur on other rotten gilled mushrooms and are not considered worthwhile as edibles. *A. parasitica* has a silky gray cap and well-developed gills; its more common relative, *A. lycoperdoides*, has deformed gills and a spore-covered cap surface (*see p.223*). Both species are found on old fruitbodies of the *Russula nigricans* group (*see p.180*). *Volvariella surrecta* occurs on gilled mushrooms, in this case on the fruitbodies of *Clitocybe nebularis*. A few small *Collybia* species also develop sclerotia on gilled mushrooms.

- **SPORE DEPOSIT** White.
- **SIZE** Cap 0.5–1.5cm (w); stem 1–3cm (h) x 0.2–0.4cm (w).
- **HABITAT** On rotten fruitbodies of *Russula* and *Lactarius* in woods.
- **RANGE** Widespread in north temperate zones; rare.

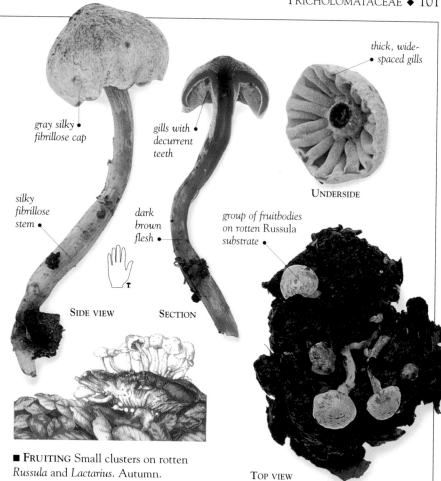

gray silky fibrillose cap

gills with decurrent teeth

thick, wide-spaced gills

UNDERSIDE

silky fibrillose stem •

dark brown flesh •

group of fruitbodies on rotten *Russula* substrate

SIDE VIEW   **SECTION**

- **FRUITING** Small clusters on rotten *Russula* and *Lactarius*. Autumn.

TOP VIEW

cap dark gray-brown when moist, drying to a paler grayish leather brown •

smooth, deeply funnel-shaped cap with inrolled margin

young grayish cream to pale brown gills, fairly crowded

strongly decurrent gills

pale brownish flesh

stem • cylindrical to clavate; longitudinally striate

TOP/SIDE VIEW

clavate • whitish base

UNDERSIDE

old discolored gills

SECTION

TOP/SIDE VIEW

- **FRUITING** Singly or in troops. Late autumn to early winter.

PSEUDOCLITOCYBE CYATHIFORMIS

The Goblet

This species is unlikely to be mistaken for any other. Clear field marks are the strongly funnel-shaped cap – hence its common name – very dark coloration, and tall stem. Also the cap is hygrophanous and the margin is inrolled. The flesh is aromatic and mild tasting, and although edible it is not recommended. The genus *Pseudoclitocybe* differs from the true *Clitocybe* species (*see p.86*) in that the spores are amyloid (giving a blue reaction in iodine reagents). *P. cyathiformis* is like a larger dark *Omphalina* species (*see p.84*). Other species of *Pseudoclitocybe* are, on the whole, smaller and paler and are often found in more open habitats.

- **SPORE DEPOSIT** Cream white.
- **SIZE** Cap 3–7cm (w); stem 6–10cm (h) x 0.5–1cm (w).
- **HABITAT** In woods, parks, and hedges, on litter in tall grass, or on extremely decayed deciduous trunks.
- **RANGE** Reported along east and west coasts in North America.

MELANOLEUCA COGNATA

Ocher-gilled Cavalier

Individual species in this genus can be difficult to identify in the field, although with a microscope *Melanoleuca* species are easily confirmed. *M. cognata* in Europe often occurs in spring when few other gilled mushrooms are above ground; this, combined with its yellowish gills, makes it one of the easier members of the genus to identify. Almost all species have umbonate caps and narrowly attached gills. All *Melanoleuca* species are edible but are not considered worthwhile for cooking.

- **SPORE DEPOSIT** Cream.
- **SIZE** Cap 5–12 cm (w); stem 3–8 cm high x 0.5–1.2cm (w).
- **HABITAT** Reliably found in summer in the spruce-fir zone of the Rockies.
- **RANGE** Widespread and frequent in Colorado Rockies.

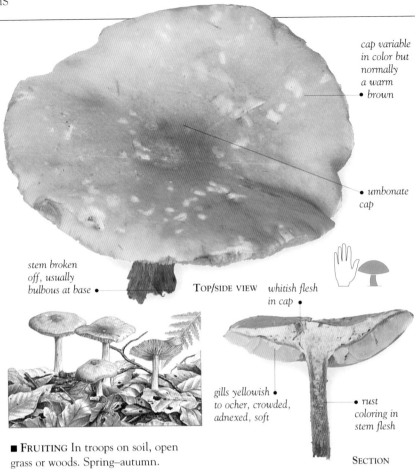

cap variable in color but normally a warm brown

umbonate cap

stem broken off, usually bulbous at base

TOP/SIDE VIEW

whitish flesh in cap

gills yellowish to ocher, crowded, adnexed, soft

rust coloring in stem flesh

SECTION

- **FRUITING** In troops on soil, open grass or woods. Spring–autumn.

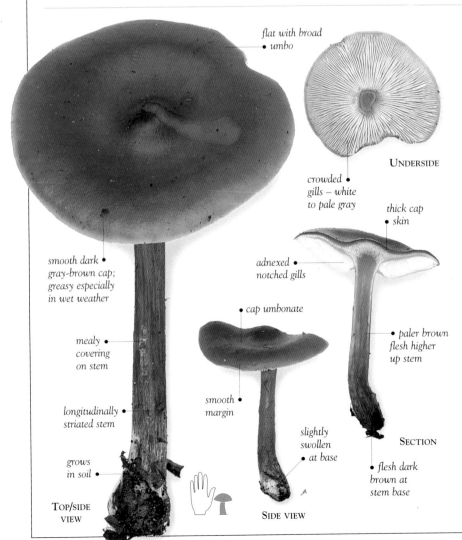

flat with broad umbo

UNDERSIDE

crowded gills – white to pale gray

thick cap skin

smooth dark gray-brown cap; greasy especially in wet weather

adnexed notched gills

mealy covering on stem

cap umbonate

paler brown flesh higher up stem

longitudinally striated stem

smooth margin

grows in soil

slightly swollen at base

SECTION

flesh dark brown at stem base

TOP/SIDE VIEW

SIDE VIEW

MELANOLEUCA POLIOLEUCA

Common Cavalier

This species has often been referred to as *M. melaleuca*, but this is now considered to be a rarer species. *M. polioleuca* abounds on roadsides and similar places throughout autumn. It is a dark species with pale gills and flesh that stains very dark brown from the stem base. It is not worthwhile as an edible.

- **SPORE DEPOSIT** Very pale cream.
- **SIZE** Cap 4–7cm (w); stem 3–8cm high x 0.5–1cm (w).
- **HABITAT** On soil in gardens, parks, and along roads in woods.
- **RANGE** Widespread and common in north temperate zones.

- **FRUITING** In troops on disturbed soil. Summer–autumn. Overwinters in CA.

COLLYBIA MACULATA

Spotted Tough-shank

A mushroom that can produce mass fruitings, making it difficult to find anything else. Very young specimens are pure white, fairly tough, and inedible. As the fruitbody matures, however, rusty spots develop. In mature, it looks like a species of *Tricholoma* (see p.92) and it is unlike most members of the genus *Collybia* – the tough-shanks. *Collybia maculata* has a woody smell and an indistinct to bitter taste. Based on the above characteristics plus the rather colored spore deposit, it has been proposed to reinstate *Rhodocollybia* for this and similar species.

■ **SPORE DEPOSIT** Cream-orange.
■ **SIZE** Cap 4–10cm (w); stem 6–12cm (h) x 1–2.5cm (w).
■ **HABITAT** On humus-rich soil in fairly acid woodland, under both conifer and deciduous trees.
■ **RANGE** Widespread and common in north temperate zones.

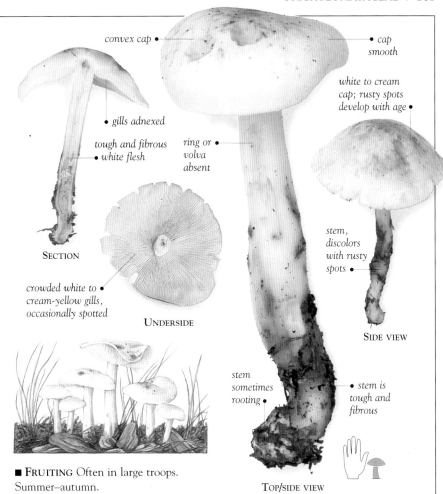

- convex cap
- cap smooth
- white to cream cap; rusty spots develop with age
- gills adnexed
- tough and fibrous white flesh
- ring or volva absent
- **SECTION**
- crowded white to cream-yellow gills, occasionally spotted
- **UNDERSIDE**
- stem, discolors with rusty spots
- **SIDE VIEW**
- stem sometimes rooting
- stem is tough and fibrous
- **TOP/SIDE VIEW**

■ **FRUITING** Often in large troops. Summer–autumn.

COLLYBIA FUSIPES

Spindle-shank

The clustered habit and deeply rooting stems with twisted fibers are distinctive features of this inedible species. A digging tool is necessary to get the entire stem out of the ground. Deep down the stems are attached to decaying roots from the host tree.

■ **SPORE DEPOSIT** White.
■ **SIZE** Cap 4–8cm (w); stem 4–8cm (h) above ground x 0.5–1.5cm (w).
■ **HABITAT** Attached to buried roots, mainly of old oak trees in parks or ancient forests.
■ **RANGE** Fairly common and widespread in the oak regions of Europe. Not reported in North America.

- cap reddish brown
- convex, umbonate, or irregular cap shape
- smooth but greasy cap surface
- stem paler in color toward cap
- very tough fox-brown stem
- cream gills with rust-brown spots
- crowded stained gills
- rooting bases fused together below ground
- pale fibrous flesh
- **SIDE VIEW**
- many smaller gills toward cap margin
- **UNDERSIDE**
- cap is darker when wet
- **TOP VIEW**
- **SECTION**

■ **FRUITING** In clusters with deeply rooting stems. Late summer–autumn.

COLLYBIA DRYOPHILA

Russet Tough-shank

A familiar mushroom complex found in most types of woodland. The cap can be distorted by a jelly fungus parasite. C. dryophila is not recommended as an edible because it has caused cases of digestive upset. There are more than a half dozen species in the C. dryophila complex. Marasmius oreades (see p.108) is also similar.

■ **SPORE DEPOSIT** Cream.
■ **SIZE** Cap 2–6 cm (w); stem 3.5–7cm (h) x 0.3–0.5cm (w).
■ **HABITAT** On litter and humus-rich soil, mostly in woods or open grassy sites.
■ **RANGE** Widespread and common in north temperate zones.

■ **FRUITING** In troops. Late spring–early winter.

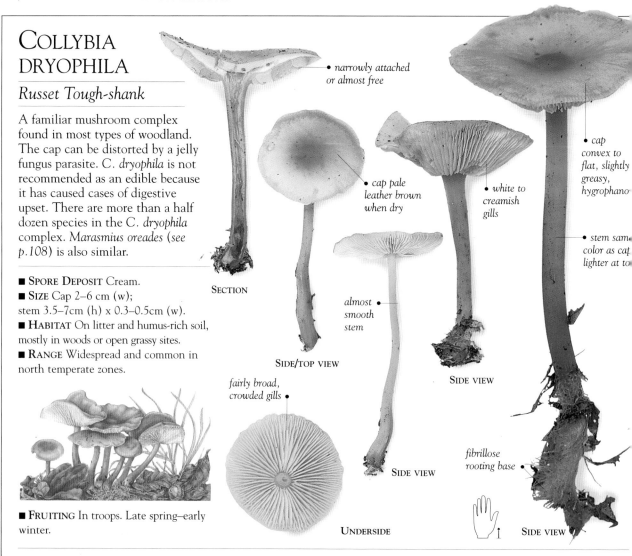

narrowly attached or almost free

cap pale leather brown when dry

white to creamish gills

cap convex to flat, slightly greasy, hygrophanous

stem same color as cap, lighter at top

SECTION

almost smooth stem

SIDE/TOP VIEW

fairly broad, crowded gills

SIDE VIEW

fibrillose rooting base

UNDERSIDE

SIDE VIEW

COLLYBIA ERYTHROPUS

Red-stemmed Tough-shank

This species is rather similar to C. dryophila (see above) except that it has a fox red stem and usually grows on mossy, decaying wood. Its smell and taste is indistinct, so it is not worthwhile as an edible. It tends to grow in clusters, whereas C. dryophila appears as separate fruitbodies. It is also less common than its russet relative. C. acervata is similar to C. erythropus in that it grows in clusters with conifers. C. erythropus could also be confused with Marasmius species (see p.107).

■ **SPORE DEPOSIT** Pale cream.
■ **SIZE** Cap 1–4cm (w); stem 3–7cm (h) x 0.2–0.5cm (w).
■ **HABITAT** On mossy stumps or springing from half-buried, decayed wood in deciduous forests.
■ **RANGE** Fairly common and widespread in Europe.

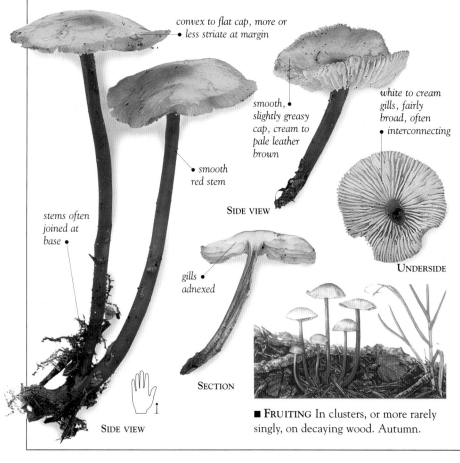

convex to flat cap, more or less striate at margin

smooth, slightly greasy cap, cream to pale leather brown

white to cream gills, fairly broad, often interconnecting

smooth red stem

stems often joined at base

gills adnexed

SIDE VIEW

UNDERSIDE

SECTION

SIDE VIEW

■ **FRUITING** In clusters, or more rarely singly, on decaying wood. Autumn.

COLLYBIA BUTYRACEA

Buttery Tough-shank

A species recognized by its greasy cap and distinctly club-shaped stem base. The cap is hygrophanous, creating zones of light and dark colors. Despite its name, it is not a worthwhile edible. Along with *C. maculata*, this is sometimes placed in the genus *Rhodocollybia*.

■ **SPORE DEPOSIT** Pale cream.
■ **SIZE** Cap 3–6cm (w); stem 4–7cm (h) x 0.5–2cm (w).
■ **HABITAT** Mostly on humus-rich soil and leaf litter in deciduous woods.
■ **RANGE** Widespread and common to abundant in north temperate zones.

■ **FRUITING** In troops on leaf litter and soil. Late summer–early winter.

greasy horn-gray cap; slightly striate •

narrowly attached gills appear almost free •

stem hollow or with soft pith •

cap darkest at distinct umbo •

• stem is similar in color to cap

club-shaped stem has litter attached • to fibrillose base

cap dries out from center • (hygrophanous)

tough and • fibrous flesh

SIDE VIEW

SECTION

smooth, crowded, white gills

SIDE VIEW

UNDERSIDE

TOP VIEW

---

dry, smooth, very pale grayish white cap •

densely • felty stem

dark brown stem of mature specimen •

SIDE VIEW

gills adnexed •

whitish to pale brown flesh •

crowded, narrow white • to cream gills

UNDERSIDE

SECTION

■ **FRUITING** In dense tufts on leaf litter in rich soils. Summer–autumn.

COLLYBIA CONFLUENS

Tufted Tough-shank

This species produces dense tufts of fruitbodies. These tufts can spring from a fairy ring on thick leaf litter in woods. The tall, slender stems are clothed in gray-white felt, and the rounded caps are smaller than those of most *Collybia* species. The smell and taste of *Collybia confluens* is faint and pleasantly aromatic, but it is not considered worthwhile as an edible. *C. acervata* also grows in clusters, but it has reddish coloring and is always associated with coniferous, never deciduous trees.

■ **SPORE DEPOSIT** Pale cream.
■ **SIZE** Cap 1–3cm (w); stem 5–9cm (h) x 0.3–0.7cm (w).
■ **HABITAT** On thick leaf litter from deciduous and coniferous trees; probably more common on rich soils.
■ **RANGE** Widespread in north temperate zones; especially in northern North America.

COLLYBIA PERONATA

Wood Woolly-foot

Not a spectacular fungus, but one that will be remembered if the acrid-tasting flesh of this inedible fungus is experienced. It also has a spicy smell. The felty, yellow stem base is another distinctive identification feature.

- **SPORE DEPOSIT** Pale cream.
- **SIZE** Cap 2.5–6cm (w); stem 4–8cm (h) x 0.3–0.5cm (w).
- **HABITAT** On leaf litter in both conifer and deciduous forests.
- **RANGE** Widespread in north temperate zones; rare in North America.

- **FRUITING** In troops or small clusters on leaf litter in forests. Autumn.

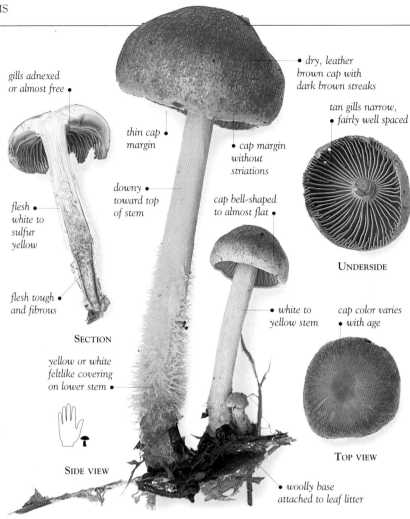

gills adnexed or almost free •

thin cap margin

• cap margin without striations

downy • toward top of stem

flesh • white to sulfur yellow

flesh tough • and fibrous

SECTION

yellow or white feltlike covering on lower stem •

SIDE VIEW

• dry, leather brown cap with dark brown streaks

tan gills narrow, • fairly well spaced

cap bell-shaped to almost flat •

UNDERSIDE

• white to yellow stem

cap color varies • with age

TOP VIEW

• woolly base attached to leaf litter

cap cream to pale leather brown •

curved stem with small scales at base •

gills whitish to pinkish cream, adnate

• pale stem; flesh tough and fibrous

broad gills with • few connections, well spaced

SECTION

SIDE VIEW

finely wrinkled and furrowed • surface

• caps convex, later flat

UNDERSIDE

pale tan stem turns reddish brown at base •

SIDE VIEW

MARASMIELLUS RAMEALIS

Twig Mummy-cap

This tiny agaric always grows in abundance along dead twigs. Its short, curved stems are clothed in pale scales at their bases. It tolerates fairly dry conditions. *M. candidus* can be distinguished from this by its whiter cap and black stem base.

- **SPORE DEPOSIT** White.
- **SIZE** Cap 0.3–1.5cm (w); stem 0.5–2cm (h) x 0.05–0.15cm (w).
- **HABITAT** Damp forests, on sticks, twigs, and cones.
- **RANGE** Widespread and common in Europe and North America.

- **FRUITING** Often in piles of sticks and canes, crowded. Summer–autumn.

MICROMPHALE FOETIDUM

Fetid Mummy-cap

Occasionally this fairly small, gilled mushroom can be detected by its smell alone, which is similar to rotten cabbages. M. *foetidum* only grows on fallen deciduous branches. Its habitat distinguishes it from the very similar-looking and smelling M. *brassicolens*, which grows on beech leaves and twigs. The gills are also paler and more crowded than in M. *foetidum*. Both species prefer damp woods on rich, calcareous soils. Another smaller species M. *perforans* occurs on needle beds. It also has a rotten smell.

- ■ **SPORE DEPOSIT** Whitish.
- ■ **SIZE** Cap 0.5–3cm (w); stem 1–4cm (h) x 0.2–0.4cm (w).
- ■ **HABITAT** On woody litter in deciduous woods on richer soil.
- ■ **RANGE** Widespread in north temperate zones.

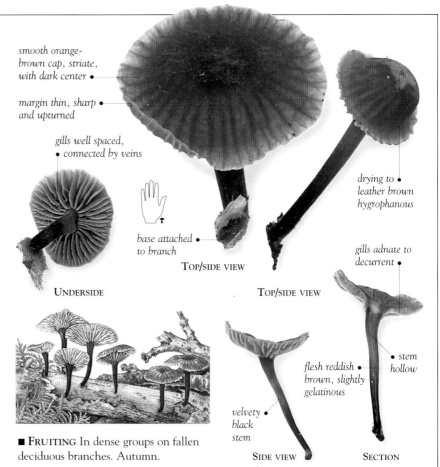

smooth orange-brown cap, striate, with dark center •

margin thin, sharp • and upturned

gills well spaced, • connected by veins

drying to • leather brown hygrophanous

base attached • to branch

TOP/SIDE VIEW

UNDERSIDE

TOP/SIDE VIEW

gills adnate to decurrent

flesh reddish • brown, slightly gelatinous

• stem hollow

velvety • black stem

SIDE VIEW

SECTION

■ **FRUITING** In dense groups on fallen deciduous branches. Autumn.

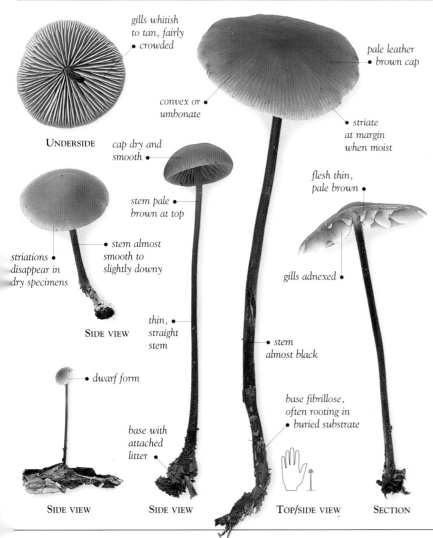

gills whitish to tan, fairly • crowded

UNDERSIDE

convex or • umbonate

cap dry and smooth •

stem pale • brown at top

stem almost • smooth to slightly downy

striations • disappear in dry specimens

SIDE VIEW

thin, • straight stem

• dwarf form

base with attached litter •

SIDE VIEW

SIDE VIEW

pale leather • brown cap

• striate at margin when moist

flesh thin, pale brown •

gills adnexed •

• stem almost black

base fibrillose, often rooting in • buried substrate

TOP/SIDE VIEW

SECTION

MARASMIUS ALLIACEUS

Wood Garlic Mummy-cap

This large species of *Marasmius* has a pungent smell reminiscent of rancid garlic. It is distinguished by a fairly pale cap and a black, almost smooth, stem. It tastes rancid, but some people use it as a spice to flavor cooking. The smaller, paler M. *scorodonius* has a similar smell.

- ■ **SPORE DEPOSIT** Whitish.
- ■ **SIZE** Cap (0.5–) 1.5–4cm (w); stem (4–) 7–15cm (h) x 0.3–0.6cm (w).
- ■ **HABITAT** On beech trunks or on buried branches in beech woods.
- ■ **RANGE** Widespread in the beech regions of Europe and nearby Asia; not reported in North America.

■ **FRUITING** Solitary or in troops in beech woods. Late summer–autumn.

MARASMIUS OREADES

Fairy-ring Mushroom

This species is known to people who have a grass lawn. Some dislike it because it causes characteristic circles in the turf. Others collect the pleasant-tasting fruitbodies that sit at the front edge of rings. It is important to know the difference between this and the poisonous *Clitocybe dealbata* (see p.89), since they occur in the same grassy habitat.

■ **SPORE DEPOSIT** Whitish.
■ **SIZE** Cap 1–5cm (w); stem 3–6cm or up to 10cm (h) x 0.3–0.7cm (w).
■ **HABITAT** Grassland including lawns.
■ **RANGE** Widespread and common in north temperate zones.

■ **FRUITING** In fairy rings in grass turf. Late spring-autumn.

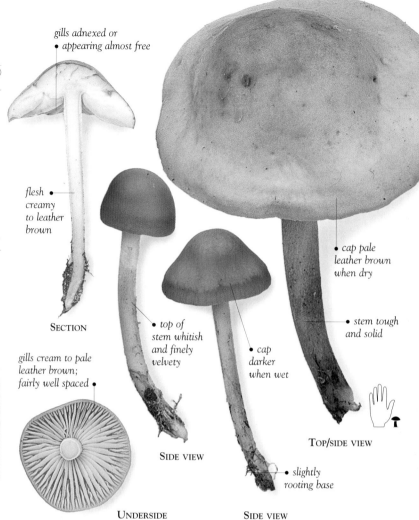

gills adnexed or appearing almost free

flesh creamy to leather brown

SECTION

gills cream to pale leather brown; fairly well spaced

UNDERSIDE

top of stem whitish and finely velvety

cap darker when wet

SIDE VIEW

slightly rooting base

SIDE VIEW

cap pale leather brown when dry

stem tough and solid

TOP/SIDE VIEW

cap ivory with dark dot in center

cap has a distinct navel and is deeply grooved

stem very tough

stem shriveled but can revive

TOP/SIDE VIEW

ivory gills attached to ring (collarium)

UNDERSIDE

flesh thin, tough, whitish

upper part of stem whitish

stem black

CAP SECTION

fruitbody growing on twig

SIDE VIEW

■ **FRUITING** In troops on forest litter. Midsummer–autumn.

MARASMIUS ROTULA

Common Wheel Mummy-cap

This is one of many *Marasmius* species that have the gills attached to a little wheel (a collarium). Most of these occur on leaf litter in tropical rain forests, but a number of tiny species can also be found in temperate zones. *M. rotula* is easy to find, since it occurs on exposed twigs and has striking white caps especially noticable after hard summer rains. The brick-red *M. graminum* is found in grass, and *M. brilliantii* occurs in swarms on leaf litter in damp forests.

■ **SPORE DEPOSIT** Whitish.
■ **SIZE** Cap 0.5–2cm (w); stem 2–4cm or up to 6cm (h) x 0.1cm (w).
■ **HABITAT** On twigs and branches in both deciduous and coniferous forests.
■ **RANGE** Widespread and common in north temperate zones.

MARASMIUS ANDROSACEUS

Horse-hair Mummy-cap

In this species the gills are attached directly to the stem. The stems are very thin and shiny but extremely tough. It has only a faint smell and a mild taste, and is not worthwhile as an edible. The fungus produces horsehairlike threads of densely interwoven hyphae in order to colonize a new substrate. These tough threads enable it to grow in windblown, inhospitable habitats. *M. androsaceus* often occurs with *Micromphale perforans*. However, *M. androsaceus* has a velvety stem and cabbagelike smell. In the tropics many related fungi produce "horse-hair," which some birds use in making nests.

■ **SPORE DEPOSIT** White.
■ **SIZE** Cap 0.3–1cm (w); stem 2.5–5cm (h) x 0.03–0.10cm (w).
■ **HABITAT** On pine needles and other fine litter in pine woods.
■ **RANGE** Widespread and common in north temperate zones.

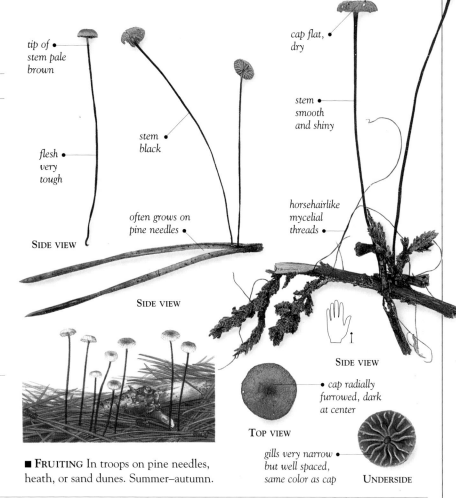

tip of stem pale brown

flesh very tough

stem black

often grows on pine needles

SIDE VIEW

SIDE VIEW

cap flat, dry

stem smooth and shiny

horsehairlike mycelial threads

SIDE VIEW

cap radially furrowed, dark at center

TOP VIEW

gills very narrow but well spaced, same color as cap

UNDERSIDE

■ **FRUITING** In troops on pine needles, heath, or sand dunes. Summer–autumn.

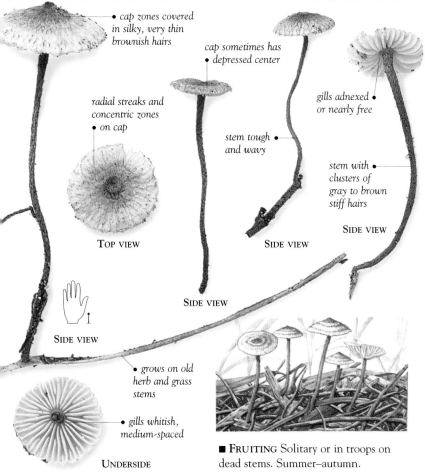

cap zones covered in silky, very thin brownish hairs

radial streaks and concentric zones on cap

TOP VIEW

SIDE VIEW

cap sometimes has depressed center

stem tough and wavy

SIDE VIEW

gills adnexed or nearly free

stem with clusters of gray to brown stiff hairs

SIDE VIEW

grows on old herb and grass stems

gills whitish, medium-spaced

UNDERSIDE

■ **FRUITING** Solitary or in troops on dead stems. Summer–autumn.

CRINIPELLIS SCABELLUS

Shaggy-foot Mummy-cap

This is another particularly tough fungus, preferring dry and exposed habitats, but unlike *Marasmius rotula* (*see opposite*) and other *Marasmius* species, it cannot revive after total desiccation. The stem has a dense covering of stiff hairs, and the cap has adpressed silky hairs, often arranged in zones. The flesh is whitish and tough. Neither the smell nor taste is noteworthy. *Crinipellis* species are found mainly in the tropics, with just a few satellite species in temperate zones. A tropical species causes severe damage to cacao trees.

■ **SPORE DEPOSIT** White.
■ **SIZE** Cap 0.5–1.5cm (w); stem 1.5–3.5cm (h) x 0.1–0.2cm (w).
■ **HABITAT** On herb and grass stems in many dry grassy areas, including unfertilized lawns.
■ **RANGE** Widespread and locally common in north temperate zones; not reported in North America.

STROBILURUS ESCULENTUS

Spruce-cone Toadstool

The various *Strobilurus* species are almost always found on the fallen, decaying cones of conifer trees. *S. esculentus* occurs only on spruce cones; *S. trullisatus* prefers Douglas fir cones, and *S. conigenoides* occurs on magnolia fruits. Species of *Strobilurus* resemble small members of the genus *Collybia* (*see p.103*), but they differ in various microscopic features. They will not rehydrate after being dried out. Some of the more vividly colored *Mycena* species also occur on cones as does *Baeospora myosura* (*see p.120*).

■ **SPORE DEPOSIT** Pale cream.
■ **SIZE** Cap 0.5–3cm (w); stem 2–5cm (h) (without roots) x 0.1–0.25cm (w).
■ **HABITAT** Mainly on buried spruce cones, in spruce stands or natural spruce forests. In damp areas, it is also found on cones lying above the ground.
■ **RANGE** Widespread and common in European spruce regions, including areas where spruce has been introduced, and in Asia; not reported in North America.

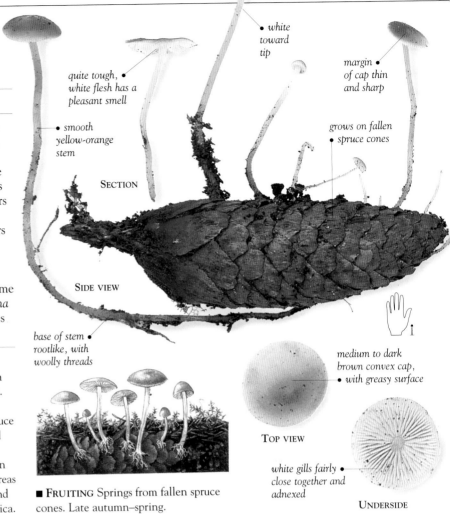

- quite tough, white flesh has a pleasant smell
- smooth yellow-orange stem
- white toward tip
- margin of cap thin and sharp
- grows on fallen spruce cones

SECTION

SIDE VIEW

- base of stem rootlike, with woolly threads

- medium to dark brown convex cap, with greasy surface

TOP VIEW

- white gills fairly close together and adnexed

UNDERSIDE

■ **FRUITING** Springs from fallen spruce cones. Late autumn–spring.

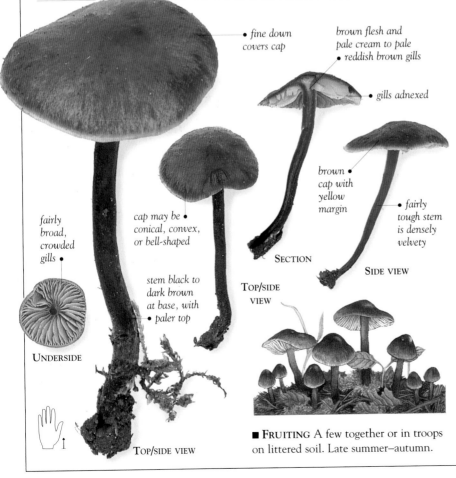

- fine down covers cap
- brown flesh and pale cream to pale reddish brown gills
- gills adnexed
- brown cap with yellow margin
- fairly tough stem is densely velvety

- fairly broad, crowded gills
- cap may be conical, convex, or bell-shaped
- stem black to dark brown at base, with paler top

UNDERSIDE

SECTION

TOP/SIDE VIEW

SIDE VIEW

TOP/SIDE VIEW

■ **FRUITING** A few together or in troops on littered soil. Late summer–autumn.

MACROCYSTIDIA CUCUMIS

Cucumber-scented Toadstool

Although its common name suggests a mild, pleasant scent, this inedible species actually has a quite strong, rancid smell that is reminiscent of rotten cucumbers – or pickled herrings. Another distinctive feature is the dark, pale-margined cap, with a velvety surface. The generic name is based on the large protruding cells, called cystidia, all over the surface of the fruitbodies. Its dark rusty ocher spore deposit is unusual within its family.

■ **SPORE DEPOSIT** Rusty ocher.
■ **SIZE** Cap 0.5–5cm (w); stem 3–7cm (h) x 0.2–0.5cm (w).
■ **HABITAT** On rich soil mixed with leaf litter or sawdust, in gardens and parks, or along forest ditches and roads.
■ **RANGE** Widespread but rather local in north temperate zones; widespread in Europe, but this species is more local in Pacific Northwest in North America.

MYCENA CROCATA

The Stainer

Also commonly known as the Orange-milking Mycena, the stem of this species exudes a saffron-colored liquid when it is cut or broken. The lower part of the stem is the same color as the liquid. *M. haemotopus* (see *p.112*) produces a bloodred milk, and the smaller *M. sanguinolenta* does the same. This species and other *Mycena* are frequently attacked by a spiky mold fungus called *Spinellus fusiger*.

■ **SPORE DEPOSIT** Pale cream.
■ **SIZE** Cap 1–3cm (w); stem 5–12cm (h) x 0.1–0.3 cm (w).
■ **HABITAT** Almost exclusively associated with the litter of beech trees, M. *crocata* is found mainly on fallen beech branches or in places with thick leaf litter.
■ **RANGE** Widespread and common in beech regions in Europe; also found in Japan. Not reported in North America.

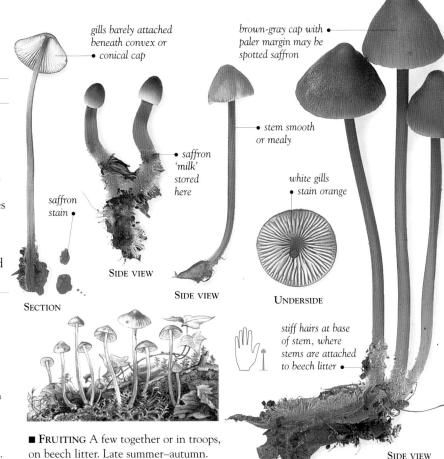

gills barely attached beneath convex or conical cap

saffron 'milk' stored here

saffron stain

SECTION

SIDE VIEW

SIDE VIEW

stem smooth or mealy

brown-gray cap with paler margin may be spotted saffron

white gills stain orange

UNDERSIDE

stiff hairs at base of stem, where stems are attached to beech litter

SIDE VIEW

■ **FRUITING** A few together or in troops, on beech litter. Late summer–autumn.

variable cap color, but mostly shades of gray

white liquid exudes from broken stem

stem dry to the touch and usually gray

grows on various kinds of litter

SIDE VIEW   **SIDE VIEW**

surface of convex cap is smooth and dry, with fine radiating lines

TOP VIEW

adnexed gills

gills white, distant, unlike most other Mycena species

SIDE VIEW   **UNDERSIDE**

SECTION

■ **FRUITING** Singly or in troops, on litter or humus-rich soil. Late summer–winter.

MYCENA GALOPUS

Milk-drop Bonnet

This highly variable *Mycena* species is best identified by the copious white liquid found in the stems of most specimens when they are broken. The base of the stem is the best place to test this characteristic. There are also completely white and black forms of this fungus, and the black form, (or black bonnet), is sometimes treated as a totally separate species and is then known as M. *leucogala*. The faint smell of M. *galopus* resembles radishes but its edibility is unknown. The gills in *Mycena galopus* are more distant than those of its look-alikes.

■ **SPORE DEPOSIT** Pale cream.
■ **SIZE** Cap 0.5–2cm (w); stem 3–7cm (h) x 0.1–0.2cm (w).
■ **HABITAT** On the litter layer – found both on the fallen needles of conifers and on the leaf litter from deciduous trees; also in semiopen habitats, including lawns.
■ **RANGE** Widespread and common throughout Europe; east and west coasts of North America.

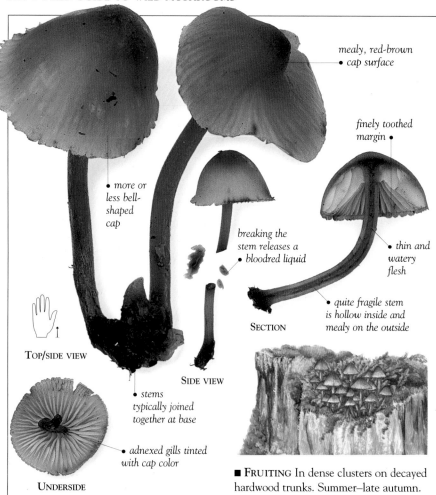

more or less bell-shaped cap

mealy, red-brown cap surface

breaking the stem releases a bloodred liquid

finely toothed margin

SECTION

thin and watery flesh

quite fragile stem is hollow inside and mealy on the outside

SIDE VIEW

TOP/SIDE VIEW

stems typically joined together at base

adnexed gills tinted with cap color

UNDERSIDE

■ FRUITING In dense clusters on decayed hardwood trunks. Summer–late autumn.

MYCENA HAEMATOPUS

Bleeding Bonnet

Usually found growing in tight clusters on wood, this species has a fine powder covering its cap surface, and the cap margin is toothed. Another distinguishing characteristic occurs when the stem is bruised or broken: it oozes a dark, blood-red liquid. M. haematopus should not be confused with the smaller M. sanguinolenta, another bleeding species, which has a more slender build and red-brown gill edges. It normally grows on leaf litter. Mycena crocata (see p.111) produces an orange milk, and Mycena inclinata produces tight clusters but no milk.

■ SPORE DEPOSIT Whitish cream.
■ SIZE Cap 0.5–3cm (w); stem 3–7cm (h) x 0.2–0.4cm (w).
■ HABITAT In most types of forests, on the stumps and fallen trunks of deciduous trees.
■ RANGE Widespread and common in north temperate zones.

MYCENA EPIPTERYGIA

Yellow-stemmed Bonnet

There are comparatively few slimy species of Mycena. This particular species is identified by a vivid yellow stem. It is quite variable in other characteristics. Size varies considerably as does the degree of rusty brown coloring on the stems. The smell is typically somewhat mealy-rancid. M. rorida is by far the slimiest Mycena species. The stem has a thick slimy envelope, thicker than the stem itself. M. belliae, which grows only on reeds, has a slightly slimy stem. Unlike M. epipterygia, the gills are strongly decurrent.

■ SPORE DEPOSIT Creamish.
■ SIZE Cap 0.5–2.5cm (w); stem 3–8cm (h) x 0.1–0.25cm (w).
■ HABITAT On plant litter, including decaying wood; mostly on conifers but also in more open habitats on acid soil with brambles and bracken.
■ RANGE Widespread and common in north temperate zones.

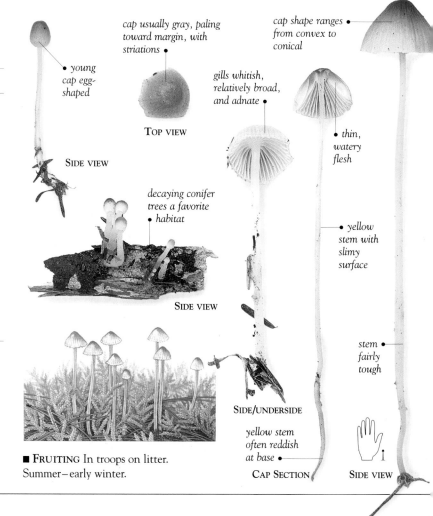

young cap egg-shaped

SIDE VIEW

cap usually gray, paling toward margin, with striations

TOP VIEW

cap shape ranges from convex to conical

gills whitish, relatively broad, and adnate

thin, watery flesh

decaying conifer trees a favorite habitat

SIDE VIEW

yellow stem with slimy surface

SIDE/UNDERSIDE

stem fairly tough

yellow stem often reddish at base

CAP SECTION

SIDE VIEW

■ FRUITING In troops on litter. Summer–early winter.

margin appears more striated when wet

purplish gray when wet; dries to pale gray-lavender

cap shape varies from convex to flat

fragile, watery flesh

purplish stem

gills broad and narrowly attached

serrated, purple-black gill edge

hollow stem

SECTION

SIDE VIEW OF GILL

SIDE VIEW

stem thicker and fibrous toward its base

SIDE VIEW

■ **FRUITING** Singly or a few together on thick beech leaf litter. Summer–autumn.

MYCENA PELIANTHINA

Serrated Bonnet

This somber species of Mycena can be identified by its large size, dark gill color, and broad gill shape. The overall impression is that of a Collybia species (see pp.103–106), but a variety of microscopic features places the species in Mycena alongside the M. pura group (see below). Gray-purple in color, the gills have an almost black, serrated edge. The cap is large and hygrophanous, becoming darker in color when wet. The smell is reminiscent of radishes and is similar to that of M. pura (see below). The entire Mycena pura group is thought to be toxic.

■ **SPORE DEPOSIT** White.
■ **SIZE** Cap 3–6cm (w); stem 4–8cm (h) x 0.4–0.8cm (w).
■ **HABITAT** On thick leaf litter, mainly from beech trees, mostly in rich, calcareous forests.
■ **RANGE** Widespread but local in Europe and adjacent Asia; across northern North America.

MYCENA PURA

Lilac Bonnet

A highly variable suspect fungus with a characteristic radish smell. Some of the many differently colored forms are considered as separate species or varieties. Most, however, have shades of purple in the cap or stem. A large pink form, Mycena rosea, has been implicated in poisonings.

■ **SPORE DEPOSIT** White.
■ **SIZE** Cap 2–6cm (w); stem 3–9cm (h) x 0.3–1cm (w).
■ **HABITAT** On humus-rich soil in both wooded and open habitats.
■ **RANGE** Common in north temperate zones; extending farther south.

gills fairly crowded

cap shape varies from convex to umbonate

UNDERSIDE

distinctly striate at margin when wet

TOP VIEW

adnexed to adnate gills may be sinuate-notched

the pinkish form is also known as M. rosea

hollow stem

springs from soil rich in humus

dry stem may have yellow hue or be paler than cap

SECTION

fine white fibers cover base of stem

SIDE VIEW

■ **FRUITING** Singly or in small groups. Late summer–early winter.

SIDE VIEW

MYCENA ACICULA

Orange-capped Bonnet

Among the various tiny *Mycena* species that favor litter, *M. acicula* is probably the easiest to identify. The vivid orange cap and slender, translucent yellow stem are its most obvious distinguishing features. Finding this fungus can however be a difficult task, since it often grows singly, hidden deep among leaves or in other sheltered places.

■ **SPORE DEPOSIT** Whitish.
■ **SIZE** Cap 0.3–1cm (w); stem 2–6cm (h) x 0.05–0.1cm (w).
■ **HABITAT** On tiny pieces of woody litter such as bark flakes, situated in moist places in woods or parks.
■ **RANGE** Widespread and fairly common in north temperate zones.

■ **FRUITING** On woody litter in gardens, hedges, and forests. Spring–winter.

cap surface dusted with a fine powder

cap shape convex or bell-shaped

TOP VIEW

orange cap with yellowish margin encloses pale yellow gills

stem has a powdery dusting, like cap

SIDE VIEW

long and very slender stem

SIDE VIEW

translucent yellow color extends along length of stem

the stem may be rooting in buried substrate

SIDE VIEW

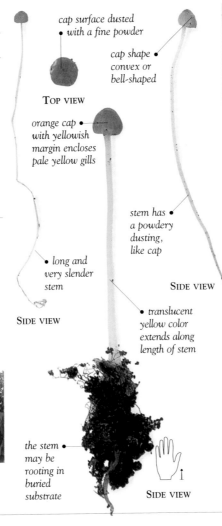

MYCENA ADONIS

Coral-pink Bonnet

A close relative of *M. flavoalba* (see below), but with a striking, coral-red cap that fades with age. The typical form has a white, translucent stem.

■ **SPORE DEPOSIT** White.
■ **SIZE** Cap 0.5–1.5cm (w); stem 2.5–4cm (h) x 0.1–0.2cm (w).
■ **HABITAT** On thick litter or among mosses on humus-rich soil, in both open and wooded areas.
■ **RANGE** Widespread in north temperate zones; west coast of North America.

■ **FRUITING** Singly or in small groups, in moss or other damp places. Autumn.

MYCENA FLAVOALBA

Yellow-white Bonnet

Circular groups of hundreds of *M. flavoalba* fruitbodies are a typical mid- to late-autumn feature on mossy lawns. They may also occur on conifer debris, where they can easily be mistaken for various other cream-colored species, especially those belonging to the genus *Hemimycena*. True to its common name, the most distinctive characteristic of *M. flavoalba* is the diluted yellow color of its convex or conical cap. It is a close relative of *M. adonis* (see above).

■ **SPORE DEPOSIT** Whitish.
■ **SIZE** Cap 0.5–2cm (w); stem 3–5cm (h) x 0.1–0.2cm (w).
■ **HABITAT** In mossy, grassy areas; on litter in conifer forests.
■ **RANGE** Widespread and common in Europe; eastern North America, the Rockies, and Pacific Northwest.

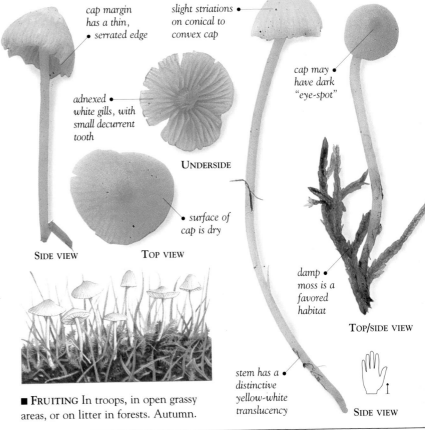

cap margin has a thin, serrated edge

slight striations on conical to convex cap

cap may have dark "eye-spot"

adnexed white gills, with small decurrent tooth

UNDERSIDE

SIDE VIEW

surface of cap is dry

TOP VIEW

damp moss is a favored habitat

TOP/SIDE VIEW

stem has a distinctive yellow-white translucency

SIDE VIEW

■ **FRUITING** In troops, in open grassy areas, or on litter in forests. Autumn.

cap dry and gray in color, sometimes with faint olive or pink hues

TOP VIEW

white to pink gills

UNDERSIDE

gills rather crowded

cap shape varies from convex to bell-like

gills narrowly attached to stem

smooth surface

stem horn-gray, or with tones of lilac

fine white fibrils at base of stem

TOP/SIDE VIEW

SECTION

favors woody debris such as fallen branches or bark

SIDE VIEW

MYCENA ARCANGELIANA

Late-season Bonnet

Not an easily identified species, the early stages of this bonnet are often characterized by a lilac stem and a dull gray cap. If kept inside a can, a strong iodine-like smell will become noticeable in minutes.

- **SPORE DEPOSIT** White.
- **SIZE** Cap 1–2.5cm (w); stem 3–7cm (h) x 0.2–0.3cm (w).
- **HABITAT** On mossy bark at the base of living trees or bushes, or on woody debris in gardens, cemeteries, parks, and forests.
- **RANGE** Widespread and common in Europe; rare but widely distributed in North America.

- **FRUITING** Often in troops on woody debris. Autumn–early winter.

MYCENA FILOPES

Iodine Bonnet

This rather nondescript species is best identified with the aid of a microscope and by the combination of fragile stem, gray coloring, and iodine smell – iodine is a compound used as an antiseptic. It can easily be confused with other gray bonnets such as M. *metata* and M. *arcangeliana* (*see above*). The former tends to have pinkish hues and prefers more acid conditions and conifer forests; the latter is slightly more robust, has a stronger color on the stem, and grows on more woody substrates.

- **SPORE DEPOSIT** White.
- **SIZE** Cap 0.8–2cm (w); stem 6–10cm (h) x 0.1–0.2cm (w).
- **HABITAT** On humus or small pieces of litter, mostly in deciduous forests but also found on needle beds beneath conifers. Often found along forest paths; prefers rich soil.
- **RANGE** Widespread and common in Europe; eastern North America and Pacific Northwest.

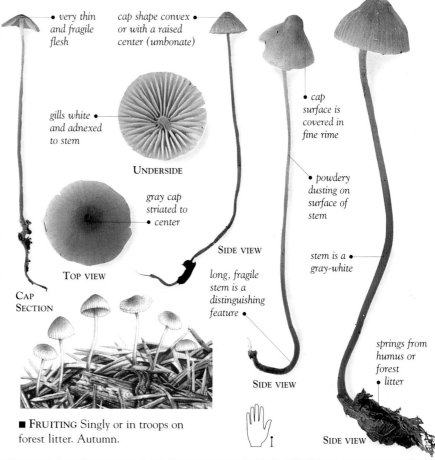

very thin and fragile flesh

cap shape convex or with a raised center (umbonate)

gills white and adnexed to stem

UNDERSIDE

gray cap striated to center

TOP VIEW

CAP SECTION

cap surface is covered in fine rime

powdery dusting on surface of stem

SIDE VIEW

stem is a gray-white

long, fragile stem is a distinguishing feature

SIDE VIEW

springs from humus or forest litter

- **FRUITING** Singly or in troops on forest litter. Autumn.

SIDE VIEW

MYCENA OLIVACEO-MARGINATA

Field Bonnet

Like its much larger relative, M. pelianthina (see p.113), this Mycena species has a distinctive olive-brown colored gill edge that provides an important identification feature. M. olivaceo-marginata is typically found in open grassy areas. The olive-brown gill edge can be difficult to detect with the naked eye and so is best seen with a hand lens, in good light. The wide variety of cap colors found in this species range from gray-brown to yellow, and even shades of pink.

- **SPORE DEPOSIT** White.
- **SIZE** Cap 0.7–1.5cm (w); stem 3–6cm (h) x 0.1–0.2cm (w).
- **HABITAT** On mossy turf in parkland and in most cut or grazed grassy areas, including those by the coast.
- **RANGE** Widespread and common in Europe; not reported in North America.

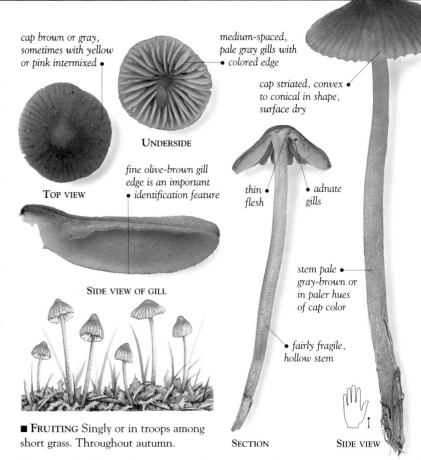

cap brown or gray, sometimes with yellow or pink intermixed •

UNDERSIDE

medium-spaced, pale gray gills with • colored edge

cap striated, convex to conical in shape, surface dry

fine olive-brown gill edge is an important • identification feature

TOP VIEW

thin • flesh

• adnate gills

stem pale • gray-brown or in paler hues of cap color

SIDE VIEW OF GILL

• fairly fragile, hollow stem

- **FRUITING** Singly or in troops among short grass. Throughout autumn.

SECTION   **SIDE VIEW**

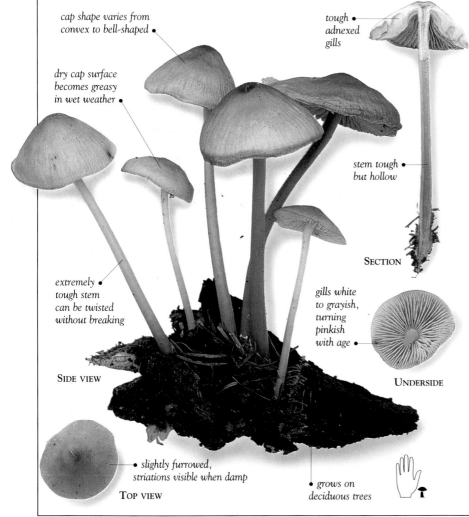

cap shape varies from convex to bell-shaped •

dry cap surface becomes greasy in wet weather •

extremely • tough stem can be twisted without breaking

SIDE VIEW

• slightly furrowed, striations visible when damp

TOP VIEW

tough • adnexed gills

stem tough • but hollow

SECTION

gills white to grayish, turning pinkish with age •

UNDERSIDE

• grows on deciduous trees

MYCENA GALERICULATA

Common Bonnet

Although one of the most abundant of all forest fungi, this species is hard to identify since it has few marked characteristics. Two notable features, however, are its unusual toughness compared to other Mycena species, and a noticeable tendency for the gills to turn a pinkish hue with age.

- **SPORE DEPOSIT** Pale cream.
- **SIZE** Cap 1–6cm (w); stem 3–8cm (h) x 0.2–0.7cm (w).
- **HABITAT** On deciduous trunks, stumps, fallen branches in forests.
- **RANGE** Widespread and common in north temperate zones, extending south. Widely distributed in North America.

- **FRUITING** In tufts and troops on deciduous trees. Summer–early winter.

MYCENA INCLINATA

Clustered Oak Bonnet

As its name suggests, this distinctive *Mycena* is found in dense clusters. Do not confuse this species with M. *maculata*, which lacks the spicy smell and toothed cap edge of this species and has a purplish brown stem.

■ **SPORE DEPOSIT** Pale cream.
■ **SIZE** Cap 1–4cm (w); stem 6–12cm (h) x 0.2–0.3cm (w).
■ **HABITAT** Mostly on stumps or dead parts of standing oak trees; sometimes on other deciduous trees. Prefers mature trees in ancient forests.
■ **RANGE** Widespread and common in Europe and North America.

■ **FRUITING** In clusters on dead wood of standing trees. Autumn–early winter.

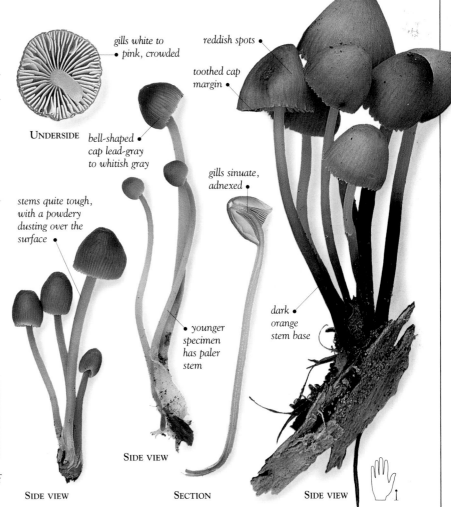

gills white to pink, crowded

UNDERSIDE

bell-shaped cap lead-gray to whitish gray

stems quite tough, with a powdery dusting over the surface

SIDE VIEW

younger specimen has paler stem

SIDE VIEW

SECTION

reddish spots

toothed cap margin

gills sinuate, adnexed

dark orange stem base

SIDE VIEW

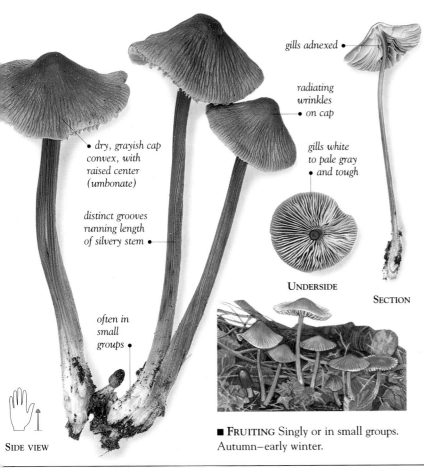

dry, grayish cap convex, with raised center (umbonate)

distinct grooves running length of silvery stem

often in small groups

SIDE VIEW

gills adnexed

radiating wrinkles on cap

gills white to pale gray and tough

UNDERSIDE

SECTION

■ **FRUITING** Singly or in small groups. Autumn–early winter.

MYCENA POLYGRAMMA

Roof-nail Bonnet

Besides its fairly large size, the silvery stem with distinct grooves running along its length is the main distinguishing feature of this tough-fleshed *Mycena*. M. *vitilis* is smaller and lacks the distinctive grooves on the stem. It occurs in the same habitat and is more common. *Mycena galericulata* (see opposite) is even tougher and also lacks stem grooves. Occasionally an entirely white form is found. Such forms can be hard to identify.

■ **SPORE DEPOSIT** White.
■ **SIZE** Cap 1–4cm (w); stem 5–12cm (h) x 0.2–0.4cm (w).
■ **HABITAT** Forests – mostly rooting to buried deciduous trees and around stumps, but also favors the base of living trees; occasionally found on conifers.
■ **RANGE** Widespread; common in Europe and adjacent Asia; also found in Japan and eastern North America.

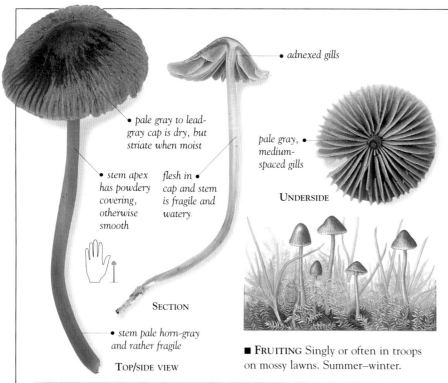

- *adnexed gills*

- *pale gray to lead-gray cap is dry, but striate when moist*

- *stem apex has powdery covering, otherwise smooth*

flesh in cap and stem is fragile and watery •

pale gray, medium-spaced gills •

UNDERSIDE

SECTION

- *stem pale horn-gray and rather fragile*

TOP/SIDE VIEW

■ **FRUITING** Singly or often in troops on mossy lawns. Summer–winter.

MYCENA LEPTOCEPHALA

Nitrous Lawn Bonnet

This nondescript, gray mushroom is one of a group of *Mycena* species that smell rather like nitric acid or chlorine. M. *leptocephala* is by far the most common. M. *stipata* has a greasier cap and is found on conifer stumps. M. *alcalina*, as it is recognized in North America, is a complex of species all smelling like chlorine.

■ **SPORE DEPOSIT** White.
■ **SIZE** Cap 0.6–1.5cm (w); stem 3–7cm (h) x 0.1–0.2cm (w).
■ **HABITAT** In mossy lawns, and among tall grass, woodland litter, or brambles.
■ **RANGE** Widespread and common throughout the north temperate zones.

MYCENA STYLOBATES

Common Disk-footed Bonnet

Most *Mycena* species have stems that are slightly rooting or inserted directly into the substrate. Some, including this species, have stem disks where they meet the substrate.

■ **SPORE DEPOSIT** White.
■ **SIZE** Cap 0.3–0.7cm, up to 1cm (w); stem 2–5cm (h) x 0.05–0.1cm (w).
■ **HABITAT** On various types of litter, in both open and sheltered habitats.
■ **RANGE** Widespread and fairly common in the north temperate zones.

■ **FRUITING** Singly or in small groups. Summer–autumn.

MYCENA CINERELLA

Arched Bonnet

This species is a uniform pale gray, but the clearest marker is seen from below – strongly arched gills running down the stem. This fungus gives off a yeasty smell when crushed. It can be separated from M. *speirea* because the latter grows on twigs, has a browner color, and lacks the yeasty smell. M. *vulgaris* also has decurrent gills but the cap, stem, and gill edges have a slimy layer. It grows on needle debris.

■ **SPORE DEPOSIT** White.
■ **SIZE** Cap 0.5–1cm, up to 1.5cm (w); stem 3–5cm (h) x 0.05–0.2cm (w).
■ **HABITAT** Mostly on needle beds but also in mossy, damp oak woods and occasionally in mossy, open areas.
■ **RANGE** Widespread in north temperate zones; reported on West Coast of US.

■ **FRUITING** Mostly in troops in sheltered, damp places. Autumn.

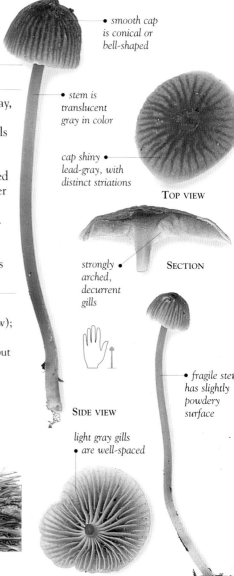

- *smooth cap is conical or bell-shaped*

- *stem is translucent gray in color*

cap shiny lead-gray, with distinct striations •

TOP VIEW

strongly arched, decurrent gills •

SECTION

SIDE VIEW

- *fragile stem has slightly powdery surface*

light gray gills are well-spaced •

UNDERSIDE   **SIDE VIEW**

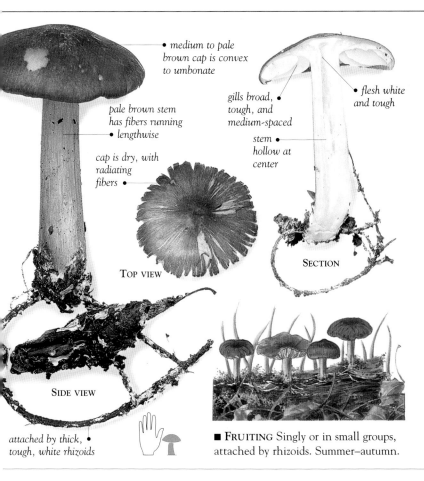

- medium to pale brown cap is convex to umbonate
- pale brown stem has fibers running lengthwise
- cap is dry, with radiating fibers
- flesh white and tough
- gills broad, tough, and medium-spaced
- stem hollow at center

TOP VIEW

SECTION

SIDE VIEW

attached by thick, tough, white rhizoids •

■ **FRUITING** Singly or in small groups, attached by rhizoids. Summer–autumn.

MEGACOLLYBIA PLATYPHYLLA

Broad-gilled Agaric

As its scientific name implies, this very broad-gilled species resembles an overgrown *Collybia* species (*see pp.103–106*). It is a tough-fleshed mushroom with extremely thick, stringlike rhizoids at the stem base, spreading far out into the substrate. The rhizoids are so strong that they can be used to lift out the fruitbody. More commonly known in North America as *Tricholomopsis platyphylla*, this species has been known to cause gastric upsets.

■ **SPORE DEPOSIT** Pale cream.
■ **SIZE** Cap 6–15cm (w); stem 5–12cm (h) x 1–2.5cm (w).
■ **HABITAT** Buried in the woodland floor on deciduous wood; often appears to be fruiting on leaf litter or growing on very rotten deciduous stumps.
■ **RANGE** Widespread and common throughout the north temperate zones.

OUDEMANSIELLA MUCIDA

Porcelain Fungus

In Europe, this is a striking feature of many beech woods. It will often appear high up in living trees where a branch has broken off. The slimy, ivory-white cap and prominent stem ring combine with its habitat to make this an unmistakable species.

■ **SPORE DEPOSIT** Pale cream.
■ **SIZE** Cap 2–15cm (w); stem 3–8cm (h) x 0.3–1cm (w).
■ **HABITAT** On standing beech or fallen branches or trunks; more rarely it can also be found growing on oak.
■ **RANGE** Widespread and fairly common in north temperate zones but absent in North America.

■ **FRUITING** In clusters or singly on beech bark and wood. Autumn.

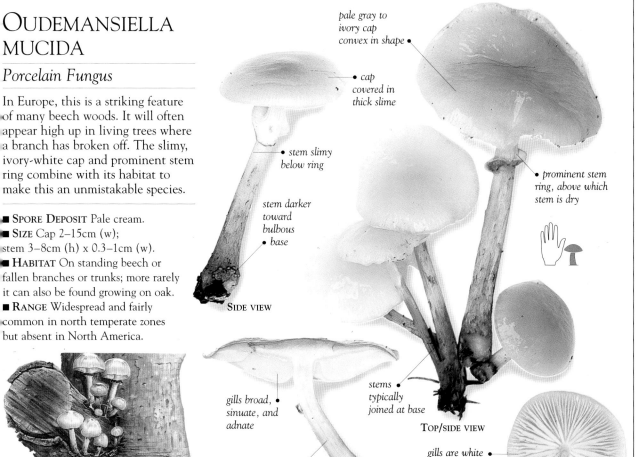

- pale gray to ivory cap convex in shape
- cap covered in thick slime
- stem slimy below ring
- stem darker toward bulbous base
- prominent stem ring, above which stem is dry

SIDE VIEW

- gills broad, sinuate, and adnate
- stems typically joined at base

TOP/SIDE VIEW

- gills are white and tough

solid to hollow stem

SECTION

UNDERSIDE

OUDEMANSIELLA RADICATA

Rooting Shank

With a bit of care and a digging tool, the very impressive rooting stem can be excavated and the tree roots from which they grow can be located. Unlike some look-alikes, such as *O. longipes* and *O. caussei*, the cap of *O. radicata* is greasy, especially in wet weather.

O. radicata is actually a complex of indistinguishable species. Many authors now consider these species to be members of the genus *Xerula*. All these species have strongly rooting stems and often a velvety covering, at least on the stem.

- **SPORE DEPOSIT** Pale cream.
- **SIZE** Cap 3–10cm (w); stem 5–15cm (h); roots 5–15cm long x 0.5–1cm (w).
- **HABITAT** Around standing trees and on deciduous stumps, especially beech, in parks and deciduous woods.
- **RANGE** As a complex, widespread in northern temperate zones; common in some regions, but extent of distribution uncertain.

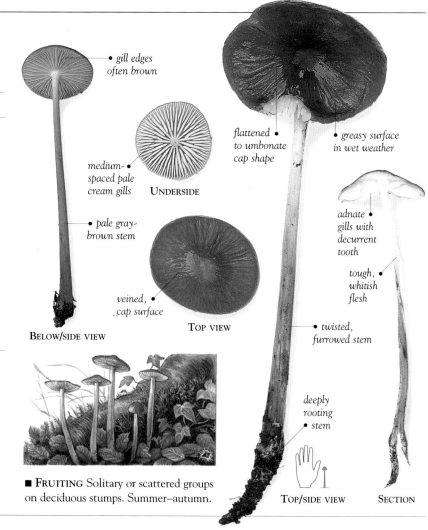

- gill edges often brown
- medium-spaced pale cream gills
- **UNDERSIDE**
- pale gray-brown stem
- veined, cap surface
- **BELOW/SIDE VIEW**
- **TOP VIEW**
- flattened to umbonate cap shape
- greasy surface in wet weather
- adnate gills with decurrent tooth
- tough, whitish flesh
- twisted, furrowed stem
- deeply rooting stem
- **TOP/SIDE VIEW**
- **SECTION**

- **FRUITING** Solitary or scattered groups on deciduous stumps. Summer–autumn.

- dry cap surface
- powdery white on pale brown stem
- gills adnexed or free of stem
- **TOP/SIDE VIEW**
- fallen conifer cone acts as substrate
- stem rises directly from cone or cone scale
- **SECTION**
- fairly narrow, crowded pale gray gills
- **UNDERSIDE**
- smooth pale brown cap
- flat to slightly umbonate cap shape
- **TOP VIEW**

- **FRUITING** A few specimens on a cone or singly on detached scales. Autumn.

BAEOSPORA MYOSURA

Cone Cap

The genus *Baeospora* is a small one. Typically, species grow on fallen cones or individual cone scales. They have dull colors or, in the case of *B. myriadophylla*, lilac gills, and very crowded, almost free gills. *B. myosura* has a musty smell and indistinct taste, so it is not worthwhile as an edible. *B. myriadophylla* grows mainly on fallen conifer trunks and is rare or absent in most regions. Other similar fungi that grow on conifer cones include *Strobilurus* species and some *Mycena* species (*see pp.111–118*), especially the striking European *M. seynii*.

- **SPORE DEPOSIT** White.
- **SIZE** Cap 0.5–2cm (w); stem 1–4cm (h) and 0.1–0.2mm (w).
- **HABITAT** On cones and cone scales from various conifers including spruce and pine in parks and woods.
- **RANGE** Widespread and common throughout the north temperate zones.

velvety, oyster-shaped cap

cap surface turns greasy in wet weather

olive color fades to dull brown with age

gills hardly developed

TOP VIEW

IMMATURE

short stem has dark scales on yellow-ocher ground

crowded cream gills

UNDERSIDE

■ **FRUITING** In rows on standing living or dead deciduous trunks. Late autumn.

PANELLUS SEROTINUS

Late Fall Oyster Mushroom

The olive and yellow coloring, oyster-fungus shape, and distinct nublike stem make this species easy to identify. The smell is faintly mushroomy, and the flesh has a mild to slightly bitter taste. Although edible, it is not worthwhile. Old or atypical specimens are often confused with *Pleurotus ostreatus* (see p.78) or *Phyllotopsis nidulans*. Some mycologists consider that *P. serotinus* belongs to the genus *Sarcomyxa*.

■ **SPORE DEPOSIT** White.
■ **SIZE** Cap 3–10cm (w); stem 0.8–1.5cm (h) x 0.5–1cm (w).
■ **HABITAT** Often near water on dead or living trunks and fallen branches.
■ **RANGE** Widespread throughout the north temperate zones.

pale leather brown fruitbodies

oyster-shaped fruitbodies

TOP/SIDE VIEW

surface slightly cracked with age

stem short and placed at margin

UNDERSIDE

crowded gills, brownish with paler edge

PANELLUS STIPTICUS

Styptic False Oyster Mushroom

A small oyster-shaped fungus with a fruity aromatic smell and a bitter astringent taste. The fruitbodies are very tough and inedible, and typically survive into spring. In North America, the gills are luminescent; in Europe they are not. It grows on deciduous trees, while on conifers the whiter and smaller *P. mitis* can be found. A very similar and luminescent, but poroid, eastern North American species is known as *P. pusillus*.

■ **SPORE DEPOSIT** Whitish.
■ **SIZE** Cap 1–4cm (w).
■ **HABITAT** On stumps of deciduous, broadleaved trees.
■ **RANGE** Widespread in north temperate zones; common in eastern North America.

■ **FRUITING** Tiers and rows on oak and beech stumps. Autumn–winter.

PHAEOLEPIOTA AUREA

Golden Cap

A spectacular fungus that can grow to an impressive size. The fruitbody is golden orange and the stem has a flaring ring. Can cause gastric upsets.

■ **SPORE DEPOSIT** Ochraceous brown.
■ **SIZE** Cap 10–25cm (w); stem 10–30cm (h) x 1.5–4cm (w).
■ **HABITAT** Prefers rich soils; along paths and other disturbed woodland sites.
■ **RANGE** Widespread in north temperate zones; found in Pacific Northwest.

■ **FRUITING** Troops of fruitbodies on rich, disturbed soil. Summer–autumn.

CYSTODERMA AMIANTHINUM

Saffron Powder-cap

This is a species with several look-alikes; *C. amianthinum* var. *Rugoso reticulatum* has a deeply wrinkled cap and pungent odor. *C. jasonis* is similar, but has darker coloring and a coarser surface.

- **SPORE DEPOSIT** Whitish.
- **SIZE** Cap 1–4cm (w); stem 2.5–6cm (h) x 0.3–0.7cm (w).
- **HABITAT** On moss in damp, mainly acid, forests; also sheltered among leaves.
- **RANGE** Widespread and common in north temperate zones.

- **FRUITING** Singly or a few together on mossy forest soil. Autumn.

CYSTODERMA TERREI

Cinnabar Powder-cap

This is a considerably larger species than *C. amianthinum* (*see left*) and is notable for its brick-red cap and reddish lower stem. Again, several sibling species occur in very similar habitats, and accurate identification requires the use of a microscope or first-hand experience with this difficult genus.

- **SPORE DEPOSIT** Whitish.
- **SIZE** Cap 2–8cm (w); stem 3–7cm (h) x 0.4–0.8cm, or up to 1cm (w).
- **HABITAT** On humus-rich soil in all kinds of acid woods and planted areas.
- **RANGE** Widespread in Europe, Japan, and North America.

- **FRUITING** Singly or a few together in acid woods and planted areas. Autumn.

- convex to umbonate cap shape
- brick-red, mealy cap
- reddish scales on base of stem

TOP/SIDE VIEW

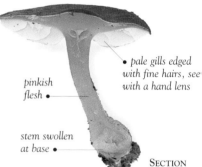

- pale gills edged with fine hairs, see with a hand lens
- pinkish flesh
- stem swollen at base

SECTION

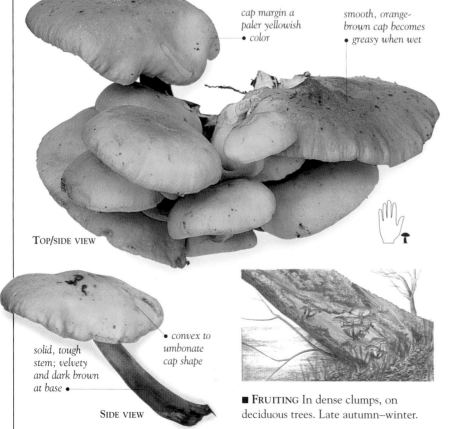

- cap margin a paler yellowish color
- smooth, orange-brown cap becomes greasy when wet

TOP/SIDE VIEW

- solid, tough stem; velvety and dark brown at base
- convex to umbonate cap shape

SIDE VIEW

- **FRUITING** In dense clumps, on deciduous trees. Late autumn–winter.

FLAMMULINA VELUTIPES

Velvet-shank

An alternative common name for *F. velutipes* is "Winter fungus," because this is one of very few species of fungus that survives frost – in fact, *Flammulina velutipes* thrives in low temperatures. Found in dense clusters on deciduous trees, its yellow cap and velvety, dark brown stem make it easy to identify. *F. velutipes* is now cultivated in the Far East, and when used in cooking, it has a mild but pleasant flavor.

- **SPORE DEPOSIT** White.
- **SIZE** Cap 1–6cm, up to 10cm (w); stem 2–7cm, up to 10cm (h) x 0.3–1cm (w).
- **HABITAT** On living, but often weakened, deciduous trees, especially willow, poplar, or elm. May be found on living trees where branches have fallen; rarely on conifers.
- **RANGE** Widespread and rather common in north temperate zones.

ENTOLOMATACEAE

CLASS: *Homobasidiomycetes*

This group of pink-spored mushrooms is characterized not only by spore color, but also by the unusual, angular shape of the spores. Other distinctive features include the spore wall – more complex than in the previous family – and the gills, which are never free, unlike the equally pink-spored *Pluteaceae* (*see p.127*). Shape and size vary greatly within this family; some species resemble large *Tricholoma* species (*see p.92*), and others look like small *Mycena* species (*see p.111*) or are oyster-shaped like *Pleurotus* species (*see p.78*).

ENTOLOMA CLYPEATUM

Roman Shield

This gilled mushroom appears in late spring beneath hawthorn trees or other members of the *Rosaceae* family. It is very fleshy and often occurs in great numbers, slightly later in the year than the *Morchella* species season (*see p.26*). Because some species of *Entoloma* are poisonous and nearly all are difficult to identify, all species in this genus, should be avoided, except for the white firm-fleshed puffball-like fruiting bodies of *E. abortivum*, a choice fall edible in eastern North American woods that is aborted by the mycelium of *Armillaria mellea*.

- **SPORE DEPOSIT** Pinkish.
- **SIZE** Cap 4–12cm (w); stem 4–10cm, up to 15cm (h) x 0.8–2.5cm (w).
- **HABITAT** On rich, often clayey soils under hawthorn and related trees and bushes (*Rosaceae*) in gardens, parks, and open forests.
- **RANGE** Widespread in Europe and North America; reported in Japan.

■ **FRUITING** In troops or clusters in parks, gardens, and woods. Spring–summer.

cap convex to funnel-shaped

SIDE VIEW

cap color very pale grayish white

surface of cap dry and matte

TOP/SIDE VIEW

base somewhat rooting

TOP/SIDE VIEW

CLITOPILUS PRUNULUS

The Miller

A strong smell of fresh bread dough, combined with pinkish gills that run down its stem and pale, gray-white coloring, are the features that distinguish C. *prunulus*. Unlike some of its much smaller relatives, it is always associated with trees. Take care not to confuse this edible with poisonous species of *Clitocybe* or *Entoloma* (*see p.89 and p.124*).

- **SPORE DEPOSIT** Pinkish.
- **SIZE** Cap 3–9cm (w); stem 2–6cm (h) x 0.4–1cm, sometimes up to 1.5cm (w).
- **HABITAT** On humus-rich soil in mostly acid types of woods; also in grassy places, but close to trees.
- **RANGE** Widespread and rather common in the north temperate zones.

■ **FRUITING** A few fruitbodies together or trooping. Autumn.

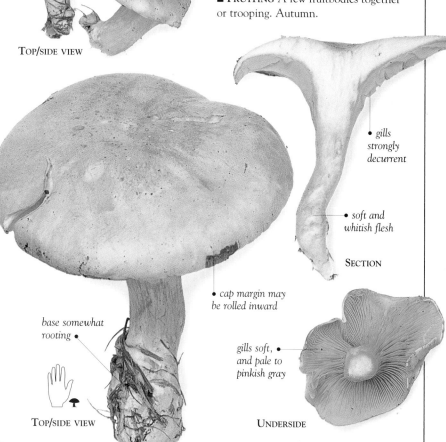

gills strongly decurrent

soft and whitish flesh

SECTION

cap margin may be rolled inward

gills soft, and pale to pinkish gray

UNDERSIDE

ENTOLOMA RHODOPOLIUM

Woodland Pink Gill 💀

The great variation within this species makes it a difficult one to identify. A number of similar species differ subtly in their coloring and in various characteristics that can be seen only with a microscope. None of the various forms of this species should be eaten, because they are poisonous. There is a slender form with a gaslike smell that was once considered a separate species but is now also known as *E. rhodopolium*.

■ **SPORE DEPOSIT** Pinkish.
■ **SIZE** Cap 4–12cm (w);
stem 6–15cm (h) x 0.5–2cm (w).
■ **HABITAT** In deciduous woods, especially beech woods, and on rich soil.
■ **RANGE** Widespread and locally common in the north temperate zones; not reported in North America.

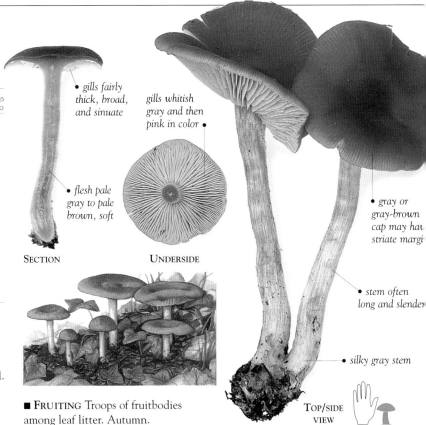

gills fairly thick, broad, and sinuate

flesh pale gray to pale brown, soft

SECTION

gills whitish gray and then pink in color

UNDERSIDE

gray or gray-brown cap may have striate margin

stem often long and slender

silky gray stem

TOP/SIDE VIEW

■ **FRUITING** Troops of fruitbodies among leaf litter. Autumn.

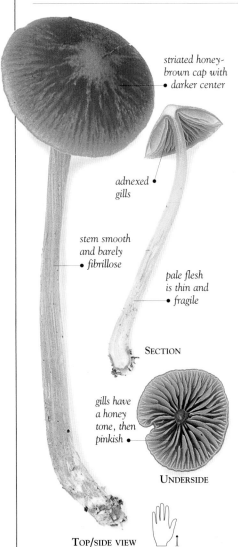

striated honey-brown cap with darker center

adnexed gills

stem smooth and barely fibrillose

pale flesh is thin and fragile

SECTION

gills have a honey tone, then pinkish

UNDERSIDE

TOP/SIDE VIEW

ENTOLOMA CETRATUM

Honey-colored Pink Gill 💀

This elegant, poisonous species occurs mainly in acid conifer woods. Its warm honey colors, striate cap and tall stature are good marks. The stem is barely fibrillose, unlike some relatives. Although not found in North America, this species illustrates the many similar mushrooms that do occur here and resemble *Collybia* species (*see pp.103–106*).

■ **SPORE DEPOSIT** Pinkish.
■ **SIZE** Cap 0.5–3cm, up to 5cm (w);
stem 5–8cm (h) x 0.2–0.4cm (w).
■ **HABITAT** On humus-rich soil under conifers but also in acid deciduous woods, and bogs.
■ **RANGE** Widespread and common in Europe; not reported in North America.

■ **FRUITING** Singly or a few together, often among debris. Summer–autumn.

ENTOLOMA EULIVIDUM

Lead Poisoner 💀

It is important to get to know this poisonous look-alike of the Wood Blewit (*see pp.90–91*). It causes about ten percent of fungus poisonings in Europe. Its gills are pale citrine yellow when young, but turn pinkish. Spore print color is a helpful marker.

■ **SPORE DEPOSIT** Pinkish.
■ **SIZE** Cap 8–20cm (w);
stem 10–18cm (h) x 2–4cm (w).
■ **HABITAT** On soil, often clayey, in mature, deciduous woods; frequently associated with oak or beech.
■ **RANGE** Widespread but localized in Europe. Replaced by a close relative in North America and East Asia.

■ **FRUITING** In small groups often near mature deciduous trees. Autumn.

ENTOLOMA CONFERENDUM

Star-spored Pink Gill ☠

This species is quite difficult to identify. Compared with some look-alikes, it has an elegant stature, with a fibrillose, silvery stem. The cap, distinctly umbonate when young, tends to be conical, becoming convex with age. The key feature is the distinct star shape of the spores. This species is also known as E. straurosporum.

- **SPORE DEPOSIT** Pinkish.
- **SIZE** Cap 2–4cm, up to 6cm (w); stem 3–6cm, up to 8cm (h) x 0.3–0.7cm (w).
- **HABITAT** Mostly in grassy places in parks and open fields and woods.
- **RANGE** Widespread and common in the north temperate zones.

- **FRUITING** Mostly in small groups of fruitbodies. Summer–autumn.

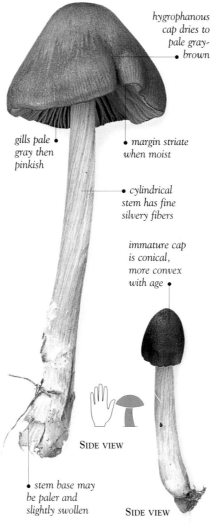

hygrophanous cap dries to pale gray-brown

gills pale gray then pinkish

margin striate when moist

cylindrical stem has fine silvery fibers

immature cap is conical, more convex with age

SIDE VIEW

stem base may be paler and slightly swollen

SIDE VIEW

ENTOLOMA SERICEUM

Silky Pink Gill ☠

Another poisonous *Entoloma* species that is difficult to identify. It is quite similar to *E. conferendum* (*see left*), but with different spores. It tends to be shorter, with a darker cap and a stronger, rancid-yeasty smell.

- **SPORE DEPOSIT** Pinkish.
- **SIZE** Cap 2–5cm, up to 7cm (w); stem 2–6cm, up to 8cm (h) x 0.2–0.6cm (w).
- **HABITAT** Tolerates some improved grasslands as well as occurring in semi-natural situations; common in lawns.
- **RANGE** Widespread and common in the north temperate zones of Europe and North America.

- **FRUITING** Mostly found in small groups of fruitbodies in grassy places. Autumn.

---

cap smooth but innately fibrillose with inrolled edge

stem is distinctly fibrillose

flesh white and solid

stem paler than cap, can be yellowish toward base

SIDE VIEW

SECTION

young cap is distinctly umbonate

fruitbody unusually pale

gills fairly crowded and either sinuate-notched or free

SIDE VIEW

- **FRUITING** Singly or in small groups. Spring–autumn.

ENTOLOMA PORPHYROPHAEUM

Porphyry Pink Gill ☠

The combination of gray-purplish coloring, very tall stature, and grassland habitat help identify this complex of quite uncommon but distinctive *Entoloma* species. A spore print will help distinguish this complex from similar purplish *Cortinarius* species. Although some sources state that this species is edible, it is probably poisonous and should be avoided.

- **SPORE DEPOSIT** Pinkish.
- **SIZE** Cap 4–8cm, up to 14cm (w); stem 7–14cm, up to 17cm (h) x 0.5–2cm (w).
- **HABITAT** In unimproved grasslands, often associated with *Hygrophoraceae* and *Clavariaceae*; also in alpine areas.
- **RANGE** As a complex, widespread, although uncommon, in Europe and eastern North America.

- *cap convex, pale grass green to greenish gold-brown*

hollow stem

gills can be either adnate or adnexed

cap margin frequently forms a wavy line

gills pinkish

SECTION

- *cap slightly depressed at center*

UNDERSIDE

- *striate at margin*

- *translucent green stem with white base*

- *flesh stains blue when bruised*

SIDE VIEW   **SIDE VIEW**

■ **FRUITING** Singly or in troops, in grass mixed with herbs. Summer–early autumn.

ENTOLOMA INCANUM

Green Pink-gill ☠

Perhaps the most striking of the smaller, possibly poisonous *Entoloma* species, this and other mainly blue species are often referred to a separate genus, *Leptonia*. Although the overall color of the fruitbody is a green or green-brown, the flesh discolors to a sky blue when bruised and the smell is striking – strongly reminiscent of mice. The coloring of this *Entoloma* species means that it blends in so well with its grassy habitats that it can often be overlooked by the forayer.

■ **SPORE DEPOSIT** Pinkish.
■ **SIZE** Cap 1–3cm, up to 4cm (w); stem 2–6cm, up to 8cm (h) x 0.2–0.4cm (w)
■ **HABITAT** On soil in calcareous grassy areas or paths in forests.
■ **RANGE** Widespread but uncommon in Europe and North America.

ENTOLOMA NITIDUM

Steel-blue Pink-gill

This is one of very few quite large, blue *Entoloma* species. Its edibility is unknown, but it should not be eaten. *E. bloxamii* is similar, but it is less slender and prefers open grassy areas.

■ **SPORE DEPOSIT** Pinkish.
■ **SIZE** Cap 1–2.5cm, up to 4cm (w); stem 2–6cm (h) x 0.2–0.4cm (w).
■ **HABITAT** Among mosses in damp, acid conifer woods or planted areas.
■ **RANGE** Widespread but mostly northern in Europe and adjacent Asia; not reported in North America.

■ **FRUITING** Singly or in small groups among moss. Throughout autumn.

ENTOLOMA SERRULATUM

Saw-gilled Blue-cap ☠

The various blue-colored *Entoloma* species are frequently placed instead within the genus *Leptonia*. They have bluish hues on the cap, or on the stem, or on both, and their flat caps may have a central depression. *E. serrulatum* has dark, almost black, coloring and a serrated, blue-black gill edge.

■ **SPORE DEPOSIT** Pinkish.
■ **SIZE** Cap 1–2.5cm, up to 4cm (w); stem 2–6cm (h) x 0.2–0.4cm (w).
■ **HABITAT** In grassland, sparse roadside vegetation, or open woods.
■ **RANGE** Widespread in Europe and North America.

■ **FRUITING** In small groups, on most soil types. Late summer–autumn.

- *gills pale blue, turning pinkish blue with age*

- *blue-black cap dry to touch, with tiny, erect scales and central depression*

UNDERSIDE

- *flesh thin and bluish, with a faint perfumed smell*

- *dark, serrated gill edge*

- *stem same color as cap or paler*

SIDE VIEW   **SECTION**

PLUTEACEAE

CLASS: *Homobasidiomycetes*

Members of this family occur mostly on decaying wood. Their pinkish spores develop on gills that tend to be crowded, soft, and free from the stem, which can be removed unbroken from the flesh of the cap. Caps may be smooth, fibrous, or hairy. The genus *Volvariella* has a veil that envelops the fruitbody, appearing as a volva at the stem base in mature specimens.

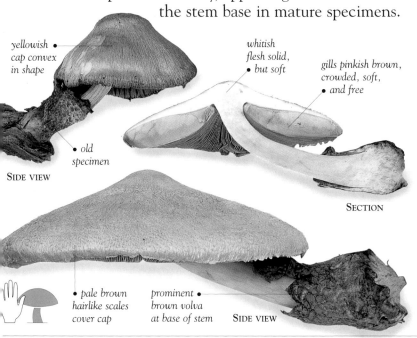

yellowish cap convex in shape

old specimen

SIDE VIEW

whitish flesh solid, but soft

gills pinkish brown, crowded, soft, and free

SECTION

pale brown hairlike scales cover cap

prominent brown volva at base of stem

SIDE VIEW

VOLVARIELLA BOMBYCINA

Silky Volvar

An easy species to identify, but not so easy to find. It has a very large, white to yellowish cap, covered in silky fibers, and a pronounced sac at the stem base. It is one of a few species of *Volvariella* found growing on dead or dying standing trees. Although edible, it is not recommended.

- **SPORE DEPOSIT** Pinkish.
- **SIZE** Cap 10–25cm (w); stem 8–20cm (h) x 1–2.5cm (w).
- **HABITAT** On standing dead trees, often elm, rarely on fallen trunks, on stored lumber, or in buildings.
- **RANGE** Widespread in north temperate zones, but mostly rather local, extending farther south.

- **FRUITING** Singly or in clusters, on dead trees. Summer–autumn.

VOLVARIELLA GLOIOCEPHALA

Stubble-field Volvar

Of all the soil-growing *Volvariella* species, this is by far the largest, and it is further characterized by a smooth, sticky cap that ranges in color between white and mouse gray. A close relative, *V. volvacea* is commercially grown on a large scale in parts of Southeast Asia. It is sold fresh in markets or canned for export. It is a synonym of, and preferred name for, *V. speciosa*. The fruitbodies do not keep well.

- **SPORE DEPOSIT** Pinkish.
- **SIZE** Cap 6–14cm (w); stem 10–25cm (h) x 0.7–1.5cm (w).
- **HABITAT** On disturbed soil with high nutrient content, such as stubble fields, compost beds, bark mulches, or haystacks.
- **RANGE** Widespread and fairly common in north temperate zones extending farther south.

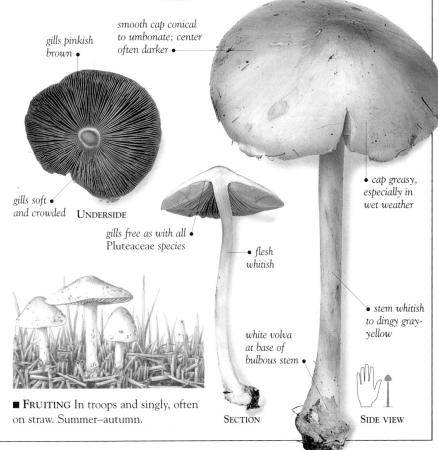

gills pinkish brown

gills soft and crowded **UNDERSIDE**

smooth cap conical to umbonate; center often darker

gills free as with all Pluteaceae species

flesh whitish

white volva at base of bulbous stem

cap greasy, especially in wet weather

stem whitish to dingy gray-yellow

FRUITING In troops and singly, often on straw. Summer–autumn.

SECTION

SIDE VIEW

PLUTEUS CERVINUS

Fawn Shield-cap

A highly variable wood-inhabiting edible species that reaches its most impressive dimensions when growing on sawdust. Typically, it has a dark brown cap, and stem fibers at the base. *P. pouzarianus* is a look-alike in Europe found on conifers.

- ■ **SPORE DEPOSIT** Pinkish.
- ■ **SIZE** Cap 4–10cm, up to 16cm (w); stem 4–10cm (h) x 0.5–1.5cm (w), up to 2cm (at base).
- ■ **HABITAT** On decaying deciduous trees in woods, parks, and gardens.
- ■ **RANGE** Widespread in north temperate zones; extending south.

- ■ **FRUITING** Singly or in small groups on decaying trees. Summer–autumn.

- cap shape ranges from convex to umbonate or flat
- gills crowded, soft, and pinkish brown

UNDERSIDE

- cap rather felty at center
- cap greasy when wet, shiny when dry
- gills free from stem
- thick white flesh
- cap usually dark brown
- fibrous stem
- white flesh has rancid smell
- dark fibers on club-shaped base

SECTION

TOP/SIDE VIEW

SIDE VIEW

PLUTEUS UMBROSUS

Velvety Shield-cap

A dark brown, velvety cap and stem surface and dark gill edges make this species easy to identify. It generally occurs near other *Pluteus* species on rotten deciduous trees.

- ■ **SPORE DEPOSIT** Pinkish.
- ■ **SIZE** Cap 4–11cm (w); stem 5–8cm, up to 12cm (h) x 0.4–2cm (w).
- ■ **HABITAT** Often on large-diameter, deciduous trunks left to decay naturally.
- ■ **RANGE** Widespread in north temperate zones; mostly uncommon.

- ■ **FRUITING** Singly or in small groups on decayed trees. Summer–autumn.

- velvety, umbonate dark brown cap
- paler cap flesh shows through in places

TOP VIEW

- fringed edge to cap
- free gills pinkish, with a downy, brown edge
- radiating vein pattern across cap
- pale stem dotted with brown
- stem swells toward base

SECTION

- found mostly on well-rotted deciduous trees
- free gills crowded and soft

UNDERSIDE

TOP/SIDE VIEW

PLUTEUS AURANTIORUGOSUS

Flame Shield-cap

Picking this species out from its close relatives is made easy by the vivid, flame red cap. The cap surface consists of round cells that make it very delicate, in contrast to the fiber-covered *P. cervinus* (see p.128).

- **SPORE DEPOSIT** Pinkish.
- **SIZE** Cap 2–5cm (w); stem 3–8cm (h) x 0.3–0.6cm (w).
- **HABITAT** On fallen trunks or trees such as poplar, ash, and elm.
- **RANGE** Widespread but uncommon in north temperate zones.

- **FRUITING** Singly or in small groups, on decaying logs. Summer–autumn.

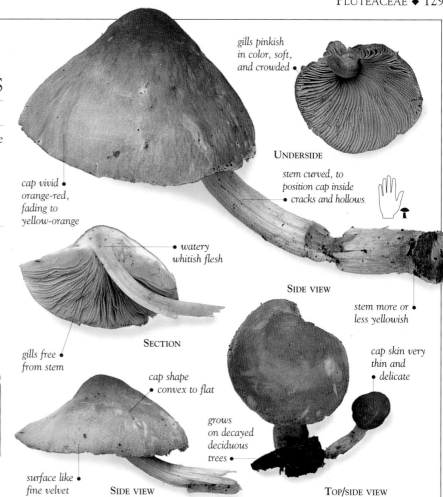

gills pinkish in color, soft, and crowded •

UNDERSIDE

stem curved, to position cap inside • cracks and hollows

cap vivid • orange-red, fading to yellow-orange

• watery whitish flesh

SIDE VIEW

stem more or • less yellowish

gills free • from stem

SECTION

cap shape • convex to flat

cap skin very thin and • delicate

surface like • fine velvet

SIDE VIEW

grows on decayed deciduous trees •

TOP/SIDE VIEW

---

cap striate • at margin when wet

cap smooth, not fiber-covered •

gills free •

flesh • whitish to yellow

SIDE VIEW

SECTION

• cap shape convex to umbonate

translucent • quality to stem

stem paler • than cap

tends to favor well-rotted deciduous trees •

SIDE VIEW

• yellowish cap color may have green tinge

• cap hygrophanous

TOP VIEW

• cap may be finely veined

UNDERSIDE

• gills pinkish, soft and crowded

PLUTEUS CHRYSOPHAEUS

Golden-green Shield-cap

Differently colored forms of this conspicuous *Pluteus* species are considered by some to be separate species. All forms have a yellowish cap with a pale yellow stem. *Pluteus romellii* has a darker cap and yellow coloring concentrated at the base.

- **SPORE DEPOSIT** Pinkish.
- **SIZE** Cap 1–6cm (w); stem 3–8cm (h) x 0.3–0.8cm (w).
- **HABITAT** On well-rotted deciduous stumps and fallen, moss-covered trunks.
- **RANGE** Widespread in Europe and eastern North America.

- **FRUITING** Singly or in small groups on stumps. Summer–autumn.

AMANITACEAE

CLASS: *Homobasidiomycetes*

This family is famous because it includes some of the deadliest gilled mushrooms. Members have white spores and typically free gills. Young fruitbodies are enclosed in a membranous egglike veil, seen as loose scales on mature caps and as a volva or remnant at the stem base. Most species have a partial veil that leaves a ring on the stem. Nearly all species form mycorrhizal associations with trees.

tawny cap smooth and grooved at the margin

stem tinted in cap color, almost smooth

cap shape conical to umbonate

TOP VIEW

flesh watery and soft

AMANITA FULVA

Tawny Grisette

The grisettes belong to a subgenus called *Amanitopsis*, identified by a furrowed cap margin and an absence of a ring on the stem. *A. fulva* has a deep tawny cap color and smooth stem. The color of the volva is important for identification.

■ **SPORE DEPOSIT** Whitish.
■ **SIZE** Cap 3–8cm (w); stem 7–15cm (h) x 0.7–1.2cm (w).
■ **HABITAT** In forests under deciduous and coniferous trees, forming a mycorrhizal association. Be careful not to confuse this species with the toxic members of this group.
■ **RANGE** Widespread in north temperate zones and throughout North America.

gills white to cream, crowded, and free

UNDERSIDE

young fruitbody breaking out of veil

SIDE VIEW

thick, rusty volva

TOP/SIDE VIEW

stem hollow and rather fragile

SECTION

■ **FRUITING** Singly or in small groups around birch trees. Summer–autumn.

cap has furrowed margin

cap smooth, rich orange, and convex to umbonate

flesh soft and whitish

stem hollow and rather fragile

stem has no ring

SECTION

gills white to cream

UNDERSIDE

gills crowded, soft, and free

thick white volva

TOP/SIDE VIEW

■ **FRUITING** Singly or in small groups, under birches. Early summer–autumn.

AMANITA CROCEA

Orange Grisette

This striking grisette differs from *A. fulva* (*see above*) in having a shiny, orange cap and especially in having thin, orange girdles on the stem. The white volva is thick and prominent. Although both *A. fulva* and *A. crocea* are found in the proximity of birch trees, the latter prefers richer soils. *Amanitopsis* species in Europe are edible but must be cooked thoroughly and not eaten raw. The fruitbodies do not keep well.

■ **SPORE DEPOSIT** Whitish.
■ **SIZE** Cap 6–12cm (w); stem 10–20cm (h) x 1–2cm (w).
■ **HABITAT** Forms mycorrhiza with birch and possibly spruce, on fairly rich soils, in lowlands and near the timber line.
■ **RANGE** Widespread in Europe and northeastern North America.

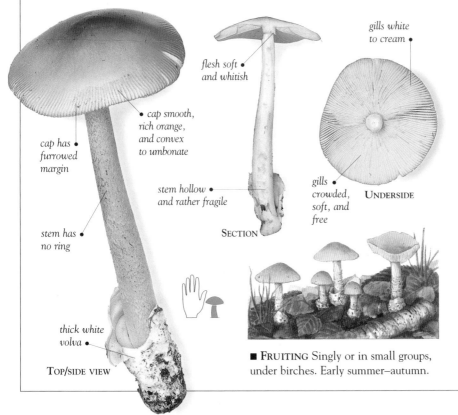

AMANITA PHALLOIDES

Death Cap ☠

It is particularly important to be familiar with this fungus, since just one mistake could be fatal. Fresh, young specimens are relatively easy to identify by their greenish colors, ringed stem, broad, free gills, and prominent white volva. Damaged specimens or older, grayer, or browner capped ones have been mistaken for species of *Russula*, *Tricholoma*, or *Volvariella*. Note that the stem ring can be missing.

- **SPORE DEPOSIT** Whitish.
- **SIZE** Cap 8–15cm (w); stem 8–16cm (h) x 1–2.5cm (w).
- **HABITAT** Mostly on rich soil forming mycorrhiza with deciduous trees.
- **RANGE** Widespread in Europe and North America.

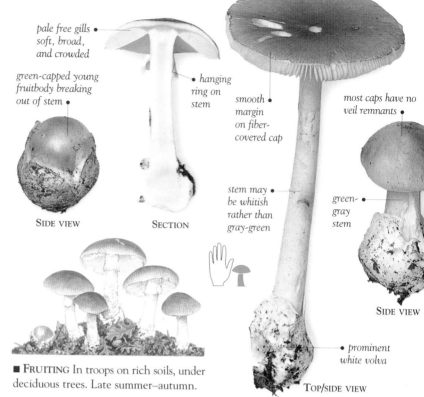

pale free gills soft, broad, and crowded

green-capped young fruitbody breaking out of stem

hanging ring on stem

smooth margin on fiber-covered cap

most caps have no veil remnants

SIDE VIEW

SECTION

stem may be whitish rather than gray-green

green-gray stem

SIDE VIEW

prominent white volva

TOP/SIDE VIEW

- **FRUITING** In troops on rich soils, under deciduous trees. Late summer–autumn.

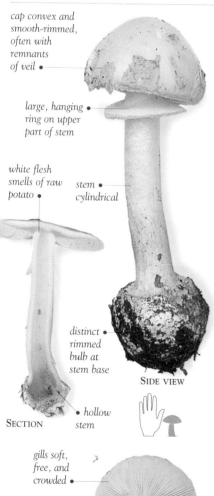

cap convex and smooth-rimmed, often with remnants of veil

large, hanging ring on upper part of stem

white flesh smells of raw potato

stem cylindrical

distinct rimmed bulb at stem base

SIDE VIEW

SECTION

hollow stem

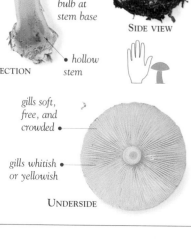

gills soft, free, and crowded

gills whitish or yellowish

UNDERSIDE

AMANITA CITRINA

False Death Cap ☠

One of the most common forest fungi in many areas, the species is only slightly toxic but should be avoided. *A. citrina* often occurs later in the year than the equally common *A. rubescens* (*see p.134*). The citrine or white colors of the fruitbody and swollen, rounded bulb at the stem base are good markers. A strong smell of raw, peeled potatoes is highly distinctive. *A. porphyria* (*see p.135*) is a grayish look-alike.

- **SPORE DEPOSIT** Whitish.
- **SIZE** Cap 5–10cm (w); stem 6–13cm (h) x 0.8–1.5cm (w); volva up to 3cm (w).
- **HABITAT** Forms mycorrhiza with various deciduous trees and conifers, mostly on acidic soils.
- **RANGE** Widespread in north temperate Europe, Asia, and eastern North America.

- **FRUITING** Singly or in troops on acidic soils. Late summer–autumn.

AMANITA COTHURNATA

Booted Amanita ☠

Considered by some to be a variety of *A. pantherina* (*see p.133*) and supposedly just as deadly poisonous. *A. pantherina* is darker in color.

- **SPORE DEPOSIT** Whitish.
- **SIZE** 3–8cm, up to 10cm (w); stem 5–12cm (h) x 0.3–1.5cm (w).
- **HABITAT** Forms mycorrhiza with deciduous trees or conifers.
- **RANGE** Local in eastern North America.

- **FRUITING** Singly or in troops on acid soil. Late summer–autumn.

AMANITA MUSCARIA

Fly Agaric ☠

Although long used in small amounts as an inebriant and visionary drug in Siberia, as a food this complex of bright red to orange to yellow-capped mushrooms is poisonous. Different cap and universal veil colors occur in different parts of the world, even in different parts of North America. Yellow to orange caps and white to off-white universal veil is common in eastern North America, while a reddish cap with yellowish veil patches occurs in western North America. The classic fairy tale book illustration of a bright red cap with white veil patches occurs in Alaska.

- ■ **SPORE DEPOSIT** Whitish.
- ■ **SIZE** Cap 6–15cm, up to 25cm (w); stem 8–20cm (h) x 1–2.5cm (w); base up to 3cm (w).
- ■ **HABITAT** Grows near trees with which it forms mycorrhiza, mostly with birch or spruce, usually on acid soils.
- ■ **RANGE** As a complex, widespread and common in the north temperate zones.

crowded gills •

hanging stem ring may have teeth at margin

• *cap margin smooth or faintly striated*

• *cap red, orange, or orange-yellow*

UNDERSIDE

prominent raised veil scales on cap vanish after heavy rain •

• *white gills free of stem*

• *flesh white to yellowish*

TOP/SIDE VIEW

• *stem base lacks loose volva, but is girdled with scales*

bulbous base •

SECTION

■ **FRUITING** In troops or rings near its partner tree. Summer–autumn.

AMANITA CAESAREA

Caesar's Mushroom

A legendary choice edible fungus that is confined to warm regions. Obviously striking characters are the golden orange cap and stem and the white, prominent, loose volva at the stem base. Note that *A. muscaria* (see above) may appear in yellow-orange form, so take great care not to confuse the two species. Nearly indistinguishable look-alikes are common in eastern North America and in the Southwest. European *A. caesarea* may not occur in North America. Although a choice mushroom in Europe, it is mediocre in North America.

- ■ **SPORE DEPOSIT** Whitish.
- ■ **SIZE** Cap 8–20cm (w); stem 8–16cm (h) x 2–3cm (w); volva up to 5cm (w).
- ■ **HABITAT** Forms mycorrhiza with deciduous trees; on sandy soils.
- ■ **RANGE** Widespread and common in North America, Europe and Asia.

striking gold-orange cap may have white veil patches •

pale yellowish flesh in cap •

cap dry, with furrowed margin •

• *orange stem has prominent ring*

gills soft and free of the stem •

large, sac-shaped white volva at base of stem •

SIDE VIEW

white stem flesh •

SECTION

• *crowded gills are cream to golden yellow*

UNDERSIDE

■ **FRUITING** Single fruitbodies or in troops on sandy soils. Summer.

AMANITA PANTHERINA

The Panther ☠

This deadly poisonous fungus has variable coloring, so beware. The bulblike stem base, with a distinct rim and a ring with no striations on the upper side, are good field-marks. Cap color is normally fairly pale brown and the scales are small and plentiful. The cap margin has fine, radial lines. *A. cothurnata* (see p.131) and *A. gemmata* (see below) are close relatives but differ in color and habitat.

- **SPORE DEPOSIT** Whitish.
- **SIZE** Cap 5–12cm (w); stem 6–12cm (h) x 0.5–1.5cm (w); bulb up to 3cm (w).
- **HABITAT** Mostly on calcareous soils, forming mycorrhiza with conifers and deciduous trees in woods and parks.
- **RANGE** As a complex, widespread and in places common in the north temperate zones.

cap dry and dull brown •

• small, whitish veil patches on cap

• stem whitish

immature • form still partly covered by white veil

SIDE VIEW

SIDE VIEW

• gills white, crowded, soft, and free

• stem has a hanging, non-striated ring

may have girdles above bulb •

rounded, bulblike base, with • distinct rim

- **FRUITING** Singly or in small groups beneath trees. Summer–autumn.

TOP/SIDE VIEW

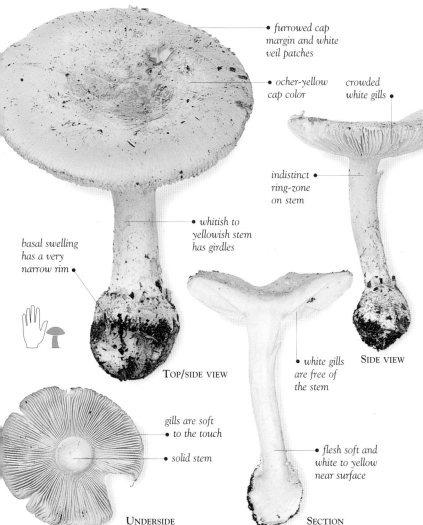

• furrowed cap margin and white veil patches

• ocher-yellow cap color

crowded white gills •

indistinct • ring-zone on stem

basal swelling has a very narrow rim •

• whitish to yellowish stem has girdles

TOP/SIDE VIEW

gills are soft • to the touch

• solid stem

UNDERSIDE

• white gills are free of the stem

SIDE VIEW

• flesh soft and white to yellow near surface

SECTION

AMANITA GEMMATA

Gemmed Agaric ☠

Resembling *A. pantherina* (see above) in its radially lined cap margin and its stature, this poisonous species differs in having a short-lived stem ring, a less prominent basal bulb, and a yellowish cap. North America boasts a wide range of forms that make accurate identification particularly difficult.

- **SPORE DEPOSIT** White.
- **SIZE** Cap 3–10cm (w); stem 5–10cm (h) x 0.5–1.5cm (w); bulb up to 2cm (w).
- **HABITAT** Associated with conifers, or in deciduous forests, on sandy soils.
- **RANGE** As a complex, widespread but local in the north temperate zones.

- **FRUITING** In small groups, typically beneath conifers. Summer–autumn.

AMANITA SPISSA

Stout Agaric

Although A. *spissa* is very similar in stature to A. *rubescens* (*see below*), it lacks that species' pinkish tinges. In color, it is closer to A. *pantherina* (*see p.133*), but the cap margin of A. *spissa* is smooth and its ring striated. A. *pantherina* can also be recognized by the rim on the bulbous stem base. Although eaten by some in Europe, cannot be recommended in North America because too little is known about its identity and edibility. A. *excelsa* is considered by some to be a separate species or variety. It has a rooting stem, is paler and odorless.

- ■ **SPORE DEPOSIT** White.
- ■ **SIZE** Cap 7–15cm (w); stem 8–14cm (h) x 2–4cm (w).
- ■ **HABITAT** Typically associated with beech or spruce trees.
- ■ **RANGE** Widespread in north temperate Europe, Asia, and eastern North America.

convex cap usually dark brown, with grayish patches of veil •

free gills white, crowded, and soft •

UNDERSIDE

prominent hanging ring has clearly defined • *grooves*

base of stem club-shaped, with brown to gray- • *brown veil gird*

TOP/SIDE VIEW

■ **FRUITING** Singly or a few together in forests. Summer–autumn.

convex cap has gray to pink veil patches of variable size

stem downy gray, white, or pink •

prominent • *hanging, striate ring on upper part of stem*

base of stem swollen and • *girdled*

SIDE VIEW

flesh white and soft; stains pink

SECTION

gills white, crowded, • soft, and free

TOP/ SIDE VIEW

UNDERSIDE

AMANITA RUBESCENS

The Blusher

Although edible in Europe, too little is known about its edibility here to recommended it. The pink-tinged coloring of the damaged flesh and the frequent white phalliclike deformity, caused by the ascomycete *Hypomyces hyalinus*, are the best identification clues.

- ■ **SPORE DEPOSIT** White.
- ■ **SIZE** Cap 6–18cm (w); stem 6–15cm (h) x 1.5–4cm (w).
- ■ **HABITAT** Associated with both deciduous and coniferous trees, often on humus-rich, acidic soils.
- ■ **RANGE** Widespread in north temperate Europe and eastern North America.

■ **FRUITING** Singly or in groups, often on acid soils. Summer–autumn.

AMANITA PORPHYRIA

Porphyry False Death-cap 💀

Although very similar in stature to *A. citrina* (see p.131), and with a similar strong smell of raw peeled potatoes, *A. porphyria* has different coloring and is found in a different habitat. Named after the color of its cap, which is "porphyrous," or grayish purple, it also has a gray ring around the stem. This species is slightly poisonous, but eating should be avoided since it could be easily confused with its deadly poisonous relatives. More *Amanita* species occur especially in North America.

- **SPORE DEPOSIT** White.
- **SIZE** Cap 5–9cm (w); stem 8–13cm (h) x 1–2cm (w); volva up to 2.5cm (w).
- **HABITAT** Found beneath conifers on acid soils; mycorrhizal.
- **RANGE** Widespread across north temperate Europe, Asia, and northern North America.

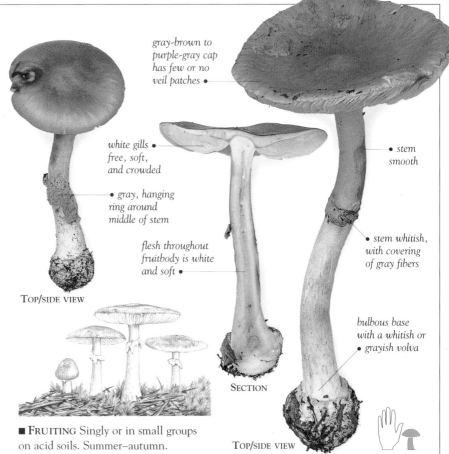

gray-brown to purple-gray cap has few or no veil patches •

white gills • free, soft, and crowded

• gray, hanging ring around middle of stem

flesh throughout fruitbody is white and soft •

• stem smooth

• stem whitish, with covering of gray fibers

bulbous base with a whitish or • grayish volva

TOP/SIDE VIEW

SECTION

TOP/SIDE VIEW

■ **FRUITING** Singly or in small groups on acid soils. Summer–autumn.

AMANITA VIROSA

Destroying Angel 💀

While not causing as many fatalities worldwide as *A. phalloides* (see p.131), this is a complex that every forager should be familiar with. Damaged specimens or specimens collected without the base (showing the saclike volva) are easily mistaken for immature specimens of *Agaricus* species. This shining white but deadly mushroom can be the most beautiful mushroom in the woods.

- **SPORE DEPOSIT** White.
- **SIZE** Cap 6–11cm (w); stem 10–20cm (h) x 1–2cm (w); volva up to 3cm (w).
- **HABITAT** Associated with trees, in deciduous and conifer forests.
- **RANGE** Widespread in north temperate zones.

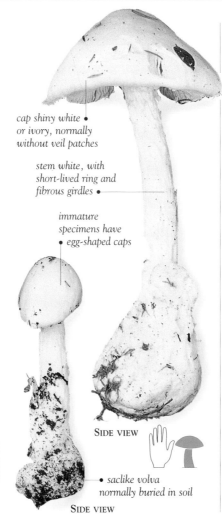

cap shiny white • or ivory, normally without veil patches

stem white, with short-lived ring and fibrous girdles •

immature specimens have • egg-shaped caps

• saclike volva normally buried in soil

SIDE VIEW

SIDE VIEW

■ **FRUITING** Singly or in groups, mostly in acid forests. Summer–autumn.

LIMACELLA GUTTATA

Weeping Slime-veil

Limacella species is distinguished from *Amanita* species by the typically slimy caps or stems and the absence of a volva at the stem base. The stem of *L. guttata* is dry; it has a prominent ring that exudes a clear liquid. It is edible but not recommended.

- **SPORE DEPOSIT** White.
- **SIZE** Cap 7–15cm (w); stem 8–14cm (h) x 1–2.5cm (w).
- **HABITAT** On rich soil in mixed forests, on thick leaf litter.
- **RANGE** Widespread but local in Europe; in the Midwest and Rockies in North America.

■ **FRUITING** On rich woodland soils. Late summer–autumn.

AGARICACEAE

CLASS: *Homobasidiomycetes*

This family includes a fairly wide variety of mushrooms – spore color varies and sizes range from tiny species of *Leucocoprinus* to huge parasols in the genus *Macrolepiota*. However, all family members have free gills, and most have a distinct ring on the stem. Some choice edible species are in this family as well as a few deadly ones.

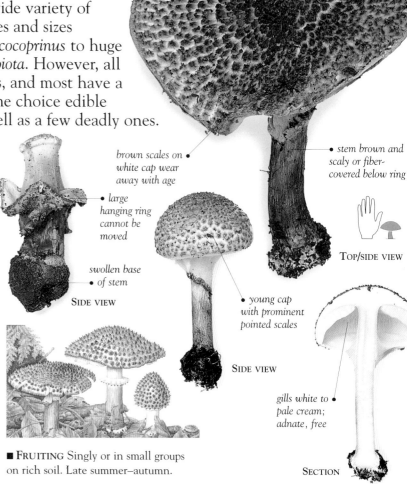

• stem brown and scaly or fiber-covered below ring

TOP/SIDE VIEW

brown scales on • white cap wear away with age

• large hanging ring cannot be moved

swollen base • of stem

SIDE VIEW

• young cap with prominent pointed scales

SIDE VIEW

LEPIOTA ASPERA

Sharp-scaled Parasol ☠

Part of a large, possibly poisonous complex of species of *Lepiota* that one should not mistake for the edible *Macrolepiota procera* (see p.138). The main features that distinguish *L. aspera* are the stem ring, which cannot be moved, and an unpleasant smell. When young, *L. aspera* has conical or pyramidal cap scales, which are good clues to identification.

■ SPORE DEPOSIT White.
■ SIZE Cap 5–15cm (w); stem 5–12cm (h) x 0.5–1.5cm (w).
■ HABITAT On rich soil along roadsides in calcareous forests.
■ RANGE Widespread in north temperate zones.

■ FRUITING Singly or in small groups on rich soil. Late summer–autumn.

gills white to • pale cream; adnate, free

SECTION

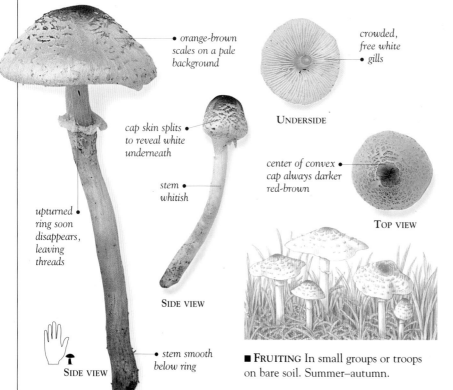

• orange-brown scales on a pale background

cap skin splits • to reveal white underneath

stem • whitish

upturned • ring soon disappears, leaving threads

SIDE VIEW

SIDE VIEW

• stem smooth below ring

crowded, free white • gills

UNDERSIDE

center of convex • cap always darker red-brown

TOP VIEW

■ FRUITING In small groups or troops on bare soil. Summer–autumn.

LEPIOTA CRISTATA

Stinking Parasol ☠

The most common of the smaller, possibly poisonous *Lepiota* species, this is best identified by its pale colors, the concentric pattern of flat orange-brown scales on the cap, and an unpleasant odor of burned rubber. The stem ring is very short-lived but can be seen as an upturned cuff on younger specimens. *L. lilacea* is a much rarer species with a similar shape but with purple to purple-brown colors. It is very poisonous.

■ SPORE DEPOSIT White.
■ SIZE Cap 1–4cm (w); stem 2.5–5cm (h) x 0.2–0.4cm (w).
■ HABITAT On fairly rich soil, in lawns, among moss, or along the edge of paths and roads in leaf litter.
■ RANGE Widespread and common in north temperate zones.

LEPIOTA CLYPEOLARIA

Shaggy-stalked Parasol

Although fairly large, this *Lepiota* species is not particularly fleshy. Its overall coloring is white to cream, and the cap may have a brownish tinge. The specimen shown here is a brown example. *Lepiota clypeolaria* has a pure white, partial veil, making the stems of the young specimens white and shaggy. The similar, and equally common, *Lepiota ventriosospora* has yellow or yellowish brown tinges to the stem veil and cap.

- **SPORE DEPOSIT** White.
- **SIZE** Cap 3–7cm (w); stem 5–12cm (h) x 0.5–1cm (w).
- **HABITAT** On better soils, among leaf litter, or on needle beds in deciduous, especially oak, or conifer forests.
- **RANGE** Widespread in north temperate zones.

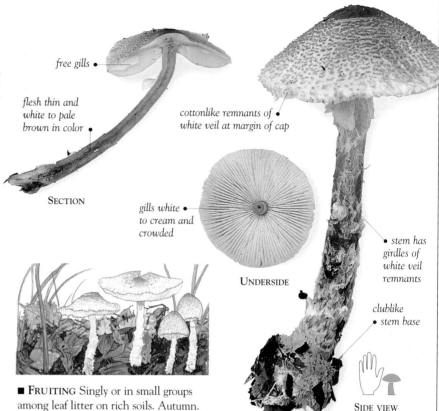

free gills

flesh thin and white to pale brown in color

SECTION

cottonlike remnants of white veil at margin of cap

gills white to cream and crowded

UNDERSIDE

stem has girdles of white veil remnants

clublike stem base

SIDE VIEW

- **FRUITING** Singly or in small groups among leaf litter on rich soils. Autumn.

---

cap with dark scales

ring soon disappears

stem with dark scales

TOP/SIDE VIEW

gills free, white, crowded

flesh pale or ocher

SECTION   UNDERSIDE

LEPIOTA CASTANEA

Chestnut Parasol

Lepiota castanea is a small and dark *Lepiota* species with dark brown scales on the stem ring. The smell is strong and rather unpleasant. Microscopic features, such as spore shape are important when identifying small *Lepiota* species. Because some are deadly and many are poisonous, and precise identification is so difficult, no small *Lepiota* should be eaten.

- **SPORE DEPOSIT** White.
- **SIZE** Cap 2–4cm (w); stem 2–5cm (h) x 0.2–0.4cm (w).
- **HABITAT** On rich soil; also on forest paths or along banks in deciduous and coniferous forests.
- **RANGE** Widespread, mostly southern in north temperate zones.

- **FRUITING** Mostly a few together along woodland rides or ditches. Autumn.

LEPIOTA BRUNNEO-INCARNATA

Deadly Lepiota Complex

Although a highly poisonous fungus, the size and rarity of this species make the likelihood of eating this species by accident unlikely. This is just one of a group of small *Lepiotas*; no small *Lepiota* should ever be eaten.

- **SPORE DEPOSIT** White.
- **SIZE** Cap 2.5–5cm (w); stem 2–3.5cm (h) x 0.5–0.8cm (w).
- **HABITAT** On rich soil, in lawns, under hedges, or along forest roads.
- **RANGE** Widespread in Europe; not reported in North America, but other equally deadly *Lepiotas* are widely distributed in North Americà.

- **FRUITING** Singly or a few together on rich soil. Late summer–autumn.

LEPIOTA OREADIFORMIS

Grassland Parasol

The scientific name of this fungus reflects its superficial similarity to the edible *Marasmius oreades* (see p.108). Differences include the thinner, free gills of *L. oreadiformis*. Unlike most *Lepiota* species, however, the stem ring is hardly visible in this species.

- ■ **SPORE DEPOSIT** White.
- ■ **SIZE** Cap 2–6cm (w); stem 3–5cm (h) x 0.8–1.2cm (w).
- ■ **HABITAT** In open, dry grassland, often at coastal sites such as sand dunes.
- ■ **RANGE** Widespread in Europe; not reported in North America.

- ■ **FRUITING** In troops among lichens and short grass. Autumn.

LEPIOTA IGNIVOLVATA ☠

Orange-girdled Parasol

This fairly fleshy *Lepiota* species is best identified by its orange-margined ring, situated low on the stem. The cap has a concentric pattern of fine, orange-brown scales and a raised, ocher-brown center. *L. ventriosospora* is similar but lacks the orange color on the veil and the stem base.

- ■ **SPORE DEPOSIT** White.
- ■ **SIZE** Cap 4–11cm, up to 14cm (w); stem 5–15cm (h) x 0.5–2cm (w).
- ■ **HABITAT** On leaf litter on calcareous soils, under conifer and deciduous trees.
- ■ **RANGE** Widespread especially in central and southern Europe; not reported in North America.

- ■ **FRUITING** In troops or singly, often deep in woodland leaf litter. Autumn.

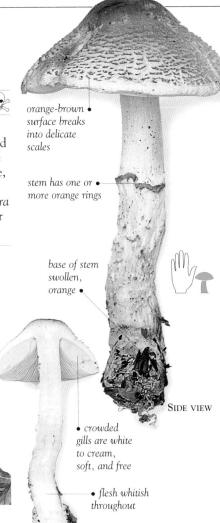

- *orange-brown surface breaks into delicate scales*
- *stem has one or more orange rings*
- *base of stem swollen, orange*

SIDE VIEW

- *crowded gills are white to cream, soft, and free*
- *flesh whitish throughout*

SECTION

MACROLEPIOTA PROCERA

Parasol Mushroom

A spectacular large mushroom, known for the beautiful snakeskin stem pattern and a large, movable ring. Unlike *M. rhacodes* (see opposite), the flesh does not change color when bruised. This may be one of the best edible mushrooms (see p.236 for recipes), although familiarity with the poisonous *Chlorophyllum molybdites* (see opposite) is vital, especially in the US. This Parasol Mushroom group includes species that lack the snakeskin stem pattern, are smaller, and have different sized spores.

- ■ **SPORE DEPOSIT** White or pinkish.
- ■ **SIZE** Cap 10–30cm, up to 40cm (w); stem 15–30cm, up to 40cm (h) x 0.8–2cm (w); stem bulb up to 4cm (w).
- ■ **HABITAT** Dunes and grassy areas.
- ■ **RANGE** As a complex, widespread in Europe and North America.

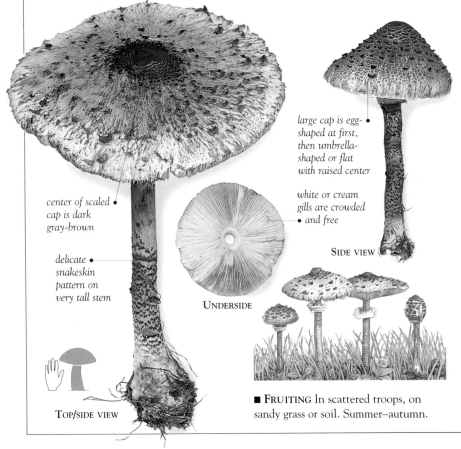

- *center of scaled cap is dark gray-brown*
- *delicate snakeskin pattern on very tall stem*

TOP/SIDE VIEW

UNDERSIDE

- *large cap is egg-shaped at first, then umbrella-shaped or flat with raised center*
- *white or cream gills are crowded and free*

SIDE VIEW

- ■ **FRUITING** In scattered troops, on sandy grass or soil. Summer–autumn.

MACROLEPIOTA RHACODES

Shaggy Parasol

Similar in many ways to M. *procera* (*see opposite*), this shaggy species is smaller and lacks the snakeskin stem pattern. Its flesh turns carrot-red when bruised, and very young specimens resemble flower bulbs. Some varieties are known to cause stomach upsets, so this fungus should only be eaten in small quantities, at least initially. Care should be taken not to confuse it with *Chlorophyllum molybdites* (*see below*).

- **SPORE DEPOSIT** White.
- **SIZE** Cap 5–15cm, up to 20cm (w); stem 10–15cm, up to 20cm (h) x 1–2cm (w).
- **HABITAT** Mostly found in parks and gardens, but also occurs on needle beds under conifers.
- **RANGE** Widespread and common throughout Europe and North America.

- **FRUITING** In troops, mostly on better soils. Summer–autumn.

cracking skin in young cap •

egg-shaped cap • in immature specimens

cap surface breaks up into scales as it matures and expands •

SIDE VIEW

leaf litter attached to bulbous base •

SIDE VIEW

SIDE VIEW

white flesh stains • carrot-red, then dark red

SECTION

prominent • double stem ring

stem lacks • snakeskin pattern of similar M. procera

• smooth to fibrillose stem is swollen at base

gills free •

hollow • stem

SIDE VIEW

• cap flattens as it expands fully

pattern of concentric, pale brown scales cover surface of cap •

TOP VIEW

• shaggy edge to cap

• free gills white to cream and crowded

UNDERSIDE

CHLOROPHYLLUM MOLYBDITES

Green-gilled Parasol ☠

The green or olive-green gills, which stain grayish or darker when handled, are the best way of distinguishing this species, although the immature gills will be white to off-white. Another marker is the green spore deposit. It is so similar to species of *Macrolepiota* (*see opposite*) that some mycologists now consider it as belonging to this genus.

- **SPORE DEPOSIT** Green to olive.
- **SIZE** Cap 10–15cm (w); stem 8–18cm (h) x 1–2.5cm (w).
- **HABITAT** On bare soil or in grass, woods, parks, and gardens.
- **RANGE** Widespread in tropical and subtropical climates; across southern US, north to New York City.

- **FRUITING** Typically, in fairy rings. All year or following summer rain.

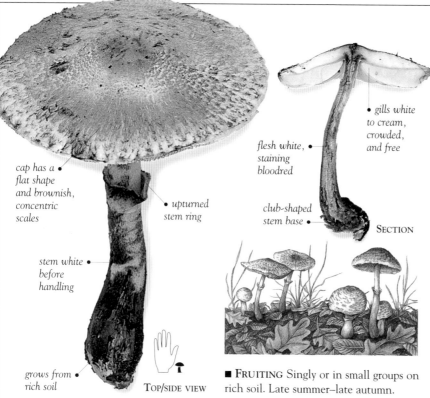

cap has a flat shape and brownish, concentric scales •

• upturned stem ring

stem white before handling •

grows from rich soil •

TOP/SIDE VIEW

• gills white to cream, crowded, and free

flesh white, staining bloodred •

club-shaped stem base •

SECTION

■ **FRUITING** Singly or in small groups on rich soil. Late summer–late autumn.

LEUCOCOPRINUS BADHAMII

Red-staining Parasol ☠

When handled, any part of this agaric turns saffron-red or a deep bloodred and, finally, nearly black. Initially it is almost white, with delicate, brownish scales on the cap. The common and edible red-staining northeastern North American *L. americana* occurs in sawdust and plant debris.

■ **SPORE DEPOSIT** White.
■ **SIZE** Cap 3–8cm (w); stem 3–7cm (h) x 0.4–0.8cm (w).
■ **HABITAT** On calcareous or nutrient-rich soils, among leaf or garden litter, or needle beds; particularly under yew but also under deciduous trees.
■ **RANGE** Widespread in Europe; not known in North America.

LEUCOCOPRINUS LUTEUS

Yellow Parasol

Best known from its occurrence in flowerpots and greenhouses, but also widespread and common throughout the southern United States. Its yellow coloring is very distinctive.

■ **SPORE DEPOSIT** White.
■ **SIZE** Cap 1–5cm (w); stem 4–10cm (h) x 0.2–0.4cm (w); base up to 0.6cm (w).
■ **HABITAT** In greenhouses; in the wild in warm, tropical climates.
■ **RANGE** Subtropical and tropical areas.

■ **FRUITING** Often growing in tufts on compost-rich soil. All year.

LEUCOAGARICUS LEUCOTHITES

Smooth Parasol ☠

This fungus is commonly mistaken for one of several *Agaricus* species, but it can be distinguished by the gills, which never turn black, and the white spore deposit. The stem ring is also slightly different from *Agaricus* species. Formerly known in Europe and North America as *Leucoagarius naucina*, this complex is now known in the United States as *L. naucinoides*. No mushroom in this group is safe to eat.

■ **SPORE DEPOSIT** White.
■ **SIZE** Cap 5–8cm (w); stem 4–8cm (h) x 0.8–2cm (w).
■ **HABITAT** Among grass along road-sides, and in parks, gardens, and sand dunes.
■ **RANGE** Widespread in Europe and North America.

■ **FRUITING** In small groups or fairy rings, mostly in grass. Late summer–autumn.

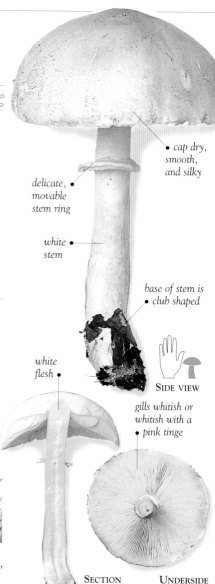

• cap dry, smooth, and silky

delicate, movable stem ring •

white stem •

base of stem is • club shaped

SIDE VIEW

white flesh •

gills whitish or whitish with a • pink tinge

SECTION   UNDERSIDE

slight reddish stain in flesh

both cap and stem stain faintly carrot-red when handled

cap white to dark brown

TOP/SIDE VIEW

ring simple, upturned when young

SECTION

chocolate-brown gills when mature

UNDERSIDE

■ **FRUITING** In troops and rings on rich soil or compost. Late summer–autumn.

AGARICUS BISPORUS

Cultivated Mushroom

Perhaps the best known of all edible mushrooms in the Western world, this species has long been cultivated on a huge scale. It belongs to the group of red-staining *Agaricus* species. Another important *Agaricus* characteristic is the position of the ring. In *A. bisporus*, it is partially upturned and quite small. Only species like Paddy Straw *Volvariella volvacea*, wood-ear (*Auricularia auricula-judae*), and shiitake *Lentinula edodes* compete in commercial importance.

■ **SPORE DEPOSIT** Chocolate-brown.
■ **SIZE** Cap 5–10cm (w); stem 3–6cm (h) x 1–2cm (w).
■ **HABITAT** By roadsides, in cemeteries, and other sites with disturbed, rich soils.
■ **RANGE** Widespread in north temperate zones.

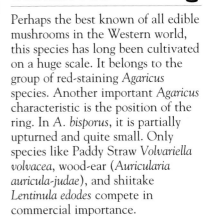

AGARICUS BITORQUIS

Spring Agaricus

Besides the habitat, *Agaricus bitorquis* is best identified by a distinct double stem ring, which is sheathed and upturned, firm flesh, which turns pink slowly; and the squared cap, which has an inrolled margin. The smell is acidic. *A. bernardii* (see p.142) is found in similar sites.

■ **SPORE DEPOSIT** Chocolate-brown.
■ **SIZE** Cap 5–12cm (w); stem 4–8cm, up to 12cm (h) x 1–3.5cm (w).
■ **HABITAT** Mostly in urban areas, in hard or packed soil, or often in schoolyard playgrounds.
■ **RANGE** Widespread and common in Europe and North America.

■ **FRUITING** A few together, emerging from soil or tarmac. Summer–autumn.

AGARICUS CAMPESTRIS

Meadow Mushroom

A very familiar mushroom with a faintly reddening fruitbody and without the characteristic almond smell found, for example, in *A. arvensis* (see p.143). The ring is small, single, and has no scales on the underside. The cap may be pinkish gray in older specimens.

■ **SPORE DEPOSIT** Chocolate-brown.
■ **SIZE** Cap 4–10cm, up to 12cm (w); stem 3–7cm (h) x 0.8–1.5cm (w).
■ **HABITAT** Almost exclusively found in the open, often in rich, manured grasslands and in city parks.
■ **RANGE** Widespread and common in north temperate zones.

■ **FRUITING** In large groups or rings in meadows. Summer–autumn.

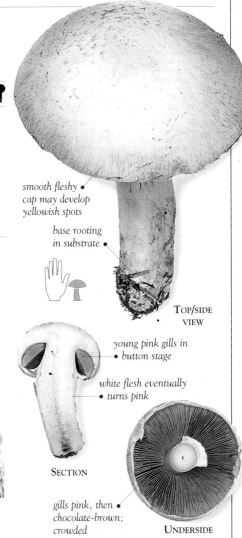

smooth fleshy cap may develop yellowish spots

base rooting in substrate

TOP/SIDE VIEW

young pink gills in button stage

white flesh eventually turns pink

SECTION

gills pink, then chocolate-brown; crowded

UNDERSIDE

cap white or gray-white •

• flattened or convex cap shape

cracks on cap form • scaly pattern

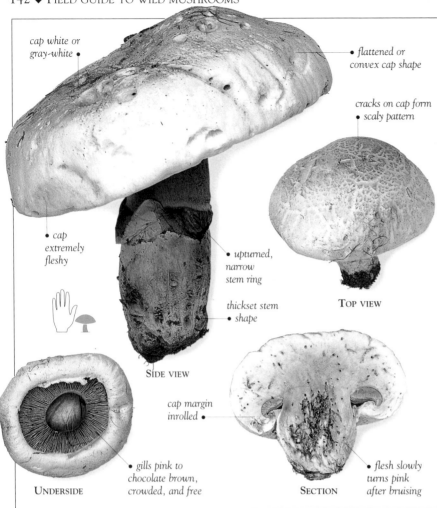

• cap extremely fleshy

• uptuned, narrow stem ring

thickset stem • shape

TOP VIEW

SIDE VIEW

cap margin inrolled •

• gills pink to chocolate brown, crowded, and free

UNDERSIDE

SECTION

• flesh slowly turns pink after bruising

AGARICUS BERNARDII

Salt-loving Mushroom

A very fleshy, foul-smelling mushroom that tolerates soils rich in, or contaminated by, salt. Its stem ring is upturned and very narrow, and the cap of A. bernardii often cracks into a scaly pattern.

■ **SPORE DEPOSIT** Chocolate brown.
■ **SIZE** Cap 7–15cm, up to 20cm (w); stem 5–10cm (h) x 2–4cm (w).
■ **HABITAT** Near the coast, or along roads that are salted in winter.
■ **RANGE** Widespread in Europe and east and west coasts of North America.

■ **FRUITING** In troops in coastal grassy areas or roads. Summer–autumn.

AGARICUS SILVATICUS

Red-staining Mushroom

This species belongs to a group that stains red, mostly after bruising. Because some red staining species cause gastric upsets, great care should be taken about precise identification before any mushroom in this group is eaten.

■ **SPORE DEPOSIT** Chocolate brown.
■ **SIZE** Cap 5–10cm (w); stem 5–10cm (h) x 0.5–1.5cm (w); base up to 2.5cm (w).
■ **HABITAT** On conifer debris in forests and parks, sometimes in damp woods.
■ **RANGE** Widespread in north temperate zones.

■ **FRUITING** In troops or rings on needle beds. Throughout autumn.

gills pale gray, turning rose pink and, finally, chocolate brown •

cap shape convex to flat with a raised center •

UNDERSIDE

flesh whitish, stains red if bruised or cut •

cap has radiating scales

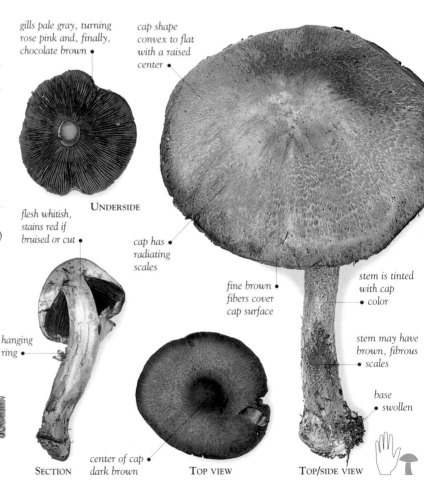

fine brown • fibers cover cap surface

stem is tinted with cap • color

hanging ring •

stem may have brown, fibrous • scales

base • swollen

SECTION

center of cap • dark brown

TOP VIEW

TOP/SIDE VIEW

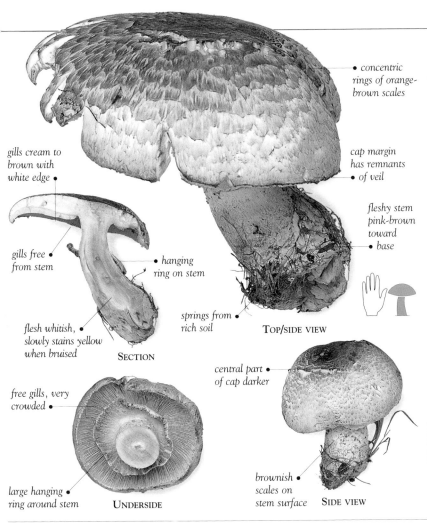

- *concentric rings of orange-brown scales*
- *cap margin has remnants of veil*
- *fleshy stem pink-brown toward base*
- *gills cream to brown with white edge*
- *gills free from stem*
- *hanging ring on stem*
- *flesh whitish, slowly stains yellow when bruised*

SECTION

- *springs from rich soil*

TOP/SIDE VIEW

- *central part of cap darker*
- *free gills, very crowded*
- *large hanging ring around stem*

UNDERSIDE

- *brownish scales on stem surface*

SIDE VIEW

AGARICUS AUGUSTUS

The Prince

The brown-scaled cap and yellow reaction of the flesh, together with a strong almond smell, distinguish this edible species. Together with its paler relatives it contains a high degree of cadmium, which does little harm but is best eaten in small bits.

- **SPORE DEPOSIT** Chocolate brown.
- **SIZE** Cap 8–15cm, up to 20cm (w); stem 7–12cm, up to 20cm (h) x 1.5–3.5cm (w).
- **HABITAT** On rich soil in all types of woods and parks, and in garden compost.
- **RANGE** Widely distributed in western North America.

- **FRUITING** A few together or in large troops on rich soil. Throughout autumn.

AGARICUS ARVENSIS

Horse Mushroom

A close relative of *A. augustus* (*see above*) but without the prominent cap scales. The stem has a hanging ring with a wheel-like pattern underneath. The flesh slowly stains ocher-yellow, and it smells similar to almonds. This edible also contains a high concentration of cadmium.

- **SPORE DEPOSIT** Chocolate brown.
- **SIZE** Cap 7–15cm, up to 20cm (w); stem 7–15cm (h) x 1–3cm (w).
- **HABITAT** In horse-grazed pasture, lawns, and parks, often near spruce.
- **RANGE** Widespread and common in north temperate zones.

- **FRUITING** Mostly in rings in grassy areas. Summer–autumn.

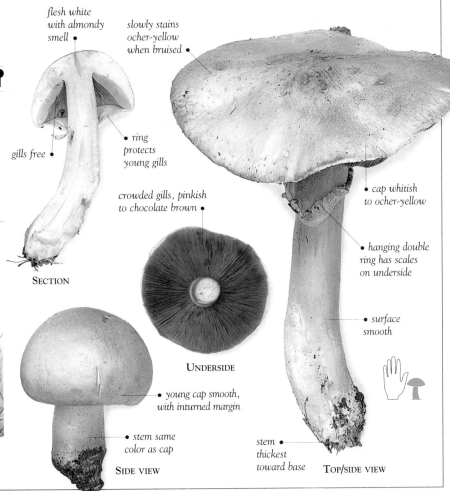

- *flesh white with almondy smell*
- *slowly stains ocher-yellow when bruised*
- *gills free*
- *ring protects young gills*

SECTION

- *crowded gills, pinkish to chocolate brown*

UNDERSIDE

- *young cap smooth, with inturned margin*
- *stem same color as cap*

SIDE VIEW

- *cap whitish to ocher-yellow*
- *hanging double ring has scales on underside*
- *surface smooth*
- *stem thickest toward base*

TOP/SIDE VIEW

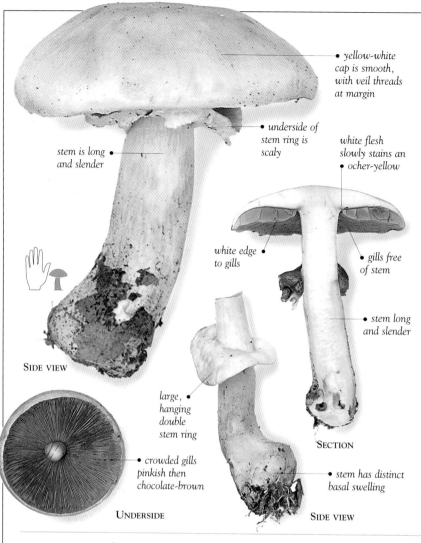

yellow-white cap is smooth, with veil threads at margin

stem is long and slender

underside of stem ring is scaly

white flesh slowly stains an ocher-yellow

white edge to gills

gills free of stem

stem long and slender

large, hanging double stem ring

crowded gills pinkish then chocolate-brown

SECTION

stem has distinct basal swelling

UNDERSIDE

SIDE VIEW

SIDE VIEW

AGARICUS SILVICOLA

Wood Mushroom

This species, which includes *A. abruptibulbus*, is a woodland form of *A. arvensis* (*see p.143*). The stem is more slender, and the bulb is usually flat. It has an almond or anise smell and yellowing flesh. Although edible, treat with caution as it contains high levels of cadmium.

■ **SPORE DEPOSIT** Chocolate-brown.
■ **SIZE** Cap 6–12cm (w); stem 8–12cm (h) x 1–2cm (w); bulb up to 3cm (w).
■ **HABITAT** On rich soil mixed with debris, under trees; sometimes in parks.
■ **RANGE** Widespread and common throughout the north temperate zones.

■ **FRUITING** A few together or occasionally in rings. Summer–autumn.

AGARICUS XANTHODERMA

Yellow-staining Mushroom ☠

Despite the yellow-staining feature, the appearance of this poisonous species is of a whiter, almost gray-white fungus compared to the other yellow-staining *Agaricus* species. The best markers are the stem base – it should be bright yellow at the very tip when cut lengthwise – and an inklike smell. It has some darker colored, equally poisonous, relatives. The edible *Agaricus* species *A. arvensis*, *A. augustus* (*see p.143*), and *A. silvicola* (*see above*) are similar, but smell of almond or anise and are slower to stain yellow.

■ **SPORE DEPOSIT** Chocolate-brown.
■ **SIZE** Cap 5–13cm (w); stem 5–10cm (h) x 1–2cm (w).
■ **HABITAT** On bare soil or in grass in parkland, cemeteries, and similar places.
■ **RANGE** Widespread but not evenly distributed throughout the north temperate zones and elsewhere.

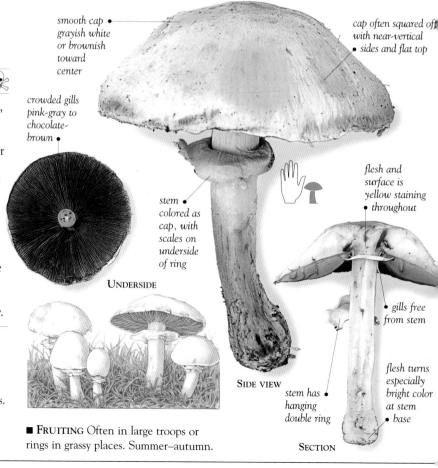

smooth cap grayish white or brownish toward center

crowded gills pink-gray to chocolate-brown

cap often squared off with near-vertical sides and flat top

stem colored as cap, with scales on underside of ring

flesh and surface is yellow staining throughout

UNDERSIDE

gills free from stem

SIDE VIEW

stem has hanging double ring

flesh turns especially bright color at stem base

SECTION

■ **FRUITING** Often in large troops or rings in grassy places. Summer–autumn.

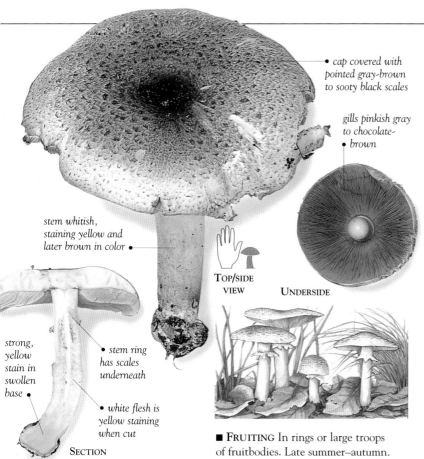

- cap covered with pointed gray-brown to sooty black scales

gills pinkish gray to chocolate-brown

stem whitish, staining yellow and later brown in color

TOP/SIDE VIEW

UNDERSIDE

strong, yellow stain in swollen base

- stem ring has scales underneath

- white flesh is yellow staining when cut

SECTION

■ **FRUITING** In rings or large troops of fruitbodies. Late summer–autumn.

AGARICUS PRAE-CLARESQUAMOSUS

Dark-scaled Mushroom

This unpleasant-smelling fungus is an ally of the yellow-staining *A. xanthoderma (see opposite)*, with similar poisonous properties and flesh that quickly stains yellow. This is the mushroom more commonly known in western North America as *Agaricus meleagris*. A similar mushroom, *A. placomyces*, is common in eastern North America. All have similar poisonous qualities that in some people can cause quite severe gastric upsets.

- ■ **SPORE DEPOSIT** Chocolate-brown.
- ■ **SIZE** Cap 5–14cm (w); stem 6–10cm (h) x 1–1.5cm (w); base up to 2.5cm (w).
- ■ **HABITAT** On rich soil in calcareous woods or in parklands.
- ■ **RANGE** As a complex, widespread, but local to rare, in north temperate zones.

AGARICUS HONDENSIS

Felt-ringed Mushroom

A North American mushroom that can cause gastric upsets. It differs from *A. praeclaresquamosus* and *A. placomyces (see above)* in having paler cap scales, a less flat-topped cap, and a thicker stem ring. It does not stain yellow when bruised, but the unpleasant smell is similar to *A. xanthoderma (see p.144)*.

- ■ **SPORE DEPOSIT** Chocolate-brown.
- ■ **SIZE** Cap 6–15cm (w); stem 6–15cm (h) x 1–2cm (w), thicker at basal bulblike swelling.
- ■ **HABITAT** On soil in woodland.
- ■ **RANGE** Pacific coast of N. America.

■ **FRUITING** In troops on mixed woodland litter. Autumn or winter.

AGARICUS CALIFORNICUS

False Meadow Mushroom

Easy to confuse with *A. campestris (see p.141)*, this poisonous species has a pungent odor and a scalier, browner cap surface. When eaten, the resultant poisonings are gastric upsets. It belongs with the group of yellow-staining mushrooms, whereas *A. campestris* differs because it stains pink.

- ■ **SPORE DEPOSIT** Chocolate-brown.
- ■ **SIZE** Cap 5–10cm (w); stem 3–10cm (h) x 1–1.5cm (w).
- ■ **HABITAT** Mostly in urban areas, among damp grass in lawns and parks.
- ■ **RANGE** California.

■ **FRUITING** In troops among grass. All year, particularly in wet areas.

AGARICUS PORPHYRIZON

Porphyry Mushroom

The combination of purplish cap colors, yellow-staining flesh, and almondy smell is found in a number of mostly small *Agaricus* species. *A. porphyrizon* is an unusually fleshy and sturdy member of the group. It grows deep in woodland leaf litter.

- ■ **SPORE DEPOSIT** Chocolate-brown.
- ■ **SIZE** Cap 5–8cm (w); stem 4–6cm (h) x 0.7–1cm, sometimes 1.5cm (w).
- ■ **HABITAT** On soil and leaf litter in deciduous woods, on conifer debris, and in gardens.
- ■ **RANGE** Widespread but local in Europe; not reported in North America.

■ **FRUITING** Singly or a few together on rich soil, among leaf litter. Autumn.

COPRINACEAE

CLASS: *Homobasidiomycetes*

The genera *Coprinus*, *Psathyrella*, and *Panaeolus* are usually placed in the *Coprinaceae*. All species have brown to black spore deposits. *Coprinus* species typically have gills that deliquesce, producing an inky liquid filled with spores. *Psathyrella* species are fragile and often elegantly shaped. *Panaeolus* have marbled gills due to clustered spores. The gills of the latter two genera do not deliquesce.

COPRINUS COMATUS

Shaggy Mane

This popular edible species has a fleshier fruitbody than most other members of the genus *Coprinus*. The shaggy wiglike caps, which tend to deliquesce quickly, are also a distinctive feature. If eating, set off early in the day and pick only young specimens. Prepare and cook the fungi as soon as you get home.

- **SPORE DEPOSIT** Black.
- **SIZE** Cap 5–20cm (h) x 2–6cm (w); stem 10–35cm (h) x 1–2cm, up to 3cm (w).
- **HABITAT** On disturbed soil, in lawns, and along roads and forest paths.
- **RANGE** Widespread and common in north temperate zones.

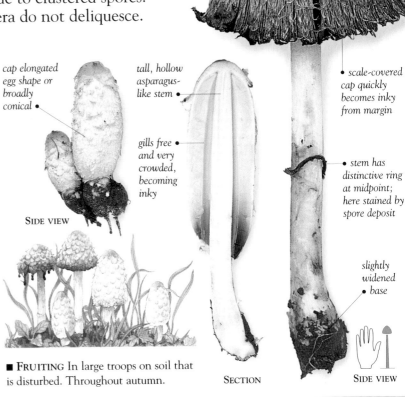

cap elongated egg shape or broadly conical ●

tall, hollow asparagus-like stem ●

● scale-covered cap quickly becomes inky from margin

gills free and very crowded, becoming inky ●

SIDE VIEW

● stem has distinctive ring at midpoint; here stained by spore deposit

slightly widened ● base

SECTION

SIDE VIEW

- **FRUITING** In large troops on soil that is disturbed. Throughout autumn.

● striking pattern on cap

cap becomes inky very quickly from margin

gills free and crowded, becoming inky from margin ● inward

young cap egg-shaped; later cylindrical or bell-shaped

hollow ● stem

SIDE VIEW

● stem white and tall, with fine floccules

SECTION

SIDE VIEW

SIDE VIEW

- **FRUITING** Singly or in small clusters among forest litter. Autumn.

COPRINUS PICACEUS

Magpie Ink-cap

An unmistakable forest fungus that occasionally occurs in great numbers where wood chips have been used as mulch. The cap pattern is caused by the white veil breaking up into scales when the cap expands. These, along with the unpleasant fetid smell, are good markers. It is not recommended as an edible.

- **SPORE DEPOSIT** Black.
- **SIZE** Cap 5–10cm (h) x 2–6cm (w); stem 8–30cm (h) x 0.6–2cm (w).
- **HABITAT** Among sawdust or wood chips in deciduous forests.
- **RANGE** Widespread but mainly found in the beech region of Europe; reported in California.

COPRINUS ATRAMENTARIUS

Alcohol Ink-cap ☠

This fleshy species often occurs in dense clusters at the base of tree stumps or dying trees. It is known to cause palpitations and nausea if taken with alcohol. Because the chemical responsible for these side effects breaks down slowly, alcohol should not be drunk for days after eating this mushroom. Although several species of *Coprinus* are eaten by some people, only the Shaggy Mane (*Coprinus comatus*) (see p.146) can be recommended for general consumption.

- **SPORE DEPOSIT** Black.
- **SIZE** Cap 3–7cm (w); stem 5–12cm, up to 17cm (h) x 0.8–1.5cm (w).
- **HABITAT** In clusters at soil level but always associated with decaying wood, usually deciduous, in woods, parks, and gardens. Often found growing on unhealthy city trees.
- **RANGE** Widespread and common in north temperate zones.

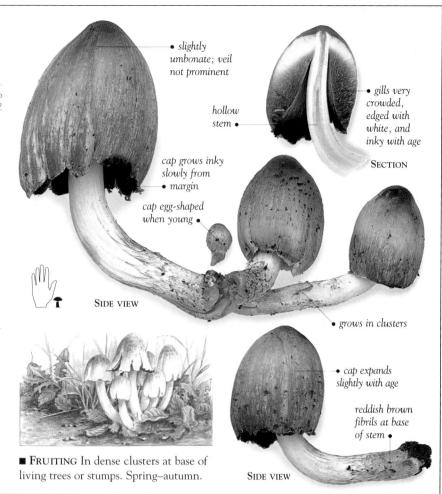

- slightly umbonate; veil not prominent
- hollow stem
- gills very crowded, edged with white, and inky with age

SECTION

- cap grows inky slowly from margin
- cap egg-shaped when young

SIDE VIEW

- grows in clusters
- cap expands slightly with age
- reddish brown fibrils at base of stem

SIDE VIEW

■ **FRUITING** In dense clusters at base of living trees or stumps. Spring–autumn.

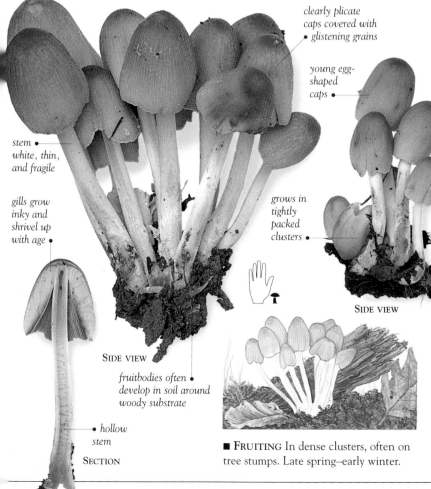

clearly plicate caps covered with glistening grains

young egg-shaped caps

stem white, thin, and fragile

gills grow inky and shrivel up with age

grows in tightly packed clusters

SIDE VIEW

fruitbodies often develop in soil around woody substrate

hollow stem

SECTION

SIDE VIEW

■ **FRUITING** In dense clusters, often on tree stumps. Late spring–early winter.

COPRINUS MICACEUS

Glistening Ink-cap

C. micaceus is so called because its cap surface is covered in small remnants of veil whose grains create a glistening effect. This highly abundant species is found both in urban areas and in the heart of forests. It was once considered poisonous. Some close relatives produce a thick orange-yellow mat known as ozonium on the substrate. One of these, *Coprinus domesticus*, is often found in damp cellars. Other species of *Coprinus* may be found in similar sites, such as behind loose tiles in bathrooms. The mycelium is able to produce numerous fruitings in one season.

- **SPORE DEPOSIT** Black.
- **SIZE** Cap 2–4cm (w); stem 4–10cm (h) x 0.2–0.5cm (w).
- **HABITAT** On and around old stumps and unhealthy living trees.
- **RANGE** Widespread and common in north temperate zones.

COPRINUS DISSEMINATUS

Fairies' Bonnets

Cream-white when young, this species turns gray with age. It only produces a little ink. *Psathyrella pygmaea* is similar, but its cap surface has neither hairs nor grains and is less plicate.

- **SPORE DEPOSIT** Black.
- **SIZE** Cap 0.5–1.5cm (w); stem 1–4cm (h) x 0.1–0.2cm (w).
- **HABITAT** On and around stumps and dying deciduous trees.
- **RANGE** Widespread and common in north temperate zones.

- **FRUITING** In huge troops around deciduous stumps. Spring–early autumn.

cap broadly egg-shaped, with plicate surface •

fine hairs • and grains on cap surface (visible with hand lens)

• flesh very thin and white; gills free

• delicate white stem

grows in • huge troops

SIDE VIEW

cap paler in color when • young

gills white to gray-black when • fully mature

stronger • color at center

SECTION   **TOP VIEW**   **TOP VIEW**   **UNDERSIDE**

---

fine, mealy cap covering may • wash off in rain

rolled-back • cap margin

gills black and inky • when mature

ring absent • from stem

UNDERSIDE

cap egg-shaped • when young

white, mealy stem slightly • swollen at base

SIDE VIEW

SIDE VIEW

COPRINUS NIVEUS

Snow-white Ink Cap

Despite its fairly small size, C. *niveus* is far from being the smallest of the *Coprinus* species. It is best identified by its snow white coloring and the loose, mealy covering over its cap, the remnants of a veil. There are other white *Coprinus* species, but C. *niveus* can be distinguished by its larger size and microscopic features.

- **SPORE DEPOSIT** Black.
- **SIZE** Cap 1–3cm (w); stem 5–8cm (h) x 0.1–0.3cm (w).
- **HABITAT** Nearly always on fairly fresh horse manure in wet grass.
- **RANGE** Widespread in Europe and North America.

- **FRUITING** A few together on horse manure. Summer–autumn.

PANACOLINA FOENISECII

Lawn Mower's Mushroom ☠

A slightly poisonous fungus that cannot be overlooked, because it is one of the most common lawn fungi. Unlike species of *Panaeolus*, which grow on dung and have smooth, blackish spores, this grows in grass and has coarsely ornamented dark brownish spores.

- **SPORE DEPOSIT** Dark brown.
- **SIZE** Cap 1–3cm (w); stem 4–6cm (h) x 0.2–0.3cm (w).
- **HABITAT** Grassy areas and lawns.
- **RANGE** Widespread and common in Europe and North America.

- **FRUITING** In troops in damp grassland and lawns. Late spring–autumn.

PANAEOLUS SPHINCTRINUS

Fringed Mottle Gill

Marbled gill sides, caused by uneven ripening of the spores, make this a very typical *Panaeolus* species. A clear marker for identifying this particular species is the triangular veil remnants at the cap margin. The cap is not hygrophanous, and older specimens can have paler caps that contrast with dark stems. *P. campanulatus*, *P. papilionaceus*, *P. retirugis*, and *P. sphinctinus* may refer to a single species composed of environmentally induced macroscopic differences in populations that are not separable microscopically.

■ **SPORE DEPOSIT** Black.
■ **SIZE** Cap 1–4cm (w); stem 4–10cm, down to 2cm (h), x 0.2–0.3cm (w).
■ **HABITAT** On old dung or in strongly manured, grazed fields and meadows.
■ **RANGE** Widespread in north temperate zones and elsewhere.

cap convex or • bell-shaped

toothed • cap margin

UNDERSIDE

blackish • gills with white edges

stem • variable but often fragile and delicate

SIDE VIEW   **TOP VIEW**

old cap • covered in black spore deposit

paler cap color • on older specimens

triangular • veil remnants just visible

broad gills • are mottled in black and gray

dark • brown stem

hollow • stem

SECTION   **SIDE VIEW**

■ **FRUITING** Singly or a few together on or near dung or manure. Summer–autumn.

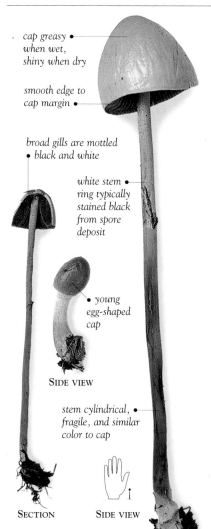

cap greasy • when wet, shiny when dry

smooth edge to cap margin •

broad gills are mottled • black and white

white stem • ring typically stained black from spore deposit

young • egg-shaped cap

SIDE VIEW

stem cylindrical, • fragile, and similar color to cap

SECTION   **SIDE VIEW**

PANAEOLUS SEMIOVATUS

Shiny Mottle Gill

Recognizable at a distance in pastureland, this species is distinguished by its sticky, later shiny, cap and its stem ring. It is always associated with the dung of grazing animals, as are nearly all species of *Panaeolus*. It has been reported as edible but not worthwhile.

■ **SPORE DEPOSIT** Black.
■ **SIZE** Cap 1–6cm (w); stem 6–10cm, or down to 2cm and up to 15cm (h) x 0.3–0.5cm (w).
■ **HABITAT** On horse dung or straw mixed with dung.
■ **RANGE** Widespread in north temperate zones throughout N.A.

■ **FRUITING** Singly or a few on each dropping. Late spring–autumn.

LACRYMARIA VELUTINA

Weeping Widow

Milklike drops seen along the edge of the young gills give this species its name. These droplets soon get filled with spores and dry as black spots. The cap is felty. There are several similar species, distinguished by size and cap color.

■ **SPORE DEPOSIT** Black.
■ **SIZE** Cap 2–10cm (w); stem 4–12cm (h) x 0.5–2cm (w).
■ **HABITAT** On disturbed, nutrient-rich soil, by roadsides and along paths.
■ **RANGE** Widespread in north temperate zones.

■ **FRUITING** In troops, along roads and paths, often near nettles. Autumn.

PSATHYRELLA PILULIFORMIS

Stump Brittle-head

The genus *Psathyrella* is a difficult one because it consists of mainly little brown mushrooms, so-called LBMs. Some, however, do have helpful field marks. *Psathyrella piluliformis*, for example, always occurs in tufts or clusters and has a distinct white veil at the cap margin. A good hand lens or microscope is helpful for positive identification. This species is also hygrophanous; the caps are a dark red-brown when wet and dry to a paler yellowish brown; it is also more commonly known as *P. hydophila*.

- **SPORE DEPOSIT** Dark purplish brown to dark reddish brown.
- **SIZE** Cap 1.5–6cm (w); stem 3–10cm, up to 15 cm (h) x 0.3–0.9cm (w).
- **HABITAT** In forests, associated with rotten deciduous trees, especially those of beech trees; often on stumps.
- **RANGE** Widespread and common in north temperate zones.

stem white and almost smooth

gills off-white to reddish brown, fairly crowded

white veil at margin stained by spores

gills adnexed, edges pale

grows in dense tufts or clusters

UNDERSIDE

SIDE VIEW

stem hollow but fairly sturdy

cap convex to bell-shaped

SIDE VIEW

SECTION

- **FRUITING** In dense clusters on and around deciduous stumps. Autumn.

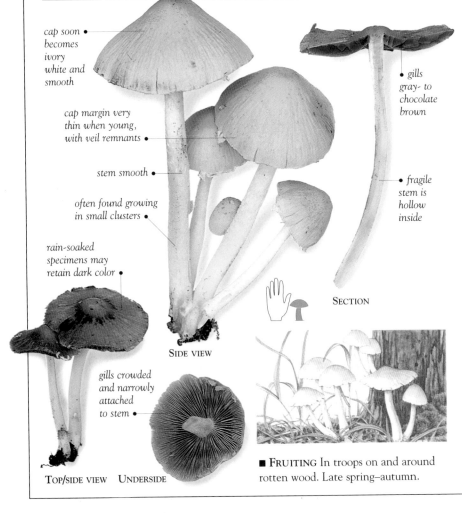

cap soon becomes ivory white and smooth

cap margin very thin when young, with veil remnants

stem smooth

often found growing in small clusters

rain-soaked specimens may retain dark color

gills gray- to chocolate brown

fragile stem is hollow inside

SECTION

SIDE VIEW

gills crowded and narrowly attached to stem

TOP/SIDE VIEW   **UNDERSIDE**

- **FRUITING** In troops on and around rotten wood. Late spring–autumn.

PSATHYRELLA CANDOLLEANA

White Brittle-head

An early-fruiting *Psathyrella* species, this is perhaps one of the most common species in the genus, often found in gardens and parks. The yellow-brown caps of *P. candolleana* dry out rapidly to an ivory white, and the threadlike veil disappears, leaving an almost smooth cap. True to its name, this species is extremely brittle when dry. As the spores mature, the gills undergo a change in color, from white, through lilac to brown. This species, formerly known as *Hypholoma incertum* is actually a complex of at least a half a dozen sibling species, that is, morphologically identical but reproductively intersterile populations.

- **SPORE DEPOSIT** Brownish purple.
- **SIZE** Cap 1.5–7cm (w); stem 3–9cm (h) x 0.2–0.6cm (w).
- **HABITAT** Close to rotten deciduous trees, in gardens, parks, and woods.
- **RANGE** Widespread and common in north temperate zones.

PSATHYRELLA MULTIPEDATA

Tufted Brittle-head

This particular species of *Psathyrella*, whose scientific name means "many footed," tends to form highly impressive, compact clusters, usually late in the season and in urban areas. There is no obvious veil, and the stems within a cluster are joined at the base and deeply rooted. The caps are hygrophanous, becoming pale yellow-brown from the center. Young moist caps are brown and striate at least halfway to the center. *P. piluliformis* (see opposite) has broader caps and grows directly on rotten stumps. Other tuft-forming species in open areas include *Lyophyllum* species (see p.99).

■ **SPORE DEPOSIT** Brownish black.
■ **SIZE** Cap 0.8–4cm (w); stem 8–14cm, or as small as 4cm (h) x 0.2–0.4cm (w).
■ **HABITAT** On rich loamy or clay soils, often in urban areas at the side of roads and in parks.
■ **RANGE** Widespread in Europe. In North America reported in the Midwest.

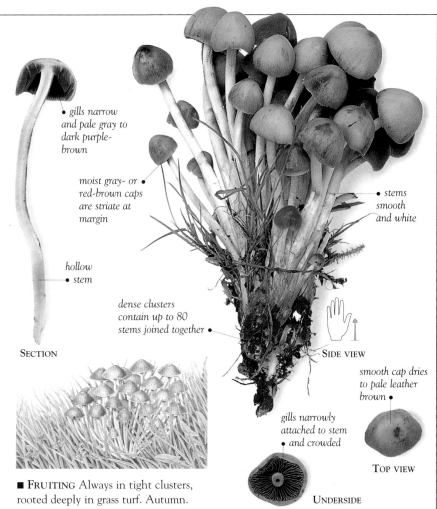

gills narrow and pale gray to dark purple-brown

moist gray- or red-brown caps are striate at margin

hollow stem

SECTION

dense clusters contain up to 80 stems joined together

stems smooth and white

SIDE VIEW

smooth cap dries to pale leather brown

gills narrowly attached to stem and crowded

TOP VIEW

UNDERSIDE

■ **FRUITING** Always in tight clusters, rooted deeply in grass turf. Autumn.

---

conical cap has no veil, but microscopic dark hairs in upper flesh

gills quite crowded and fragile

UNDERSIDE

very tall, fragile stem

gills narrow and gray to black, with whitish edge

stem is hollow inside

often found on woody debris

white stem has touches of cap color near base

SIDE VIEW

SECTION

stem is smooth on the surface

rich dark brown cap dries to a pale yellow-brown

TOP VIEW

SIDE VIEW

■ **FRUITING** In troops or scattered, on soil. Late summer–autumn.

PSATHYRELLA CONOPILUS

Cone Brittle-head

A species of *Psathyrella* known for its tall, elegant stature and its dark, reddish brown cap, which in dry weather dries out to a pale ocher-yellow. The cap is conical in shape, smooth, and striated at the margin. The cap skin and flesh have dark, thick-walled hairs – a unique feature, but visible only with a good hand lens, good lighting, and luck. A number of similar species are smaller, paler, and often have pinkish tinges. All are very thin-fleshed and fragile. *Psathyrella* is a large genus of mostly inconspicuous mushrooms, all looking more or less alike.

■ **SPORE DEPOSIT** Black.
■ **SIZE** Cap 2–6cm (w); stem 9–19cm (h) x 0.2–0.3cm (w); base up to 0.5cm (w).
■ **HABITAT** On disturbed soil, especially among wood chips and debris, along roadsides and paths, and in parks.
■ **RANGE** Widespread in Europe and North America.

BOLBITIACEAE

CLASS: *Homobasidiomycetes*

This family of gilled mushrooms is fairly small but quite diverse. One notable feature is the cap surface, which is made up of rounded cells that cause the skin to crack in dry weather. The spore deposits are a dull clay brown. A veil may also be present, either at the cap margin or as a stem ring. Some species are well known edibles, but a few are highly toxic.

• cap is smooth or cracked, usually without veil remnants at margin

AGROCYBE CYLINDRACEA

Poplar Field-cap

A very fleshy member of the family, this differs from *A. praecox* (*see below*) in size and habit. The stem ring is well developed, and the cap skin often cracks in dry weather, a feature common to most *Agrocybe* species. *A. cylindracea* is cultivated and eaten in southern Europe.

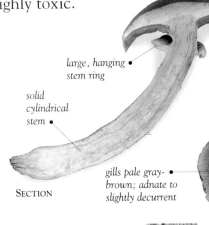

large, hanging • stem ring

solid cylindrical stem •

SECTION

gills pale gray-brown; adnate to slightly decurrent

whitish stem • becomes browner with age

TOP/SIDE VIEW

UNDERSIDE

convex cap is an ocher-tinged shade of white

• stem slightly striated, even more so above ring

SIDE VIEW

- **SPORE DEPOSIT** Clay brown.
- **SIZE** Cap 6–15cm (w); stem 8–15cm (h) x 1–3cm (w).
- **HABITAT** On or inside dead willows and poplar trees.
- **RANGE** Widespread in warm north temperate to subtropical zones, and reported in southeastern US.

■ **FRUITING** Mostly in tufts or singly on dead wood. Late spring–autumn.

• cap brown when wet, drying to a pale ocher

hanging • stem ring stained by brown spores

striations • along stem

SIDE VIEW

flesh white to buff in color •

adnexed • to adnate gills have a decurrent tooth

SECTION

stem slender • and fairly solid

• ring still attached to cap margin

SECTION

stem slightly swollen at base •

SIDE VIEW

■ **FRUITING** In small groups on soil, in grass, or on wood chips. Spring–summer.

AGROCYBE PRAECOX

Spring Wood Chip Field Cap

This highly variable fungus can be eaten, but it often has an unpleasant bitter taste. It usually has a stem ring, and sometimes the veil is attached to the cap margin. It is hygrophanous and dries quickly to a uniform, yellowish gray-white. The stem base may be swollen. *Agrocybe dura* fruits in spring in grassy areas and lacks a well-developed ring.

- **SPORE DEPOSIT** Tobacco brown.
- **SIZE** Cap 3–7cm, up to 14cm (w); stem 4–10cm (h) x 0.6–1cm (w).
- **HABITAT** Among rotting wood chips; in woods, parklands, and lawns.
- **RANGE** Widespread and common in north temperate zones.

ocher-yellow cap becomes slightly greasy in wet weather

grows in grass turf

SIDE VIEW

gills adnate

gills well spaced with whitish edge

stem cylindrical, solid, and straight

stem surface has a few fine hairs

UNDERSIDE   **SECTION**

■ **FRUITING** In troops in grassy areas. Summer–autumn.

AGROCYBE PEDIADES

Lawn Cap

Fairly nondescript in appearance, this fungus fruits in the early summer months. It is normally completely smooth – it lacks a veil – with a gently convex, yellowish ocher cap. According to some experts, *A. pediades* can be divided into several species, defined mainly according to spore size and habitat. Rarely, a veil and ring will develop on some specimens, and some others may never develop spores.

■ **SPORE DEPOSIT** Tobacco brown.
■ **SIZE** Cap 1–3.5cm (w); stem 2.5–5cm (h) x 0.3–0.5cm (w).
■ **HABITAT** Typically grows in lawns and other types of grassy areas, but can also grow on manured mulch.
■ **RANGE** Widespread and common in north temperate zones.

CONOCYBE LACTEA

Milky Cone Cap

Most *Conocybe* species are difficult to tell apart without the aid of a microscope. *C. lactea* stands out because of its very elongated cap and ivory coloring. Together with *Agrocybe pediades* and *Panaeolina foenisecii*, these three are our most conspicuous late spring lawn fungi.

■ **SPORE DEPOSIT** Orange-brown.
■ **SIZE** Cap 1–2.2cm (h) x 1–1.5cm (w); stem 5–11cm (h) x 0.01–0.03cm (w).
■ **HABITAT** In grass on good soils, scattered in great numbers; disappears by mid-day.
■ **RANGE** Widespread and common in north temperate zones; northern North America, Gulf Coast, California.

■ **FRUITING** In troops in wet grass, after summer rains. Summer–autumn.

elongated cap ivory white in color

cap finely striate toward margin when moist

gills adnexed at first, becoming free

smooth cap surface wrinkles slightly with age

SIDE VIEW

very slender stem, hollow and fragile

ivory white stem has faint striations

SECTION   **SIDE VIEW**

CONOCYBE PERCINCTA

Deadly Conocybe Complex ☠

One group of *Conocybe*, often separated as *Pholiotina*, has veil remnants in the form of scales at the cap margin or as stem rings, and many species contain deadly amatoxins. *C. percincta* is a poisonous group member with a movable, easily lost stem ring.

■ **SPORE DEPOSIT** Rusty brown.
■ **SIZE** Cap 0.5–1.2cm (w); stem 3–5cm (h) x 0.1–0.15cm (w).
■ **HABITAT** On rich, disturbed soil.
■ **RANGE** Widespread but exact distribution not known.

■ **FRUITING** Singly or a few together on rich black soil. Throughout autumn.

STROPHARIACEAE

CLASS: *Homobasidiomycetes*

Species in *Strophariaceae* have microscopic threadlike cells in their cap skin. All have either brownish, purplish brown, or black spores. Those in the genus *Stropharia* often have bright colors and a slimy cap, whereas *Psilocybe* species (*see p.156*) tend to be duller. Several species have mild to strong hallucinogenic properties.

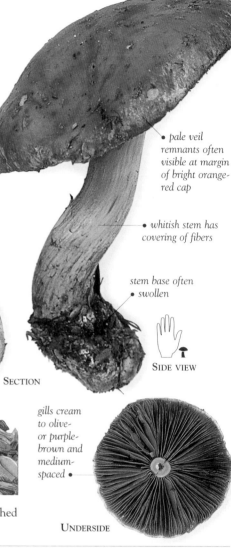

- pale veil remnants often visible at margin of bright orange-red cap
- whitish stem has covering of fibers
- stem base often swollen

SIDE VIEW

STROPHARIA AURANTIACA

Red Slime-head

This distinctive species is best identified by the sturdy, red-capped fruitbodies and its occurrence on wood chips. *Psilocybe squamosa* var. *thrausta*, sometimes considered a *Stropharia* species, has similar coloring and thinner flesh.

- **Spore Deposit** Purplish brown.
- **Size** 1.5–6cm (w); stem 2–6cm (h) x 0.2–0.8cm (w).
- **Habitat** Mostly on decaying wood chips or sawdust mixed with soil.
- **Range** Widespread and currently spreading in Europe; reported from California.

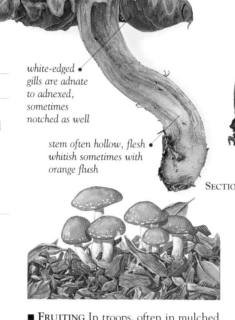

- white-edged gills are adnate to adnexed, sometimes notched as well
- stem often hollow, flesh whitish sometimes with orange flush

SECTION

- gills cream to olive- or purple-brown and medium-spaced

UNDERSIDE

- **Fruiting** In troops, often in mulched flowerbeds. Summer–autumn.

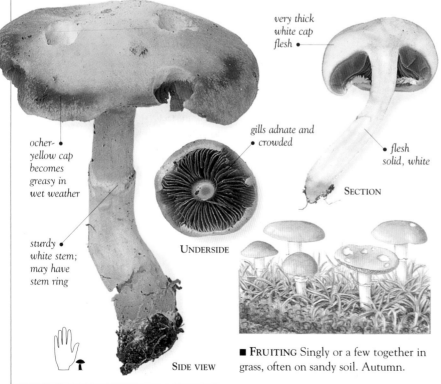

- ocher-yellow cap becomes greasy in wet weather
- sturdy white stem; may have stem ring

SIDE VIEW

- very thick white cap flesh
- gills adnate and crowded

UNDERSIDE

- flesh solid, white

SECTION

- **Fruiting** Singly or a few together in grass, often on sandy soil. Autumn.

STROPHARIA CORONILLA

Garland Slime-head

This fairly small but sturdy gilled mushroom has a very dark spore deposit and a thick, narrow stem ring. The gills are whitish to violet-gray turning dark purple-brown. The white cap flesh is extremely thick. Recent reports suggest it could be poisonous. Fruitbodies with different spores have been separated as distinct species.

- **Spore Deposit** Dark purplish brown.
- **Size** Cap 1.5–6cm (w); stem 2.5–4cm, sometimes up to 5cm (h) x 0.4–1cm (w).
- **Habitat** Common in grassy areas in drier situations, including gardens, parks, and sand dunes.
- **Range** Widespread in north temperate zones.

STROPHARIA SEMIGLOBATA

Dung Slime-head

In common with many of its close relatives, this species has a greasy cap when wet and a tiny, often inconspicuous stem ring, which is often stained black by deposited spores. The overall appearance is rather elegant, with a long, slender stem that is also slimy and a smooth, often hemispherical cap and stem. It is one of a range of fungi that grow on herbivore dung at different stages of decay. *S. semiglobata* prefers old dung in open sites.

- **SPORE DEPOSIT** Brownish black.
- **SIZE** Cap 0.5–4cm, up to 6cm (w); stem 2–8cm, up to 10cm (h) x 0.2–0.5cm (w).
- **HABITAT** On all kinds of dung but mainly found on horse, cow, and sheep manure, in grassy areas and pastures.
- **RANGE** Widespread in north temperate zones and elsewhere.

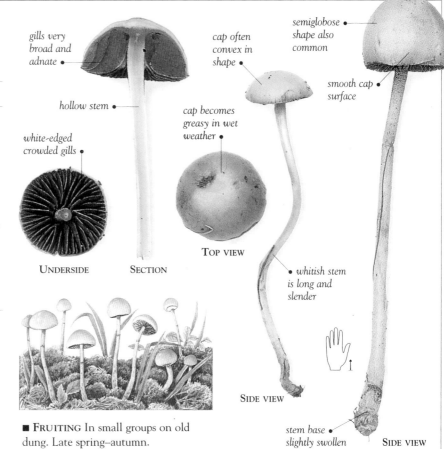

- gills very broad and adnate
- hollow stem
- white-edged crowded gills
- cap often convex in shape
- cap becomes greasy in wet weather
- semiglobose shape also common
- smooth cap surface

UNDERSIDE   **SECTION**

TOP VIEW

- whitish stem is long and slender

SIDE VIEW

- stem base slightly swollen

SIDE VIEW

- **FRUITING** In small groups on old dung. Late spring–autumn.

STROPHARIA CYANEA

Blue-green Slime-head

There are several species of *Stropharia* with blue-green colors. This particular one has a fairly pale brown spore deposit and gills that are not edged with white. The very similar *S. aeruginosa* has darker spores and gills and a white gill edge. *S. pseudocyanea* has a distinct smell of freshly ground black pepper.

- **SPORE DEPOSIT** Dark tobacco brown.
- **SIZE** Cap 3–7cm (w); stem 4–8cm (h) x 0.4–1cm (w).
- **HABITAT** Mostly among leaf litter; often found in beech woods in Europe on calcareous soils.
- **RANGE** As a complex, widespread in north temperate zones.

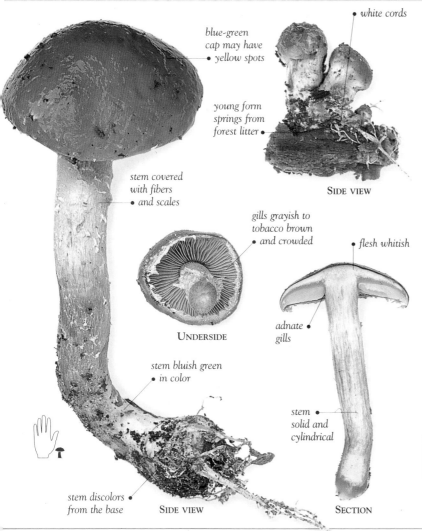

- blue-green cap may have yellow spots
- white cords
- young form springs from forest litter
- stem covered with fibers and scales
- gills grayish to tobacco brown and crowded
- flesh whitish
- adnate gills
- stem bluish green in color
- stem solid and cylindrical
- stem discolors from the base

UNDERSIDE

SIDE VIEW

SIDE VIEW

SECTION

- **FRUITING** In small groups or singly, among forest leaf litter. Autumn.

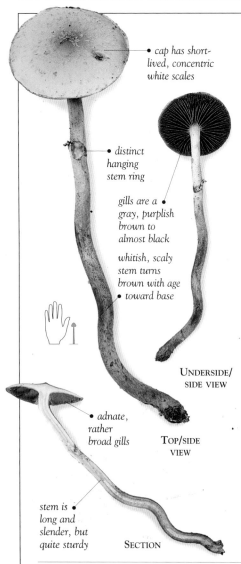

- cap has short-lived, concentric white scales
- distinct hanging stem ring
- gills are a gray, purplish brown to almost black
- whitish, scaly stem turns brown with age toward base

UNDERSIDE/SIDE VIEW

- adnate, rather broad gills

TOP/SIDE VIEW

stem is long and slender, but quite sturdy

SECTION

PSILOCYBE SQUAMOSA

Scaly-stalked Psilocybe

Its similarity to some *Stropharia* species (*see p.154*) indicates the close relationship between these two genera, sometimes lumped together as a single genus. A northern North American variant with a brick-red cap is called *P. thrausta*. Neither is known to be either edible or poisonous.

- ■ **SPORE DEPOSIT** Purple-brown.
- ■ **SIZE** Cap 2–5cm (w); stem 10–15cm (h) x 0.3–0.5cm (w).
- ■ **HABITAT** In woods and forests, springing from buried or half-buried wood chips or sawdust.
- ■ **RANGE** Widespread and fairly common in the north temperate zones.

■ **FRUITING** In small groups or single fruitbodies, on wood debris. Autumn.

PSILOCYBE CAERULIPES

Blue-footed Liberty Cap ☠

This easily overlooked little brown mushroom is a woodland wood decomposer whose claim to fame is its psyhcoactivity. Its cap margin and stem base bruise blue or greenish blue, a sign in gill mushrooms that they probably contain psilocybin or a related indole alkaloid. Although hallucinogenic, it rarely occurs in collectible amounts.

- ■ **SPORE DEPOSIT** Dark purplish brown.
- ■ **SIZE** Cap 2.5–10cm (w); stem 3–6cm (h) x 0.2–0.4cm (w).
- ■ **HABITAT** On rotten wood or wood chips in woods and parks.
- ■ **RANGE** Eastern North America.

■ **FRUITING** In troops or clusters of fruitbodies on wood debris. Autumn.

PSILOCYBE CYANESCENS

Blue-rimmed Liberty Cap ☠

A hallucinogenic species that discolors a distinct dark blue where handled, especially at the cap margin. The hygrophanous cap becomes greasy in wet weather and often has a wavy, flat shape. Frequently joined at the bases, the whitish stems stain blue and have no ring. The gills are adnate and fairly well spaced. It is readily dispersed by transporting wood chip mulch.

- ■ **SPORE DEPOSIT** Dark purplish brown.
- ■ **SIZE** Cap 2–4cm (w); stem 3–6cm (h) x 0.3–0.8cm (w).
- ■ **HABITAT** Mostly found in disturbed sites, such as flower-bed mulch that contains wood chips, preferably made from conifers.
- ■ **RANGE** Widespread but rather local, in the north temperate zones.

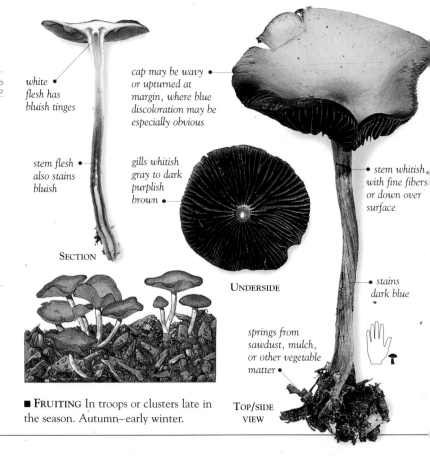

- white flesh has bluish tinges
- cap may be wavy or upturned at margin, where blue discoloration may be especially obvious
- stem flesh also stains bluish
- gills whitish gray to dark purplish brown

SECTION

UNDERSIDE

- stem whitish with fine fibers or down over surface
- stains dark blue

springs from sawdust, mulch, or other vegetable matter

TOP/SIDE VIEW

■ **FRUITING** In troops or clusters late in the season. Autumn–early winter.

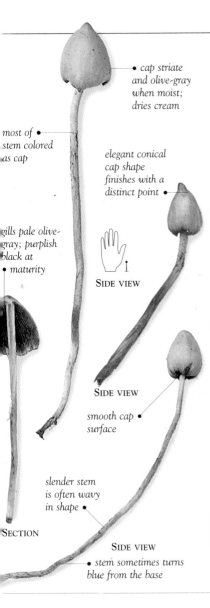

- cap striate and olive-gray when moist; dries cream

- most of stem colored as cap

elegant conical cap shape finishes with a distinct point •

gills pale olive-gray; purplish black at • maturity

SIDE VIEW

SIDE VIEW

smooth cap • surface

slender stem is often wavy in shape •

SECTION

SIDE VIEW

• stem sometimes turns blue from the base

PSILOCYBE SEMILANCEATA

Liberty Cap ☠

This is a relatively weak hallucinogenic mushroom in northwestern North America, where it is common in pastureland. It grows in and about clumps of tall grass and is unmistakable by its sharply conic, often nippled cap, whose margin (and stem base) is sometimes tinged green or blue.

- **SPORE DEPOSIT** Purplish black.
- **SIZE** Cap 0.5–2cm (w); stem 4–10cm (h) x 0.2–0.3cm (w).
- **HABITAT** In fertilized grassland, both in densely grazed or mown sites and hidden in deep clumps of grass.
- **RANGE** Widespread and common in the Pacific Northwest.

- **FRUITING** Singly or in large troops in grassland. Summer–autumn.

PSILOCYBE CUBENSIS

San Isidro Liberty Cap ☠

This potent hallucinogen resembles a *Stropharia* (see p.154); it is large, has an umbonate cap, a hanging stem ring, and deep purple-brown gills when mature. It is known as "San Isidro" among the Mazatec Indians.

- **SPORE DEPOSIT** Dark purplish brown.
- **SIZE** Cap 2–12cm (w); stem 5–15cm (h) x 0.5–1.2cm (w).
- **HABITAT** Primarily, on cow dung in subtropical to tropical pastureland, during the wet seasons.
- **RANGE** Caribbean and Gulf coast of US and elsewhere in the tropics.

- **FRUITING** Several or singly on relatively fresh droppings. All year.

HYPHOLOMA CAPNOIDES

Conifer Tuft 🍄

Unlike *H. fasciculare* (see p.158), this species lacks greenish yellow tinges on the gills, which are a pale gray to purplish black. It has a very mild, pleasant taste. It is one of the few gilled mushrooms that can be found almost all year in temperate zones, and always on conifers. Also known as *Naematoloma capnoides*. Some mycologists place *Hypholoma* species, along with *Stropharia*, in the *Psilocybe* genus. It has a rooting stem and a strong, aromatic smell.

- **SPORE DEPOSIT** Wine-brown.
- **SIZE** Cap 3–7cm (w); stem 5–8cm (h) x 0.5–1cm (w).
- **HABITAT** On strongly decayed conifer stumps.
- **RANGE** Widespread and common in north temperate zones.

UNDERSIDE

• gills pale gray to purplish brown, adnate, and crowded

cap greasy and darker in wet weather

TOP VIEW

yellowish to pale orange-brown cap has velar remnants at edge •

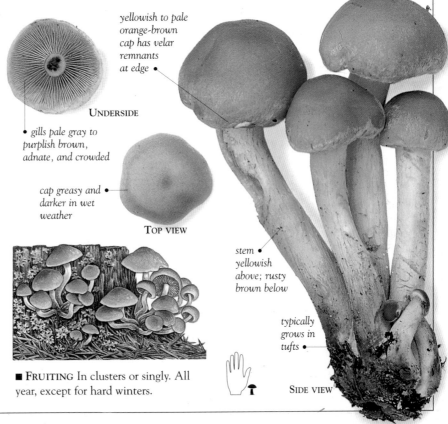

stem yellowish above; rusty brown below

typically grows in tufts •

SIDE VIEW

- **FRUITING** In clusters or singly. All year, except for hard winters.

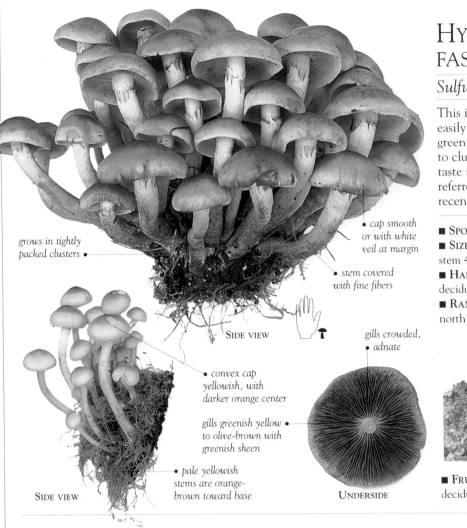

grows in tightly packed clusters •

cap smooth or with white veil at margin •

stem covered with fine fibers •

SIDE VIEW

convex cap yellowish, with darker orange center •

gills greenish yellow to olive-brown with greenish sheen •

pale yellowish stems are orange-brown toward base •

SIDE VIEW

gills crowded, adnate •

UNDERSIDE

HYPHOLOMA FASCICULARE

Sulfur Tuft

This inedible gilled fungus can be easily identified by the mixture of greenish yellow gills and a tendency to cluster on dead wood. The bitter taste is another good mark. Species referred to as *Hypholoma* were, until recently, *Naematolomas*.

■ **SPORE DEPOSIT** Purplish brown.
■ **SIZE** Cap 3–7cm, down to 1cm (w); stem 4–10cm (h) x 0.3–1cm (w).
■ **HABITAT** On rotten wood such as deciduous stumps and upturned roots.
■ **RANGE** Widespread and common in north temperate zones.

■ **FRUITING** In clusters on rotten deciduous wood. Late spring–early winter.

HYPHOLOMA SUBLATERITIUM

Brick Tops

This species of *Hypholoma* is best identified by its large size, the lack of green color in the gills, and the distinct brick red hue of its cap. Compared with *H. fasciculare* (see above), *H. sublateritium* is a milder tasting and popular edible where it is a common fall clustered stump mushroom in eastern North America. A range of much smaller *Hypholoma* species, including *H. udum* and *H. elongatum*, occur in boggy places, sometimes among sphagnum moss, and *H. dispersum* occurs in large troops on needle beds or on the remains of conifers.

■ **SPORE DEPOSIT** Purplish brown.
■ **SIZE** Cap 5–10cm, or down to 3.5cm (w); stem 5–10cm (h) x 0.5–1.5cm (w).
■ **HABITAT** On deciduous stumps or buried roots in woods or parks.
■ **RANGE** Widely distributed in eastern North America.

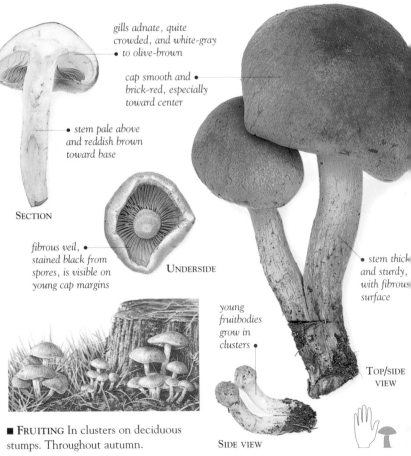

gills adnate, quite crowded, and white-gray to olive-brown •

cap smooth and brick-red, especially toward center •

stem pale above and reddish brown toward base •

SECTION

fibrous veil, stained black from spores, is visible on young cap margins •

UNDERSIDE

stem thick and sturdy, with fibrous surface •

young fruitbodies grow in clusters •

TOP/SIDE VIEW

SIDE VIEW

■ **FRUITING** In clusters on deciduous stumps. Throughout autumn.

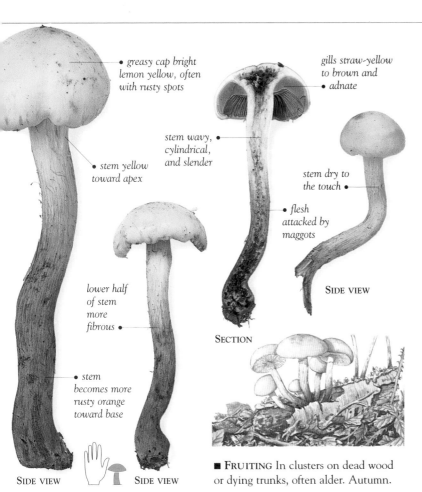

• greasy cap bright
lemon yellow, often
with rusty spots

gills straw-yellow
to brown and
• adnate

• stem yellow
toward apex

stem wavy,
cylindrical,
and slender •

stem dry to
the touch •

• flesh
attacked by
maggots

SIDE VIEW

lower half
of stem
more
fibrous •

SECTION

• stem
becomes more
rusty orange
toward base

SIDE VIEW   SIDE VIEW

■ **FRUITING** In clusters on dead wood
or dying trunks, often alder. Autumn.

PHOLIOTA ALNICOLA

Alder Scale-head

In this and some other *Pholiota*
species, the cap scales are not
particularly conspicuous, but they
can usually be seen more clearly in
young specimens, as veil scales at
the cap margin. The yellow caps –
or yellow with some green
intermixed – and densely tufted
habit are the main distinguishing
features. The stems are almost
smooth. The form that grows on
willows has a bitter taste and is
sometimes separated as *P. salicicola*,
and the coniferous form is also
separated and is known as *P. flavida*.

■ **SPORE DEPOSIT** Brown.
■ **SIZE** Cap 3–7cm, up to 10cm (w);
stem 8–15cm (h) x 0.6–1cm (w).
■ **HABITAT** On dead or dying deciduous
trees, such as alder and birch, rarely on
conifers, and often in damp places.
■ **RANGE** Widespread in north temperate
zones; exact distribution unknown.

PHOLIOTA AURIVELLA

Golden Scale-head

This is part of a large complex of
Pholiotas that is very common in the
fall. The mushrooms have slimy caps
and stems and occur densely clustered
on wood. Many species have been
named, but no reliable criteria
exist for delineating species
in this complex.

■ **SPORE DEPOSIT** Brown.
■ **SIZE** Cap 7–15cm, down to 5cm (w);
stem 8–15cm (h) x 1–2.5cm (w).
■ **HABITAT** On logs, in holes in trees,
and in clusters on deciduous trees.
■ **RANGE** As a complex, widespread
in north temperate zones.

■ **FRUITING** In clusters on mostly living
deciduous trees. Autumn.

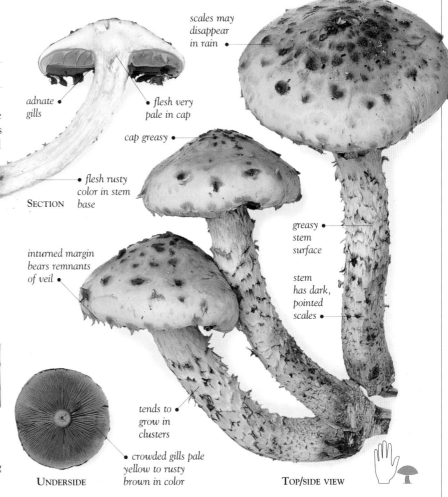

scales may
disappear
in rain •

adnate •
gills

• flesh very
pale in cap

cap greasy •

SECTION

• flesh rusty
color in stem
base

greasy •
stem
surface

inturned margin
bears remnants
of veil •

stem
has dark,
pointed
scales •

tends to •
grow in
clusters

UNDERSIDE

• crowded gills pale
yellow to rusty
brown in color

TOP/SIDE VIEW

PHOLIOTA SQUARROSA

Shaggy Dry Scale-head ☠

The dense, upturned scales on both cap and stem make it difficult to mistake this dry-skinned *Pholiota* species. It will fruit in dense tufts year after year on old deciduous trees, often the same aspen or birch. The similar but smaller and paler *P. squarrosoides* also occurs on deciduous trees. It also differs in being highly viscid beneath the scales. *P squarrosa*, especially populations with a distinct garlicky odor, is known to cause gastric upsets if eaten often or with alcohol. An eastern North American look-alike is *Floccularia (Armillaria) decorosa*.

- ■ **SPORE DEPOSIT** Brown.
- ■ **SIZE** Cap 5–15cm (w); stem 6–15cm (h) x 1–2cm (w).
- ■ **HABITAT** At the base of living deciduous trees or on stumps.
- ■ **RANGE** Widespread in north temperate zones, particularly North America.

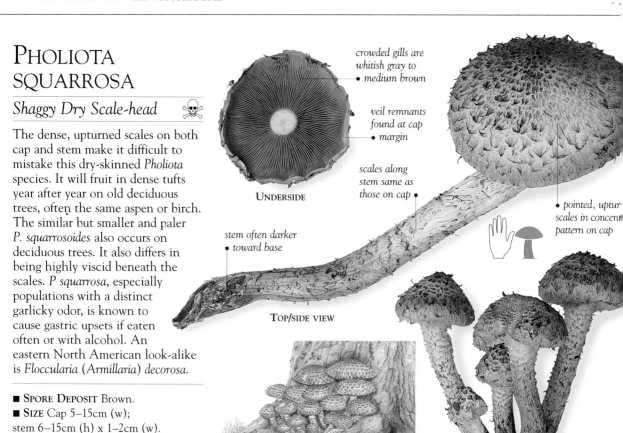

crowded gills are whitish gray to medium brown

veil remnants found at cap margin

scales along stem same as those on cap

UNDERSIDE

stem often darker toward base

TOP/SIDE VIEW

pointed, uptur scales in concent pattern on cap

grows in dense clusters

SIDE VIEW

- ■ **FRUITING** In clusters around living trees or stumps. Autumn–early winter.

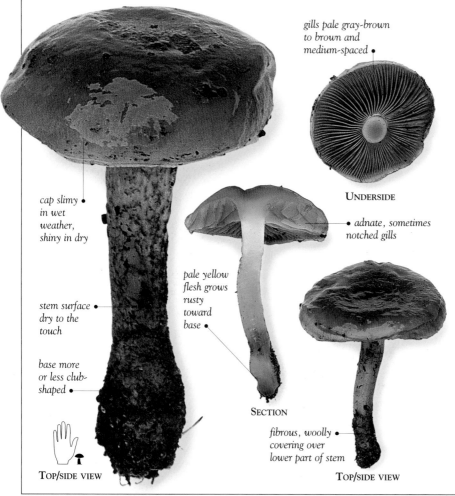

cap slimy in wet weather, shiny in dry

stem surface dry to the touch

base more or less club-shaped

TOP/SIDE VIEW

pale yellow flesh grows rusty toward base

SECTION

fibrous, woolly covering over lower part of stem

TOP/SIDE VIEW

gills pale gray-brown to brown and medium-spaced

UNDERSIDE

adnate, sometimes notched gills

PHOLIOTA HIGHLANDENSIS

Charcoal Scale-head

This inedible gilled mushroom is notable not only for favoring bonfire sites, but also for having a fairly fleshy orange-brown fruitbody with a slimy cap, especially in wet weather. Other gilled mushrooms found on bonfire sites are, on the whole, smaller.

- ■ **SPORE DEPOSIT** Brown.
- ■ **SIZE** Cap 2–6cm (w); stem 2–6cm (h) x 0.4–1cm (w).
- ■ **HABITAT** On bonfire sites or in woods where a fire has occurred.
- ■ **RANGE** Widespread in north temperate zones.

- ■ **FRUITING** In swarms or small clusters on old bonfire sites. Almost all year.

PHOLIOTA GUMMOSA

Ocher-green Scale-head

Although *P. gummosa* often seems to be fruiting on soil, it has probably sprung from a piece of wood buried below the soil. Pale ocher-greenish caps, brown gills, and a whitish, scaly stem are its principal field marks. It is slimy only in wet weather.

- **SPORE DEPOSIT** Brown.
- **SIZE** Cap 2–6cm (w); stem 4–9cm (h) x 0.4–1cm (w).
- **HABITAT** Often along roadsides, mostly from woody sources underground.
- **RANGE** Widespread in north temperate zones; not reported in North America.

- **FRUITING** Often in large troops or clusters on disturbed soil. Autumn.

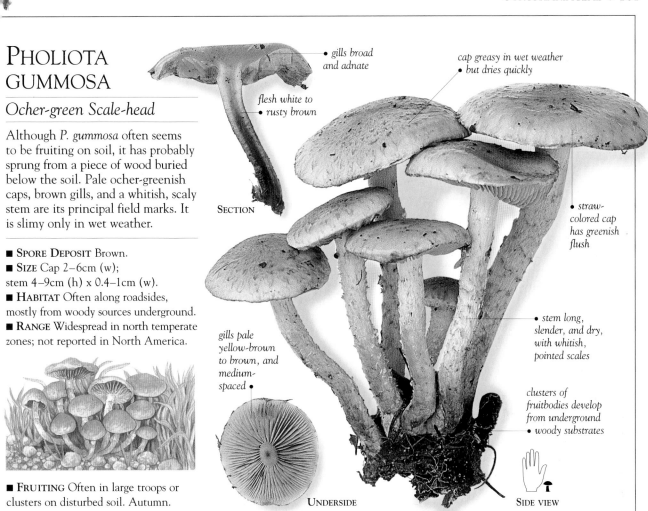

gills broad and adnate

flesh white to rusty brown

SECTION

cap greasy in wet weather but dries quickly

straw-colored cap has greenish flush

stem long, slender, and dry, with whitish, pointed scales

clusters of fruitbodies develop from underground woody substrates

gills pale yellow-brown to brown, and medium-spaced

UNDERSIDE

SIDE VIEW

---

cap whitish, grayish or yellowish

cap margin turned slightly inward with inconspicuous veil remnants

stem mealy at top, with scaly, fibrous covering

base of stem often club-shaped

gills yellowish to brown and fairly crowded

springs from woody debris in leaf litter

SIDE VIEW

UNDERSIDE

gills adnate and notched to slightly decurrent

SECTION

rust-colored flesh at stem base

cap very slimy in wet weather

TOP VIEW

PHOLIOTA LENTA

Beech-litter Scale-head

The pale yellowish gills and greasy cap are good indicators to help identify this inedible species. The greenish components of *P. gummosa* (*see above*) are lacking, and the cap is normally totally smooth.

- **SPORE DEPOSIT** Brown.
- **SIZE** Cap 4–8cm (w); stem 5–8cm (h) x 0.7–1.2cm (w).
- **HABITAT** On woody debris among leaf litter, typically in deciduous woods but also in mixed woods under conifers; mostly from woody sources underground.
- **RANGE** Widespread in north temperate zones.

- **FRUITING** Singly or in small groups among leaf litter. Late autumn.

CREPIDOTACEAE

CLASS: *Homobasidiomycetes*

These brown-spored gilled mushrooms, often resemble small oyster mushrooms (*see p78*), and are all associated with dead plant remains. Unlike many *Cortinariaceae* (*see p.163*), they never form mycorrhizal associations. Opinions differ over what to include in the family, and some have abandoned it, combining it with *Cortinariaceae*.

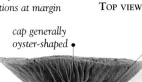

cap is hygrophanous

greasy cap surface in wet conditions

dries out paler from center

wet cap shows clear striations at margin

TOP VIEW

CREPIDOTUS MOLLIS

Soft Slipper Toadstool

Unlike many, mostly smaller, *Crepidotus* species, C. mollis has gelatinous cap skin and gelatinous underlying flesh. It is hygrophanous, with a striate cap margin when wet. A closely related species, C. calolepis, has brownish scales toward the point where the fungus is attached to its deciduous substrate.

■ **SPORE DEPOSIT** Tobacco brown.
■ **SIZE** Fan-shaped cap 2–7cm (w).
■ **HABITAT** On dead deciduous trunks, for example, elm, ash, and beech.
■ **RANGE** Widespread in north temperate zones.

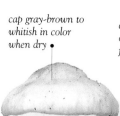

cap gray-brown to whitish in color when dry

SIDE VIEW

cap generally oyster-shaped

gills pale gray-brown and medium-spaced

SIDE VIEW

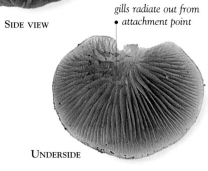

gills radiate out from attachment point

UNDERSIDE

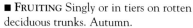

■ **FRUITING** Singly or in tiers on rotten deciduous trunks. Autumn.

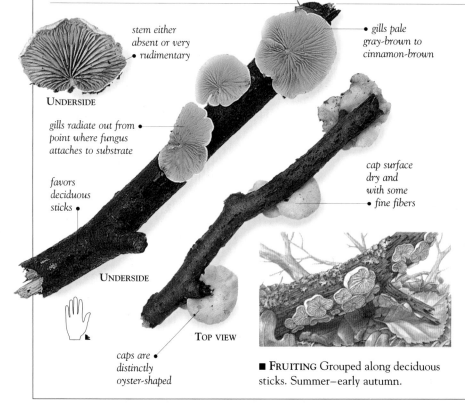

stem either absent or very rudimentary

UNDERSIDE

gills radiate out from point where fungus attaches to substrate

favors deciduous sticks

UNDERSIDE

TOP VIEW

caps are distinctly oyster-shaped

gills pale gray-brown to cinnamon-brown

cap surface dry and with some fine fibers

■ **FRUITING** Grouped along deciduous sticks. Summer–early autumn.

CREPIDOTUS VARIABILIS

Varied Slipper

This species is one of several small, whitish oysterlike fungi with tobacco brown spores. They are best distinguished by spore characteristics that can only be seen with the aid of a microscope. The most distinctive species in the genus is C. cinnabarinus, which has a cinnabar-red cap; it occurs in eastern North America, but it is rarely reported.

■ **SPORE DEPOSIT** Tobacco brown.
■ **SIZE** Fan-shaped cap 0.5–3cm (w); stem absent or rudimentary.
■ **HABITAT** On deciduous sticks, often among brush piles in damp forests.
■ **RANGE** Widespread and common in north temperate zones; in North America from the Midwest west.

CORTINARIACEAE

CLASS: *Homobasidiomycetes*

The large number of different forms in this huge family has made it extremely difficult to name species in many of the genera. *Cortinariaceae* consists of both agarics that have mycorrhizal associations with trees – including *Inocybe*, *Hebeloma*, *Rozites*, and *Cortinarius* – and those without such relationships, such as *Galerina* and *Gymnopilus*. Almost all members have rusty brown spores.

distinct striations on cap extend almost to center •

• smooth stem is a translucent yellow-brown

• flesh very thin and brownish

cap honey-brown and smooth •

stem • extremely long and thin

SIDE VIEW

• stem color darkest toward base

CAP SECTION

SIDE VIEW   SIDE VIEW

GALERINA CALYPTRATA

Tiny Pixie Cap

A slender species, with honey brown coloring and a striate cap. It is found rooting in moss tussocks. G. *calyptrata* can be reliably differentiated from G. *hypnorum* by spore characters. G. *sphagnosum* grows in sphagnum moss and has a ring zone on the stem.

■ **SPORE DEPOSIT** Ocher-brown.
■ **SIZE** Cap 0.3–0.8cm, up to 1.5cm (w); stem 3–4cm (h) x 0.1–0.2cm (w).
■ **HABITAT** On moss in lawns or in damp forests on sphagnum moss.
■ **RANGE** Widespread, but not reported in North America.

gills pale brown and rather widely spaced •

UNDERSIDE

TOP VIEW

• hygrophanous cap tiny and convex in shape

found growing only in tussocks of moss •

■ **FRUITING** Singly or in small groups on mossy ground. Summer–autumn.

---

stem has ring toward top and is fibrous, but not scaly, below •

rich brown hygrophanous cap dries to a pale yellow-brown •

gills pale gray to rust-brown, and medium-spaced •

• may be joined at stem bases

UNDERSIDE

grows in swarms • on deciduous trees

SIDE VIEW

■ **FRUITING** Mostly in dense swarms on dead wood. Summer–winter.

GALERINA UNICOLOR

Deadly Galerina Complex ☠

This *Galerina* complex looks similar to the edible *Kuehneromyces mutabilis* (*see p.164*), but has no scales below the stem ring. This complex is also a deadly look-alike for the Honey Mushroom complex, *Armillaria mellea* (*see p.98*), but produces a brown rather than a white spore print. G. *autumnalis*, G. *marginata*, and G. *venenata* contain deadly amatoxins and can cause fatalities.

■ **SPORE DEPOSIT** Rust-brown.
■ **SIZE** Cap 1–5cm, sometimes up to 7cm (w); stem 3–7cm (h) x 0.3–0.7cm, sometimes up to 1cm (w).
■ **HABITAT** As a complex on rotten stumps and trunks in mixed woods.
■ **RANGE** As a complex, widespread in north temperate zones.

cap umbonate;
honey brown to
leathery yellow

stem dark and scaly
below ring, paler
and smooth above

springs in clusters from
rotten deciduous trees

gills decurrent

pale brown,
aromatic flesh

medium-
spaced gills

SIDE VIEW

SECTION   UNDERSIDE

cap typically
two-toned, drying
from center
(hygrophanous)

TOP VIEW

KUEHNEROMYCES MUTABILIS

Two-toned Wood-tuft

The strongly hygrophanous cap gives this species its two-tone appearance. Pointed stem scales are another mark, found below a ring often stained brown from spores. Care is needed to avoid confusion with deadly *Galerina* species such as *G. unicolor* (see p.163). This species is also placed by some in *Pholiota* and *Galerina*.

- **SPORE DEPOSIT** Ocher-brown.
- **SIZE** Cap 2–7cm (w); stem 3–7cm, up to 10cm (h) x 0.4–1cm (w).
- **HABITAT** On rotten deciduous trees and also on conifers deep in woods.
- **RANGE** Widespread and common in western North America.

- **FRUITING** In dense troops of individual clusters, on dead wood. Almost all year.

GYMNOPILUS PENETRANS

Freckled Gym

A fairly uniformly orange-brown species with distinct rusty flecks on the gills. It can be confused with *Gymnopilus picreus*, which has a darker stem and much more vivid yellow gills. Some authors prefer to divide the species into two additional species, *G. hybridus* and *G. sapineus*. All species in the genus occur on both deciduous and conifer dead wood or dead plant remains, unlike related species of *Cortinarius* (see pp.166–173) where all species live in mycorrhizal association with living trees.

- **SPORE DEPOSIT** Rust-brown.
- **SIZE** Cap 3–8cm (w); stem 4–7cm (h) x 0.4–1cm (w).
- **HABITAT** On dead conifer and deciduous trees in woods and parks.
- **RANGE** Widespread in north temperate zones.

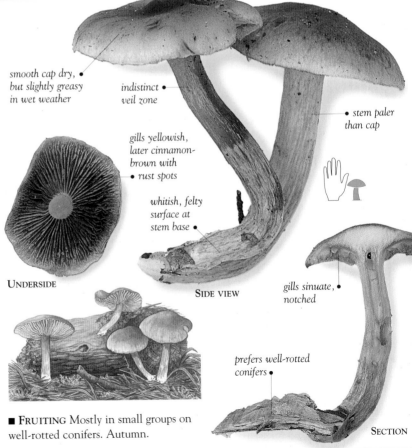

smooth cap dry,
but slightly greasy
in wet weather

indistinct
veil zone

stem paler
than cap

gills yellowish,
later cinnamon-
brown with
rust spots

whitish, felty
surface at
stem base

UNDERSIDE

SIDE VIEW

gills sinuate,
notched

prefers well-rotted
conifers

SECTION

- **FRUITING** Mostly in small groups on well-rotted conifers. Autumn.

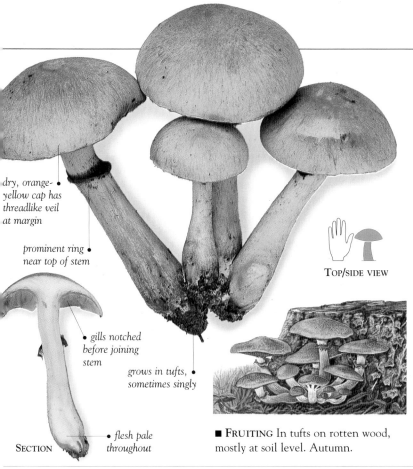

dry, orange-yellow cap has threadlike veil at margin

prominent ring near top of stem

 TOP/SIDE VIEW

gills notched before joining stem

grows in tufts, sometimes singly

SECTION

flesh pale throughout

■ **FRUITING** In tufts on rotten wood, mostly at soil level. Autumn.

GYMNOPILUS SPECTABILIS

Big Laughing Gym

This striking species complex is distinguised by growing in tufts on wood. Some species in this complex also bruise greenish. This large, fleshy *Gymnopilus* species complex is intensely bitter and contains hallucinogens. *Phaeolepiota aurea* (*see p.121*) resembles this complex in size and color but occurs on soil. Another look-alike, *Armillaria mellea* (*see p.98*), produces a white spore print.

■ **SPORE DEPOSIT** Rust-orange.
■ **SIZE** Cap 5–15cm (w); stem 5–15cm (h) x 1–3.5cm (w).
■ **HABITAT** On rotten or dying deciduous trees or stumps.
■ **RANGE** As a complex, widespread in north temperate zones.

CORTINARIUS CINNAMOMEUS

Cinnamon Cort

Similar to *C. semisanguineus* (*see right*) seen from above, the gill color of this species differs markedly if it is viewed from below. *C. cinnamomeus* has orangish gills that turn rusty or cinnamon-brown from maturing spores. *C. cinnamomeus* is a term used in North America covering a number of species that are extremely hard to differentiate.

■ **SPORE DEPOSIT** Rust-brown.
■ **SIZE** Cap 2–5cm (w); stem 2–7cm (h) x 0.5–1cm (w).
■ **HABITAT** Mycorrhizal association with both deciduous trees and conifers.
■ **RANGE** Widespread in north temperate zones.

■ **FRUITING** In troops under trees, with which it forms mycorrhiza. Autumn.

CORTINARIUS SEMISANGUINEUS

Red-gilled Cort

Species of *Cortinarius* with bright red or yellow coloring are classified separately as a group called *Dermocybe*. Although none of these should be eaten, most are excellent sources of fabric dye. *C. semisanguineus* is best told by its yellow-cinnamon to orange-brown cap and stalk and bloodred gills. *C. sanguineus* has bloodred cap, stalk, and gills.

■ **SPORE DEPOSIT** Rust-brown.
■ **SIZE** Cap 2–7cm (w); stem 4–10cm (h) x 0.5–1cm (w).
■ **HABITAT** Exclusively found under, and forming mycorrhiza with conifers; rarely reported in purely deciduous woods.
■ **RANGE** Widespread in north temperate zones.

■ **FRUITING** In troops under conifers, often on moss tussocks. Autumn.

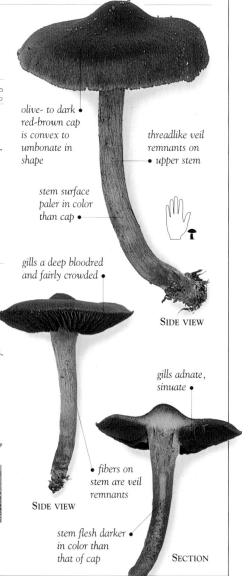

olive- to dark red-brown cap is convex to umbonate in shape

threadlike veil remnants on upper stem

stem surface paler in color than cap

gills a deep bloodred and fairly crowded

SIDE VIEW

gills adnate, sinuate

fibers on stem are veil remnants

SIDE VIEW

stem flesh darker in color than that of cap

SECTION

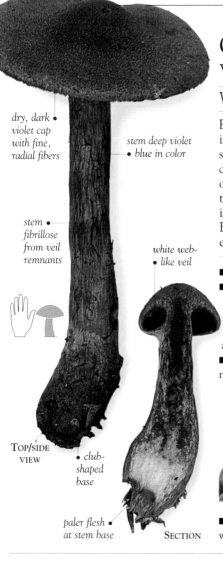

dry, dark violet cap with fine, radial fibers

stem deep violet blue in color

stem fibrillose from veil remnants

white web-like veil

TOP/SIDE VIEW

club-shaped base

paler flesh at stem base

SECTION

CORTINARIUS VIOLACEUS

Violet Cort

Every part of this striking species is a deep violet-blue except for the spores, which produce a rusty brown deposit. There are two forms, one occurring under deciduous trees and the other under conifers. The latter is also referred to as *C. hercynicus*. Both are locally common and edible, but not recommended.

■ **SPORE DEPOSIT** Rusty brown.
■ **SIZE** Cap 6–15cm (w); stem 6–14cm (h) x 1–2.5cm (w).
■ **HABITAT** In damp woods, forming mycorrhiza with both deciduous and coniferous trees.
■ **RANGE** Widespread but local in north temperate zones.

■ **FRUITING** In small groups in damp woods or by bogs. Summer–autumn.

CORTINARIUS ORELLANUS

Deadly Cort

A red-brown species with a strongly fibrillose, umbonate cap and reddish gills. The stem has threadlike veil traces but no girdles, unlike its close relative, *C. rubellus* (see p.167). A similar cort in the Pacific Northwest is *C. rainierensis*. This is an extremely deadly fungus, causing severe kidney damage. Symptoms typically appear a long time after eating.

■ **SPORE DEPOSIT** Rusty brown.
■ **SIZE** Cap 3–6cm, up to 8cm (w); stem 4–9cm (h) x 1–2cm (w).
■ **HABITAT** In acid soils and under oaks.
■ **RANGE** Widespread in warm temperate parts of Europe; absent in North America.

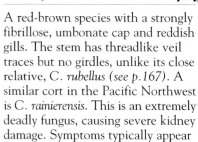

■ **FRUITING** In troops on mostly acid soil, under oaks. Autumn.

CORTINARIUS BOLARIS

Red-dappled Cort

Cortinarius species can be extremely difficult to identify, but *Cortinarius bolaris* has a very distinctive appearance, with its red scales on both cap and stem. It is a fairly short-stemmed, sturdy-looking species and may be quite common in localized areas. The veil is cobweblike and is typical for the genus. Its remains can be seen as fine threads at the cap margin.

■ **SPORE DEPOSIT** Rusty brown.
■ **SIZE** Cap 3–6cm (w); stem 3–6cm (h) x 0.8–1.5cm (w).
■ **HABITAT** In mixed woods on rather acid soils; forms mycorrhizal relationships with deciduous trees, especially with oak and birch.
■ **RANGE** Widespread and locally common in north temperate zones in eastern North America.

broadly convex in shape

cap thick-fleshed

gills gray-brown to cinnamon, with reddish flecks

whitish flesh turns yellow to orange toward stem base

SECTION

red scales and girdles on stem

TOP/SIDE VIEW

cap has f[...] reddish sca[...]

stem paler and smoothe[...] toward apex

TOP/SID[...] VIEW

often occurs on mossy ground

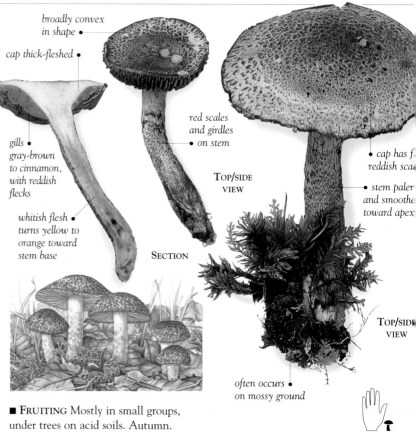

■ **FRUITING** Mostly in small groups, under trees on acid soils. Autumn.

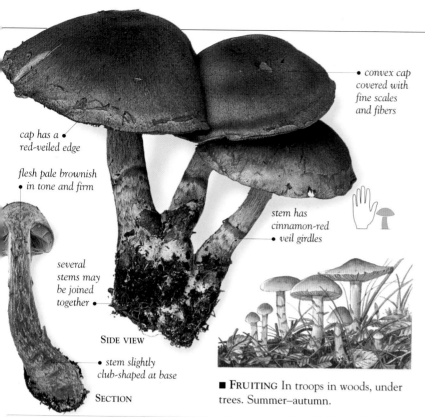

- *convex cap covered with fine scales and fibers*

cap has a red-veiled edge

flesh pale brownish in tone and firm

several stems may be joined together •

SIDE VIEW

stem has cinnamon-red veil girdles •

• *stem slightly club-shaped at base*

SECTION

■ **FRUITING** In troops in woods, under trees. Summer–autumn.

CORTINARIUS ARMILLATUS

Bracelet Cort

This readily identifiable *Cortinarius* species has prominent red veil girdles on its tall, sturdy stem and a large, thick-fleshed cap with fine, orange-brown scales. The slightly smaller *C. paragaudis* (also called *C. haematochelis*) has stem girdles that are more of a dirty red color. It is not associated with birch.

■ **SPORE DEPOSIT** Rusty brown.
■ **SIZE** Cap 5–12cm (w); stem 7–15cm (h) x 1–3cm (w).
■ **HABITAT** Forming mycorrhiza with birch and possibly other trees, in damp woods and boggy places.
■ **RANGE** Widespread and locally common in north temperate zones.

CORTINARIUS PHOLIDEUS

Scaly Cort

The well-marked characteristics of this particular *Cortinarius* species include the violet-colored gills, combined with a scaly cap and brown-girdled stem. Birch is the typical mycorrhizal host, but it may also occur with other trees. The flesh also has violet tinges and has a faint smell reminiscent of fresh tangerines. The cap is more or less convex when young but is flat with a pointed center.

■ **SPORE DEPOSIT** Rusty brown.
■ **SIZE** Cap 3–8cm (w); stem 5–12cm (h) x 0.5–1cm, up to 1.5cm (w).
■ **HABITAT** In mixed woods, favors acid soils, forming mycorrhizal relationships with deciduous trees, especially birches, and some conifers.
■ **RANGE** Widespread and locally common in north temperate zones.

■ **FRUITING** In small groups on mossy, acid soil, often under birches. Autumn.

thin, pointed scales on brownish cap •

fibrous girdles on stem •

gills violet to violet-brown •

• *top of stem often more violet-colored*

TOP/SIDE VIEW

• *solid stem*

cap often fairly pointed •

SECTION   **SIDE VIEW**

CORTINARIUS RUBELLUS

Foxy-orange Cort

A reddish species with veil bands on the stem, a fairly pointed cap, and the typical *Cortinarius* spore color. As deadly as *C. orellaneus*, this has been confused with chanterelles (*see pp.47–48*) in the UK.

■ **SPORE DEPOSIT** Rusty brown.
■ **SIZE** Cap 3–8cm (w); stem 5–11cm (h) x 0.8–1.5cm (w); base up to 2cm (w).
■ **HABITAT** Mycorrhizal with conifers.
■ **RANGE** Widespread and locally common in Europe and parts of Asia.

■ **FRUITING** Singly or in troops on acid soil. Summer–autumn.

CORTINARIUS TORVUS

Sheathed Cort

The stem sheath or "stocking" is a strong identification feature for this species, combined with fairly pale coloring, a very fleshy cap, and widely spaced gills. In Europe, *C. subtorvus* is darker and occurs with willows and *Dryas* in mountain areas.

- **SPORE DEPOSIT** Rusty brown.
- **SIZE** Cap 4–8cm, up to 10cm (w); stem 4–9cm (h) x 0.5–1.5cm (w); stem base up to 2cm (w).
- **HABITAT** Mycorrhizal with beech or pine, on a variety of soils.
- **RANGE** Widespread in Europe and eastern North America.

- **FRUITING** Singly or a few fruitbodies together, among leaf litter. Autumn.

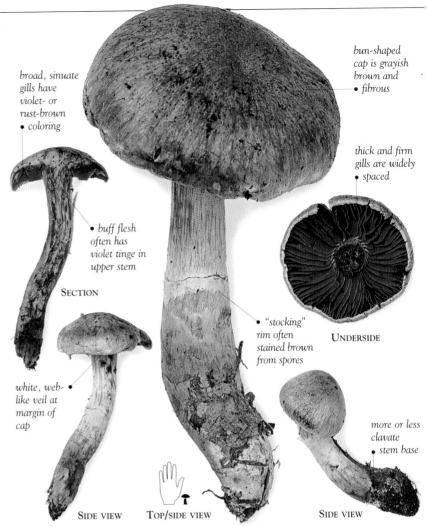

broad, sinuate gills have violet- or rust-brown coloring

bun-shaped cap is grayish brown and fibrous

buff flesh often has violet tinge in upper stem

SECTION

thick and firm gills are widely spaced

UNDERSIDE

white, web-like veil at margin of cap

"stocking" rim often stained brown from spores

more or less clavate stem base

SIDE VIEW   **TOP/SIDE VIEW**   **SIDE VIEW**

CORTINARIUS ALBOVIOLACEUS

Silvery Violet Cort

True to its common name, the entire fruitbody of this species is a silvery violet color – except for the gills and the rusty brown spores, which are often deposited around the veil zone found in the upper part of the stem. This also describes *Sericexybe*, a small subgenus of Corts. *C. malachius* (*see p.171*), grows with conifers and has a slightly scaly cap. *C. camphoratus* and *C. traganus*, also grow with conifers; the former smells like strong cheese, the latter like gas and has a yellow-brown flesh. Another form, *C. pyriodorus*, smells like canned pears.

- **SPORE DEPOSIT** Rust-brown.
- **SIZE** Cap 5–8cm, down to 3cm (w); stem 5–12cm (h) x 1–2cm (w).
- **HABITAT** Mycorrhizal with conifers and deciduous trees, often on acid soil.
- **RANGE** Widespread in eastern North America.

sinuate gills are light gray-blue to cinnamon in color

cap is dry, convex, and silvery violet

flesh is tinged with violet

immature form has button-shaped cap

veil on stem is often stained brown from spores

medium-spaced gills

UNDERSIDE   **SECTION**

stem clavate at base

SIDE VIEW

SIDE VIEW

- **FRUITING** Singly or a small group together, among leaf litter. Autumn.

CORTINARIUS FLEXIPES

Pixy Cort

This is one of a large group of *Cortinarius* species that belong to a subgenus called *Telamonia*. Most of these fungi are small, and they are usually very difficult to identify. *C. flexipes* has no smell, and the slender shape and gray-brown coloring mean that it is easily confused with various other species of *Cortinarius* not included here.

- **SPORE DEPOSIT** Rusty brown.
- **SIZE** Cap 2–4cm (w); stem 5–10cm (h) x 0.4–0.5cm (w).
- **HABITAT** Mycorrhizal with spruce.
- **RANGE** Widespread, reported in northeastern North America.

- **FRUITING** In troops and clusters. Throughout summer–autumn.

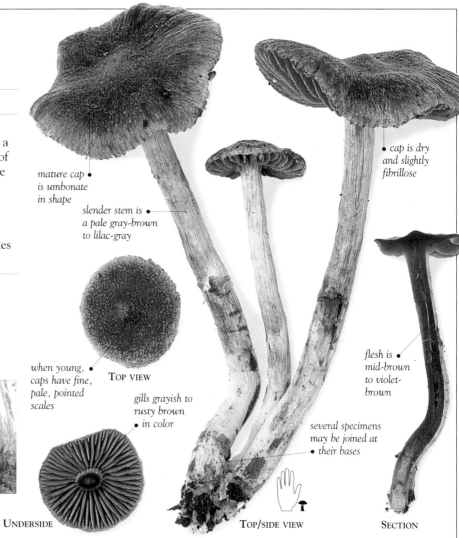

mature cap is umbonate in shape

slender stem is a pale gray-brown to lilac-gray

cap is dry and slightly fibrillose

when young, caps have fine, pale, pointed scales

TOP VIEW

gills grayish to rusty brown in color

flesh is mid-brown to violet-brown

several specimens may be joined at their bases

UNDERSIDE

TOP/SIDE VIEW

SECTION

---

dark brown cap dries much paler

stem may have thin ring, and white veil girdles may be visible

flesh is umber in color

umbonate cap shape

cap dry, with fine, pointed, whitish scales

TOP VIEW

remnants of white veil at cap margin

medium-spaced gills

UNDERSIDE

SIDE VIEW   **SECTION**

- **FRUITING** In troops, often among moss and fallen needles. Summer–autumn.

CORTINARIUS PALEACEUS

Geranium Cort

Although not a distinctive species, this fungus is best told by the fine, pale scales on its rather pointed cap and the fact that it gives off a smell reminiscent of geranium plants. Its edibility is unknown. On some specimens, the scales are almost absent or the margin striated. The gills may be tinged with violet when young, and the stem is girdled with pale veil bands. *Cortinarius hemitrichus* is another very similar species, but it lacks an odor.

- **SPORE DEPOSIT** Rusty brown.
- **SIZE** Cap 1–3cm, up to 5cm (w); stem 4–7cm (h) x 0.3–0.5cm (w).
- **HABITAT** Mycorrhizal and found mainly in damp conifer woods, but also under deciduous trees in a wide range of woodland habitats.
- **RANGE** Reported in eastern N. A. Throughout north temperate zones.

- *orange-yellow cap greasy in wet weather*
- *yellow girdles stained brown by fallen spores*
- *gills gray to blue-white, later brown*

TOP/SIDE VIEW

thick and sturdy stem has pointed base •

SIDE VIEW

CORTINARIUS TRIUMPHANS

Yellow-girdled Cort

A fleshy, impressive species with prominent yellow veil girdles on its sturdy stem. The greasy cap is an attractive yellow color and often has veil remnants at the edge. *C. saginus, C. cliduchus,* and *C. olidus* are similar.

- **SPORE DEPOSIT** Rusty brown.
- **SIZE** Cap 8–15cm (w); stem 10–15cm, down to 5cm (h) x 1–3cm (w).
- **HABITAT** Mycorrhizal with birches, especially among grass in woods and in lawns in gardens and parks.
- **RANGE** Widespread but local in Europe, parts of Asia, and reported in northeastern North America.

- **FRUITING** In troops under birches, among grass. Summer–autumn.

CORTINARIUS CALOCHROUS

Lilac-gilled Cort

This member of the *Phlegmacium* group is best characterized by its small size, lilac gills, mild taste, and stem bulb. It is one of the more distinctive species in this group, where many others lack readily diagnosable differences.

- **SPORE DEPOSIT** Rusty brown.
- **SIZE** Cap 4–6cm (w); stem 3–6cm (h) x 0.6–1cm (w); stem bulb up to 3cm (w).
- **HABITAT** On better soils, often in leaf litter, and mycorrhizal with beeches; some varieties prefer conifers.
- **RANGE** Widespread and locally common in north temperate zones.

- **FRUITING** Singly or a few together under beech trees. Autumn.

CORTINARIUS ANSERINUS

Plum-scented Cort

Typical of beech woodland *Cortinarius*, this fleshy species belongs to the greasy-capped subgenus *Phlegmacium*. It can be confused with *Cortinarius calochrous* (see above), which is smaller and has whitish flesh unlike the lilac stem flesh found in *C. anserinus*. The smell is fruity, reminiscent of plums, and the cap skin has a bitter taste. The flesh is mild tasting. Taste and smell are important characters for identifying *Phlegmacium* although they are best avoided as edibles.

- **SPORE DEPOSIT** Rusty brown.
- **SIZE** Cap 6–12cm (w); stem 6–12cm (h) x 1–2.5cm (w); bulb up to 4cm (w).
- **HABITAT** Mycorrhizal with beech, growing in leaf litter on calcareous soils.
- **RANGE** Widespread and locally common in Europe; not reported in North America.

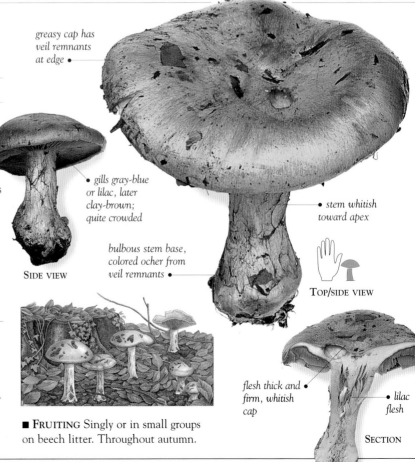

greasy cap has veil remnants at edge •

SIDE VIEW

- *gills gray-blue or lilac, later clay-brown; quite crowded*

bulbous stem base, colored ocher from veil remnants •

• *stem whitish toward apex*

TOP/SIDE VIEW

flesh thick and firm, whitish cap •

• *lilac flesh*

SECTION

- **FRUITING** Singly or in small groups on beech litter. Throughout autumn.

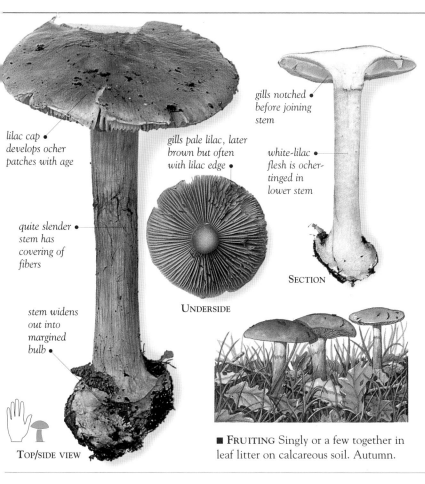

lilac cap develops ocher patches with age

gills pale lilac, later brown but often with lilac edge

gills notched before joining stem

white-lilac flesh is ocher-tinged in lower stem

quite slender stem has covering of fibers

stem widens out into margined bulb

UNDERSIDE

SECTION

TOP/SIDE VIEW

■ **FRUITING** Singly or a few together in leaf litter on calcareous soil. Autumn.

CORTINARIUS SODAGNITUS

Bitter Lilac Cort

Cortinarius sodagnitus is a striking member of the *Phlegmacium* group, with bright violet coloring on both cap and stem. This color does, however, turn to an ocher-buff from the center of the cap as the fungus matures. The stem has a prominent, sharply defined bulb at the base. The cap skin has a bitter taste. The flesh is mild, but it and its relatives cannot be recommended as edibles. *C. dibaphus* is even more colorful and more bitter, and it occurs in Europe under conifers.

■ **SPORE DEPOSIT** Rusty brown.
■ **SIZE** Cap 4–10cm (w); stem 6–10cm (h) x 0.5–1.5cm (w); stem bulb up to 3cm (w).
■ **HABITAT** Mainly associated with beech on calcareous soils.
■ **RANGE** Widespread in north temperate zones; reported in Colorado.

CORTINARIUS MALACHIUS

Blue-buff Cort

Reminiscent of *C. alboviolaceus* (*see p.168*) in stature and in its immature coloring, this species can be told apart by its preference for conifers and by the fact that it soon loses its mauve tones and becomes buffish. A copious white veil also makes the cap more scaly. *C. camphoratus*, also a coniferous species, can be recognized by its smell.

■ **SPORE DEPOSIT** Rusty brown.
■ **SIZE** Cap 4–8cm, up to 12cm (w); stem 5–12cm (h) x 1–2cm (w).
■ **HABITAT** Mycorrhizal with conifers.
■ **RANGE** Widespread but local in Europe; not reported in North America.

■ **FRUITING** In troops on needle beds and moss, under conifers. Autumn.

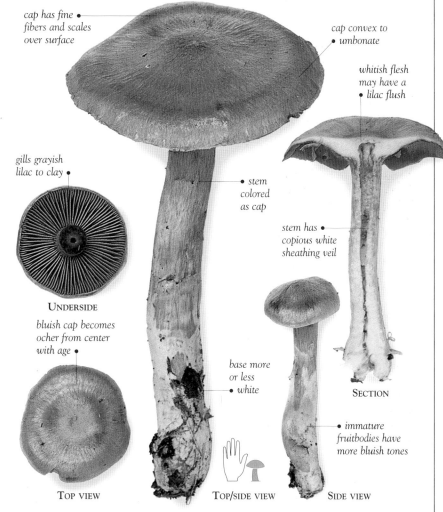

cap has fine fibers and scales over surface

cap convex to umbonate

whitish flesh may have a lilac flush

gills grayish lilac to clay

stem colored as cap

stem has copious white sheathing veil

UNDERSIDE

bluish cap becomes ocher from center with age

base more or less white

SECTION

immature fruitbodies have more bluish tones

TOP VIEW

TOP/SIDE VIEW

SIDE VIEW

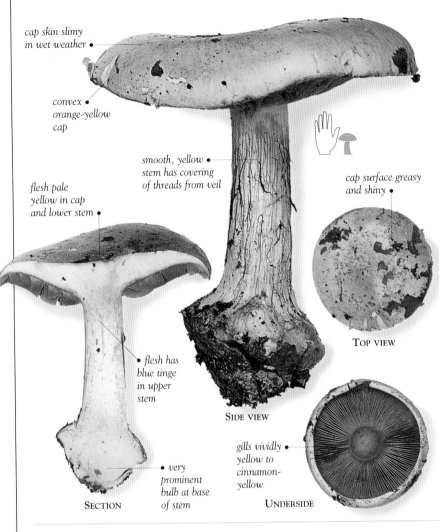

- *cap skin slimy in wet weather*
- *convex orange-yellow cap*
- *smooth, yellow stem has covering of threads from veil*
- *flesh pale yellow in cap and lower stem*
- *flesh has blue tinge in upper stem*

SIDE VIEW

- *very prominent bulb at base of stem*

SECTION

- *cap surface greasy and shiny*

TOP VIEW

- *gills vividly yellow to cinnamon-yellow*

UNDERSIDE

CORTINARIUS ELEGANTISSIMUS

Elegant Cort ☠

Quite similar in some physical ways to C. *splendens* (*see below*), this species is larger, with some blue in the stem flesh and a different smell. It is worth noting that there are also several other *Cortinarius* species with which C. *elegantissimus* could fairly easily be confused.

- ■ **SPORE DEPOSIT** Rusty brown.
- ■ **SIZE** Cap 6–10cm (w); stem 6–10cm (h) x 2–3cm (w); bulb up to 5cm (w).
- ■ **HABITAT** Mycorrhizal with beech trees, on calcareous soils.
- ■ **RANGE** Widespread but local in Europe; not reported in North America.

- ■ **FRUITING** Singly or a few together, in leaf litter on calcareous soil. Autumn.

CORTINARIUS SPLENDENS

Splendid Cort ☠

There are several yellow *Phlegmacium* species with distinct stem bulbs, and they can be told apart only with some difficulty. This striking, aptly named *Cortinarius* species is a relatively small and very brightly colored member of the group. Its yellow flesh reacts with potassium hydroxide and turns reddish pink. Yellow species of *Cortinarius* may also resemble edible *Tricholoma* species (*see pp.92–97*), but there is a difference in spore color.

- ■ **SPORE DEPOSIT** Rusty brown.
- ■ **SIZE** Cap 3–7cm (w); stem 4–9cm (h) x 0.7–1.4cm (w); bulb up to 3.5cm (w).
- ■ **HABITAT** Mycorrhizal, commonly with beech trees, on calcareous soils.
- ■ **RANGE** Widespread and locally common in Europe; not reported in North America.

- *yellow cap often more orange-brown toward center*
- *veil remnants form fibrous covering on stem*
- *prominent bulb at base of stem*
- *flesh bright yellow*

SECTION

TOP/SIDE VIEW

- *gills bright yellow, turning rusty yellow with age*

UNDERSIDE

- ■ **FRUITING** Singly or a few together, on calcareous soils. Autumn.

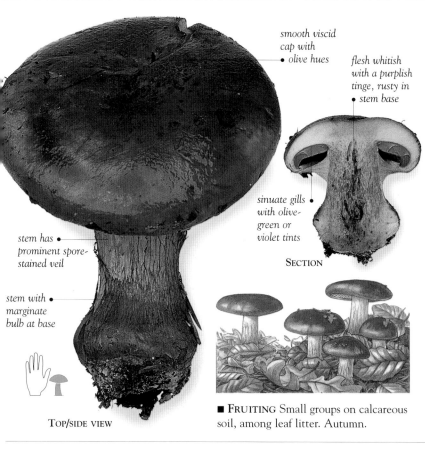

smooth viscid cap with olive hues

flesh whitish with a purplish tinge, rusty in stem base

stem has prominent spore-stained veil

sinuate gills with olive-green or violet tints

stem with marginate bulb at base

SECTION

TOP/SIDE VIEW

■ **FRUITING** Small groups on calcareous soil, among leaf litter. Autumn.

CORTINARIUS RUFO-OLIVACEUS

Red and Olive Cort

This is a large *Phlegmacium* with the usual greasy cap, but here the cap has rhubarb coloring or some olive at the margin. The stem – typically long and slender but bulbous – has many color components, and the gills can be either greenish or lilac. The unique color combination makes it easily identifiable. Several other *Phlegmacium* species are olive colored, including the visually striking fungus *C. atrovirens*.

■ **SPORE DEPOSIT** Rusty brown.
■ **SIZE** Cap 6–10cm, up to 12cm (w); stem 7–12cm (h) x 1.5–2cm (w); bulb up to 3cm (w).
■ **HABITAT** Forms mycorrhizal relationships, especially with beech and oak trees, on calcareous soils.
■ **RANGE** Widespread but local in Europe; not reported in North America.

CORTINARIUS CAERULESCENS

Large Blue Cort

Although this is an impressive blue *Cortinarius* species, with white veil patches and a prominent, bulbous stem base, it is not the only one. For most corts, all stages of fruitbody development must be observed before any species identification can be attempted.

■ **SPORE DEPOSIT** Rusty brown.
■ **SIZE** Cap 5–12cm (w); stem 4–8cm, up to 10cm (h) x 1.5–2.5cm (w); bulb up to 4cm (w).
■ **HABITAT** Mycorrhizal with deciduous trees on calcareous soils, in leaf litter.
■ **RANGE** Widespread but local in Europe; reported in southern Appalachians.

■ **FRUITING** Small groups among leaf-litter on calcareous soils. Autumn.

CORTINARIUS MUCOSUS

Orange Slime Cort

This shiny, orange-brown species belongs to a group of *Cortinarius* where both the cap and stem are slimy. *C. mucosus* has a white stem and a fairly dark reddish to orange-brown cap; it forms mycorrhiza with pine trees. The similar *C. collinitus* has a blue tinge to the stem slime and occurs under spruce. There are also several other similar species.

■ **SPORE DEPOSIT** Rusty brown.
■ **SIZE** Cap 6–10cm, up to 15cm (w); stem 7–12cm, up to 15cm (h) x 1–2.5cm (w).
■ **HABITAT** As a group, mycorrhizal with both conifers and deciduous trees.
■ **RANGE** As a group widespread in north temperate zones.

■ **FRUITING** Singly or a few together underneath pines. Summer–autumn.

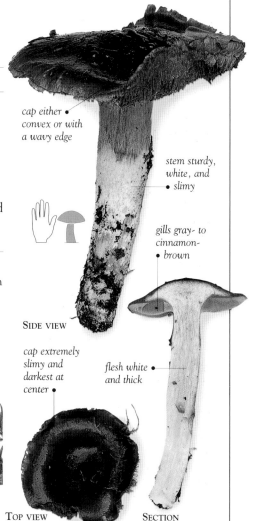

cap either convex or with a wavy edge

stem sturdy, white, and slimy

gills gray- to cinnamon-brown

SIDE VIEW

cap extremely slimy and darkest at center

flesh white and thick

TOP VIEW   **SECTION**

HEBELOMA MESOPHAEUM

Veiled Fairy Cake ☠

Hebeloma species can be divided into several groups. This one belongs to the veiled group and has several very close relatives, best told with the aid of a microscope. The veil can be seen as fine, whitish threads and patches near the cap margin and as threads on the upper stem. Most *Hebeloma* species also have a radishlike smell.

- **SPORE DEPOSIT** Tobacco-brown.
- **SIZE** Cap 2–5cm, up to 7.5cm (w); stem 2–6cm, up to 9cm (h) x 0.3–0.7cm, up to 1.8cm (w).
- **HABITAT** In mixed woods; mycorrhizal with both conifers and deciduous trees.
- **RANGE** Widespread and common in north temperate zones.

- **FRUITING** In troops under trees. Autumn.

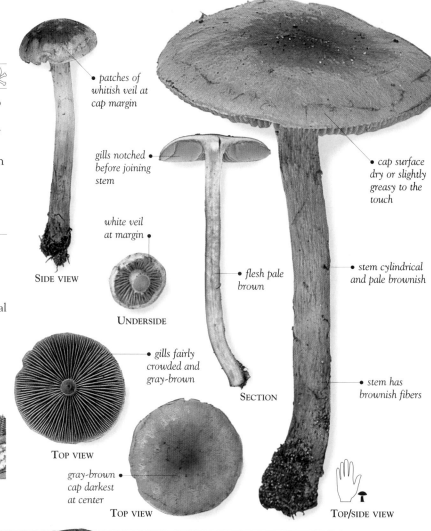

patches of whitish veil at cap margin •

gills notched before joining stem

white veil at margin •

SIDE VIEW

UNDERSIDE

gills fairly crowded and gray-brown •

TOP VIEW

gray-brown cap darkest at center •

TOP VIEW

• flesh pale brown

SECTION

• cap surface dry or slightly greasy to the touch

• stem cylindrical and pale brownish

• stem has brownish fibers

TOP/SIDE VIEW

---

distinctive ring near apex of stem •

stem widens out at soil level •

stem typically has scaly surface

long stem is very deep rooting •

SECTION

TOP/SIDE VIEW

stem colored as cap or paler •

• cap greasy, with concentric brown scales

gills clay-brown • and crowded

UNDERSIDE

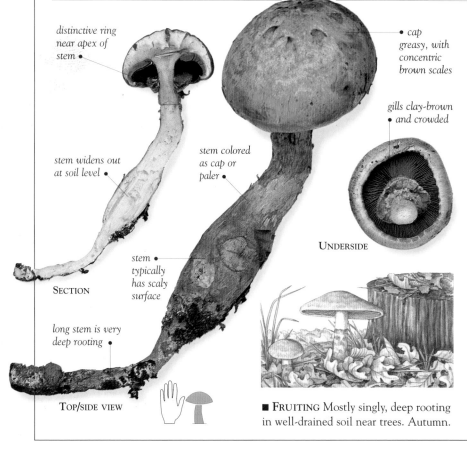

- **FRUITING** Mostly singly, deep rooting in well-drained soil near trees. Autumn.

HEBELOMA RADICOSUM

Rooting Fairy Cake ☠

An unusual and large *Hebeloma* species with a very strong marzipan or bitter almond smell, and a stem that roots deep underground to vole nests. Both the cap and stem have distinct brown scales. The prominent stem ring is an unusual feature in the genus. This species could be confused with *Pholiota* (see pp.159–161), but none of these have such a distinctive smell.

- **SPORE DEPOSIT** Snuff-brown.
- **SIZE** Cap 5–12cm (w); stem 6–20cm (h) x 1.5–2.5cm (w).
- **HABITAT** Mycorrhizal with deciduous trees; associated with underground vole nests and campsite latrines in deciduous woods in well-drained soil.
- **RANGE** Widespread but uncommon in north temperate zones; not reliably reported in North America.

HEBELOMA PALLIDOLUCTUOSUM

Sweet Scented Fairy Cake ☠

A small group of *Hebeloma* species has very strong, sweet, aromatic to almost sickly smells. The most common species is *H. pallidoluctuosum*. This group in the US is usually referred to as *H. saccharioleus*. The caps are viscid and smooth, except for the felty surface of *H. tomentosum*.

- **SPORE DEPOSIT** Snuff-brown.
- **SIZE** Cap 2–8cm (w); stem 2.5–5cm (h) x 0.4–0.8cm (w).
- **HABITAT** Mycorrhizal with deciduous trees on richer soils, in parks and woods.
- **RANGE** Widespread and fairly common as a species complex in north temperate zones.

- **FRUITING** In troops under deciduous trees, especially oak. Autumn.

HEBELOMA CRUSTULINIFORME

Poison Pie ☠

A fairly fleshy species with no veil, and gill edges that exude drops of a clear liquid. These drops later trap mature spores and, when dry, produce a dark spotting on the gill edge. Other related species have a similar radishlike smell. Caution: Do not confuse with a pale Blewit (*see p.91*).

- **SPORE DEPOSIT** Snuff-brown.
- **SIZE** Cap 4–9cm (w); stem 3–8cm (h) x 0.8–2cm (w).
- **HABITAT** Mycorrhizal, with conifers and deciduous trees in woods and parks.
- **RANGE** Widespread and common in north temperate zones.

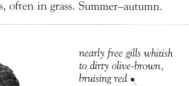

- **FRUITING** In troops or rings beneath trees, often in grass. Summer–autumn.

fleshy, buff cap almost white at margin

whitish stem has mealy covering

TOP/SIDE VIEW

gray or clay gills rather broad, with drop-exuding edge

UNDERSIDE

stem widens slightly at base

SIDE VIEW

INOCYBE ERUBESCENS

Deadly Fiber Cap ☠

This deadly, early-fruiting European species is also known as *I. patouillardii*. It is fairly squat in stature and stains red all over when older or if handled. The cap has distinct radial fibers, as do other members of the genus. *I. pudica* also stains red, but has more slender, whiter fruitbodies. *I. godeyi* (*see p.176*) stains red and has a bulbous stem base. It can be mistaken for the edible *Calocybe gambosa* (see p.99).

- **SPORE DEPOSIT** Snuff-brown.
- **SIZE** Cap 3–9cm (w); stem 4–7cm, up to 12cm (h) x 1–2cm (w).
- **HABITAT** Mycorrhizal with beech and linden, on richer clay or calcareous soils.
- **RANGE** Widespread but local in Europe and parts of Asia; not reported in North America.

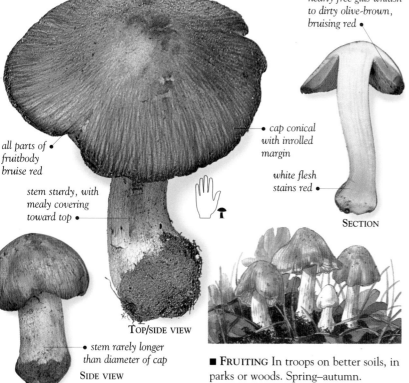

all parts of fruitbody bruise red

stem sturdy, with mealy covering toward top

TOP/SIDE VIEW

stem rarely longer than diameter of cap

SIDE VIEW

nearly free gills whitish to dirty olive-brown, bruising red

cap conical with inrolled margin

white flesh stains red

SECTION

- **FRUITING** In troops on better soils, in parks or woods. Spring–autumn.

INOCYBE HAEMACTA

Green and Pink Fiber Cap ☠

Inocybe species tend to be fairly dull in color and only rarely have greenish tones, as in this species. *I. haemacta* smells similar to urine or a stable. Found in Europe, it is reportedly hallucinogenic.

- **SPORE DEPOSIT** Tobacco-brown.
- **SIZE** Cap 3–6.5cm (w); stem 2–8cm (h) x 0.4–0.6cm (w).
- **HABITAT** Mycorrhizal with deciduous trees on rich soil, in forests and parks.
- **RANGE** Widespread but local to rare in Europe; this species has not been reported in North America.

- **FRUITING** Singly or a few together, often on soil at roadsides. Autumn.

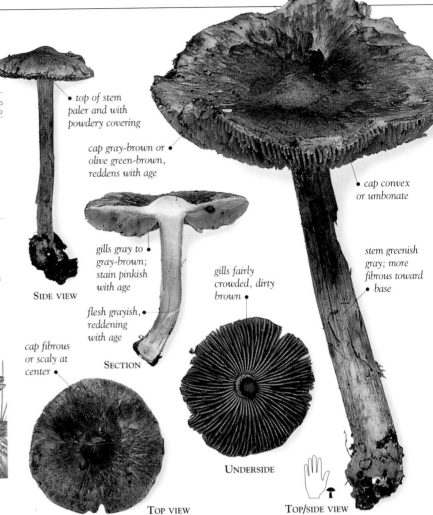

top of stem paler and with powdery covering

cap gray-brown or olive green-brown, reddens with age

cap convex or umbonate

SIDE VIEW

gills gray to gray-brown; stain pinkish with age

gills fairly crowded, dirty brown

stem greenish gray; more fibrous toward base

flesh grayish, reddening with age

SECTION

cap fibrous or scaly at center

UNDERSIDE

TOP VIEW

TOP/SIDE VIEW

INOCYBE GODEYI

Blushing Fiber Cap ☠

A creamish white to pale ocher species that soon turns bright orange-red. Another good marker is the bulbous stem base. *I. pudica*, found along the Pacific Northwest, another white species that turns pinkish, but it lacks the stem bulb.

- **SPORE DEPOSIT** Tobacco-brown.
- **SIZE** Cap 1.5–5cm (w); stem 2–7cm (h) x 0.3–0.6cm (w); bulb up to 0.8cm (w).
- **HABITAT** On calcareous soil, mycorrhizal with deciduous trees.
- **RANGE** Widespread in Europe; reported in eastern North America.

cap conical in shape, creamish at first

gills creamish to reddish brown

whole length of stem covered in a fine down

cap turns a vivid orange-red

SECTION

gills adnexed and medium-spaced

stem base has distinct bulb

SIDE VIEW

TOP/SIDE VIEW

UNDERSIDE

- **FRUITING** Typically, a few together on soil, along path edges. Autumn.

INOCYBE GEOPHYLLA

White Fiber Cap ☠

Perhaps the most common *Inocybe* species, it occurs in two color forms: one is white, and the other is lilac all over except for its brown gills. In all forms, the cap is conical to umbonate and the stem straight, without a bulb. Caution: Do not confuse the lilac form with *Laccaria amethystina* (see p.85).

■ **SPORE DEPOSIT** Brown.
■ **SIZE** Cap 1–4cm (w); stem 2–5cm (h) x 0.3–0.5cm (w).
■ **HABITAT** On rich soil, often bare and disturbed, such as along ditches or roads; mycorrhizal with conifers and deciduous trees.
■ **RANGE** Widespread and common in north temperate zones.

■ **FRUITING** A few together or in troops on soil or between needles. Autumn.

lilac form of species

LILAC FORM

TOP VIEW

gills adnexed

silky, smooth cap has covering of fine fibers

WHITE FORM

cap may have clearly pointed, raised area in center

upper part of stem downy on surface

flesh whitish and slightly watery

lower part of stem has fibrous covering

whitish form may have ocher tinges

SIDE VIEW   **SECTION**

TOP/SIDE VIEW

UNDERSIDE

gills pale gray to gray-brown and fairly crowded

SIDE VIEW

---

pointed cap flares upward and tears at edge with age

stem whitish or flushed with cap color; downy toward top

TOP VIEW

stem thicker at base but not bulbous

SIDE VIEW

gills yellowish gray to yellowish brown

pale flesh

distinctive, radiating fibers over cap

SECTION

■ **FRUITING** Mostly in small groups on good soils, under trees. Summer–autumn.

INOCYBE RIMOSA

Straw-colored Fiber Cap ☠

It usually takes time to get to know this variable, more or less yellowish species well. Its distinctively pointed cap has coarse, radiating fibers and, with age, the cap margin turns upward and gets torn very easily. The stem widens toward the base but is not bulbous, and only the upper part is finely downy. Typically, the gills will have a yellow flush. *I. maculata*, a similar species, has a cap; this is darker reddish brown and has patches of whitish veil. The stem is fairly pale and may have a small basal bulb.

■ **SPORE DEPOSIT** Tobacco-brown.
■ **SIZE** Cap 3–7cm (w); stem 6–10cm (h) x 0.5–1cm (w).
■ **HABITAT** Mycorrhizal, mostly with deciduous trees on richer, often disturbed, soil, along woodland paths.
■ **RANGE** Widespread and locally common in north temperate zones.

INOCYBE GRISEOLILACINA

Gray and Lilac Fiber Cap ☠

This species is best told by the small, brownish scales on its cap and the pale lilac stem. The cap may also have a lilac flush. *I. cincinnata* is quite similar but typically has a darker cap, and the lilac stem color is concentrated near the apex.

- ■ **SPORE DEPOSIT** Brown.
- ■ **SIZE** Cap 0.8–4cm (w); stem 4–7cm, down to 2cm (h) x 0.2–0.6cm (w).
- ■ **HABITAT** Mycorrhizal with deciduous trees growing on richer soils; often along roadsides like other close relatives.
- ■ **RANGE** Widespread in north temperate zones, but exact distribution not yet known.

- ■ **FRUITING** In troops or small groups on soil near deciduous trees. Autumn.

ocher-brown cap may have lilac tinge near margin •

convex cap covered with distinctive, small brown scales

cylindrical stem base not bulbous •

stem • tinted lilac

fibrous, scaly stem •

TOP/SIDE VIEW

flesh eaten by larvae •

pale flesh with or without lilac flush •

SIDE VIEW

gills ocher • to pale brown with a white edge

SECTION

UNDERSIDE

stem color darker toward base •

TOP/SIDE VIEW

---

fibers and scales cover surface • of cap

dull • brown cap

cap flesh typically pale •

gills gray-brown with whitish • edge

UNDERSIDE

grayish brown to dark brown cap is convex • in shape

stem has • covering of brownish fibers

stem darkest at non-bulbous base •

SECTION

• flesh darker toward stem base

SIDE VIEW

SIDE VIEW

INOCYBE LACERA

Torn Fiber Cap ☠

This variable species is not easy to identify without a microscope. It is dull brown to dark brown with a fibrillose, scaly cap. There is a veil at the cap edge in young specimens. This is most commonly found in hard-packed soil along forest trails.

- ■ **SPORE DEPOSIT** Tobacco-brown.
- ■ **SIZE** Cap 1–4.5cm (w); stem 2.5–6cm, up to 10cm (h) x 0.2–0.6cm (w).
- ■ **HABITAT** Mycorrhizal with a variety of trees such as willows and conifers.
- ■ **RANGE** Widespread and common in north temperate zones.

- ■ **FRUITING** A few together or in troops, often on poor soils. Spring–autumn.

INOCYBE ASTEROSPORA

Star-spored Fiber Cap 💀

Some *Inocybe* species have smooth spores and some rough. An extreme form of the latter type is *I. asterospora* with its star-shaped spores. Its largish fruitbodies have flattened stem bulbs and strongly fibrillose caps.

- **SPORE DEPOSIT** Tobacco-brown.
- **SIZE** Cap 3–7cm (w); stem 4–9cm (h) x 0.5–1.2cm (w); bulb up to 2cm (w).
- **HABITAT** Mycorrhizal with deciduous trees, especially hazel or beech.
- **RANGE** Widespread and common in north temperate zones; locally common in eastern North America.

- **FRUITING** Singly or a few together, often on bare soil under trees. Autumn.

cap paler underneath fibers

pale flesh in cap

cap covered in radiating dark red-brown fibers

gills tobacco-brown •

UNDERSIDE

TOP/SIDE VIEW

TOP/SIDE VIEW

cap slightly • umbonate

stem downy • along whole length

stem flesh • browner than cap

SECTION

SIDE VIEW

whitish, • flattened bulb at base of stem

---

yellow-brown convex to umbonate cap •

white veil remnants often cover center of cap •

TOP VIEW

medium-spaced pale brown gills •

UNDERSIDE

narrow, prominent, and striated • ring on stem

stem solid and • fibrous inside

SECTION

cap surface furrowed or wrinkled •

SIDE VIEW

adnexed gills have toothed edge •

stem smooth • under ring

TOP/SIDE VIEW

ROZITES CAPERATA

Gypsy 🍄

A relative of *Cortinarius* species (*see pp.165–173*), but with pale brown spores and a membranous stem ring. Initially, the wrinkled cap is egg-shaped and lilac-gray.

- **SPORE DEPOSIT** Pale brown.
- **SIZE** Cap 5–12cm (w); stem 5–15cm (h) x 1–2cm (w).
- **HABITAT** Mycorrhizal with both deciduous trees and conifers.
- **RANGE** Widespread in areas of the north temperate zones; local in eastern and northwestern North America.

- **FRUITING** In troops or small groups on acid soil beneath trees. Summer–autumn.

RUSSULACEAE

CLASS: *Homobasidiomycetes*

The two traditional genera in this family are *Lactarius* and *Russula*. Both have crumbly flesh; most *Russulas* have brittle gills. The cut flesh of *Lactarius* exudes clear, milky, or colored latex. *Russula's* often have brighter cap colors. While mild-tasting *Russulas* are thought to be edible, and some peppery *Russula* and *Lactaria* species are eaten in Europe, only a few North American species can be safely eaten.

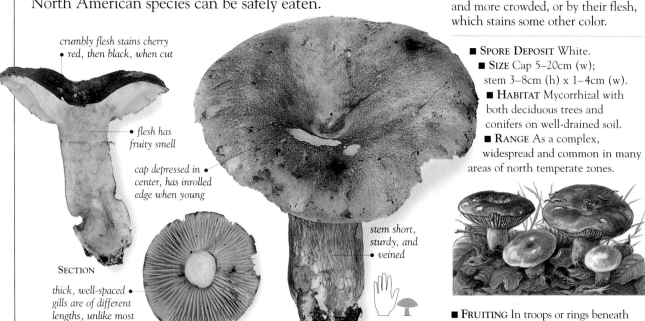

crumbly flesh stains cherry • red, then black, when cut

flesh has • fruity smell

cap depressed in center, has inrolled edge when young

SECTION

thick, well-spaced • gills are of different lengths, unlike most Russula species

UNDERSIDE

stem short, sturdy, and • veined

TOP/SIDE VIEW

RUSSULA NIGRICANS

Blackening Brittle Gills

A very large and firm-fleshed species that reddens at first and then turns completely black. The caps of old fruitbodies are often host to fruiting of *Asterophora* (see p.101). Some in this complex can be told apart by their gills, which are thinner and more crowded, or by their flesh, which stains some other color.

■ **SPORE DEPOSIT** White.
■ **SIZE** Cap 5–20cm (w); stem 3–8cm (h) x 1–4cm (w).
■ **HABITAT** Mycorrhizal with both deciduous trees and conifers on well-drained soil.
■ **RANGE** As a complex, widespread and common in many areas of north temperate zones.

■ **FRUITING** In troops or rings beneath deciduous trees. Summer–autumn.

RUSSULA DELICA

White Milk Cap Brittle Gills

Known as *R. brevipes* in North America, this *Lactarius vellereus* look-alike (see p.189) is often found pushing its way up through soil and leaf litter, which conceals its overall cream-white coloring. The gills of this large, firm-fleshed fungus are well-spaced. *R. chloroides* in Europe and *R. brevipes* var. *acrior* in North America tend to have a turquoise zone at the top of the stem. This complex is often parasitized by another fungus, the orange Lobster Mushroom, *Hypomyces lactifluorum*.

■ **SPORE DEPOSIT** White to cream.
■ **SIZE** Cap 5–15cm (w); stem 2–5cm (h) x 1.5–3cm (w).
■ **HABITAT** Mycorrhizal with both conifers and deciduous trees.
■ **RANGE** As a complex, widespread and common in many areas of the north temperate zones.

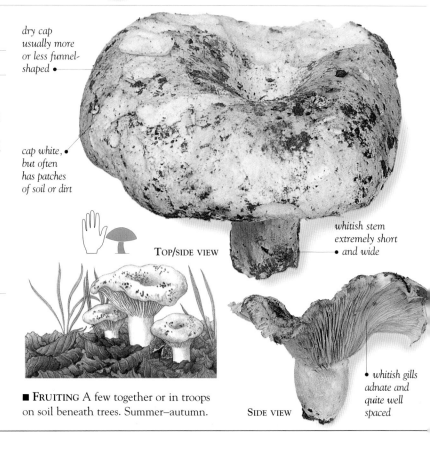

dry cap usually more or less funnel-shaped •

cap white, • but often has patches of soil or dirt

TOP/SIDE VIEW

whitish stem extremely short • and wide

■ **FRUITING** A few together or in troops on soil beneath trees. Summer–autumn.

SIDE VIEW

• whitish gills adnate and quite well spaced

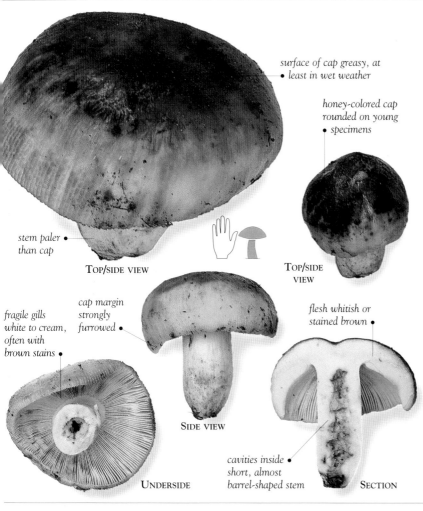

surface of cap greasy, at least in wet weather

honey-colored cap rounded on young specimens

stem paler than cap

TOP/SIDE VIEW

TOP/SIDE VIEW

cap margin strongly furrowed

fragile gills white to cream, often with brown stains

flesh whitish or stained brown

SIDE VIEW

cavities inside short, almost barrel-shaped stem

SECTION

UNDERSIDE

RUSSULA FOETENS
Fetid Brittle Gills

Marked by a rancid smell, this fleshy, orange-brown species also has a greasy cap with a grooved edge. R. subfoetens is similar, but the flesh stains yellow with potassium hydroxide. Some other species in this complex have a sweet marzipan smell when young but a disagreeable flavor.

- **SPORE DEPOSIT** Cream.
- **SIZE** Cap 8–15cm, down to 6cm (w); stem 6–12cm (h) x 1.5–3cm (w).
- **HABITAT** In woods, mycorrhizal with conifers and deciduous trees.
- **RANGE** As a complex, widespread and common in north temperate zones.

- **FRUITING** Singly or in troops in woodland. Summer–autumn.

RUSSULA FELLEA
Geranium Brittle Gills ☠

Growing under deciduous trees, this species can be recognized by the beige-brown coloring of the fruitbodies and gills, its small size, and very bitter taste. In North America, the similar R. simillima occasionally has the geranium scent of R. fellea.

- **SPORE DEPOSIT** Whitish.
- **SIZE** Cap 3–6cm, up to 8cm (w); stem 3–7cm (h) x 1–2cm (w).
- **HABITAT** In deciduous woods, mycorrhizal with trees, especially beech, mostly on well-drained, acid soil.
- **RANGE** Widespread and common in Europe.

- **FRUITING** Singly or in groups under mycorrhizal partner. Summer–autumn.

striations visible on margin of smooth, dry cap

gills rather crowded

gills pale, and tinted with cap color

UNDERSIDE

smooth stem tinted with cap color

flesh is whitish throughout fruitbody

stem expands slightly toward base

SECTION

springs from well-drained, acid soils

TOP/SIDE VIEW

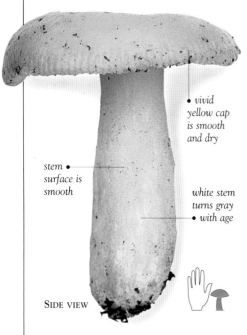

*vivid
yellow cap
is smooth
and dry*

*stem
surface is
smooth*

*white stem
turns gray
with age*

SIDE VIEW

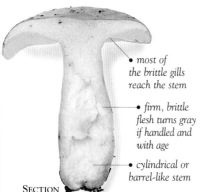

*most of
the brittle gills
reach the stem*

*firm, brittle
flesh turns gray
if handled and
with age*

*cylindrical or
barrel-like stem*

SECTION

RUSSULA CLAROFLAVA

Graying Yellow Brittle Gills

The highly attractive, brightly
colored *R. claroflava* is found only in
wet birch woodland – often so wet
that sphagnum moss covers the
ground. Apart from the vivid yellow
color of the cap, it can be told by its
white, mild-tasting flesh – which
turns gray with age and when
bruised – and its ocher spore deposit.

■ **SPORE DEPOSIT** Ocher.
■ **SIZE** Cap 5–10cm (w);
stem 4–10cm (h) x 1–2cm (w).
■ **HABITAT** On wet ground; forms
mycorrhizal associations with birch.
■ **RANGE** Widespread and rather
common in the north temperate zones.

■ **FRUITING** In troops or singly, under
birch trees. Summer–autumn.

RUSSULA VINOSA

Graying Vinaceous Brittle Gills

Although highly regarded in
Europe, there are too many look-
alikes in North America to
recommend this as a safe edible.
The cap has a winelike color, the
firm flesh turns gray when cut or
with age, and it occurs in sandy
pine woods. It has a pleasant taste.

■ **SPORE DEPOSIT** Ocher.
■ **SIZE** Cap 4–12cm (w);
stem 3–8cm (h) x 1.5–2.5cm (w).
■ **HABITAT** Mycorrhizal with conifers.
■ **RANGE** Widespread in north temperate
zones; common and widely distributed
in northeastern North America.

■ **FRUITING** Scattered on sandy soil with
moss and lichens. Summer–autumn.

RUSSULA OCHROLEUCA

Yellow-ocher Brittle Gills

One of the most common woodland
fungi in Europe, this species is
marked by its ocher-yellow cap and
white gills. The taste is bland –
neither bitter nor hot – and the
fungi are inedible. In eastern North
America, this species is replaced
with *R. ochraleucoides*, which is
common at times in open oak
woods, and bitterish to taste.
The bruised flesh of *R. ochraleucoides*
does not turn ashy gray, unlike
R. claroflava (see above)
and *R. ochroleuca*.

■ **SPORE DEPOSIT** White.
■ **SIZE** Cap 5–12cm (w);
stem 3–8cm (h) x 1–2.5cm (w).
■ **HABITAT** In woods, mycorrhizal with
both conifers and deciduous trees.
■ **RANGE** Widespread and common in
Europe, parts of Asia.

*most of the
gills reach
the stem*

SECTION

*gills whitish
and rather
crowded*

UNDERSIDE

*yellow-ocher
cap is matte
and smooth;
skin peels back
a long way
when pulled*

*base turns
slightly grayish
with age or
handling*

TOP/SIDE VIEW

■ **FRUITING** Singly or in troops, mostly
on well-drained soil. Summer–autumn.

cap color varies greatly from green to wine-red or is a mix of the two

cap is smooth and slightly greasy

TOP VIEW

gills are pliable and oily to the touch

chunky stem is a whitish color

cap soon flattens out toward margin

TOP/SIDE VIEW

SECTION

stem is firm but brittle

white gills are crowded close together

UNDERSIDE

RUSSULA CYANOXANTHA

Charcoal Burner

This odd common name comes from the French word *charbonnier*. It is a much sought-after large species in Europe that tends to be early-fruiting. In North America, this species and the similar but forked gill *R. variata* are edible but not choice.

■ **SPORE DEPOSIT** White.
■ **SIZE** Cap 5–15cm (w); stem 5–10cm (h) x 1–3cm (w).
■ **HABITAT** Mycorrhizal with deciduous trees, especially beech, but also with conifers. It prefers acid soil.
■ **RANGE** Widespread and common in in parts of the north temperate zone.

■ **FRUITING** Singly or in troops, on well-drained soil under trees. Summer–autumn.

RUSSULA VESCA

Bare-toothed Brittle Gills

A distinctive cap margin has given this species its common name – the cap skin is too short to reach the margin, so the gills are left exposed. *R. vesca*'s coloring tends toward wine-red, mixed with brown, and its pointed stem often has brown spots at the base. It has a nutty taste.

■ **SPORE DEPOSIT** White.
■ **SIZE** Cap 5–10cm (w); stem 3–6cm, up to 8cm (h) x 1.5–2.5cm (w).
■ **HABITAT** Mycorrhizal with conifers and deciduous trees, on well-drained soil.
■ **RANGE** Widespread in north temperate zones; common in Europe.

■ **FRUITING** Singly or in troops on well-drained soils. Summer–autumn.

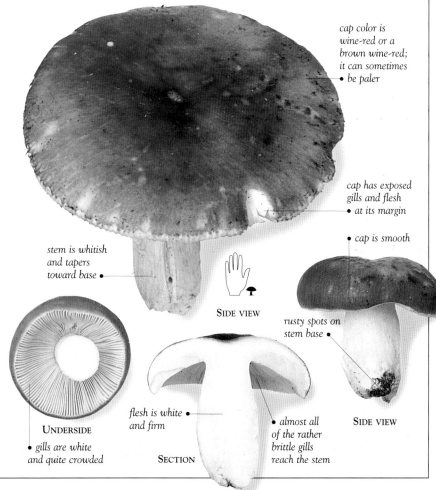

cap color is wine-red or a brown wine-red; it can sometimes be paler

cap has exposed gills and flesh at its margin

cap is smooth

stem is whitish and tapers toward base

SIDE VIEW

rusty spots on stem base

UNDERSIDE

gills are white and quite crowded

flesh is white and firm

SECTION

almost all of the rather brittle gills reach the stem

SIDE VIEW

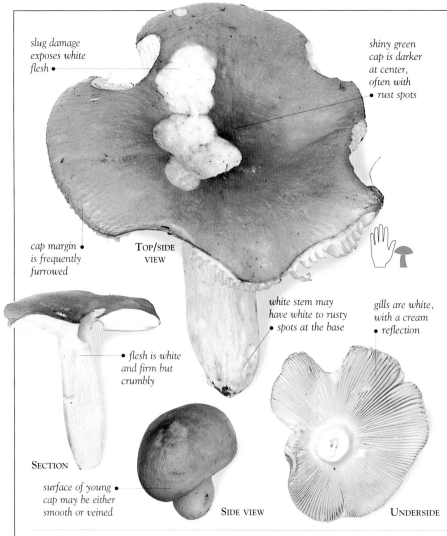

slug damage exposes white flesh •

shiny green cap is darker at center, often with • rust spots

cap margin is frequently furrowed

TOP/SIDE VIEW

white stem may have white to rusty • spots at the base

gills are white, with a cream • reflection

• flesh is white and firm but crumbly

SECTION

surface of young • cap may be either smooth or veined

SIDE VIEW

UNDERSIDE

RUSSULA AERUGINEA

Tacky Green Brittle Gills

This is one of a small number of green-capped *Russulas*. *R. cyanoxantha* (*see p.183*) often has other colors besides green in the cap; *R. variata* has forked gills; *R. crustosa* is like *R. virescens* but with yellowish to ocher areas on the green caps.

- **SPORE DEPOSIT** Cream.
- **SIZE** Cap 4–9cm (w); stem 4–7cm (h) x 1–2.5cm (w).
- **HABITAT** Mycorrhizal with birch, especially under oak, live oak, aspen, lodgepole pine, and other conifers.
- **RANGE** Widely distributed in north temperate zones.

- **FRUITING** In troops among grass and leaf litter. Summer–autumn.

RUSSULA PUELLARIS

Yellow-staining Brittle Gills

A thin-fleshed *Russula* species that stains yellow all over with age. The purplish to reddish brown coloring is gradually replaced with ocher-yellow hues. Initially, the cap may be almost black at the center, but always with a paler, furrowed margin. The cap skin can be peeled almost to the center. This is at best a mediocre edible, with rather thin, mild-flavored flesh. Little to nothing is known about the edibility of particular pinkish to wine red capped *Russulas* in North America.

- **SPORE DEPOSIT** Dark cream.
- **SIZE** Cap 3–6cm (w); stem 3–6cm (h) x 0.7–1.5cm (w).
- **HABITAT** Mycorrhizal with both conifers and deciduous trees.
- **RANGE** Widespread in most of the north temperate zones including Europe and northern North America.

shiny, slightly greasy cap contains many colors, becoming more yellow with age •

cream to yellow gills are medium-spaced •

UNDERSIDE

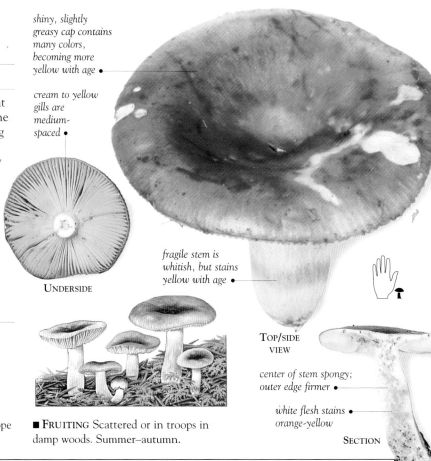

fragile stem is whitish, but stains yellow with age •

TOP/SIDE VIEW

center of stem spongy; outer edge firmer •

white flesh stains • orange-yellow

SECTION

- **FRUITING** Scattered or in troops in damp woods. Summer–autumn.

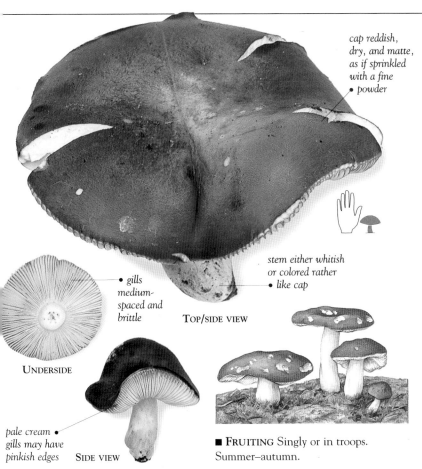

cap reddish, dry, and matte, as if sprinkled with a fine • powder

• gills medium-spaced and brittle

TOP/SIDE VIEW

UNDERSIDE

stem either whitish or colored rather • like cap

pale cream • gills may have pinkish edges

SIDE VIEW

■ **FRUITING** Singly or in troops. Summer–autumn.

RUSSULA ROSEA
Firm-fleshed Brittle Gills

Although hard to describe, this inedible species is easy to identify among the many red or reddish species of *Russula*. The flesh is very hard, and the red color is diluted. Also, the cap skin is extremely thin and does not peel. The taste of this species has been compared to the wood of a pencil and so, despite its appealing texture, it is not considered a worthwhile edible. *R. velutipes* is perhaps the most similar *Russula*, but unlike *R.rosea* it has cap skin that can be peeled and more fragile flesh.

■ **SPORE DEPOSIT** Pale cream.
■ **SIZE** Cap 4–12cm (w); stem 3–8cm (h) x 1–3cm (w).
■ **HABITAT** On well-drained soil in deciduous woods, often forms mycorrhizal associations with beech.
■ **RANGE** Widespread and common in European beech regions, reported in northeastern North America.

RUSSULA INTEGRA
Almond Brittle Gills

A highly regarded edible in parts of Scandinavia, the nutty flavor of this species is reminiscent of almonds. The gills of *R. integia* are thick and well spaced; the gills flake apart on handing. Because this is a complex of species, it is difficult to recognize reliably in North America. Its edibility is not reported on here, so it cannot be recommended as an edible.

■ **SPORE DEPOSIT** Yellow.
■ **SIZE** Cap 6–12cm (w); stem 5–10cm (h) x 1.5–3cm (w).
■ **HABITAT** Mycorrhizal with conifers.
■ **RANGE** As a complex, widespread in boreal parts of north temperate zones.

■ **FRUITING** Scattered or in troops in conifers. Summer–autumn.

RUSSULA TURCI
Iodine Brittle Gills

Another mild-tasting *Russula*, this particular species is typically associated with pines and is identified by its winelike cap coloring and distinct iodine smell, especially at the stem base. It belongs to the group of *Russula* species with yellow or pale ocher spores. The cap is depressed at the center in mature specimens, and the margin may have a finely dusty coating.

■ **SPORE DEPOSIT** Pale ocher.
■ **SIZE** Cap 3–10cm (w); stem 3–7cm (h) x 1–2.5cm (w).
■ **HABITAT** Mycorrhizal with pines (mainly two-needled) and possibly spruce.
■ **RANGE** Widespread in Europe; across northern North America.

■ **FRUITING** In troops, mainly under pine trees. Summer–autumn.

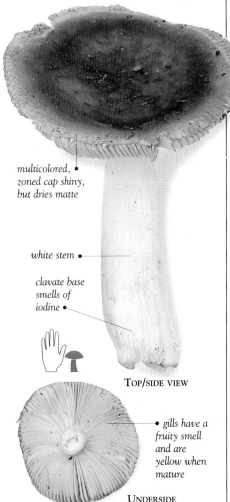

multicolored, • zoned cap shiny, but dries matte

white stem •

clavate base smells of iodine •

TOP/SIDE VIEW

• gills have a fruity smell and are yellow when mature

UNDERSIDE

cap varies in color from • red with black center to green and brownish purple

• gills very fragile

• margin smooth

• flesh turns dark green with iron sulfate

• flesh white, staining brownish

SECTION

SIDE VIEW

smooth cap • may have central depression

swollen or cylindrical stem is white, pinkish, or red •

TOP/SIDE VIEW

■ FRUITING In troops under trees or with creeping willow. Summer–autumn.

RUSSULA XERAMPELINA

Crab-scented Brittle Gills

This *Russula* species has a smell reminiscent of shellfish, which intensifies as it ages. It can be divided into a number of closely related species, although here it is treated as one. *R. xerampelina* varies greatly in color, from dark red to pure dark green. Its stem often has rusty spots, and the whole fruitbody may stain brownish with maturity. The different species occur in different habitats with various mycorrhizal partners.

■ **SPORE DEPOSIT** Ocher.
■ **SIZE** Cap 6–15cm (w); stem 4–8cm (h) x 1.5–3cm (w).
■ **HABITAT** In woods; mycorrhizal with conifers and deciduous trees.
■ **RANGE** Widespread in the north temperate zones and common when the species is taken in a broad sense.

RUSSULA PALUDOSA

Tall Brittle Gills

A large and splendid species that happens to be as good to eat as it is to admire, at least in Europe. Taller than most species of *Russula*, the fruitbody colors are similar to those of the *R. emetica (see right)*, but with less red in the cap and yellow discoloration from the center.

■ **SPORE DEPOSIT** Pale ocher.
■ **SIZE** Cap 8–16cm, down to 4cm and up to 20cm (w); stem 10–15cm, down to 6cm (h) x 1.5–4cm (w).
■ **HABITAT** Mycorrhizal with conifers, often among sphagnum in boggy areas.
■ **RANGE** Widespread and locally common in north temperate zones.

■ **FRUITING** In troops or scattered under conifers. Summer–autumn.

RUSSULA EMETICA

The Sickener

The coloring of this striking fungus makes it reminiscent of *Amanita muscaria (see p.132)*, but it does not have veil patches on the cap, a stem ring, or a bulb. Despite its name, it is not highly poisonous, and it has such a hot taste that anyone eating it will soon be alerted. In this complex, the common open or dry woodland species in North America is called *Russula silvicola*.

■ **SPORE DEPOSIT** White.
■ **SIZE** Cap 3–8cm (w); stem 5–8cm (h) x 1–2cm (w).
■ **HABITAT** Mycorrhizal with conifers, or in mixed woods in dry forest lands and in sphagnum bogs.
■ **RANGE** As a complex, widespread and common in north temperate zones.

■ **FRUITING** In troops or singly with conifers. Summer–autumn.

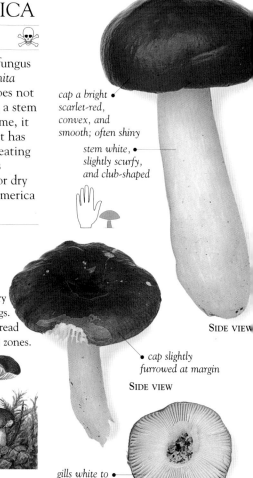

cap a bright • scarlet-red, convex, and smooth; often shiny

stem white, • slightly scurfy, and club-shaped

SIDE VIEW

• cap slightly furrowed at margin

SIDE VIEW

gills white to • pale cream

UNDERSIDE

specimen with signs of slug activity

cap convex in shape and a vivid scarlet-red

smooth stem

slightly club-shaped

TOP/SIDE VIEW

SIDE VIEW

white gills medium-spaced and brittle

surface of cap matte and smooth

stem whitish

UNDERSIDE

SIDE VIEW

TOP VIEW

RUSSULA MAIREI

Beechwood Sickener

Similar to *R. emetica* (*see opposite*), but smaller and with a different, sweetish smell. The cap is also a strong red color but less shiny. *R. fageticola*, which is also found under beech trees, is closer in appearance to *R. emetica*. Both are very hot when tasted.

■ **SPORE DEPOSIT** White.
■ **SIZE** Cap 3–7cm (w); stem 3–5cm (h) x 0.7–2cm (w).
■ **HABITAT** In woodland, mycorrhizal with beech trees on well-drained soils.
■ **RANGE** Widespread and common in beech areas of Europe and neighboring Asia.

■ **FRUITING** In troops or singly, under beech. Summer–autumn.

RUSSULA FRAGILIS

Serrated Brittle Gills

A hand lens is a useful aid for those attempting to identify this smallish, slightly poisonous *Russula* species. When magnified, the gill edge is clearly serrated. The cap color is a mixture of reds and purple, with a touch of green. The taste is very hot.

■ **SPORE DEPOSIT** White.
■ **SIZE** Cap 2–5cm, up to 8cm (w); stem 3–7cm (h) x 0.5–2cm (w).
■ **HABITAT** In woodland, mycorrhizal with trees, often birch and oak.
■ **RANGE** Widespread and locally common in north temperate zones.

■ **FRUITING** In troops under hardwood trees. Summer–autumn.

center of cap darkest in color; cap edge slightly furrowed

cap purplish, purplish red, or with a touch of olive

TOP VIEW

stem white and slightly club-shaped

cap convex or depressed in center

gills white to cream and medium-spaced

flesh white and fairly firm

TOP/SIDE VIEW

UNDERSIDE

SECTION

gills with serrated edge seen clearly with hand lens

SIDE VIEW

- **blood-red and thin-skinned cap**
- **stem streaked bloodred; grayish pink with age**

TOP/SIDE VIEW

- **fragile gills cream to ocher; wide-spaced**

UNDERSIDE

- **gills slightly decurrent**
- **flesh white, cumbly**

SECTION

RUSSULA SANGUINEA

Rosy Brittle Gills ☠

Known as R. rosacea in North America, this vivid red-capped, slightly poisonous species with a rather thin-skinned cap can be distinguished from look-alikes by the rosy blush on its stem, its moderately hot taste, fragile, yellowish gills, pale ocher spore deposit, and its association with conifers, mostly pine trees.

- **SPORE DEPOSIT** Pale ocher.
- **SIZE** Cap 5–10cm (w); stem 4–7cm (h) x 1–2cm, up to 3cm (w).
- **HABITAT** In woodland, mycorrhizal with conifers, mostly pines.
- **RANGE** Widespread in north temperate zones.

- **FRUITING** Singly or in troops on acid soil under conifers. Summer–autumn.

RUSSULA ATROPURPUREA

Blackish Purple Brittle Gills

This very dark-colored, fleshy, and short-stemmed Russula species has a white spore deposit and a tardily but persistent hot taste. The center of its cap is almost black, the rest of the fruitbody is purple, often with yellow spots. In North America this complex is generally referred to as R. krombholzii or R. vinacea; it is one of the earliest appearing Russulas.

- **SPORE DEPOSIT** White.
- **SIZE** Cap 4–10cm (w); stem 3–6cm (h) x 1–2.5cm (w).
- **HABITAT** Mycorrhizal with oaks, rarely with other trees, mostly acid soils.
- **RANGE** Widespread in the north temperate zones.

- **FRUITING** In troops, under oaks in woodland. Summer–autumn.

RUSSULA SARDONIA

Pungent Brittle Gills ☠

An attractive species with lemon-yellow gills contrasting with a dark purple, shiny cap. Although its common name suggests a pungent smell, R. sardonia has, in fact, a slightly fruity scent. Associated strictly with pine trees, R. sardonia is one of the larger species in its genus. R. queletii can be distinguished from R. sardonia by its smaller stature, paler gills, and paler spore deposit, but it tastes just as hot. The flesh and gills of R. sardonia also turn pink when chemically tested using ammonia vapor.

- **SPORE DEPOSIT** Pale ocher.
- **SIZE** Cap 4–10cm, up to 12cm (w); stem 4–10cm (h) x 1–2.5cm (w).
- **HABITAT** Mycorrhizal with pines.
- **RANGE** Widespread in parts of Europe; reported in western N.A.

- **cap dark purplish to a rich wine-red**
- **gills distinctively lemon to lemon-ocher**
- **gills quite crowded**

UNDERSIDE

- **stem purple to wine-colored with gray**
- **cap shiny and convex**

TOP/SIDE VIEW

SIDE VIEW

- **FRUITING** In troops under pine trees. Throughout autumn.

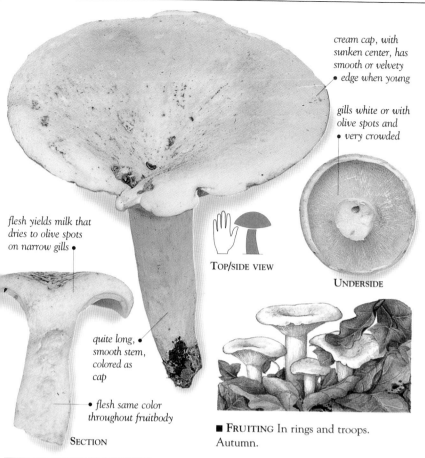

cream cap, with sunken center, has smooth or velvety edge when young

gills white or with olive spots and very crowded

flesh yields milk that dries to olive spots on narrow gills

TOP/SIDE VIEW

UNDERSIDE

quite long, smooth stem, colored as cap

flesh same color throughout fruitbody

SECTION

■ **FRUITING** In rings and troops. Autumn.

LACTARIUS PIPERATUS

Peppery Milk Cap

A large, fleshy *Lactarius* species, best identified by its whitish fruitbody, crowded, whitish gills and almost smooth cap. The milk has a very hot, peppery taste. At least one close relative has a white latex that dries green on the gills. This is a complex that is easy to recognize but difficult to delineate. In parts of Scandinavia and eastern Europe it is treated to be made edible. This involves a slow salting process, which cannot be recommended as either safe or desirable.

■ **SPORE DEPOSIT** Whitish.
■ **SIZE** Cap 8–20cm (w); stem 8–20cm (h) x 2–4cm (w).
■ **HABITAT** In woodland, mycorrhizal with both conifers and deciduous trees.
■ **RANGE** As a complex, widespread and rather common in north temperate zones, eastern N.A. to Michigan

LACTARIUS VELLEREUS

Fleecy Milk Cap

A very large *Lactarius* species that has a dense felt on its cap, a clear central depression, and well-spaced gills. More common in eastern North America is *L. deceptivus*, which has a cottony roll around its cap margin.

■ **SPORE DEPOSIT** Whitish.
■ **SIZE** Cap 10–25cm (w); stem 4–8cm (w) x 2–5cm (w).
■ **HABITAT** In woodland, mycorrhizal with deciduous trees such as beech but also found with various conifers.
■ **RANGE** As a complex, widespread worldwide in north temperate zones; exact range unknown.

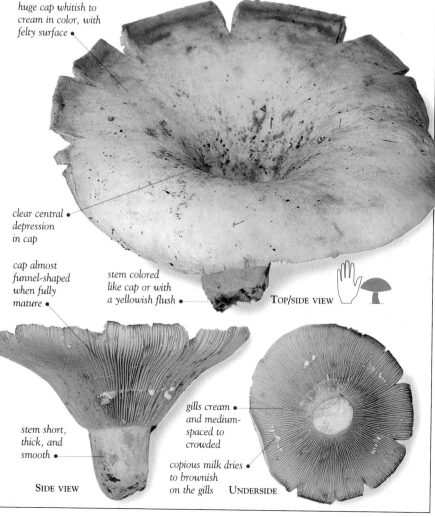

huge cap whitish to cream in color, with felty surface

clear central depression in cap

cap almost funnel-shaped when fully mature

stem colored like cap or with a yellowish flush

TOP/SIDE VIEW

stem short, thick, and smooth

gills cream and medium-spaced to crowded

copious milk dries to brownish on the gills

SIDE VIEW

UNDERSIDE

■ **FRUITING** In rings and troops among leaf litter, under trees. Autumn.

LACTARIUS CONTROVERSUS

Pink Gill Milk Cap

This uncommon and inedible species is strictly associated with willows and poplars. Its overall coloring is whitish, but the cap is faintly zoned. The gills are very crowded, as in *L. piperatus* (*see p.189*), and salmon-pink in color, which immediately separates it from other whitish *Lactarius* species.

- **SPORE DEPOSIT** Whitish.
- **SIZE** Cap 7–20cm, up to 25cm (w); stem 2–7cm (h) x 1.5–4cm (w).
- **HABITAT** In woodland and sand dunes; forms mycorrhizal associations with both willows and poplars.
- **RANGE** Widespread in north temperate zones.

- **FRUITING** Singly or in rings or troops near willows or poplars. Autumn.

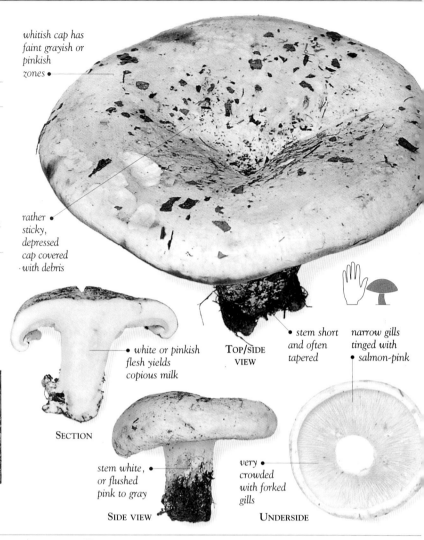

whitish cap has faint grayish or pinkish zones •

rather • sticky, depressed cap covered with debris

TOP/SIDE VIEW

• stem short and often tapered

narrow gills tinged with • salmon-pink

• white or pinkish flesh yields copious milk

SECTION

stem white, or flushed pink to gray

SIDE VIEW

very • crowded with forked gills

UNDERSIDE

LACTARIUS NECATOR

Mutagen Milk Cap

A very somber looking, dark olive-green fungus, *L. necator* remains well-hidden among leaf litter, but it is often found fruiting out in the open, in the grass under birch trees. Unlike *L. blennius* (*see p.192*), the cap is unzoned and the margin is felty and inrolled in young specimens. It has rather pale gills, which develop brown spots on their edges with age. The very hot copious milk is white. In parts of eastern Europe, it is eaten salted but it is not recommended as an edible because it is thought to cause cancer

- **SPORE DEPOSIT** Whitish.
- **SIZE** Cap 6–15cm (w); stem 4–7cm (h) x 1–2.5cm (w).
- **HABITAT** Mycorrhizal with birch and spruce, in woods, parks, and gardens.
- **RANGE** Widespread from Europe to the Far East. Absent in North America.

somber black- or gray-olive cap colors •

cap depressed in center and rather sticky •

crowded, narrow gills are whitish to yellowish •

• fairly short stem

TOP/SIDE VIEW

• stem mostly paler than cap

SIDE VIEW

margin of • cap rolls under in young specimens

UNDERSIDE

- **FRUITING** Singly, a few fruitbodies together, or in troops. Summer–autumn.

LACTARIUS TORMINOSUS

Woolly Milk Cap

The distinct zonation and shagginess of the depressed cap are the best markers for this species, which also produces white, very hot-tasting milk. This is a popular edible in parts of northern Europe, where it is eaten only after preserving in salt. Like many hot-tasting Milk Caps, it can cause severe gastric distress, especially if eaten simply sautéed. *L. pubescens* is similar and equally common in northern birch woods, but it can be distinguished by its paler colors, smaller size, and a cap that is less shaggy, with fainter zones.

■ **SPORE DEPOSIT** Pale yellowish.
■ **SIZE** Cap 5–15cm (w); stem 3–6cm (h) x 1–3cm (w).
■ **HABITAT** Mycorrhizal with birch and often found in open, grassy places.
■ **RANGE** As a complex, widespread in north temperate zones.

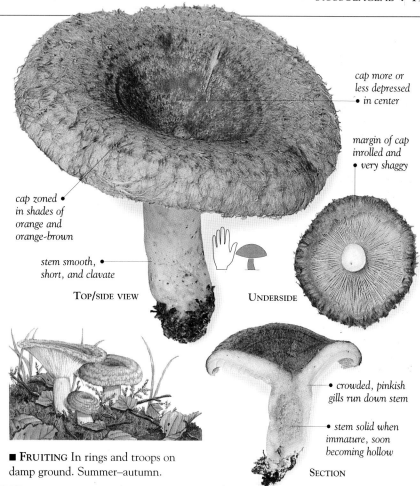

cap more or less depressed in center

margin of cap inrolled and very shaggy

cap zoned in shades of orange and orange-brown

stem smooth, short, and clavate

TOP/SIDE VIEW

UNDERSIDE

crowded, pinkish gills run down stem

stem solid when immature, soon becoming hollow

SECTION

■ **FRUITING** In rings and troops on damp ground. Summer–autumn.

LACTARIUS DELICIOSUS

Saffron Milk Cap

Also known as *L. deterrimus*, this is one of several *Lactarius* species with orange to red milklike latex and flesh that bruises greenish. Many are popular edibles, especially in Europe and Asia. It is a mediocre edible. *L. rubrilacteus* has red milk and occurs in western Douglas fir forests.

■ **SPORE DEPOSIT** Whitish.
■ **SIZE** Cap 5–15cm (w); stem 3–7cm (h) x 1–3cm (w).
■ **HABITAT** Mycorrhizal with pines, often on calcareous, sandy soils.
■ **RANGE** As a complex, widespread in north temperate zones.

short stem covered with fine orange depressions

cap slightly zoned, in tones of brownish orange

cap either greasy or dry and smooth, with inrolled margin

TOP/SIDE VIEW

red flesh yields orange milk

SECTION

crowded gills colored as cap

UNDERSIDE   **TOP/SIDE VIEW**

■ **FRUITING** In groups or troops in grass or on pine litter. Autumn.

LACTARIUS FULIGINOSUS

Sooty Milk Cap

This inedible species belongs to a group of brown *Lactarius* species, which can be identified by cutting the fruitbody to expose a white milk that turns pink. The time the milk takes to change color varies from one species to another. *L. fuliginosus* has slow-reacting milk.

- ■ **SPORE DEPOSIT** Pale ocher.
- ■ **SIZE** Cap 6–10cm (w); stem 4–7cm (h) x 1–1.5cm (w).
- ■ **HABITAT** As a complex, with both conifers and deciduous trees.
- ■ **RANGE** As a complex, widespread in north temperate zones.

- ■ **FRUITING** Mostly singly, or a few together, with deciduous trees. Autumn.

cap medium to dark brown with slightly velvety feel; often depressed •

well-spaced gills •

• margin inrolled in young specimens

UNDERSIDE

pale • ocher gills bruise pinkish brown

• whitish flesh turns dirty pink-brown where exposed

SECTION

• stem solid

• stem pale brown or almost white

TOP/SIDE VIEW

cap margin is • not furrowed

stem base • whitish

SIDE VIEW

LACTARIUS BLENNIUS

Slimy Milk Cap

Although the fruitbody color varies, *L. blennius* typically has a ring of dark spots near its smooth cap margin. Its overall hue is typically a mixture of brown, gray, and olive. *L. blennius* produces a white milk that dries to an olive-gray on the gills as does the white milk of the edible *L. trivialis* (see opposite). Although *L. blennius* is considered to be inedible, it has been eaten after boiling or salting. Just as there are many species of *Lactarius* in North America not known to occur in Europe, there are a good many common species in Europe not known in North America.

- ■ **SPORE DEPOSIT** Pale yellowish.
- ■ **SIZE** Cap 4–9cm, up to 12cm (w); stem 3–7cm (h) x 1–2.5cm (w).
- ■ **HABITAT** Mycorrhizal with beech.
- ■ **RANGE** Widespread in Europe; unreported in North America.

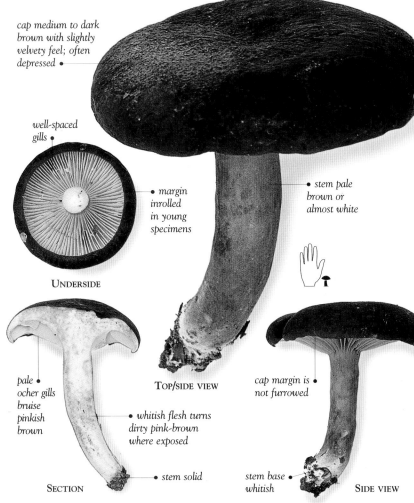

• olive-brown to green-gray cap has spots near margin

gills slightly • decurrent

whitish • gills have green-gray spots from dried milk

UNDERSIDE

cap smooth, with central depression •

stem smooth, and paler than cap •

TOP/SIDE VIEW

• flesh firm, white with copious white milk

SECTION

- ■ **FRUITING** Mostly in troops, among leaf litter under beeches. Summer–autumn.

LACTARIUS PYROGALUS

Zebra-spored Milk Cap

The milk produced by *L. pyragalus* is so hot-tasting that, if just one tiny drop is tried on the tongue, the after taste will remain for hours. Its well-spaced ocher gills and zebra-striped spores are other good markers. *L. circellatus* var. *borealis* is quite similar in appearance, but it grows under conifers and birch trees and has more crowded gills and more dense, well-marked zones on the cap. *L. vietus* is more violet gray, less zoned, and has dingy pinkish buff gills that turn gray.

- **SPORE DEPOSIT** Pale ocher-yellow.
- **SIZE** Cap 4–10cm (w); stem 3–7cm (h) x 0.5–2cm (w).
- **HABITAT** Mycorrhizal with hazel in Europe; in North America, reported in deciduous and mixed woods.
- **RANGE** Widespread and fairly common in Europe, Asia, and eastern North America.

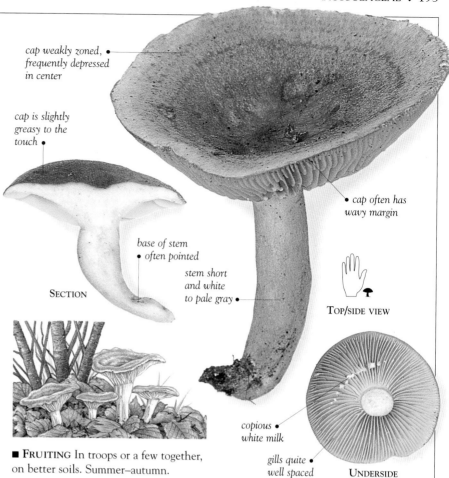

cap weakly zoned, frequently depressed in center

cap is slightly greasy to the touch

base of stem often pointed

stem short and white to pale gray

cap often has wavy margin

SECTION

TOP/SIDE VIEW

copious white milk

gills quite well spaced

UNDERSIDE

■ **FRUITING** In troops or a few together, on better soils. Summer–autumn.

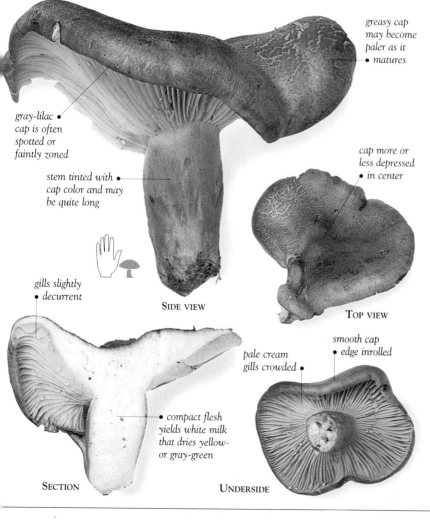

greasy cap may become paler as it matures

gray-lilac cap is often spotted or faintly zoned

stem tinted with cap color and may be quite long

gills slightly decurrent

SIDE VIEW

cap more or less depressed in center

TOP VIEW

pale cream gills crowded

smooth cap edge inrolled

compact flesh yields white milk that dries yellow- or gray-green

SECTION

UNDERSIDE

LACTARIUS TRIVIALIS

Slimy Lead Milk Cap

A large, fleshy, hot-tasting *Lactarius* species with a range of colors, from violet- to yellow-gray. In eastern North American oak woods, *L. argillaceifolius* is the mushroom most similar to European *L. trivialis*. Not a safe edible in North America.

- **SPORE DEPOSIT** Pale yellowish.
- **SIZE** Cap 6–20cm, up to 25cm (w); stem 4–10cm (h) x 1–3cm (w).
- **HABITAT** Associated with conifers and birch, often in damp woods.
- **RANGE** Widespread in north temperate zones; reported in Pacific Northwest in North America.

■ **FRUITING** In troops or a few together, under trees. Summer–autumn.

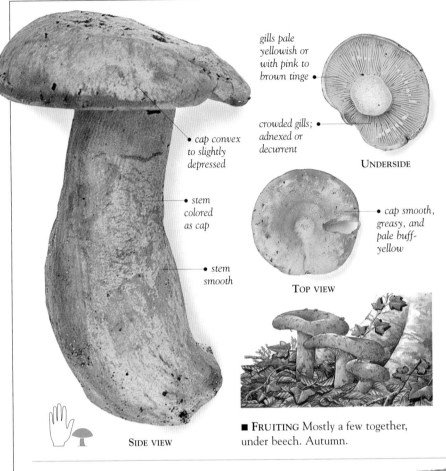

gills pale yellowish or with pink to brown tinge •

crowded gills; adnexed or decurrent

UNDERSIDE

• cap smooth, greasy, and pale buff-yellow

TOP VIEW

• cap convex to slightly depressed

• stem colored as cap

• stem smooth

SIDE VIEW

■ **FRUITING** Mostly a few together, under beech. Autumn.

LACTARIUS PALLIDUS

Pallid Milk Cap

In some ways this somewhat large species looks similar to a washed-out specimen of *L. blennius* (see p.192), and, like *L. blennius*, it is mycorrhizal with beech. However, *L. pallidus* has a pinkish-tinged fruitbody, hardly any zonation, and it produces a copious amount of white milk that does not stain gray-green. The flesh of *L. pallidus* tastes mild to slightly bitter, and it has a very faint smell. *L. musteus* is also somewhat similar in appearance and mild tasting, but, unlike *L. pallidus*, it is found growing under conifers.

■ **SPORE DEPOSIT** Pale ocher.
■ **SIZE** Cap 5–12cm (w); stem 3–8cm (h) x 0.5–2cm (w).
■ **HABITAT** Mycorrhizal with beech, in woods and parks.
■ **RANGE** Widespread in Europe; unreported in North America.

LACTARIUS GLYCIOSMUS

Coconut-scented Milk Cap

This scented species smells similar to freshly baked coconut cookies. It has subtle coloring that is not distinctive. *L. mammosus*, called *L. hibbardae* in northeastern North America, has the same coconut smell but can be told apart by its much darker color and by the fact that it grows under conifers.

■ **SPORE DEPOSIT** Pale yellowish.
■ **SIZE** Cap 2–6cm (w); stem 2–7cm (h) x 0.5–1cm (w).
■ **HABITAT** Mycorrhizal with birch, often in damp places among leaf litter.
■ **RANGE** Widespread and common in many areas of the north temperate zones.

■ **FRUITING** In troops among leaf litter, under birch. Summer–autumn.

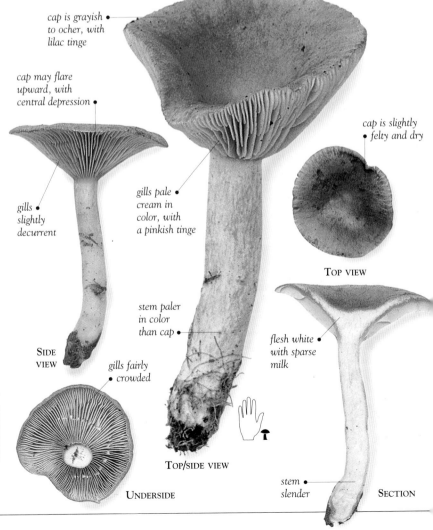

cap is grayish • to ocher, with lilac tinge

cap may flare upward, with central depression •

gills • slightly decurrent

gills pale • cream in color, with a pinkish tinge

cap is slightly • felty and dry

TOP VIEW

stem paler in color than cap •

flesh white with sparse milk

SIDE VIEW

gills fairly • crowded

UNDERSIDE

TOP/SIDE VIEW

stem • slender

SECTION

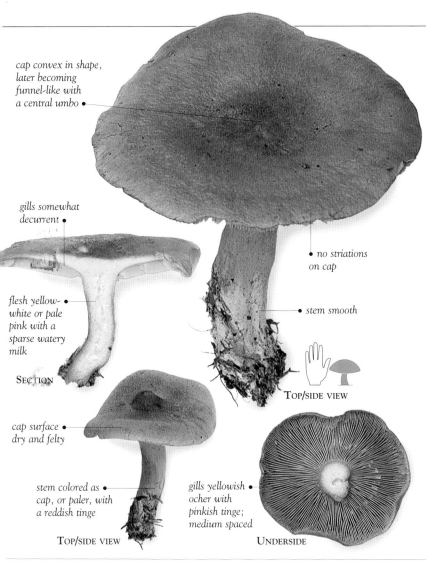

cap convex in shape, later becoming funnel-like with a central umbo •

gills somewhat decurrent •

flesh yellow-white or pale pink with a sparse watery milk

SECTION

• no striations on cap

• stem smooth

TOP/SIDE VIEW

cap surface • dry and felty

stem colored as • cap, or paler, with a reddish tinge

TOP/SIDE VIEW

gills yellowish • ocher with pinkish tinge; medium spaced

UNDERSIDE

LACTARIUS HELVUS

Spice-scented Milk Cap

This species is best told by its strong, spicy smell similar to curry or the herbs lovage and fenugreek. Also, the mild-tasting milk is more sparse and watery than in most *Lactarius* species. It is fairly large, and ultimately funnel-shaped. It has a North American equivalent known as *L. aquifluus*.

■ **SPORE DEPOSIT** Pale yellow to yellowish cream-pink.
■ **SIZE** Cap 5–16cm (w); stem 5–13cm (h) x 0.7–3cm, up to 4.5cm (w).
■ **HABITAT** Mycorrhizal with birch, pine, and spruce, often in sphagnum moss.
■ **RANGE** As *L. aquifluus*, in eastern and northern North America.

■ **FRUITING** In troops in wet, acid sites, under trees. Summer–autumn.

LACTARIUS MITISSIMUS

Mild Milk Cap

A smallish, orange-capped species with a mild taste and flesh that produces copious amounts of white, nonstaining milk. It is smaller than *L. volemus (see p.196)*, and relatives of a similar size tend to be darker, less vividly orange, or with more or less hot-tasting milk. A further distinguishing feature is the depression that develops in the convex cap as the fruitbody matures. The slimy-capped *L. luculentus*, found under conifers in western North America, is closest to this European species.

■ **SPORE DEPOSIT** Creamish pink.
■ **SIZE** Cap 2–6cm (w); stem 2–5cm (h) x 0.3–0.8cm (w).
■ **HABITAT** Mycorrhizal with conifer and deciduous trees.
■ **RANGE** Widespread in Europe; similar closely related forms are found in other north temperate zones.

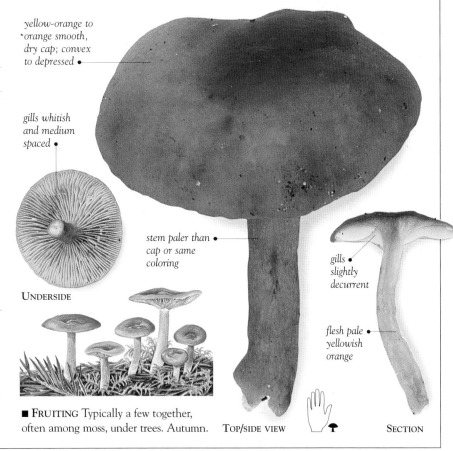

yellow-orange to orange smooth, dry cap; convex to depressed •

gills whitish and medium spaced •

UNDERSIDE

stem paler than • cap or same coloring

gills • slightly decurrent

flesh pale • yellowish orange

■ **FRUITING** Typically a few together, often among moss, under trees. Autumn.

TOP/SIDE VIEW

SECTION

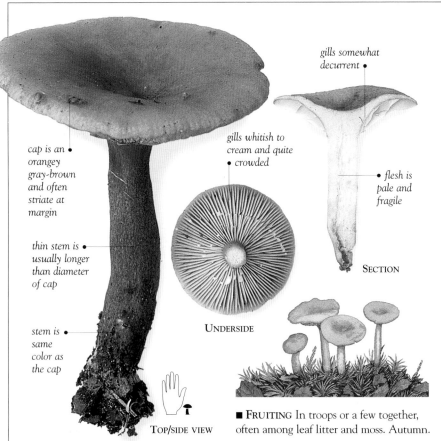

- cap is an orangey gray-brown and often striate at margin
- thin stem is usually longer than diameter of cap
- stem is same color as the cap

TOP/SIDE VIEW

- gills whitish to cream and quite crowded

UNDERSIDE

- gills somewhat decurrent
- flesh is pale and fragile

SECTION

■ FRUITING In troops or a few together, often among leaf litter and moss. Autumn.

LACTARIUS THEIOGALUS

Yellow-staining Milk Cap

A white handkerchief is a useful aid when attempting to identify smallish, orange-brown *Lactarius* species. A drop of white milk from *L. theiogalus* turns yellow after about half a minute. This is a rather pale species, often with a striate cap margin and thin flesh that is mild tasting. The possibly poisonous eastern North American *L. vinaceorufescen's* has a pinkish cinnamon water-spotted cap.

■ SPORE DEPOSIT Whitish to pale cream with pinkish tinge.
■ SIZE Cap 2–5cm (w); stem 3–8cm (h) x 0.4–1cm (w).
■ HABITAT Mycorrhizal with both conifers and deciduous trees, often in acid, damp environments.
■ RANGE Widespread and common in many areas of north temperate zones.

LACTARIUS VOLEMUS

Fishy Milk Cap

This matte and very fleshy orange *Lactarius* species produces copious white milk that dries to a brownish stain. As it matures, it smells strongly of shellfish. A similar but odorless mushroom with nonstaining wide-spaced gills, *L. hygrophoroides*, grows in the same places and is equally choice.

■ SPORE DEPOSIT Whitish.
■ SIZE Cap 6–12cm (w); stem 4–12cm (h) x 1–4cm (w).
■ HABITAT Mycorrhizal, mostly with deciduous trees such as oak and beech.
■ RANGE Widespread in north temperate zones; common in eastern N.A.

■ FRUITING Trooping or a few together. Late spring–autumn.

LACTARIUS CAMPHORATUS

Fragrant Milk Cap

A very dark reddish brown *Lactarius* species with a rather thin stem and a strong spicy smell, reminiscent of camphor, which develops as it dries. The flesh has a bitter aftertaste. In western North America there is a very similar, fragrant species called Candy Caps (*L. fragilis* var. *rubidus*), used in making cookies and pancakes.

■ SPORE DEPOSIT White to creamish.
■ SIZE Cap 3–6cm (w); stem 3–6cm (h) x 0.4–0.8cm, up to 1cm (w).
■ HABITAT Mycorrhizal, under deciduous trees or conifers. Sometimes found on decayed, moss-covered stumps.
■ RANGE Widespread and common in north temperate zones; eastern N.A.

■ FRUITING In troops or small groups, often with moss. Autumn.

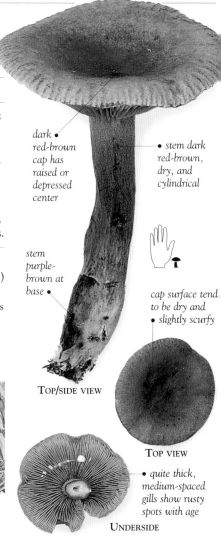

- dark red-brown cap has raised or depressed center
- stem purple-brown at base
- stem dark red-brown, dry, and cylindrical
- cap surface tend to be dry and slightly scurfy

TOP/SIDE VIEW

TOP VIEW

- quite thick, medium-spaced gills show rusty spots with age

UNDERSIDE

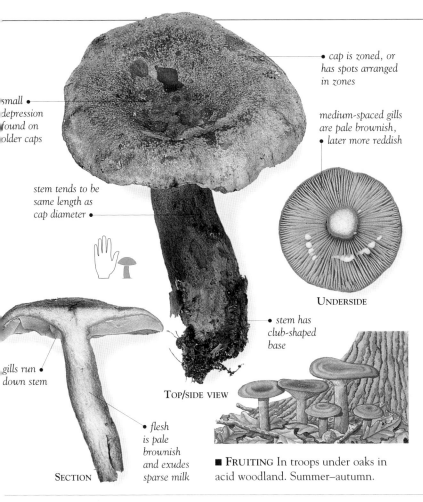

- *small depression found on older caps*
- *cap is zoned, or has spots arranged in zones*
- *medium-spaced gills are pale brownish, later more reddish*
- *stem tends to be same length as cap diameter*

UNDERSIDE

- *stem has club-shaped base*

TOP/SIDE VIEW

- *gills run down stem*
- *flesh is pale brownish and exudes sparse milk*

SECTION

■ **FRUITING** In troops under oaks in acid woodland. Summer–autumn.

LACTARIUS QUIETUS

Oak Milk Cap

Key characteristics of this species are its strict association with oak trees, its zoned cap, and its creamish, sparse milk. The characteristic oily smell is another useful identification feature. *L. chrysorrheus* has the same mycorrhizal partner but is paler, more yellowish in color, and has copious white milk that quickly turns sulfur-yellow. In eastern North America, *L. quietus* var. *incanus* is said to differ from the typical European variety by the latex not staining white paper a yellow color.

■ **SPORE DEPOSIT** Cream with a pale pinkish tinge.
■ **SIZE** Cap 4–8cm, up to 12cm (w); stem 3–7cm (h) x 0.5–1.5cm, up to 2cm (w).
■ **HABITAT** In mostly acid woodland, mycorrhizal with oaks.
■ **RANGE** Very common in Europe and parts of neighboring Asia.

LACTARIUS RUFUS

Red-hot Milk Cap

L. rufus has all-over reddish brown coloring and a raised center on the caps of most specimens. It typically tastes very hot after half a minute delay. It is taller than *L. camphoratus* (*see p.196*), has a more reddish hue, and lacks that species' distinctive spicy smell. Although it is eaten in Europe after salting, it cannot be recommended in this country.

■ **SPORE DEPOSIT** Whitish.
■ **SIZE** Cap 3–10cm (w); stem 5–10cm (h) x 0.5–2cm (w).
■ **HABITAT** Mycorrhizal with both conifers and deciduous trees, especially birch, mostly on acid soils.
■ **RANGE** Widespread and common in many regions of the north temperate zone.

■ **FRUITING** In troops or a few together, under conifers or birch. Summer–autumn.

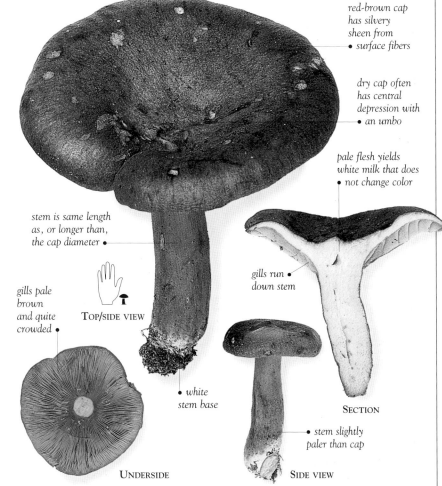

- *red-brown cap has silvery sheen from surface fibers*
- *dry cap often has central depression with an umbo*
- *pale flesh yields white milk that does not change color*
- *stem is same length as, or longer than, the cap diameter*
- *gills pale brown and quite crowded*

TOP/SIDE VIEW

- *gills run down stem*
- *white stem base*

UNDERSIDE

SECTION

- *stem slightly paler than cap*

SIDE VIEW

LACTARIUS HEPATICUS

Liver-colored Milk Cap

This *Lactarius* species, with its dull liver-brown coloring, is confined to very acid pine woods. It has become more common because of the increased incidence of acid rain. Its copious white milk turns yellow if squeezed onto a handkerchief, or if it is left to dry on the flesh of the fungus. *L. rufus (see p.197)* often occurs in the same pinewood habitat. The flesh tastes hot and is not recommended as an edible. *L. theiogalus (see p.196)* has the same yellow milk reaction if squeezed onto a handkerchief.

- **SPORE DEPOSIT** Cream.
- **SIZE** Cap 3–6cm (w); stem 4–6cm (h) x 0.6–1cm (w).
- **HABITAT** Associated with conifers, often in mossy or boggy areas.
- **RANGE** As a complex, widespread and common in regions of the north temperate zones.

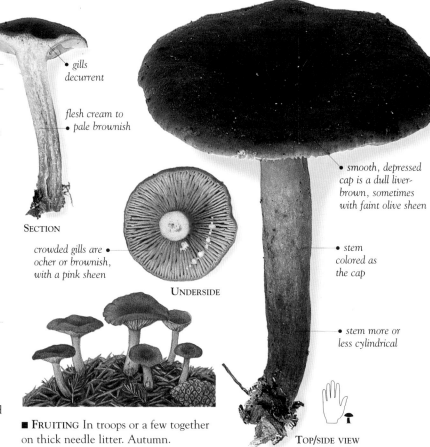

gills decurrent

flesh cream to pale brownish

SECTION

crowded gills are ocher or brownish, with a pink sheen

UNDERSIDE

smooth, depressed cap is a dull liver-brown, sometimes with faint olive sheen

stem colored as the cap

stem more or less cylindrical

TOP/SIDE VIEW

- **FRUITING** In troops or a few together on thick needle litter. Autumn.

LACTARIUS SUBDULCIS

Dull Milk Cap

A lack of distinctive characteristics makes this species difficult to identify. Important markers revolve around negative features: its milk does not turn yellow, it does not have a hot taste, and it is not associated with a particular species of tree, although it is a typical feature of beech forests.

- **SPORE DEPOSIT** Cream–pinkish cream.
- **SIZE** Cap 3–7cm (w); stem 3–6cm (h) x 0.5–1cm (w).
- **HABITAT** Mycorrhizal association with deciduous trees, chiefly beech.
- **RANGE** Widespread and common in Europe; not reliably reported in N.A.

dull cap is convex, slightly depressed, or slightly raised

stem similar in color to cap, darker toward base

often mycorrhizal with beech

gills are medium-spaced

pale brown gills are decurrent

SECTION

UNDERSIDE

occasionally two fruitbodies may fuse together

TOP/SIDE VIEW

TOP/SIDE VIEW

- **FRUITING** Typically a few together with beech trees. Summer–autumn.

PAXILLACEAE

CLASS: *Homobasidiomycetes*

These brown and white spored gilled fungi look similar to *Clitocybe* (*see p.86*), *Lepista* (*see p.90*), or *Pleurotus* (*see p.78*) species. They are classified here in the same family because they contain related compounds and are believed to be more closely related to each other than to other gilled mushrooms.

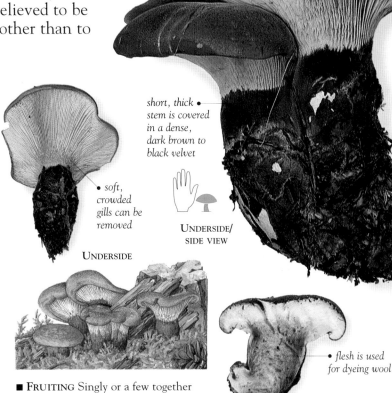

large, fleshy cap rolls under at margin

cap has a finely velvety, dark brown surface

short, thick stem is covered in a dense, dark brown to black velvet

soft, crowded gills can be removed

UNDERSIDE/ SIDE VIEW

UNDERSIDE

flesh is used for dyeing wool

SECTION

PAXILLUS ATROTOMENTOSUS

Velvet Pax

A very fleshy species with a thick stem that is usually attached to the side of the cap. The stem is covered in a thick velvet, and the dark brown cap has a much finer velvety surface. *P. panuoides* is similar but has no real stem, is thinner and paler, and occurs on conifer wood.

■ **SPORE DEPOSIT** Yellowish brown.
■ **SIZE** Cap 10–25cm (w); stem 5–10cm (h) x 2–5cm (w).
■ **HABITAT** Woods and parks; on and around conifer stumps.
■ **RANGE** Widespread and common in many regions of north temperate zones.

■ **FRUITING** Singly or a few together around tree stumps. Summer–autumn.

PAXILLUS INVOLUTUS

Poison Pax ☠

All forayers should take time to learn to recognize this very common and highly poisonous species. The strongly inrolled cap, with its downy margin, is a particularly clear marker. So are the soft removable gills, which stain brown where they have been touched. This "species" is actually a complex of indistinguishable intersterile populations.

■ **SPORE DEPOSIT** Yellowish brown.
■ **SIZE** Cap 6–15cm (w); stem 4–8cm (h) x 1–2cm (w).
■ **HABITAT** Forms mycorrhizal associations with conifers and birch, in woods, parks, and gardens.
■ **RANGE** As a complex, widespread and common in north temperate zones.

yellow- to red-brown cap has a felty to smooth surface

pale yellow to pale brown flesh

soft, easy-to-remove decurrent gills

SECTION

inrolled cap margin covered in fine down

pale yellow gills stain brown where touched

UNDERSIDE

stem base often has attached clump of litter and soil

SIDE VIEW

short, felty stem colored as cap

■ **FRUITING** In troops, rings, or a few together, under trees. Summer–autumn.

OMPHALOTUS OLEARIUS

Jack O'Lantern ☠

This is a complex of bright orange mushrooms whose gills glow in the dark. Their coloring and shape have led people to confuse Jack O'Lanterns with the chanterelle, *Cantharellus cibarius* (*see p.47*). Chanterelle gills, however, are thick-edged, forked, and more veinlike. The Jack O'Lantern complex is found growing in clusters over the base of dying tree trunks, while chanterelles grow unclustered at the base and on the ground.

- **SPORE DEPOSIT** Whitish.
- **SIZE** Cap 6–14cm (w); stem 6–15cm (h) x 0.8–2cm, up to 3cm.
- **HABITAT** On dead or dying trees and stumps on olive trees and oaks in Europe; on oaks in North America. Causes a white rot.
- **RANGE** As a complex, widespread in eastern North America and California.

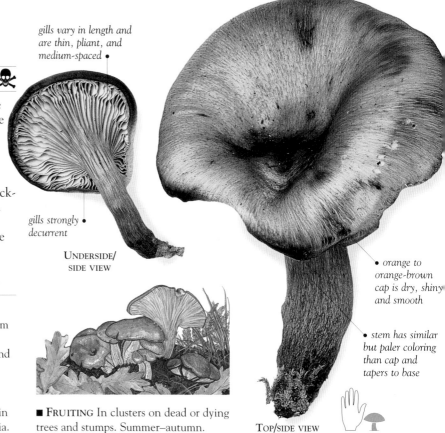

gills vary in length and are thin, pliant, and medium-spaced

gills strongly decurrent

UNDERSIDE/SIDE VIEW

orange to orange-brown cap is dry, shiny and smooth

stem has similar but paler coloring than cap and tapers to base

TOP/SIDE VIEW

- **FRUITING** In clusters on dead or dying trees and stumps. Summer–autumn.

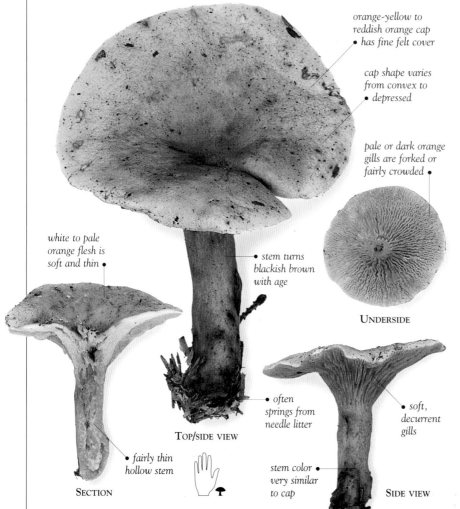

white to pale orange flesh is soft and thin

fairly thin hollow stem

SECTION

stem turns blackish brown with age

often springs from needle litter

TOP/SIDE VIEW

orange-yellow to reddish orange cap has fine felt cover

cap shape varies from convex to depressed

pale or dark orange gills are forked or fairly crowded

UNDERSIDE

soft, decurrent gills

stem color very similar to cap

SIDE VIEW

HYGROPHOROPSIS AURANTIACA

False Chanterelle

Many beginners have picked a whole basket of this fungus, believing it to be the choice *Cantharellus cibarius* (*see p.47*). Its true, soft gills fork like the veins of *C. cibarius*, but the impostor is hardly worth eating. Its flesh is much thinner and its colors more reddish. Be careful not to confuse this species with the poisonous *Omphalotus olearius*.

- **SPORE DEPOSIT** Whitish.
- **SIZE** Cap 2–8cm (w); stem 2–5cm (h) x 0.3–0.8cm (w).
- **HABITAT** Not mycorrhizal; found on needle litter, rotten wood, or sawdust.
- **RANGE** Widespread and common in north temperate zones.

- **FRUITING** In troops or a few together, on litter or wood. Summer–winter.

GOMPHIDIACEAE

CLASS: *Homobasidiomycetes*

This conifer-loving family of mainly slimy-veiled species of gilled mushrooms forms obligate mycorrhizae with conifers in the pine family. No species in this family occurs in the absence of a pine tree. Some species can be considered to be good edibles.

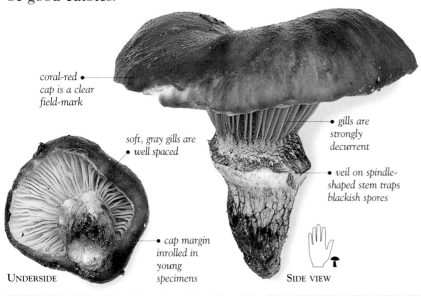

coral-red cap is a clear field-mark

soft, gray gills are well spaced

gills are strongly decurrent

veil on spindle-shaped stem traps blackish spores

cap margin inrolled in young specimens

UNDERSIDE

SIDE VIEW

GOMPHIDIUS ROSEUS

Rosy Spike Cap

An unmistakable species with a coral-red cap and spindle-shaped stem. A slimy veil is present on the stem and is often stained black by the spores. Its closest North American look-alike is *Gomphidus subroseus*, a paler species.

- **SPORE DEPOSIT** Almost black.
- **SIZE** Cap 1.5–5cm (w); stem 2–4cm (h) x 0.5–1cm (w).
- **HABITAT** Under pines near *Suillus bovinus* (see p.213), on sandy soils.
- **RANGE** Widespread in north temperate zones; not reported in North America.

- **FRUITING** A few together among moss, lichens, and pine litter. Autumn.

GOMPHIDIUS GLUTINOSUS

Viscid Spike Cap

The whole fruitbody of this species resembles a tent peg. It is covered in a transparent, slimy veil, which is best removed before cooking. The stem has an indistinct ring-zone, often colored black by spores. The stem base is lemon colored.

- **SPORE DEPOSIT** Almost black.
- **SIZE** Cap 4–10cm, up to 13cm (w); stem 5–10cm (h) x 1–2cm (w).
- **HABITAT** Usually under spruce trees.
- **RANGE** Widespread in north temperate zones.

- **FRUITING** A few together or in troops under spruce. Summer–autumn.

CHROOGOMPHUS RUTILUS

Pine Spike Cap

Species of *Chroogomphus* have less slimy caps than *Gomphidius*, and *C. rutilus* has a greasy cap only in wet weather. The veil consists of reddish threads that form zones on the stem. It is not a choice edible.

- **SPORE DEPOSIT** Almost black.
- **SIZE** Cap 4–8cm, up to 12cm (w); stem 4–10cm, up to 12cm (h) x 0.5–1cm, up to 1.5cm (w).
- **HABITAT** In woods and under pine; mycorrhizal with pines, on sandy soil.
- **RANGE** Widespread and locally common in north temperate zones.

- **FRUITING** In small groups or troops among moss, and pine needles. Autumn.

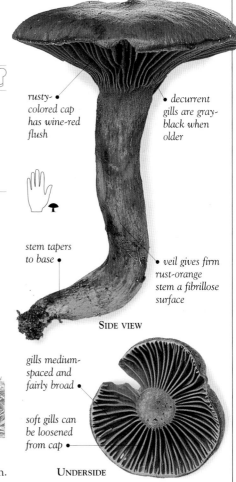

rusty-colored cap has wine-red flush

decurrent gills are gray-black when older

stem tapers to base

veil gives firm rust-orange stem a fibrillose surface

SIDE VIEW

gills medium-spaced and fairly broad

soft gills can be loosened from cap

UNDERSIDE

BOLETACEAE

CLASS: *Homobasidiomycetes*

Fungi commonly referred to as boletes do not all belong to the *Boletaceae*. A few are classified in the family *Gomphidiaceae* (*see p.211*) and the *Strobilomyceteaceae* (*see p.215*). Boletes are soft-fleshed fungi with pores rather than gills. Some species turn blue, black, or red when cut. Nearly all *Boletus* species form mycorrhiza with trees. Oak and pine woods are the best places to look for edible species. A few boletes are poisonous.

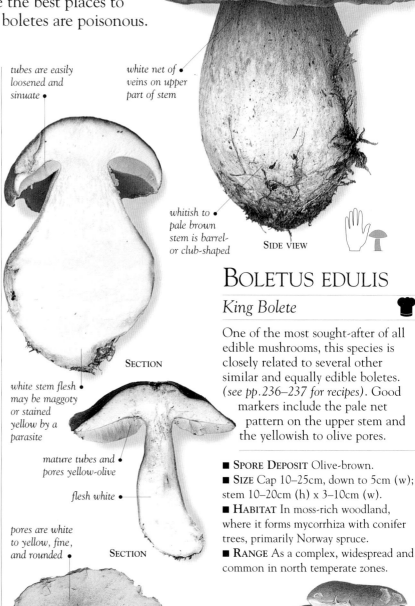

smooth, slightly greasy feel to surface of cap •

pale or dark brown cap is bun-shaped, with skin slightly • overhanging

white net of • veins on upper part of stem

whitish to • pale brown stem is barrel- or club-shaped

SIDE VIEW

tubes are easily loosened and sinuate •

white stem flesh • may be maggoty or stained yellow by a parasite

mature tubes and • pores yellow-olive

flesh white •

pores are white to yellow, fine, and rounded •

SECTION

SECTION

UNDERSIDE

BOLETUS AEREUS

Bronzy Bolete ♟

This bolete can look very similar to *B. edulis* (*see right*). However, its cap is often a darker dull chestnut color, with a fine, velvety surface texture somewhat like the cap skin of *B. aestivalis* (*see p.203*). The stem is also darker brown, often with a brownish to rust-colored net. As the stem is nearly as thick as the cap diameter, the fruitbody has a squat, almost rounded shape, and its white flesh does not change color when cut. It is a very high quality edible, mainly enjoyed by those living in central to southern Europe since this species of bolete is rare in other parts of the world.

- ■ SPORE DEPOSIT Brownish olive.
- ■ SIZE Cap 7–15cm, up to 30cm (w); stem 6–10cm (h) x 4–8cm (w).
- ■ HABITAT Mycorrhizal with mature deciduous trees, often oak or beech.
- ■ RANGE Widespread in north temperate zones; reported from California.

- ■ FRUITING Singly, a few together, or in troops. Summer–autumn.

BOLETUS EDULIS

King Bolete ♟

One of the most sought-after of all edible mushrooms, this species is closely related to several other similar and equally edible boletes. (*see pp.236–237* for recipes). Good markers include the pale net pattern on the upper stem and the yellowish to olive pores.

- ■ SPORE DEPOSIT Olive-brown.
- ■ SIZE Cap 10–25cm, down to 5cm (w); stem 10–20cm (h) x 3–10cm (w).
- ■ HABITAT In moss-rich woodland, where it forms mycorrhiza with conifer trees, primarily Norway spruce.
- ■ RANGE As a complex, widespread and common in north temperate zones.

- ■ FRUITING Singly or in troops on well-drained soil. Summer–autumn.

BOLETUS APPENDICULATUS

Spindle-stemmed Bolete

The most striking feature of this fleshy *Boletus* species is its vivid lemon-yellow tubes. It also has a similarly colored net over the stem, which is usually wider in the middle, tapering sharply toward the base. This stem base is often found to be rooting. A fine felt covers the golden reddish brown cap skin, and both the tubes and the flesh stain slightly bluish. It is a quality edible, distinguishable from *B. radicans*, which has a paler cap and bitter taste.

- **SPORE DEPOSIT** Olive-brown.
- **SIZE** Cap 8–20cm (w); stem 7–15cm (h) x 2.5–6cm (w).
- **HABITAT** In woods, mycorrhizal with deciduous trees such as oaks.
- **RANGE** Widespread in southern Europe; reported from California.

tubes lemon-yellow to brownish yellow; stain bluish •

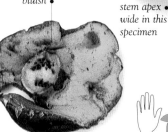

stem apex • wide in this specimen

UNDERSIDE   **SIDE VIEW**

• bun-shaped cap has fine yellow- to orange-brown skin

• yellowish net covers strongly tapering, often rooting, stem

- **FRUITING** Singly or a few together, under deciduous trees. Summer–autumn.

tubes 10–25mm • long, with fine, rounded pores

flesh pale yellow • and firm, tends to stain slightly blue   **SECTION**

---

warm orange-brown cap skin tends to overhang •

cap surface is dry and dull, often • with fine cracks

white net • covers pale brown, barrel-shaped stem

SIDE VIEW

• tubes 10–15mm long and sinuate

• white firm flesh is attacked by maggots

SECTION

BOLETUS AESTIVALIS

Summer Bolete

This species is very similar to *B. edulis* (*see opposite*), but the cap skin cracks and is a paler color. The stem net is more pronounced and extensive. *B. aestivalis* tends to occur some weeks before the main flush of *B. edulis* and *B. aereus* (*see opposite*), but in some areas fruits alongside *B. luridiformis* (*see p.204*).

- **SPORE DEPOSIT** Olive-brown.
- **SIZE** Cap 7–15cm, up to 25cm (w); stem 6–15cm (h) x 2–5cm (w).
- **HABITAT** Woods, mycorrhizal with deciduous trees, such as beech and oak.
- **RANGE** Widespread in north temperate zones; not reliably reported in N. A.

- **FRUITING** In troops or a few together, under deciduous trees. Summer–autumn.

BOLETUS PINOPHILUS

Pinewood King Bolete

Another *B. edulis* look-alike (*see opposite*), but with a much richer brown cap and stem. Also the net extends farther down the stem. As its common name suggests, this excellent edible is exclusively found with pine trees, on sandy soil.

- **SPORE DEPOSIT** Olive-brown.
- **SIZE** Cap 10–20cm, up to 25cm (w); stem 10–15cm, up to 20cm (h) x 4–8cm, up to 10cm (w).
- **HABITAT** In woods, mycorrhizal with pine trees, on sandy soils.
- **RANGE** Widespread in Europe and other north temperate zones.

- **FRUITING** Singly or a few together, on sandy soil. Summer–autumn.

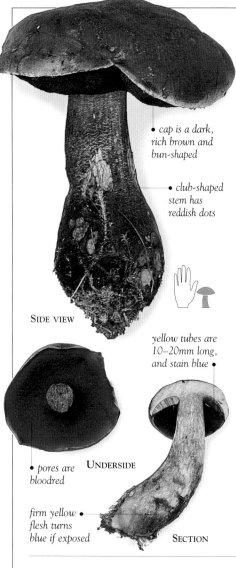

SIDE VIEW

- cap is a dark, rich brown and bun-shaped
- club-shaped stem has reddish dots

yellow tubes are 10–20mm long, and stain blue •

UNDERSIDE

• pores are bloodred

firm yellow • flesh turns blue if exposed

SECTION

BOLETUS LURIDIFORMIS

Dotted-stem Bolete

B. luridiformis belongs to a small group of boletes whose pores are red and whose flesh turns blue when cut. Its cap is a rather dark brown color and its pores are bloodred. *B. erythropus* and *B. subvelutipes* are two nearly indistinguishable species reported from North America.

- ■ **SPORE DEPOSIT** Brown to olive-brown.
- ■ **SIZE** Cap 5–20cm (w); stem 5–15cm (h) x 2–6cm (w).
- ■ **HABITAT** Myrorrhizal with a range of trees in well-drained, mostly acid and moss-rich woodlands.
- ■ **RANGE** Widespread and common in Europe; this species not reported from North America.

- ■ **FRUITING** Singly or a few together, in well-drained soil. Summer–autumn.

BOLETUS LURIDUS

Lurid Bolete

This striking, early-fruiting species is best identified by its dark and very prominent stem net, flesh that turns blue, (as do the orange pores), and red flesh underneath the tube layer. No bolete with red or orange pores and flesh that bruises blue should be eaten.

- ■ **SPORE DEPOSIT** Olive-brown.
- ■ **SIZE** Cap 10–20cm (w); stem 8–16cm, up to 20cm (h) x 2–5cm (w).
- ■ **HABITAT** Mycorrhizal with a range of trees in woods or on woody plants in alkaline soil.
- ■ **RANGE** Widespread and common in Europe; locally common in northeastern North America.

- ■ **FRUITING** Singly, a few, or rarely in large masses. Early summer–autumn.

BOLETUS BADIUS

Bay Bolete

In many ways, this fungus resembles *B. edulis* (see p.202), but its uniformly brown stem is more cylindrical and lacks any net pattern. Also, the pores stain blue when touched, but this disappears during cooking (see pp.236–237 for recipes). Although a popular edible in Europe, there is a confusing complex of similar forms in North America, and one should proceed with caution before eating American forms of unknown edibility. Some mycologists include this fungus with *B. chrysenteron* (p.207) in the genus *Xerocomus*.

- ■ **SPORE DEPOSIT** Olive-brown.
- ■ **SIZE** Cap 4–15cm (w); stem 4–12cm (h) x 1–4cm (w).
- ■ **HABITAT** In woods and parklands, mycorrhizal with pines, but also found with deciduous trees.
- ■ **RANGE** As a complex, widespread in eastern North America.

smooth, rather greasy cap is dark chestnut brown and bun-shaped •

tubes and pores are white to • yellowish olive

pores turn blue if • pressed

UNDERSIDE

finely streaked stem is paler than cap, • and has no net

often spring from • ground under pines

sinuate tubes 6–15mm long, with • fine, rounded pores

TOP/SIDE VIEW

firm white flesh • tends to stain slightly blue

SECTION

- ■ **FRUITING** Singly or in scattered groups with pine trees. Late autumn.

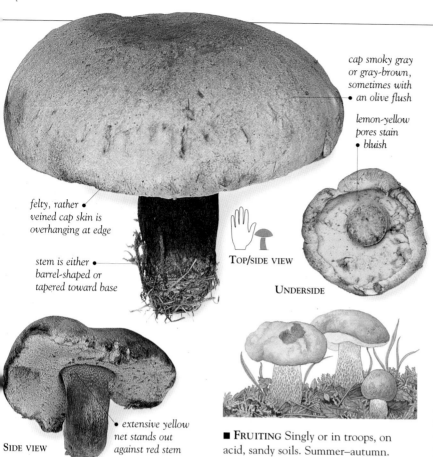

cap smoky gray or gray-brown, sometimes with an olive flush

lemon-yellow pores stain bluish

felty, rather veined cap skin is overhanging at edge

stem is either barrel-shaped or tapered toward base

TOP/SIDE VIEW

UNDERSIDE

extensive yellow net stands out against red stem

SIDE VIEW

■ **FRUITING** Singly or in troops, on acid, sandy soils. Summer–autumn.

BOLETUS CALOPUS

Scarlet-stemmed Bolete

This inedible and possibly slightly poisonous *Boletus* species is similar to the poisonous *B. satanas* (*see below*). However, the species is clearly smaller, with yellow pores and bitter-tasting, yellowish flesh, which turns pale blue when cut. Other pale-capped and red-stemmed boletes such as *B. satanas*, *B. legaliae*, and *B. pulcherrimus* tend to have red pores. Two similar bitter boletes can be found under conifers in western North America, both with blue-staining yellow pores, are *B. frustosus* and *B. coniferarum*.

■ **SPORE DEPOSIT** Olive-brown.
■ **SIZE** Cap 6–14cm, up to 20cm (w); stem 6–10cm (h) x 3–5cm (w).
■ **HABITAT** Mycorrhizal with both conifers and deciduous trees
■ **RANGE** Widespread but local in north temperate zones; not reported from North America.

BOLETUS SATANAS

Satan's Bolete

A fleshy, fat-stemmed, and pale-capped bolete, *B. satanas* can be identified by its bloodred pores and the prominent red net pattern on the stem. The flesh and pores stain only slightly blue. Mature fruitbodies have an unpleasant smell. The taste is mild, but they are slightly poisonous, causing gastrointestinal problems.

■ **SPORE DEPOSIT** Olive-brown.
■ **SIZE** Cap 10–25cm (w); stem 5–15cm (h) x 4–12cm (w).
■ **HABITAT** Mycorrhizal with deciduous trees such as beech and oak.
■ **RANGE** Widespread in southern Europe; reported in California.

■ **FRUITING** Singly, a few together, or in troops. Summer–early autumn.

BOLETUS PULCHERRIMUS

Pretty Poison Bolete

This is one of a series of beautiful but poisonous boletes. It is recognizable by its bloodred pores that bruise blue-black, its reddish brown cap, its thick yellow flesh that turns blue on cutting, and a swollen, but not abruptly bulbous reddish brown stem with a dark red net over the upper portion.

■ **SPORE DEPOSIT** Brown.
■ **SIZE** Cap 7.5–25cm (w); stem 7.5–15cm (h) x 10cm (w) at base.
■ **HABITAT** In mixed forests of tanbark oak, Douglas fir, and giant fir.
■ **RANGE** West coast of North America and New Mexico.

■ **FRUITING** Singly, or in troops in mixed forests. Late summer–autumn.

BOLETUS LEGALIAE

Le Gal's Bolete

This spectacular species belongs to a very bewildering group of reddish, net-stemmed boletes. A darker cap distinguishes it from *B. satanas* (*see left*), and the smell is much more pleasant. The whitish to yellowish flesh bruises light blue but pinkish in the stem base. *B. rhodoxanthus* is also a very close relative.

■ **SPORE DEPOSIT** Olive-brown.
■ **SIZE** Cap 5–15cm (w); stem 8–16cm (h) x 2.5–5cm (w).
■ **HABITAT** Mycorrhizal with deciduous trees; preference for calcareous soils.
■ **RANGE** Widespread in southern Europe; not reported in North America.

■ **FRUITING** Singly, a few together, or rarely in troops. Summer–early autumn.

BOLETUS RUBELLUS

Red-capped Bolete

This is one of a complex of smallish boletes with dry red cap and stems, and yellowish pores and flesh that bruise blue or greenish blue. Many of these occur in grassy areas after heavy rains. Although this species is eaten in Europe, none in this complex can be recommended in North America because of the difficulty of identification and the lack of local experience eating this group.

- **Spore Deposit** Olive-brown.
- **Size** Cap 3–6cm (w); stem 3–8cm (h) x 0.5–1cm, up to 1.5cm (w).
- **Habitat** Mycorrhizal with deciduous trees, often in open woods.
- **Range** As a complex, widespread in eastern North America.

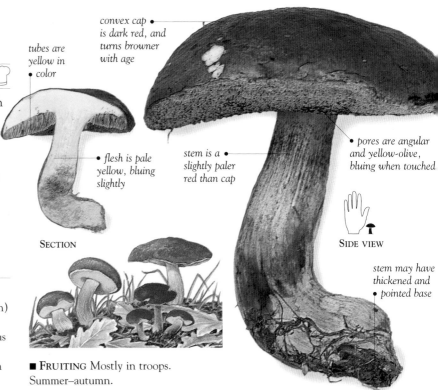

tubes are yellow in color

convex cap is dark red, and turns browner with age

flesh is pale yellow, bluing slightly

stem is a slightly paler red than cap

pores are angular and yellow-olive, bluing when touched

SECTION

SIDE VIEW

stem may have thickened and pointed base

- **Fruiting** Mostly in troops. Summer–autumn.

BOLETUS SENSIBILIS

Deceptive Bolete

This compex of mild tasting, yellow-pored boletes stains blue on bruising. *Boletes bicolor*, a large, fleshy North American species with a dry red cap and stem, and pale yellow flesh is a popular edible. Take care to avoid the reportedly poisonous *sensibilis* group, because mushrooms in this group can easily be confused with the edible *B. bicolor*.

- **Spore Deposit** Olive-brown.
- **Size** Cap 6–15cm (w); stem 8–12cm (h) x 1–3cm (w).
- **Habitat** Mycorrhizal with deciduous trees, often on sandy soils.
- **Range** As a complex, widespread in eastern North America.

- **Fruiting** In small groups on sandy soils. Summer–autumn.

BOLETUS POROSPORUS

White-cracking Bolete

This species is very similar to *B. chrysenteron* and *B. subtomentosus* (*see opposite*). However, it lacks the red color in the lower cap skin, and the stem tends to be much darker. Viewing the spores under a microscope will reveal the most accurate means of identification – the truncated shape of the spores.

- **Spore Deposit** Olive-brown.
- **Size** Cap 4–10cm (w); stem 4–10cm (h) x 0.5–2cm (w).
- **Habitat** Mycorrhizal with deciduous trees in various types of woods.
- **Range** As a complex, including the similar *B. truncatus*, widespread in north temperate zones.

- **Fruiting** Singly or a few fruitbodies together. Summer–autumn.

BOLETUS PULVERULENTUS

Midnight Blue Bolete

A rather distinctive bolete, with an intense, immediate reaction in all parts – turning dark blue – when bruised. The dotted stem resembles that of *B. erythropus* (*see p.204*), but is yellow rather than red, thinner, and more pointed. Dull yellow pores and a brown to red-brown cap are other features. Edible but not choice.

- **Spore Deposit** Olive-brown.
- **Size** Cap 4–10cm (w); stem 4–10cm (h) x 1–3cm (w).
- **Habitat** Mycorrhizal with deciduous trees, on better soils, often with oaks.
Range Widely distributed in northern temperate zones.

- **Fruiting** Singly, a few together, or rarely in troops. Summer–autumn.

BOLETUS CHRYSENTERON

Red-cracking Bolete

This is one of the smaller, less fleshy *Boletus* species. The cap skin tends to crack early, revealing a red layer underneath, and the stem is thin, cylindrical, and lacking any distinct pattern. Such species can be placed in the genus *Xerocomus*. Although edible, it is not choice.

■ **SPORE DEPOSIT** Olive-brown.
■ **SIZE** Cap 3–10cm (w); stem 3–10cm (h) x 0.5–2cm (w).
■ **HABITAT** Mycorrhizal with deciduous trees, on soils rich in humus, which have been formed under acid conditions; under conifers in California.
■ **RANGE** Widespread and common in parts of the northern temperate zones.

■ **FRUITING** Often in large troops but also singly. Summer–autumn.

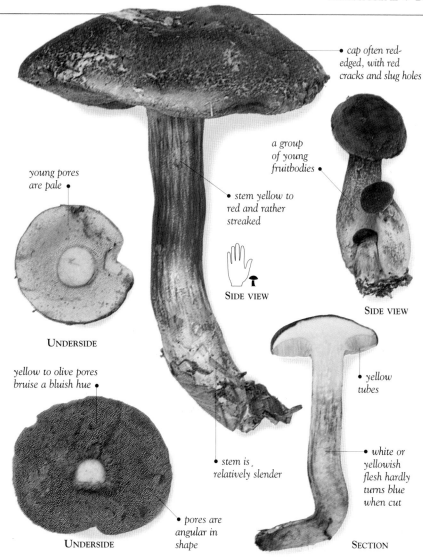

young pores are pale •

UNDERSIDE

• *cap often red-edged, with red cracks and slug holes*

a group of young fruitbodies •

• *stem yellow to red and rather streaked*

SIDE VIEW

SIDE VIEW

yellow to olive pores bruise a bluish hue •

UNDERSIDE

• *stem is relatively slender*

• *pores are angular in shape*

• *yellow tubes*

• *white or yellowish flesh hardly turns blue when cut*

SECTION

---

tubes are yellow in color •

rather soft-fleshed, olive-brown cap is felty and bun-shaped •

large yellow to olive pores barely bruise blue •

yellowish stem has faint lines and is often • *pointed*

SIDE VIEW

UNDERSIDE

• *yellowish flesh staines faintly blue*

SECTION

■ **FRUITING** Singly or a few with all trees. Summer–autumn.

BOLETUS SUBTOMENTOSUS

Yellow-cracking Bolete

Larger than *B. chrysenteron* (*see above*), the soft-fleshed, brownish cap of this species usually does not crack, or only does so with age, despite its common name. The stem is also brownish, and the angular pores stain slightly blue when bruised. *B. subtomentosus*, *B. chrysenteron*, and *B. rubellus* can be classified in the genus *Xerocomus*. Although it is edible, *Boletus subtomentosus* is not choice because the flavor is bland at best.

■ **SPORE DEPOSIT** Olive-brown.
■ **SIZE** Cap 6–10cm (w); stem 6–10cm (h) x 1–2.5cm (w).
■ **HABITAT** Mycorrhizal with deciduous trees and conifers.
■ **RANGE** Widespread and fairly common in northern temperate zones, extending to subarctic and alpine regions.

BOLETUS PARASITICUS

Earth Ball Bolete

A small, fairly uniformly ocher-brown *Boletus* species with an unusual lifestyle – it grows on the fruitbodies of *Scleroderma citrinum* (*see p.225*). In spite of its scientific name, it does no harm to its host. It is not recommended as an edible because its host is toxic.

- **SPORE DEPOSIT** Olive-brown.
- **SIZE** Cap 2–7cm (w); stem 3–6cm (h) x 0.8–1.5cm (w).
- **HABITAT** In association with *Scleroderma citrinum* (*see p.225*), forming mycorrhiza with deciduous trees.
- **RANGE** Widespread in Europe and reported in eastern North America.

- **FRUITING** In clusters on *Scleroderma citrinum*. Summer–autumn.

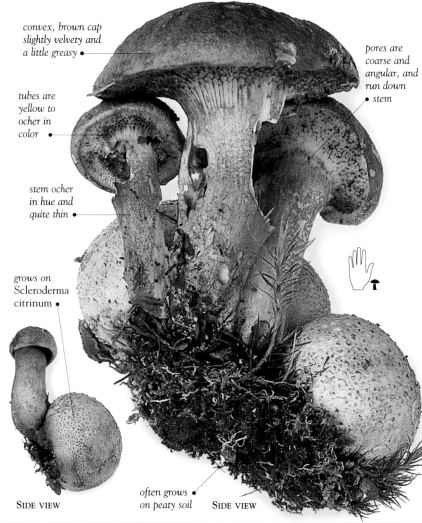

convex, brown cap slightly velvety and a little greasy

tubes are yellow to ocher in color

stem ocher in hue and quite thin

grows on Scleroderma citrinum

pores are coarse and angular, and run down stem

often grows on peaty soil   SIDE VIEW

SIDE VIEW

---

cap is cinnamon or tinged reddish, with slightly greasy skin

dry, cinnamon-colored stem is slender

stem tapers toward base

SIDE VIEW

tubes are pale cinnamon

chrome-yellow flesh

angular pores are cinnamon to rust

SECTION

UNDERSIDE

- **FRUITING** Mostly a few together or singly. Summer–autumn.

CHALCIPORUS PIPERATUS

Peppery Bolete

A very small, inedible bolete with cinnamon coloring throughout, except for the lemon-chrome flesh in the stem. The rather soft flesh has an intensely hot and peppery flavor. Although not a true edible, it has sometimes been used as a spice. *C. piperatoides* is similar but can be distinguished by the blue bruising of its cap, tubes, and pores. It is also a much rarer, warm-loving species, found under deciduous trees. *C. amarellus* is even closer, but may be told apart by its pinker colors and a milder, less peppery taste.

- **SPORE DEPOSIT** Rusty brown.
- **SIZE** Cap 3–5cm, up to 7cm (w); stem 4–6cm, up to 8cm (h) x 0.3–1cm (w).
- **HABITAT** Mycorrhizal with conifers and deciduous trees.
- **RANGE** Widespread in north temperate zones.

GYROPORUS CASTANEUS

Chestnut Bolete

Gyroporus species can be recognized by their pale spores and fragile, chambered stems. G. *castaneus* is a distinctively rich orange-brown and its flesh does not stain when it is cut. The tubes are virtually free of the stem. The taste is pleasantly nutty. A similar but apparently poisonous species from coastal Portugal has recently been publicized. Note that the so-called boletes (sometimes referred to as sponge-caps) are dispersed among several families and within these families some species have gills rather than tubes.

■ **SPORE DEPOSIT** Pale yellowish.
■ **SIZE** Cap 3–8cm, up to 12cm (w); stem 4–7cm (h) x 1–3cm (w).
■ **HABITAT** Mycorrhizal with deciduous trees, especially oaks, and also with pines. Often found on sandy soil.
■ **RANGE** Widespread and locally common in the north temperate zones.

whitish tubes are 3–6mm long; pores are whitish to pale brown •

brittle whitish flesh does not stain •

stem smooth and pale orange-brown •

• stem is chambered inside

SECTION

UNDERSIDE/SIDE VIEW

• convex to flat cap is rich orange-brown

• cap surface has velvety feel

TOP VIEW

■ **FRUITING** Singly or a few together under deciduous trees. Summer–autumn.

GYROPORUS CYANESCENS

Cornflower Bolete

A surprise awaits those who slice this *Gyroporus* species; the flesh and tubes immediately turn from a whitish color to cornflower blue. As in other *Gyroporus* species, the flesh is fragile and chambered in the stem. The bulbous base of the stem abruptly tapers to a basal point. The tubes are almost free of the stem and the pores are small and rounded. This "species" is a complex of forms, including one that turns greenish blue before blue and another (G. *subalbellus*) that does not turn blue at all.

■ **SPORE DEPOSIT** Pale yellowish.
■ **SIZE** Cap 5–8cm, up to 12cm (w); stem 6–10cm (h) x 2–3cm (w).
■ **HABITAT** In woods and forests on sandy soil, mycorrhizal with conifers and deciduous trees.
■ **RANGE** Widespread and locally common in north temperate zones; in eastern North America.

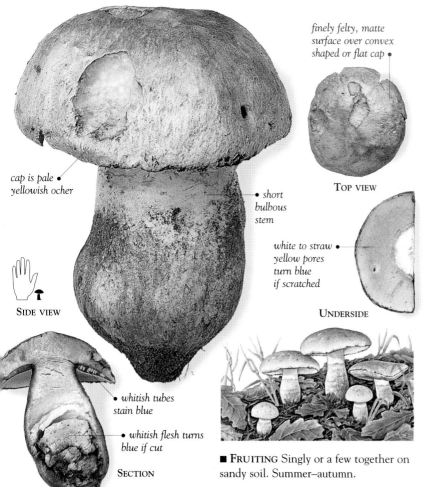

cap is pale • yellowish ocher

finely felty, matte surface over convex shaped or flat cap •

TOP VIEW

• short bulbous stem

white to straw • yellow pores turn blue if scratched

UNDERSIDE

SIDE VIEW

• whitish tubes stain blue

• whitish flesh turns blue if cut

SECTION

■ **FRUITING** Singly or a few together on sandy soil. Summer–autumn.

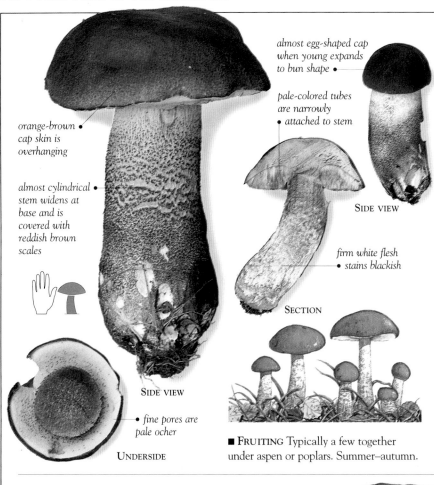

orange-brown cap skin is overhanging

almost cylindrical stem widens at base and is covered with reddish brown scales

almost egg-shaped cap when young expands to bun shape

pale-colored tubes are narrowly attached to stem

SIDE VIEW

firm white flesh stains blackish

SECTION

SIDE VIEW

fine pores are pale ocher

UNDERSIDE

LECCINUM AURANTIACUM

Red Aspen Bolete

As the name implies, this fungus is associated with aspen trees. It belongs to a red-capped group of *Leccinum* species and is further distinguished by having brown scales on the stem. The flesh is firm and of better quality than that in the *L. scabrum* group (see p.211). Also known as *L. rufum*, this red- to orange-capped group is a complex of species that occur under different kinds of trees and shrubs. Some nearly indistinguisable ones grow under oaks, others under conifers, madrones, or bearberry in California.

- **SPORE DEPOSIT** Ocher-brown.
- **SIZE** Cap 8–15cm, up to 20cm (w); stem 10–15cm (h) x 1.5–3cm (w).
- **HABITAT** In woods, mycorrhizal with aspen and poplar trees.
- **RANGE** As a complex, widely distributed in North America.

■ **FRUITING** Typically a few together under aspen or poplars. Summer–autumn.

LECCINUM VERSIPELLE

Orange Birch Bolete

A handsome *Leccinum* species, whose orange cap contrasts with its tall, black-scaled stem. It is more pleasant to eat than species in the *Leccinum scabrum* group because of its firm flesh, but it lacks the quality of many boletes. More commonly known here as *L. testaceoscabrum*.

- **SPORE DEPOSIT** Ocher-brown.
- **SIZE** Cap 8–15cm, up to 20cm (w); stem 10–18cm (h) x 1.5–4cm, up to 5cm (w).
- **HABITAT** In damp woods, forms mycorrhizal associations with birch.
- **RANGE** Widespread and common in northeastern North America.

■ **FRUITING** Singly or a few together in damp woods. Summer–autumn.

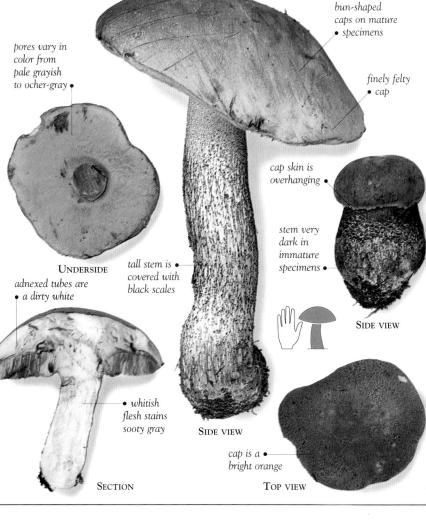

pores vary in color from pale grayish to ocher-gray

bun-shaped caps on mature specimens

finely felty cap

cap skin is overhanging

stem very dark in immature specimens

UNDERSIDE

adnexed tubes are a dirty white

tall stem is covered with black scales

whitish flesh stains sooty gray

SECTION

SIDE VIEW

SIDE VIEW

cap is a bright orange

TOP VIEW

LECCINUM CROCIPODIUM

Yellow-pored Scaber Stalk

This stands out as being quite unusual among *Leccinum* species because it has yellow pores and yellow coloring on the stem and cap – although the cap is more of a yellow-brown. The flesh stains a sooty color with age, and the slightly velvety cap skin soon cracks, which is another unusual feature for this genus. All species of *Leccinum* should be cooked thoroughly before eating.

- **SPORE DEPOSIT** Olive-ocher.
- **SIZE** Cap 4–10cm (w); stem 5–12cm (h) x 1–3cm (w).
- **HABITAT** Mycorrhizal with oak, with a preference for better soils.
- **RANGE** Mostly in warmer parts of Europe and eastern North America.

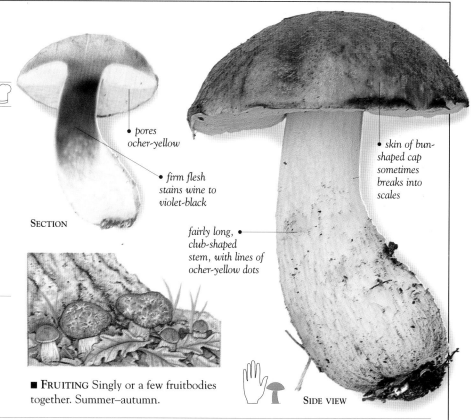

pores ocher-yellow

firm flesh stains wine to violet-black

SECTION

skin of bun-shaped cap sometimes breaks into scales

fairly long, club-shaped stem, with lines of ocher-yellow dots

- **FRUITING** Singly or a few fruitbodies together. Summer–autumn.

SIDE VIEW

---

bun-shaped cap has slightly overhanging skin

stem covered with gray to black scales

SIDE VIEW

stem is sturdy and clavate

tubes soft, gray-white, and sinuate

SIDE VIEW

firm, fibrous stem flesh hardly changes color

SECTION

LECCINUM SCABRUM

Brown Birch Scaber Stalk

Gray-white pores, gray-black stem scales, and a brown cap mark this birch-associated species. The flesh is soft in the cap but fibrous in the stem, and, unlike some relatives, it hardly stains. The borderline between near relatives is unclear, and *L. scabrum* is often used as a collective name for the whole group of brown-capped *Leccinum* species. *Leccinum scabrum* is edible but not choice. It does not keep well.

- **SPORE DEPOSIT** Ocher-brown.
- **SIZE** Cap 6–15cm, up to 20cm (w); stem 10–20cm (h) x 1–3cm (w).
- **HABITAT** Mycorrhizal with birches, often on damp ground.
- **RANGE** Widespread in north temperate zones; throughout eastern North America.

- **FRUITING** Singly, a few together, or in troops. Summer–autumn.

LECCINUM VARIICOLOR

Varied Birch Scaber Stalk

Another edible birch-associated *Leccinum* species. The cap is sooty brown, but with paler and darker areas intermixed. Another feature is the pink and turquoise staining of the stem flesh after a few minutes. A bluish stain can normally be seen from the outside at the stem base.

- **SPORE DEPOSIT** Ocher-brown spores, with distinct reddish tinge.
- **SIZE** Cap 7–12cm, up to 18cm (w); stem 8–15cm (h) x 1–3cm (w).
- **HABITAT** Mycorrhizal with birch, on damp ground.
- **RANGE** Widespread in Europe and adjacent Asia and eastern North America.

- **FRUITING** Typically singly or a few together. Summer–autumn.

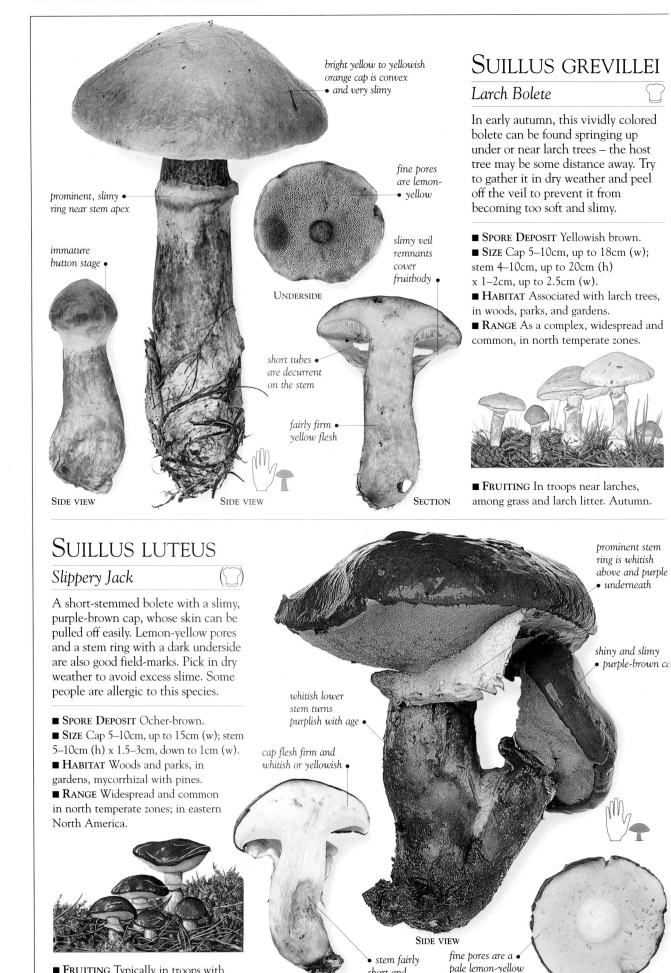

bright yellow to yellowish orange cap is convex and very slimy

SUILLUS GREVILLEI

Larch Bolete

In early autumn, this vividly colored bolete can be found springing up under or near larch trees – the host tree may be some distance away. Try to gather it in dry weather and peel off the veil to prevent it from becoming too soft and slimy.

■ **SPORE DEPOSIT** Yellowish brown.
■ **SIZE** Cap 5–10cm, up to 18cm (w); stem 4–10cm, up to 20cm (h) x 1–2cm, up to 2.5cm (w).
■ **HABITAT** Associated with larch trees, in woods, parks, and gardens.
■ **RANGE** As a complex, widespread and common, in north temperate zones.

■ **FRUITING** In troops near larches, among grass and larch litter. Autumn.

prominent, slimy ring near stem apex

fine pores are lemon-yellow

slimy veil remnants cover fruitbody

UNDERSIDE

immature button stage

short tubes are decurrent on the stem

fairly firm yellow flesh

SIDE VIEW

SIDE VIEW

SECTION

SUILLUS LUTEUS

Slippery Jack

A short-stemmed bolete with a slimy, purple-brown cap, whose skin can be pulled off easily. Lemon-yellow pores and a stem ring with a dark underside are also good field-marks. Pick in dry weather to avoid excess slime. Some people are allergic to this species.

■ **SPORE DEPOSIT** Ocher-brown.
■ **SIZE** Cap 5–10cm, up to 15cm (w); stem 5–10cm (h) x 1.5–3cm, down to 1cm (w).
■ **HABITAT** Woods and parks, in gardens, mycorrhizal with pines.
■ **RANGE** Widespread and common in north temperate zones; in eastern North America.

■ **FRUITING** Typically in troops with pine trees. Late summer–autumn.

prominent stem ring is whitish above and purple underneath

shiny and slimy purple-brown ca

whitish lower stem turns purplish with age

cap flesh firm and whitish or yellowish

stem fairly short and thick

SIDE VIEW

SECTION

fine pores are a pale lemon-yellow

UNDERSIDE

• soft-fleshed, convex to flat cap has orange rusty brown coloring

compound pores are more or less olive in color •

TOP/SIDE VIEW

UNDERSIDE

cap is only greasy and slimy in wet weather conditions

1CM

PORE SURFACE

very short stem is dry, smooth, and covered with fibers •

■ **FRUITING** In troops, often with moss and pine litter. Late summer–autumn.

SUILLUS BOVINUS

European Cow Bolete

The Latin name for this European and Asian mushroom translates as "swine cow." *S. bovinus* is usually a small species with an olive-hued pore surface that has compound pores. The pore layer is subdivided into an angular, coarse-pored layer and a lower, fine-pored layer. The ringless stems are very short and often barely visible before picking. *S. bovinus* is often found with *S. variegatus* (*see p.214*) and the much rarer *Gomphidius roseus* (*see p.201*). *S. bovinus* is edible but it is hardly of culinary interest because it is small and lacks flavor.

■ **SPORE DEPOSIT** Brownish olive.
■ **SIZE** Cap 3–7cm, up to 15cm (w); stem 3–6cm (h) x 0.5–1cm (w).
■ **HABITAT** Mycorrhizal with pines on a variety of soils, often sandy soils.
■ **RANGE** Widespread and common in Europe and parts of Asia including Japan; absent in North America.

SUILLUS GRANULATUS

Dotted-stalk Bolete

Unlike *S. luteus* (*see p.212*), this species has no ring on its distinctively dotted stem. Very young fruitbodies exude milky droplets from the pores and from the top of the stem. The cap color is somewhere between *S. grevillei* and *S. luteus* (*see p.212*), while the stem is pale yellow and pointed at the base. *S. granulatus* can be told apart from *S. collinitus* by the darker cap and the pink stem base of the latter. The flesh of *S. granulatus* is firm in young specimens and the mild nutty flavor makes it a popular edible in Europe. It is similar to the edible *S. placidus* (*see p.214*).

■ **SPORE DEPOSIT** Brownish.
■ **SIZE** Cap 4–10cm, up to 15cm (w); stem 4–8cm, up to 10cm (h) x 1–1.5cm, up to 2cm (w).
■ **HABITAT** Mycorrhizal with pines, on more or less calcareous soils.
■ **RANGE** As a complex, widespread in north temperate zones; in eastern North America and on West Coast.

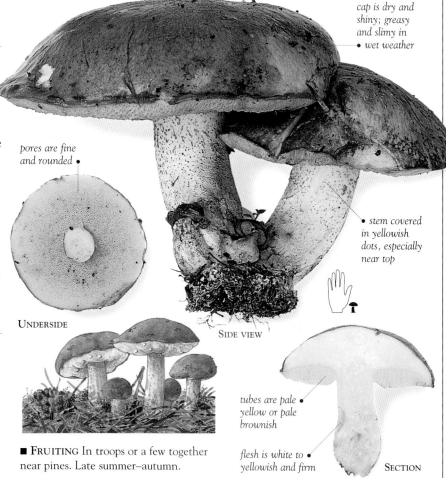

cap is dry and shiny; greasy and slimy in • wet weather

pores are fine and rounded •

• stem covered in yellowish dots, especially near top

UNDERSIDE

SIDE VIEW

tubes are pale • yellow or pale brownish

flesh is white to • yellowish and firm

SECTION

■ **FRUITING** In troops or a few together near pines. Late summer–autumn.

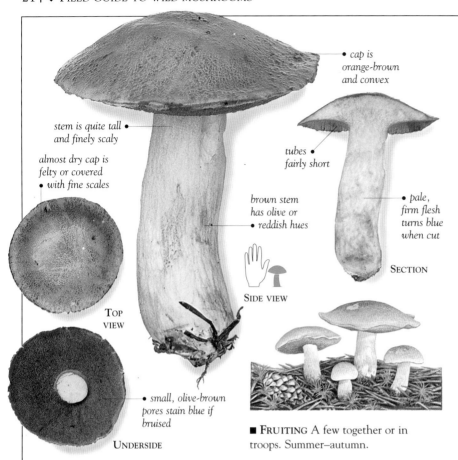

stem is quite tall and finely scaly •

almost dry cap is felty or covered • with fine scales

cap is orange-brown and convex •

tubes • fairly short

brown stem has olive or • reddish hues

• pale, firm flesh turns blue when cut

SECTION

SIDE VIEW

TOP VIEW

• small, olive-brown pores stain blue if bruised

UNDERSIDE

■ FRUITING A few together or in troops. Summer–autumn.

SUILLUS VARIEGATUS

Variegated Bolete

This rather tall-stemmed, fleshy *Suillus* species rarely exhibits the slimy cap characteristic of species in this genus. This cap has a felty to finely scaly surface. The small pores are brown to olive-brown and, like the flesh, stain blue when pressed. A nearly transcontinental "replacement" species in North America is *S. tomentosus*, found under pine trees. Although edible, it has an unpleasant taste.

■ **SPORE DEPOSIT** Brownish olive.
■ **SIZE** Cap 7–13cm, down to 5cm (w); stem 6–10cm, down to 4cm and up to 12cm (h) x 1.5–2cm, up to 3cm (w).
■ **HABITAT** Mycorrhizal with pines, often on sandy soils, with acid-loving plants.
■ **RANGE** Widespread and common in Europe and nearby Asia; absent in North America.

SUILLUS PLACIDUS

Ivory Bolete

A species best identified by its almost pure white, very slimy cap, its dark, strongly dotted and scaled stem, and its occurrence under five-needled pines. This is one of a number of species of *suillus* restricted to five-needled pine in North America. Other species include the eastern *S. americanus*, the western *S. sibiricus*, and the dry, red, scaly-capped *S. pictus* (*S.spraguei*).

■ **SPORE DEPOSIT** Yellow-brown.
■ **SIZE** Cap 4–8cm, up to 12cm (w); stem 6–9cm, up to 15cm (h) x 1–2cm (w).
■ **HABITAT** Mycorrhizal with five-needled pines, such as *Pinus strobus*.
■ **RANGE** Widespread in north temperate zones.

■ **FRUITING** In troops or a few together, among needle litter. Summer–autumn.

SUILLUS AERUGINASCENS

Gray Larch Bolete

The dingy olive coloring of this slimy bolete is less attractive than that of *S. grevillei* (*see p.212*). Its cap is a mix of hues, and its margin has a membranous white veil attached. *Fuscoboletinus* is a genus recognized by some in North America for *Suillus*-like boletes with wine-brown spore prints.

■ **SPORE DEPOSIT** Wine-brown.
■ **SIZE** Cap 5–12cm (w); stem 5–10cm (h) x 1–2cm (w).
■ **HABITAT** Mycorrhizal with larch, on better quality soils.
■ **RANGE** Widespread in Europe and Asia; across northern North America.

■ **FRUITING** In troops, often in grass near larch. Summer–autumn.

SUILLUS PLORANS

Cembra-Pine Bolete

This *Suillus* species resembles both *S. granulatus* (*see p.213*) and *S. collinitus* in exuding copious milky droplets when young. It differs in its mycorrhizal partner and in having a different color mix. The stem base is tinted pink, as it is in *S. collinitus*, and the pores are olive. It is edible but not easy to find in sufficient quantity.

■ **SPORE DEPOSIT** Brown.
■ **SIZE** Cap 3–8cm, up to 15cm (w); stem 5–7cm, up to 10cm (h) x 1–2cm (w).
■ **HABITAT** Mycorrhizal with five-needled pines such as *Pinus cembra*, at higher altitudes, among moss and needle litter.
■ **RANGE** Local in central Europe and parts of Asia; absent in North America.

■ **FRUITING** A few together or in troops. Summer–autumn.

STROBILOMYCETACEAE

CLASS: *Homobasidiomycetes*

Most of the species in this family are tropical boletes, typically with very dark coloring and pink, purplish, or black spores. The different genera can be identified by the shape of their spores, as well as by other marks. They are strongly ornamented in *Strobilomyces* and not so in the others.

UNDERSIDE

- long tubes have fine pores that become deep pink with age

- immature pores are whitish in color

UNDERSIDE

- dry cap has a texture like fine suede

- dark, coarse, and prominent net over length of thick stem

TOP/ SIDE VIEW

TYLOPILUS FELLEUS

Bitter Bolete

This large, brown-capped bolete has a dark netlike stalk pattern and slightly pinkish pores (when mature). It looks very similar to *Boletes edulis*, but it is too bitter to be edible.

- **SPORE DEPOSIT** Dingy pink.
- **SIZE** Cap 6–15cm, up to 20cm (w); stem 5–12cm (h) x 2.5–5cm, down to 1.5cm (w).
- **HABITAT** On acid soils under both conifers and deciduous trees; on rotting hemlock logs.
- **RANGE** Widespread and common in eastern North America.

- **FRUITING** Singly or in troops on well-drained, acid soil. Summer–autumn.

---

convex, gray-black cap resembles a pine cone

tough, fibrous, and scaly stem is colored as cap

SIDE VIEW

- very long tubes have quite fine pores that stain when touched

- tough, grayish flesh turns pink and then black when cut

SECTION

STROBILOMYCES STROBILACEUS

Old-man-of-the-woods

Also known as *S. floccopus*, this mushroom cannot be mistaken in Europe, but in North America and eastern Asia there are several look-alikes. The flesh bruises red. It can be eaten while very young, but it is hardly worthwhile.

- **SPORE DEPOSIT** Purplish black.
- **SIZE** Cap 5–10cm, up to 15cm (w); stem 8–16cm (h) x 1–2cm (w).
- **HABITAT** Found with both deciduous trees and conifers, on better soils.
- **RANGE** Widespread and common in eastern North America.

- **FRUITING** Often singly or a small group together. Summer–autumn.

PORPHYRELLUS PORPHYROSPORUS

Bluing Chocolate Bolete

This mushroom has been placed in different genera and is recognized by various authors as a complex of several species. This species has an unpleasant taste and has been reported to be poisonous.

- **SPORE DEPOSIT** Purple-brown.
- **SIZE** Cap 5–15cm (w); stem 5–12cm (h) x 1–3cm (w).
- **HABITAT** Found with both conifers and deciduous trees.
- **RANGE** As a complex, widespread across north temperate zones.

- **FRUITING** Singly or in troops, often in deep litter. Summer–autumn.

PHALLACEAE

CLASS: *Homobasidiomycetes*

Distinctive phallic shapes and foul-smelling fruitbodies have made this family famous. The putrid smell derives from the spore mass and serves to attract insects such as flies and beetles to disperse the spores; rain also helps. The young fruitbody is enclosed in an egglike structure, which breaks open as the stem emerges.

spores are found within putrid, olive-green slime that covers thimble-shaped cap

white, spongy stem has a cellular structure and is hollow inside

PHALLUS IMPUDICUS

Shameless Stinkhorn

Most people have spotted this species; at least they will have noticed the foul smell. Three similar stinkhorns are the granular-headed *P. ravenelii* and the skirt-stalked *Dictyophora duplicata* of eastern North America, and the more widely distributed pink egg *P. hadriani*.

■ SPORE MASS Olive-brown.
■ SIZE Egg up to 6cm (h); stem 15–20cm (h) x 1.5–3cm, up to 4cm (w).
■ HABITAT In acid deciduous or conifer woods and in sand dunes.
■ RANGE As a genus, widespread and common in the north temperate zones.

olive spore mass

thick white stem almost ready to emerge from egg

intact egg with thin leathery skin

SECTION

white cord runs down into substrate

SIDE VIEW

beneath the slime, cap is honeycomb-like and white in color

SIDE VIEW

volva around base is thin and papery

the volva is what is left of the skin of the egg

SIDE VIEW

■ FRUITING Singly or in troops, often around stumps. Summer–autumn.

spore mass is sticky, putrid, and olive in color

stem tip is orange beneath the spore mass

stem whitish to dirty orange in color

remnants of egg skin around stem base

SIDE VIEW   SIDE VIEW

stem emerging from egg

hollow stem has a sponge-like texture

leathery skin

thick, gelatinous layer

white cord anchors egg in substrate

SECTION

egg is whitish in color and narrowly egg-shaped

SIDE VIEW   SIDE VIEW

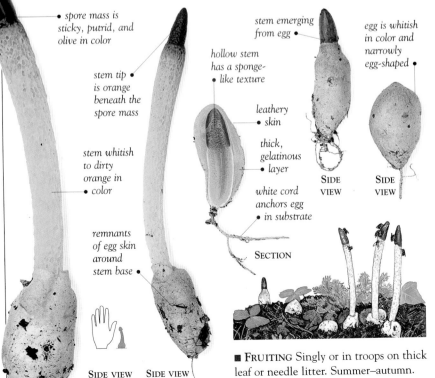

■ FRUITING Singly or in troops on thick leaf or needle litter. Summer–autumn.

MUTINUS CANINUS

Dog Stinkhorn

This resembles a smaller, more slender *Phallus impudicus* but without a well-formed head. The common eastern North American species found in wood mulch is *Mutinus elegans*, which has an orange-pink stalk and a long-tapered, green-slime covered top. While not reported to be poisonous, it is not worthwhile as an edible.

■ SPORE MASS Olive.
■ SIZE Egg up to 4cm (h); stem 6–12cm (h) x 1–1.5cm (w).
■ HABITAT On thick leaf or needle litter, often around rotten stumps.
■ RANGE As a genus, common in Europe and North America from Quebec to Florida, west to Michigan.

CLATHRACEAE

CLASS: *Homobasidiomycetes*

Like the *Phallaceae*, members of this family give off strong, putrid odors, and their spores are found in a slimy mass and are dispersed by flies. They have remarkable shapes and are mostly very vividly colored. Some of the most spectacular species originated in Australia and New Zealand.

CLATHRUS ARCHERI

Devil's Fingers

This inedible, foul-smelling species is now well established in Europe. It has four to eight spreading arms, united at the base. A similar stinkhorn, *Pseudocolus fusiformis*, is found in North America in the mid-Atlantic states, but it has only three to four arms fused at the tips.

■ **SPORE MASS** Olive-brown.
■ **SIZE** Egg 3–6cm (h); arms 5–10cm, up to 18cm (h).
■ **HABITAT** Among leaf litter, on sawdust or wood chips, in flower-beds.
■ **RANGE** Inadvertently introduced into Europe and North America with exotic plant materials. Reported in California.

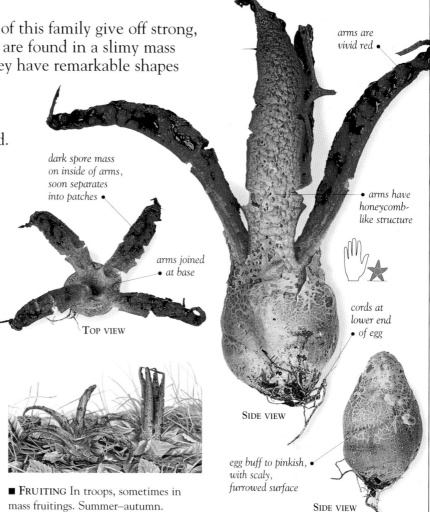

dark spore mass on inside of arms, soon separates into patches •

arms joined • at base

TOP VIEW

arms joined at tips at first, and • separate later

arms are vivid red •

• arms have honeycomb-like structure

cords at lower end • of egg

SIDE VIEW

egg buff to pinkish, • with scaly, furrowed surface

SIDE VIEW

■ **FRUITING** In troops, sometimes in mass fruitings. Summer–autumn.

spore mass on inner surface of spherical • cage

bright color and spongy • texture

• cords

latticelike cage shape just visible through the egg skin •

SIDE VIEW

• remains of the white or buff egg skin at base

SIDE VIEW

■ **FRUITING** In small groups or troops. All year round.

CLATHRUS RUBER

Red Cage Fungus

An unusual inedible fungus that immediately attracts attention. The obvious features of the mature fruitbodies are their striking red coloring and spherical, cagelike structure, which emerges from an egg. Inside, it is smeared with a putrid, olive-brown spore mass. About 17 species have been found worldwide, mostly in tropical climates. Some, like *C. ruber*, are red, while others are white.

■ **SPORE MASS** Olive-brown.
■ **SIZE** Egg 3–6cm (h); mature fruitbody up to 12cm (h) x 9cm (w).
■ **HABITAT** On leafy and woody litter, in gardens; likes warmer areas.
■ **RANGE** See *C. archeri* above; reported in southeastern US and California.

NIDULARIACEAE

CLASS: *Homobasidiomycetes*

The *Nidulariaceae* have a unique approach to propagation. Spores form within "eggs" and are released when the egg wall rots away or breaks down in an animal's gut. In *Cyathus* and *Crucibulum* species, the egg is catapulted out by the force of a falling raindrop and attaches itself to vegetation with a sticky thread.

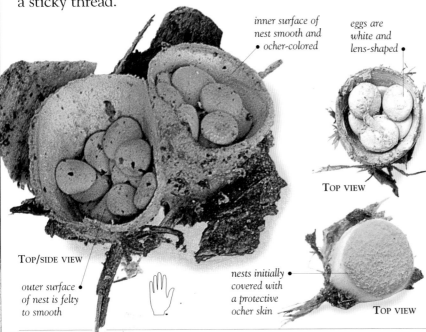

inner surface of nest smooth and ocher-colored •

eggs are white and lens-shaped •

TOP VIEW

TOP/SIDE VIEW

outer surface • of nest is felty to smooth

nests initially • covered with a protective ocher skin

TOP VIEW

CRUCIBULUM LAEVE

White-egg Bird's Nest

This, the only common species of *Crucibulum*, has cylindrical "nests," unlike the trumpet-shaped ones in the genus *Cyathus* (*see below*). Each egg is attached to the nest by a tiny cord. Immature nests are covered with a protective skin, and when this withers, the eggs are dispersed by drops of rain.

■ **SPORE COLOR** White.
■ **SIZE** Cups 0.5–1cm (h) x 0.5–0.8cm (w); eggs 0.15–0.2cm (w).
■ **HABITAT** In woods and gardens, on litter, mulch, and sawdust.
■ **RANGE** Widespread and fairly common in the north temperate zones.

■ **FRUITING** In troops, on decaying vegetation or wood. Autumn.

CYATHUS STRIATUS

Fluted Bird's Nest

Grooved striations running down the inside of the "nest" form the most distinctive feature of *C. striatus*. On the outside, the nests are covered in a brown fur, and when immature they are covered by a thin skin, which later breaks. The "eggs" are then dispersed by raindrops splashing into the cup and forcing them out. At the same time, a slimy thread is released, by which the eggs attach themselves to the vegetation. *C. olla* is similar, but has no striations and occurs mainly in open habitats.

■ **SPORE COLOR** White.
■ **SIZE** Cup 0.8–1.5cm (h) x 0.6–0.8cm (w); eggs 1–2mm (w).
■ **HABITAT** In woods, on half-buried deciduous sticks, often deep in litter.
■ **RANGE** Widespread and rather common in the north temperate zones from Alaska south to Mexico.

immature specimens have skin over • the nest

each nest is shaped like an inverted cone •

outside of nest is covered with a dark fur •

SIDE VIEW

pale gray • eggs are situated at bottom of nest

TOP VIEW

• nest is gray and striated on the inside

• eggs are attached to nest wall by thin, sticky cords

SECTION

■ **FRUITING** In clusters, on deciduous sticks. Throughout autumn.

GEASTRACEAE

CLASS: *Homobasidiomycetes*

In this small, distinctive family, the skin of the fruitbody splits and curves back in a star-shaped pattern, lifting up an inner, spore-containing ball. The ball contracts and expands when raindrops hit its surface, and this releases the spores through a tiny hole, occasionally multiple holes, at the top. Some *Geastrum* species curl up in dry weather and expand when it is wet, saving the spores for favorable conditions.

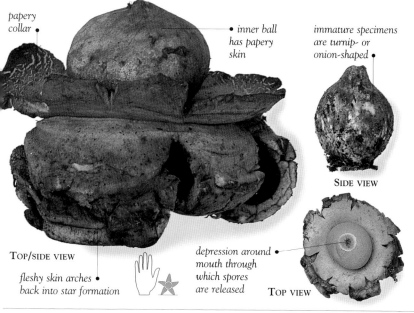

papery collar •

• inner ball has papery skin

immature specimens are turnip- or onion-shaped •

SIDE VIEW

TOP/SIDE VIEW

fleshy skin arches • back into star formation

depression around mouth through which spores are released

TOP VIEW

GEASTRUM TRIPLEX

Collared Earth Star

Perhaps the best known *Geastrum* species, this is certainly one of the most widely distributed. It is larger and fleshier than most of its close relatives, and the outer skin typically splits into two, producing a collar around the inner ball. The opening on top through which the spores are released is finely fibrous and defined by a faint, circular depression.

- ■ SPORE MASS Chocolate-brown.
- ■ SIZE Expanded fruitbody 4–12cm (w).
- ■ HABITAT In gardens and woods, on rich soil, mixed with litter.
- ■ RANGE Widespread and fairly common in warmer regions in the north temperate zones; almost cosmopolitan.

- ■ FRUITING In groups or fairy rings, on humus or rich soil. Autumn.

GEASTRUM FIMBRIATUM

Sessile Earth Star

This species, also known as *G. sessile*, is similar in some ways to a small version of *G. triplex* (see above). However, it lacks an inner collar, since the outer skin remains intact, and the unexpanded fruitbody is shaped more like a globe than an onion. The area around the mouth is less marked in *G. fimbriatum*. *G. rufescens* has a pink tinge and develops a tiny stalk on the inner ball when dry.

- ■ SPORE MASS Chocolate-brown.
- ■ SIZE Expanded fruitbody 2–6cm (w).
- ■ HABITAT Mostly on litter on calcareous soil, under both conifer and deciduous trees.
- ■ RANGE Widespread in the north temperate zones; widely distributed and common throughout eastern North America.

• inner ball pale gray to gray-buff in color

TOP/ SIDE VIEW

when compressed, papery inner ball releases • spores

outer skin • yellow-brown or pale brown

fully expanded • fruitbodies have 5 to 9 rays

SIDE VIEW

• mouth is fimbriate – edged with fine hairs

TOP VIEW

- ■ FRUITING In small groups or fairy rings on or among litter. Autumn.

GEASTRUM SCHMIDELII

Dwarf Earth Star

Apart from its small size and tendency to grow in open, grassy places, G. *schmidelii* is identified by the beaklike, furrowed, and striated mouth of the inner ball that holds the spores. It is also distinguished by the skin of the inner ball, which is smooth in this species.

■ **SPORE MASS** Chocolate-brown.
■ **SIZE** Expanded fruitbody 1.5–3.5cm (w).
■ **HABITAT** On calcareous sand in fields, dunes, or in open parts of coniferous forests.
■ **RANGE** Widespread and common throughout Europe and neighboring Asia; reported in southeastern and midwestern North America.

■ **FRUITING** In rings or a few together, often deep in sandy grass turf. Autumn.

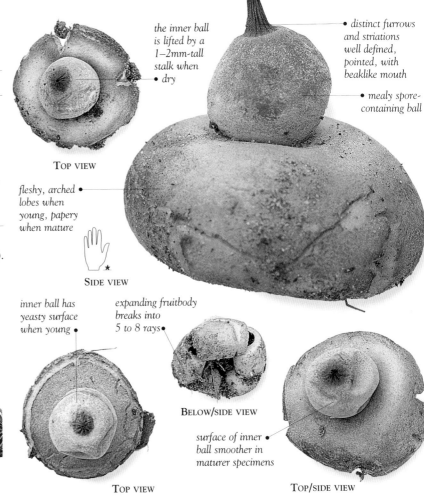

the inner ball is lifted by a 1–2mm-tall stalk when dry

TOP VIEW

distinct furrows and striations well defined, pointed, with beaklike mouth

mealy spore-containing ball

fleshy, arched lobes when young, papery when mature

SIDE VIEW

inner ball has yeasty surface when young

expanding fruitbody breaks into 5 to 8 rays

BELOW/SIDE VIEW

surface of inner ball smoother in maturer specimens

TOP VIEW

TOP/SIDE VIEW

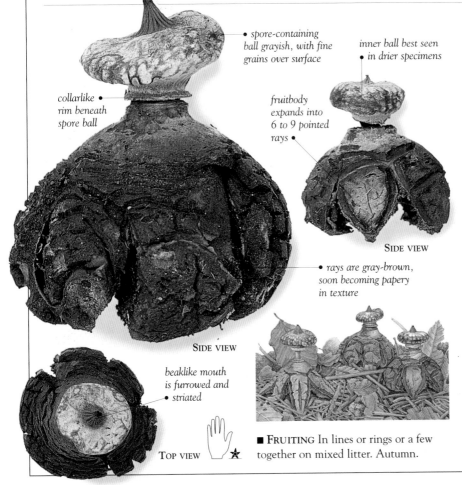

spore-containing ball grayish, with fine grains over surface

inner ball best seen in drier specimens

collarlike rim beneath spore ball

fruitbody expands into 6 to 9 pointed rays

SIDE VIEW

rays are gray-brown, soon becoming papery in texture

SIDE VIEW

beaklike mouth is furrowed and striated

TOP VIEW

■ **FRUITING** In lines or rings or a few together on mixed litter. Autumn.

GEASTRUM STRIATUM

Striated Earth Star

In this species, the inner, spore-ball is raised on a short stem. Inserted into a collarlike rim underneath the ball, the stem is seen clearly in dry specimens. The surface of the inner ball is grayish white and finely grainy. G. *pectinatum* is similar – it also has a furrowed, striated, and beaklike mouth and is larger than G. *schmidelii* (see above). It lacks the collar of G. *striatum*. It grows mainly under conifers. G. *berkeleyi* is another similar but rare species that can be identified by the sandpaper-like texture of the inner surface of the spore ball.

■ **SPORE MASS** Chocolate-brown.
■ **SIZE** Expanded fruitbody 3–6.5cm (w)
■ **HABITAT** On better soils, often under conifers in gardens, and also in mixed or conifer woods.
■ **RANGE** Widespread in Europe; world distribution uncertain.

LYCOPERDACEAE

CLASS: *Homobasidiomycetes*

All kinds of interesting folklore surrounds these distinctive, ball-shaped fungi, which release a cloud of brown spores when disturbed – but beware of getting them in your eyes, since they can cause an allergic reaction. The different genera can be distinguished by looking at microscopic characters and the way in which the skin layers of the fruitbodies either persist or rot away. All the species within this family are saprophytes, meaning that they obtain nutrients from dead plant matter.

CALVATIA UTRIFORMIS

Mosaic Puffball 🍄

Also known as C. *bovista*, this large *Calvatia* species is never taller than it is broad. Its fruitbodies are covered in coarse, yeasty scales, which are lost at maturity. Finally, the top skin rots away to reveal the chocolate-brown, powdery spore mass. The lower, sterile part changes from white to brown with age. It is unusual in having smooth spores. It is edible when very young and fresh, but not particularly tasty. There are various similar species, some of which have a lilac-tinted spore mass, as in C. *cyathiformis*, common in eastern North America. *Mycenastrum corium* is found in dry continental areas. It is big, thick-skinned, and splits into a starlike shape.

■ **SPORE MASS** Brown, but can be seen with or without olive tinges.
■ **SIZE** Fruitbody 5–10cm (h) x 5–15cm (w).
■ **HABITAT** Among grass, on roadsides, and in pastures.
■ **RANGE** Widespread in the north temperate zones; reported in eastern North America.

■ **FRUITING** Mostly in small groups in open habitats. Summer–autumn.

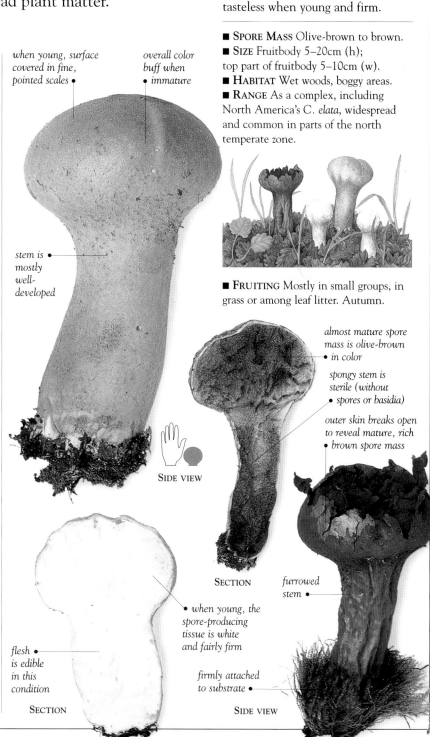

when young, surface covered in fine, pointed scales •

overall color buff when • immature

stem is • mostly well-developed

SIDE VIEW

flesh • is edible in this condition

SECTION

• when young, the spore-producing tissue is white and fairly firm

SECTION

CALVATIA EXCIPULIFORMIS

Pestle-shaped Puffball 🍄

Typical tall-stemmed specimens of this pestle-shaped *Calvatia* species are easy to identify. Those with short stems are similar to species of *Lycoperdon*, especially L. *molle*. Once mature, this species loses the skin that protects its spore-producing tissue, and the spores are then dispersed by wind and raindrops. The fruitbodies are edible, but tasteless when young and firm.

■ **SPORE MASS** Olive-brown to brown.
■ **SIZE** Fruitbody 5–20cm (h); top part of fruitbody 5–10cm (w).
■ **HABITAT** Wet woods, boggy areas.
■ **RANGE** As a complex, including North America's C. *elata*, widespread and common in parts of the north temperate zone.

■ **FRUITING** Mostly in small groups, in grass or among leaf litter. Autumn.

almost mature spore mass is olive-brown • in color

spongy stem is sterile (without • spores or basidia)

outer skin breaks open to reveal mature, rich • brown spore mass

SECTION

furrowed stem •

firmly attached to substrate •

SIDE VIEW

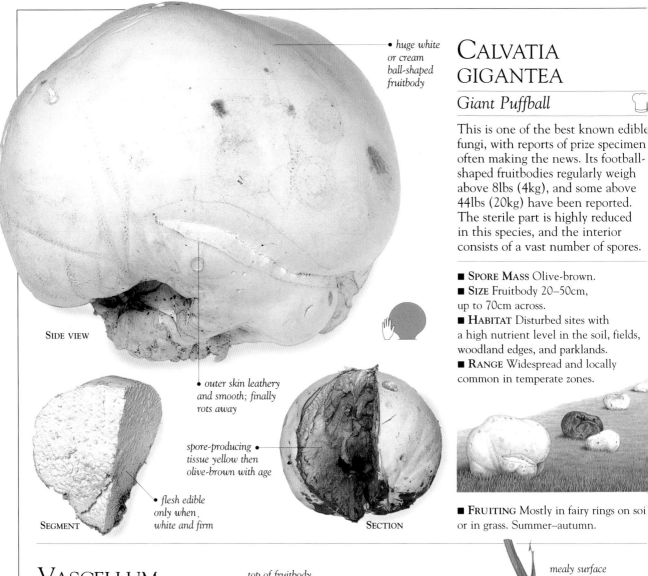

SIDE VIEW

• huge white
or cream
ball-shaped
fruitbody

• outer skin leathery
and smooth; finally
rots away

spore-producing •
tissue yellow then
olive-brown with age

• flesh edible
only when
white and firm

SEGMENT

SECTION

CALVATIA GIGANTEA

Giant Puffball

This is one of the best known edible
fungi, with reports of prize specimen
often making the news. Its football-
shaped fruitbodies regularly weigh
above 8lbs (4kg), and some above
44lbs (20kg) have been reported.
The sterile part is highly reduced
in this species, and the interior
consists of a vast number of spores.

■ **SPORE MASS** Olive-brown.
■ **SIZE** Fruitbody 20–50cm,
up to 70cm across.
■ **HABITAT** Disturbed sites with
a high nutrient level in the soil, fields,
woodland edges, and parklands.
■ **RANGE** Widespread and locally
common in temperate zones.

■ **FRUITING** Mostly in fairy rings on soil
or in grass. Summer–autumn.

VASCELLUM PRATENSE

Meadow Puffball

The uninitiated often find this
species difficult to identify. Its key
characteristic, a kind of membrane
that separates the fertile globe-
shaped part and the short, sterile
stem part, can be very difficult to
see. The globe usually has a rather
flattened top with a large opening,
through which the spores disperse
as a result of raindrops or other
pressure. The lower, sterile part
persists for a long period of time.
Firm, fresh specimens can be eaten.
Older fruitbodies are best avoided.

■ **SPORE MASS** Gray-olive–olive-brown.
■ **SIZE** Fruitbody 1.5–3.5cm (h)
x 2–4.5cm, up to 6cm (w).
■ **HABITAT** On soil and humus in grassy
areas such as lawns, open parks, golf
courses, and pastures.
■ **RANGE** Virtually cosmopolitan,
absent in lowland tropics.

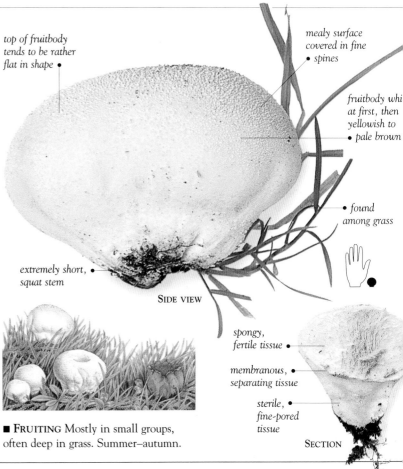

top of fruitbody
tends to be rather
flat in shape •

mealy surface
covered in fine
• spines

fruitbody whi
at first, then
yellowish to
• pale brown

• found
among grass

extremely short, •
squat stem

SIDE VIEW

spongy,
fertile tissue •

membranous, •
separating tissue

sterile, •
fine-pored
tissue

SECTION

■ **FRUITING** Mostly in small groups,
often deep in grass. Summer–autumn.

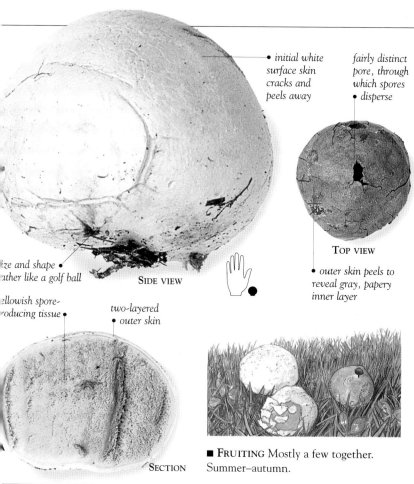

- initial white surface skin cracks and peels away

fairly distinct pore, through which spores disperse

TOP VIEW

- outer skin peels to reveal gray, papery inner layer

ze and shape ather like a golf ball

SIDE VIEW

ellowish spore-roducing tissue

two-layered outer skin

SECTION

■ **FRUITING** Mostly a few together. Summer–autumn.

BOVISTA PLUMBEA

Lead-gray Bovista

Bovista species do not have a sterile base, and the spores are blown out from a more or less distinct pore at the top. Before maturity, the outer skin peels off, like the shell of an egg, and it is the color of the inner layer that characterizes this species. The inner covering layer of *B. pila* is dark brown to bronze. The structure inside the ball is the same as the upper and inner part of *Lycoperdon* and *Calvatia* species. *Bovista* fungi often get detached at maturity, so spores are dispersed as the fruitbodies blow about. They are not of great culinary interest.

■ **SPORE MASS** Olive- to sepia-brown.
■ **SIZE** Fruitbody 1–3cm, sometimes up to 5cm across.
■ **HABITAT** Confined to grassland, especially dry grassland; tolerates fairly high fertilizer levels in the soil.
■ **RANGE** Cosmopolitan except for humid lowland tropics.

LYCOPERDON PYRIFORME

Stump Puffball

One of the easier *Lycoperdon* species to identify, field-marks include its elongated pear shape and grainy to smooth surface at maturity, white cords at the base, and its presence on woody substrates – unlike others in the genus. Often found in huge numbers on rotting wood.

SPORE MASS Olive-brown.
SIZE Fruitbody 1.5–6cm (h) 1–2.5cm (w).
HABITAT On rotten deciduous wood and, more rarely, conifers, in woods, open parks, and gardens.
RANGE Almost cosmopolitan, absent extreme climatic zones.

FRUITING Clustered on rotten wood. Autumn to winter.

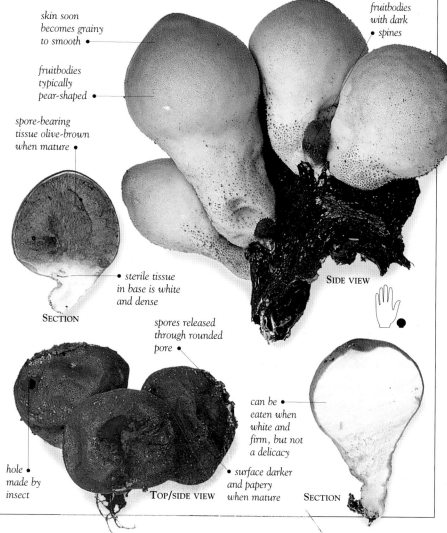

skin soon becomes grainy to smooth

fruitbodies typically pear-shaped

spore-bearing tissue olive-brown when mature

fruitbodies with dark spines

sterile tissue in base is white and dense

SECTION

SIDE VIEW

spores released through rounded pore

hole made by insect

TOP/SIDE VIEW

can be eaten when white and firm, but not a delicacy

surface darker and papery when mature

SECTION

LYCOPERDON ECHINATUM

Hedgehog Puffball

Long spines on its outer skin have given this fungus its common name. When these spines fall off, they leave a distinctive net pattern in their wake. The chocolate-brown spore mass is another diagnostic feature.

■ **SPORE MASS** Chocolate-brown, with more or less evident lilac tints.
■ **SIZE** Fruitbody 3–7cm, sometimes up to 10cm (h) x 1–3cm, sometimes up to 6cm (w).
■ **HABITAT** The eastern North American replacement species, *L. americanum*, occurs on humus in wooded areas.
■ **RANGE** Widespread in the warmer parts of Europe and nearby Asia.

■ **FRUITING** A few together, often among litter on ditch banks. Autumn.

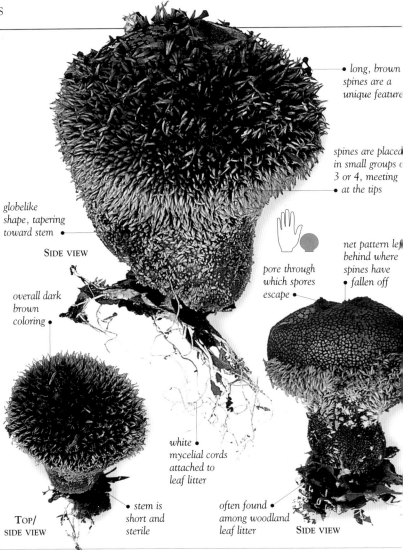

• long, brown spines are a unique feature

spines are placed in small groups of 3 or 4, meeting at the tips

net pattern left behind where spines have fallen off

pore through which spores escape •

globelike shape, tapering toward stem •

SIDE VIEW

overall dark brown coloring •

white • mycelial cords attached to leaf litter

often found • among woodland leaf litter

SIDE VIEW

TOP/ SIDE VIEW

• stem is short and sterile

• projection where central pore will form

spines • are lost with age

• spines are in groups: one large conical spine surrounded by smaller ones

SIDE VIEW

• mature specimens are not edible

• central pore

spongy spore-producing tissue darkens with age •

sterile stem • tissue is spongy but firm

SECTION

SIDE VIEW

SECTION

• stem tends to be well-developed

spore mass • brown and powdery when mature

■ **FRUITING** In dense groups and clusters, or occasionally singly. Autumn.

LYCOPERDON PERLATUM

Common Puffball

As with *L. echinatum* (see above), the much shorter, wartlike spines on this *Lycoperdon* species leave a regular pattern on the outer skin when they fall off. These spines extend over the typical, well-developed stem, but less densely. A central projection is situated where the spore-dispersing pore eventually forms. This small, white, terrestrial puffball, along with the densely clustered, wood-inhabiting *L. pyriforme* (see p.223), are the two most common species encountered across North America.

■ **SPORE MASS** Yellowish to olive-brown
■ **SIZE** Fruitbody 4–7cm, sometimes as little as 2cm and up to 9cm (h) x 2–4cm (w).
■ **HABITAT** On soil, mainly in woods but also found in grassland.
■ **RANGE** Widespread across the world, common in north temperate zones.

SCLERODERMATACEAE

CLASS: *Homobasidiomycetes*

Although seemingly similar to the *Lycoperdaceae* (*see pp.222–224*), these species rely on the wind to disperse their powderlike spore mass, which is blackish and metallic-smelling. They are further separated by forming mycorrhiza with trees. All species are poisonous.

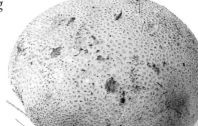

fruitbody looks somewhat like a potato

SCLERODERMA CITRINUM

Common Earth Ball 💀

This hard and scaly potato-sized fungus – with its thick skin and spores with interconnecting spines – is a familiar feature of damp woodland. The black, somewhat marbled interior is a distinctive feature, as is the strong, metallic smell. Take care not to confuse this poisonous species with the edible *Lycoperdon* species (*see p.222*) or *Tuber* species (*see p.34*).

yellowish skin has brown scales **TOP/SIDE VIEW**

very thick outer skin

firm, blackish spore-bearing tissue is powdery when mature

SECTION

- **SPORE MASS** Purplish black.
- **SIZE** Fruitbody 4–10cm, sometimes up to 15cm (w); skin 0.2–0.5cm thick.
- **HABITAT** Mycorrhizal with deciduous trees; in eastern N.A. sometimes found with *Boletus parasiticus*.
- **RANGE** Widespread and common in north temperate zones.

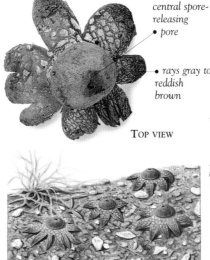

- **FRUITING** Often in clusters among moss. Summer–autumn.

SCLERODERMA VERRUCOSUM

Scaly Earth Ball 💀

The large size and scaly appearance, combined with a prominent, stem-like projection and thinnish skin, are the best field-marks of this species. At up to 1mm, the skin is much thinner than that of *S. citrinum* (*see left*) but similar to the skin of *S. areolatum* and *S. bovista*, which primarily differ microscopically.

- **SPORE MASS** Purple-black.
- **SIZE** Fruitbody 5–10cm, up to 12cm (h), including stem, x 2–5cm, up to 8cm (w).
- **HABITAT** Mycorrhizal with deciduous trees such as oak and beech, in woods and open parks.
- **RANGE** As a complex, widespread and common in eastern North America.

- **FRUITING** Mostly a few together or singly, often on bare soil. Autumn.

ASTRAEUS HYGROMETRICUS

Barometer Earth Star 💀

Bearing a strong similarity to some *Geastrum* species (*see pp.218–219*), *A. hygrometricus* has been compared to a barometer because of its amazing hygroscopic properties – it curls into a ball in dry weather and expands its rays in wet weather. The spores are released only by raindrops.

- **SPORE MASS** Brown.
- **SIZE** Expanded fruitbody 5–9cm (w).
- **HABITAT** Mycorrhizal, mostly in dry, open woods; prefers sandy soils.
- **RANGE** Virtually cosmopolitan but absent in cold temperate to arctic areas.

central spore-releasing pore

rays gray to reddish brown

TOP VIEW

inner ball has rough surface

TOP VIEW

whitish scales over surface of rays

- **FRUITING** In small groups. Autumn, but can be found in dry state all year.

COOKING WITH WILD MUSHROOMS

If your passion is indulging in the culinary delights of wild mushrooms, the following pages will explain how to find the best edible species and provide step-by-step advice on cleaning and preparing them. Mouth-watering recipes for a host of species are presented, plus advice on freezing and storing so that you can enjoy wild mushrooms all year.

HUNTING AND GATHERING
COLLECTING EDIBLE WILD MUSHROOMS

FORAYING IN WOODS, fields, and parklands is totally absorbing and, once experienced, you are sure to be hooked on finding mushrooms. Although luck plays a part, knowing which weather conditions are favorable for fruiting and being aware of the preferred habitats of the best edible species will greatly increase your chances of finding good specimens.

WHEN TO LOOK

Some species of fungi are present throughout the year, but the best time of year to hunt for edible mushrooms is spring, when a few species – notably the morels – appear, and from mid- or late summer throughout autumn to just before the first frosts. Autumn is the season traditionally associated with mushroom forays as the climate – warm weather followed by rain – provides the perfect humid environment for the underground mycelium to produce a flush of fruitbodies. Although rain is vital for mushroom growth, avoid collecting fungi in the rain or just after, since all fruitbodies absorb water; soggy fungi lack both texture and taste. The optimum time to go foraying is a day or two after rain, when the sun has come out again and warmed the earth. One way to be fairly sure that you do not pick a deadly or poisonous mushroom by mistake is to dig up the entire fungus, including the base, which may be under the ground. More fruitbodies will almost certainly appear in the same place after a few days. The mycelium can live for years; it is worth taking note of a good site so that you can return the following season. But be warned, the mycelium does not necessarily produce fruitbodies every season. Although frost signals the end of the hunting season, there are a few edible species, such as oyster mushrooms (*see p.78*), that thrive in winter.

EQUIPMENT TO TAKE

Before you go on a foray, gather up some basic equipment: an open-weave basket or trug, so that the mushrooms you collect can breathe; a small sharp knife, to give the fungi a preliminary cleaning and, if necessary, to cut the mushroom stems; and a stick to part the undergrowth. It is also useful to take a notepad and pen or pencil with you to jot down habitat details to help you identify species.

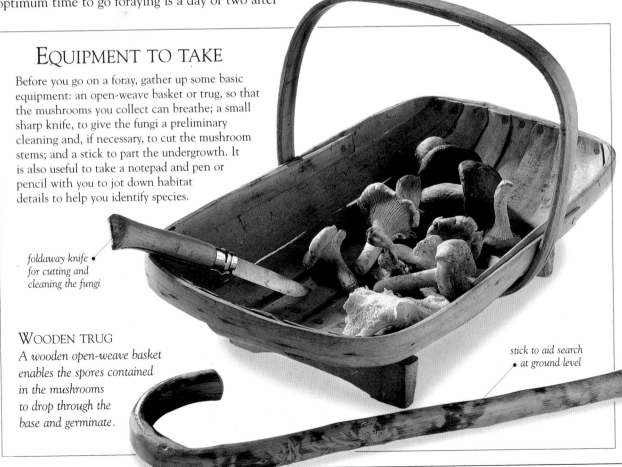

*foldaway knife •
for cutting and
cleaning the fungi*

WOODEN TRUG
*A wooden open-weave basket
enables the spores contained
in the mushrooms
to drop through the
base and germinate.*

*stick to aid search
• at ground level*

WHERE TO LOOK

Broadly speaking, most mushrooms grow in earth that is rich in humus, and in places that are not too marshy or covered with tall vegetation. Although most fungi prefer warm, damp places, there are exceptions, notably the field mushrooms that grow in open fields. Fruitbodies that appear in these places are easy to find, while roadside fungi require more effort to uncover because they are often hidden among plants. The same is true of forest fungi, which grow at ground level or up to or above head height.

BOLETE AMONG PINE
Bay boletes prefer growing under pine. As you search in the woods, look for clues such as pine cones.

CHICKEN-OF-THE-WOODS
An edible species that grows high in deciduous and conifer trees, such as yew. Its sulfur-yellow color is hard to miss.

FALLEN TREES AND LOGS
Watch for oyster mushrooms on fallen wood, where they grow quite visibly in large clusters.

KNOW YOUR TREES

Knowledge of the specific types of habitat and preferred substrate of the edible mushroom species, be it living or decaying wood, soil, or compost, will increase your chances of success on a foray. By familiarizing yourself with these details (*see Field Guide to Wild Mushrooms pp.22–225*) you can focus your search on likely looking places amid the most appropriate vegetation. The ability to tell the difference between deciduous trees, such as oak, maple, and ash, and conifers, like pine or larch, helps you recognize edible wild mushroom species, since several of these mushrooms form symbiotic relationships with just one specific tree, or with a few similar trees, in the forest.

OPEN-FIELD SITE
The football shape of puffballs makes them easy to spot in an open field.

GARDEN FINDS
The rich nutrient content of a compost heap is a popular site for wood blewit.

PICKING MUSHROOMS BY HAND
Identify your mushroom by viewing the base; then break stem at ground level.

CUTTING STUBBORN STEMS
Except for the boletes, dig up the entire mushroom with a sharp knife.

PICKING WILD MUSHROOMS

When you come across fungi on your foray, take time before picking to write down the details of their surroundings; this information will be invaluable for identification purposes and will act as reference for future forays. Note the trees and the soil type, and whether the place is shady and damp or open and sunny. Note whether the specimen is growing in isolation or whether it sits among a small cluster of other similar or different fruitbodies. If you find prize specimens in a specific location, look for some permanent landmark, such as a tree or rock. Write down specific directions so you can find that part of the woods or field again.

Back home, deal with your finds immediately. Until you are really experienced, take your fungi to an expert for identification. Even though only a handful of poisonous species are fatal, there are quite a few mildly toxic fungi, which will cause stomach upsets. Beginners should study the poisonous species very carefully (*see species entries marked with ☠, ☠ or ⌣) pp.22–225*). Avoid picking fungi that even vaguely resemble suspect species. If in doubt about what you have picked, throw it away.

FORAY CHECKLIST

At first it may be difficult to spot fungi in the landscape since the majority are small and their predominantly brown caps camouflage them well. When scanning a meadow or foraying in woods, it helps to crouch down on your hands and knees so that your eye is at soil level. It is amazing how once you've "tuned in," you will start to see fungi in the shadows under trees and shrubs and among grass and leaf litter. As you search, try to be methodical and keep your eyes open for clues, such as the scattered remains of fungi. Remember: just because a mushroom has been eaten by an animal does not mean that it is fit for human consumption – most animals have very different digestive systems from ours. Easy-to-spot mushrooms can also be used as pointers to less visible edible species. For example, the bright red toadstool, the fly agaric (*Amanita muscaria*), often grows in the same sites as edible boletes (*shown here*).

WHAT TO DO

1. Go on as many forays as possible to increase your general knowledge of edible and poisonous species.
2. Take a notebook and pen on forays and make a note of the places where you find the fungi, whether they are growing singly or in troops, note their smell, color and texture, and whether they bruise when pressed.
3. Pick only young, but not too young, fresh specimens and arrange them carefully in your basket or wrap each specimen separately in wax paper or a small paper bag.
4. Once home, spread out your fungi on a table. Sort them out according to species, size, and condition.
5. Refrigerate your finds as soon as possible after sorting and cleaning.

WHAT TO AVOID

1. Avoid picking any fungi that look slightly old, soggy, or eaten away by animals or insects.
2 Do not tear fungi from the ground or you will disturb the mycelium underground. This may disrupt formation of new fruitbodies.
3. Do not collect fungi in plastic bags; this provides an ideal environment for bacterial growth and increases the chance of food poisoning.
4. Do not put fungi that you cannot positively identify next to ones that you intend to eat.

RETURNING HOME

I used to be very daring and taste most species that I knew were not highly toxic. I've learned to be much more cautious since being ill after eating raw shaggy parasols. When you try wild mushrooms for the first time, always cook them and then eat only a small amount because you might be allergic to their proteins. Young children and the elderly are most susceptible and should eat only a few wild fungi. Some species, although edible, are bland or too thin-fleshed to be worth eating. Be choosy and, most importantly, be cautious.

SHAGGY PARASOLS
Shaggy parasols (Macrolepiota rhacodes) above left, can cause gastric upsets. Their woolly cap scales, shorter stems, and red-staining flesh will help you tell them apart from the parasol mushroom (M. procera), right, a good edible.

HUNTING IN WOODS
Take a stick to help you part the undergrowth. This way you can find fungi without having to scramble around. A map of the area will help you keep track of your whereabouts.

saffron milk cap •

• parasol

• wood blewit

THE BASKET
Ensure that only species you know to be edible sit side-by-side in the basket, preferably in one layer for ventilation.

• only fresh specimens should reach your basket

Preparing wild mushrooms
Cleaning and Preserving

To make sure your fungi remain in good condition, try to sort and clean them as soon as you reach home. First spread out your fungi on the table and carefully inspect each specimen, checking against the species information in this book. To be safe, throw away any mushrooms you cannot identify with certainty. Depending on the quality and quantity of each species you have collected, decide which ones you want to cook right away and which you would like to preserve by pickling, freezing, or drying, so that you can use fungi throughout the year.

Cleaning

All fungi need careful cleaning to remove dirt, but pay particular attention to those fruitbodies with folded, hollow heads where dirt becomes embedded, such as cauliflower fungus (*see p.51*) and morels (*see p.26*). Use a small piece of muslin or paper towel to wipe the cap and stem clean. If necessary, dampen the cloth to remove stubborn dirt. Avoid rinsing fungi under water because they tend to lose their flavor.

Step 1
Using a small sharp knife, carefully scrape dirt and debris off the length of the stem and then trim off the end.

Step 2
Take time to gently wipe the cap surface and stem with a piece of paper towel. Dampen to remove stubborn dirt.

◁ Step 1
Using a small sharp knife, cut off the stem. Slice the cap into neat ⅛ in/3mm vertical slices. Discard any slices that show signs of maggot infestation or do not feel firm to the touch.

Step 2 ▷
Inspect large stems to see if they are solid and fleshy. Discard any that are fibrous, woody, or hollow. Using a sharp knife, cut the fleshy stems into thin vertical slices, ⅛ in/3mm thick.

Slicing

After cleaning, it is a good idea to slice up the fruitbodies since some fungi are deceptive; on the outside they look sound, but when you cut into them, their flesh can be riddled with small maggot holes. Maggots begin by attacking the base of the stem and working outward. You may be able to save part of the cap; have a good look and decide. If small, cut the fungus vertically into thin slices. If large, detach the cap from the stem, and slice it vertically. If the large stem feels solid, slice it lengthwise, or discard it. On the whole, the cap is the best part to eat.

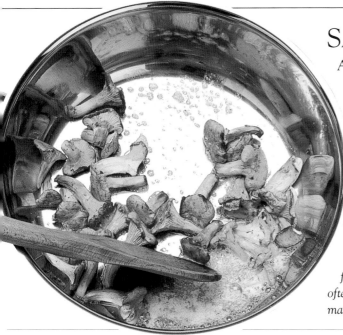

SAUTEING WILD MUSHROOMS

A quick and simple way to enhance the distinct flavor of certain fungi, such as chanterelles, is to sauté them in butter. (*See p.235 for other suitable fungi.*) If you cannot eat them right away, let them cool, and then put them into a clearly labeled airtight plastic container and place them in the deep freeze. Sauté them again before eating for best results.

HOW TO SAUTE CHANTERELLES
Heat a pat of butter and two tablespoons of olive oil in a skillet until hot. Add the whole or sliced fungi and fry quickly until no more watery liquid comes out. Stir often but not constantly with a wooden spoon. Sautéing makes the outside of the chanterelle slightly crisp.

BLANCHING

Some wild fungi need blanching (parboiling in salted water until almost tender) before being preserved. This rids them of any toxic properties that are present when raw and helps maintain their color and shape. It also prevents the thawed fungi from tasting "frostbitten." Saffron milk caps (*shown here*) need blanching before being pickled or frozen. (*See p.235 for other fungi that require this treatment.*)

STEP 1
Salt the water and bring it to a rolling boil. Plunge a few fungi at a time into the saucepan. Boil for 1 minute.

STEP 2
Retrieve the fungi with a slotted spoon and transfer onto paper towels to dry. Repeat this method for all the fungi.

STEP 2 ▷
Place a bay leaf on top of the fungi and pour on a mild, extra virgin olive oil. Fill the jar so that all the ingredients are immersed in oil. Seal the airtight jar and store in a cool, dark place.

◁ STEP 1
Clean and slice 1lb/450g wild fungi and cultivated button mushrooms. Boil the fungi in ½pt/300ml water with ½c/200ml wine vinegar for 8 minutes. Put half a cinnamon stick, 6 peppercorns, 2 cloves, 1 garlic clove and the fungi into an airtight jar.

PRESERVING IN OIL

Before the advent of freezers, the method of preserving fungi in oil or brine was very popular. Today it is not so common, although it is the process used industrially to produce the jars of bottled fungi you can buy in gourmet shops and delicatessens. The important step when bottling is to sterilize the jars, and to make sure the whole process is not interrupted. The only mushrooms worth considering for bottling are young specimens. I prefer to preserve fungi in olive oil rather than brine, which competes with the delicate and subtle flavor of the mushrooms.

FREEZING

All fungi freeze well, although they are best eaten within two months in order to enjoy their flavor. Boletes (*see pp.202–214*) and horse mushrooms (*see p.143*) freeze very well raw, while others need to be prepared beforehand by sautéing or blanching (*see p.233*). When freezing raw specimens, select small, firm fungi, clean and dry them well (*see p.232*). Use ordinary freezer bags. or airtight containers.

◁ FREEZING RAW FUNGI
To freeze raw boletes, place about six to eight small fungi in a freezer bag. Squeeze out all the air and seal. Freeze blanched mushrooms in the same way, but make sure that the specimens are bone dry before bagging the fungi to prevent them from icing up.

FREEZING SAUTEED MUSHROOMS ▷
Before freezing, sauté chanterelles (see p.47) and chicken-of-the-woods (see p.69) in butter (see p.233). Place in an airtight box and seal the lid.

FREEZING MIXED FUNGI

A clever way to keep fungi leftovers, for adding a concentrated mushroom flavor to sauces and soups, is to make what the French call *duxelles* – a finely chopped mushroom mix. To prepare *duxelles*, first sauté the fungi (*see p.233*) and then dice them in a food processor. Store the *duxelles* in the fridge for a two or three days, or spoon into trays and freeze.

◁ STEP 1
Sauté the fungi in plenty of unsalted butter – 2½oz/75g for each lb of fungi.

STEP 2 ▷
Process the sautéed fungi until they are the size of rice grains.

◁ STEP 3
Spoon into ice-cube trays and freeze. Two cubes will flavor any sauce or soup

DRYING

Drying wild fungi is a popular method of preserving and usually only takes a few days in a cool oven with the door ajar, or in a fruit dehydrator. Fungi are 90% water, so their weight loss when dried is considerable – 2lbs/1kg of fresh boletes produce only 3oz/100g of dried boletes – but the flavor is very concentrated. You must choose good specimens and clean them. Before cooking, reconstitute the fungi in hot water. Two tablespoons of dried boletes can flavor an entire dish (*see p.237 for recipe*).

DRYING SMALL FUNGI
To dry small fungi, such as horn of plenty (see p.48) or chanterelles (shown here), thread them onto string, making a knot between each piece so that they do not touch. Hang them up in a warm, well-ventilated place. When dry, store in airtight jars.

△ DRYING LARGE FUNGI
Clean and slice up the caps and stems (see p.232). Arrange them on a tray and dry them in a cool oven or use a food dehydrator.

WHICH COOKING METHOD WORKS BEST?

All edible wild fungi are best eaten freshly cooked after picking, but sometimes you simply cannot eat them right away. The following checklist covers some of the popular edibles you may find, and outlines the best method to use for preserving their flavors and textures in both the short- and long-term. Remember that many mushrooms, which are delicious cooked, can be acutely indigestible if eaten raw.

PERIGORD TRUFFLE ▷

◁ WHITE TRUFFLE

BLANCHED

Parasol (*Macrolepiota procera*)
Shaggy ink-cap (*Coprinus comatus*)
Saffron milk cap (*Lactarius deliciosus*)

△ PARASOL

FROZEN
(BLANCHED FIRST)

Hedgehog fungus
(*Hydnum repandum*)
Saffron milk caps
(*Lactarius deliciosus*)

SHAGGY INK-CAP ▷

◁ CHANTERELLE

SAUTEED

Chanterelle (*Cantharellus cibarius*)
Honey Fungus (*Armillaria mellea*)

◁ BAY BOLETE

FROZEN
(SAUTEED FIRST)

Chanterelle (*Cantharellus cibarius*)
Chicken-of-the-woods
(*Laetiporus sulphureus*)
Honey fungus (*Armillaria mellea*)

△ GIANT PUFFBALL

PICKLED IN OIL
OR VINEGAR

Morel (*Morchella esculenta*)
Boletes (*Boletus species*)
Giant puffball (*Calvatia gigantea*)

△ CHICKEN-OF-THE-WOODS

△ SAFFRON MILK CAP

MOREL ▷

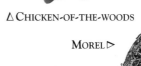

DRIED

Morel (*Morchella esculenta*)
Chanterelle (*Cantharellus cibarius*)
Bolete (*Boletus edulis* and *B. badius*)
Horn-of-plenty (*Cantharellus cornucopioides*)

△ HONEY FUNGUS

HORN OF PLENTY ▷

◁ KING BOLETE

Boletes

The wonderful taste, smell, texture, and appearance of boletes contribute to their reputation for being the most prized of edible wild fungi. Sautéed in extra virgin olive oil, garlic, and chopped parsley, their delicate flavor is brought to the fore. You can eat young boletes raw, thinly sliced, and drizzled with olive oil, lemon juice, and flakes of Parmesan.

Boletus badius
(see p.204)

Boletus edulis
(see p.202)

Crispy Bolete Caps

This simple recipe is my favorite way to cook bay boletes. Select large caps but make sure they are fresh specimens. Serves 2 as an appetizer or 4 as an accompaniment.

Ingredients

4 TBSP DRIED WHITE BREAD CRUMBS
3 TBSP CHOPPED FLAT-LEAF PARSLEY
1 GARLIC CLOVE, VERY FINELY CHOPPED
1 ANCHOVY FILLET, VERY FINELY CHOPPED
6 TBSP OLIVE OIL
FRESHLY GROUND BLACK PEPPER
4 LARGE BAY BOLETE CAPS
SALT, TO TASTE

Preparation

1 - Put the bread crumbs, parsley, garlic, and anchovy in a bowl. Add 3 tablespoons of olive oil and freshly ground black pepper. Let stand for about 1 hour. Preheat the oven to 350°F/180°C.

2 - Brush a roasting pan with some of the remaining olive oil. Wipe the bolete caps clean with damp paper towels and place them in the roasting pan, one next to the other, roundside down.

3 - Sprinkle a little salt over each cap, and put a tablespoon of the bread crumb and parsley mixture into each one. Spread the mixture evenly inside the cap and drizzle with olive oil.

4 - Bake in the oven for 35–40 minutes, or until crisp. Serve the caps warm. Tomatoes stuffed with the same mixture make a good accompaniment.

Alternatively Use

FIELD MUSHROOMS, pp.141, 240
HORSE MUSHROOMS, pp.143, 240

POTATO, CELERIAC, AND CEPE HATS

~

Fungi are a perfect match for both potato and celeriac. Here I have combined cèpes with these ingredients in an adaptation of a delicious pie recipe, originally devised by Caroline Liddell. Serves 2 as a main course.

INGREDIENTS

4 TBSP/60G UNSALTED BUTTER
1 SMALL ONION, VERY FINELY SLICED
10OZ/300G RED POTATOES
½LB/225G CELERIAC
SALT AND FRESHLY GROUND BLACK PEPPER
PINCH OF GRATED NUTMEG
2 TBSP FRESHLY GRATED PARMESAN
5OZ/150G CEPES, SLICED
1 TBSP CHOPPED PARSLEY
1 TBSP CHOPPED TARRAGON
¼LB/125G FROZEN PUFF PASTRY, THAWED

FOR THE GLAZE

1 EGG YOLK
1 TBSP MILK
¼ TSP SALT

PREPARATION

1 - Preheat the oven to 400°F/200°C. Put half the butter and all the onion in a skillet and cook for 10 minutes. Peel, wash, and dry the potatoes and celeriac. Slice them both into thin wafers.

2 - Add the potatoes and celeriac to the onion and sauté for 10 minutes. Turn the wafers from time to time to prevent them from sticking together. Season with salt, pepper, and grated nutmeg, and sprinkle with Parmesan.

3 - In a separate pan, melt the remaining butter and add the cèpes. Sauté over a high heat for 5 minutes and then add the herbs and seasoning. Mix the cèpes with the potato and celeriac and taste to check the seasoning. Set aside to cool while you prepare the pastry.

4 - Divide the pastry into 4 portions: two larger and two smaller. Roll out the smaller portions and cut into rounds. Place the pastry rounds on a greased baking sheet. Pile the vegetable mixture evenly in the middle of each round, leaving a border about 1¼in (2cm) wide around the edge. Make a glaze by mixing egg yolk, milk, and salt, and then brush this over the edges of the pastry.

5 - Roll out the larger portions of pastry and drape them over each mound. Shape the dough gently over the vegetable mixture with your hands. Seal the edges of the pie with the tines of a fork. Brush each pie with glaze and cut a steam hole in the top.

6 - Bake the pies in the oven for 15 minutes, turn the heat down to 325°F/150°C and continue baking for 10–15 minutes. Serve the pies hot, with a fresh green salad.

ALTERNATIVELY USE

FIELD MUSHROOMS MIXED WITH DRIED CEPES, pp.141, 232, 240

PARASOLS

Of the two parasol species, Macrolepiota procera *is best for cooking and has a flavor reminiscent of cèpes. The large cup-shaped cap of mature specimens is ideal for stuffing and then broiling, or for roasting.* Macrolepiota rhacodes, *the shaggy parasol, is less flavorful and can cause gastric upsets.*

MACROLEPIOTA
PROCERA
(see p.138)

STUFFED PARASOL CAPS

This recipe, more than any other for parasols, requires small, young caps that are firm and fresh and will not collapse during cooking. Serves 2 as an appetizer.

INGREDIENTS

1OZ/30G SMOKED HAM, THICKLY SLICED
4 TBSP GARDEN PEAS, COOKED
4 PARASOL CAPS, 2IN/5CM IN DIAMETER

FOR THE BECHAMEL SAUCE

1 TBSP/15G UNSALTED BUTTER
2 TBSP/15G FLOUR
½ CUP/125ML WHOLE MILK
GRATED NUTMEG
SALT AND FRESHLY GROUND BLACK PEPPER
1½ TBSP GRATED GRUYERE
1½ TBSP FRESHLY GRATED PARMESAN

PREPARATION

1 - Preheat the oven to 350°F/180°C. First make the béchamel sauce. Melt the butter in a saucepan, stir in the flour and cook for 1 minute, stirring constantly. Remove the pan from the heat and gradually add milk. When all the milk has been incorporated, return to the heat and bring slowly to a boil, stirring all the time for at least 5 minutes.

2 - Cook the béchamel sauce for 5 minutes longer, then let the sauce simmer gently for 10 minutes, stirring occasionally. Season the sauce with nutmeg and salt and freshly ground black pepper to taste. Stir in the Gruyère and Parmesan cheese.

3 - Mix the ham and the peas into the béchamel sauce. Taste to check the seasoning. Set the sauce aside to thicken, stirring occasionally to prevent a skin from forming on the surface.

4 - Wipe the caps clean with a damp paper towel. Even off the bottom of the caps with a knife so that you can stand them upright on a plate for filling. If you cut through the cap, cover the hole with the disk you sliced off, to prevent the béchamel sauce from leaking out.

5 - Cut out four 8in (20cm) square pieces of baking parchment or foil and lightly grease each one with butter. Spoon béchamel sauce into each cap and wrap each one in paper or foil. Place the bundles in a roasting pan and put them in the oven.

6 - Cook the bundles for 30–40 minutes, remove, and then allow them to cool a little. Serve two bundles on each plate, to be opened at the table.

MORELS

The morel, a tasty wild fungus that appears in spring, is highly valued, especially in France where it is combined with cream to make rich sauces. Its chambered head needs careful cleaning, and it is advisable to check the hollows for insects. This is a fungus that should always be cooked: never eat it raw. It dries well and, once reconstituted, even a small amount gives a full flavor.

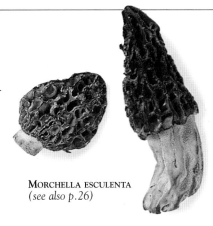

MORCHELLA ESCULENTA
(see also p.26)

MORELS WITH YELLOW PEPPERS

The mouth-watering taste of morels, which is on a par with boletes, makes them ideal candidates for a variety of recipes. In this earthy colored dish, they are combined with yellow peppers, whose flavor complements the richness of the fungi. Serves 2 as an accompaniment.

INGREDIENTS

10OZ/300G MORELS, SLICED VERTICALLY
1½OZ/40G PROSCIUTTO, CUT INTO THIN STRIPS
1 SHALLOT, VERY FINELY CHOPPED
4 TBSP EXTRA VIRGIN OLIVE OIL
SALT AND FRESHLY GROUND BLACK PEPPER
PINCH OF GRATED NUTMEG
½ CUP/120ML DRY WHITE WINE
½ YELLOW PEPPER, CUT INTO THIN STRIPS
1 TBSP CHOPPED FLAT-LEAF PARSLEY

ALTERNATIVELY USE

HORN OF PLENTY pp.48, 243
BOLETES pp.203, 204, 236

PREPARATION

1 - Clean the morels thoroughly, paying particular attention to hollows in the flesh. Cut each morel in half lengthwise.

2 - Put the ham and shallot in a saucepan and sauté in the oil for about 5 minutes, or until the shallot is soft. Add the morels and season with salt, pepper, and nutmeg. Sauté for 2 minutes, then pour over the white wine. Simmer gently for 5 minutes longer.

3 - Add the yellow pepper strips and continue cooking for about 5 minutes, until the peppers begin to soften but are still crisp. Check the seasoning and scatter chopped flat-leaf parsley over the dish. Serve immediately.

FIELD MUSHROOMS

Agaricus campestris is the wild species from which the widely cultivated open-cup mushroom derives. Small specimens can be eaten raw; others can be sautéed, used in duxelles, or in cream sauces. Agaricus arvensis – the horse mushroom – is similar in appearance but larger and has a stronger aniseed taste than A. campestris. The caps of this larger specimen are well suited to broiling and frying.

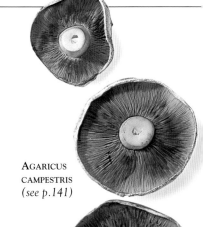

AGARICUS CAMPESTRIS *(see p.141)*

RADICCHIO LEAVES FILLED WITH FIELD MUSHROOMS

Of all the hundreds of ways to cook field mushrooms, this is my favorite. The purple radicchio leaves make a crisp, pretty container for the sautéed fungi. Serves 2 as an appetizer.

INGREDIENTS

1 LARGE RADICCHIO HEAD
9OZ/250G FIELD MUSHROOMS
4 TBSP EXTRA VIRGIN OLIVE OIL
3 TBSP CHOPPED FLAT-LEAF PARSLEY
2 ANCHOVY FILLETS, CHOPPED
1 GARLIC CLOVE, VERY FINELY CHOPPED
½ DRIED CHILI, SEEDED AND CHOPPED
SALT, TO TASTE
JUICE OF ½ LEMON
1 TSP TRUFFLE OIL (OPTIONAL)

PREPARATION

1 - Unfold four large leaves of radicchio. Wash and pat the leaves dry. Arrange two leaves on each plate. Clean the mushrooms thoroughly with damp paper towels and scrape off any earth and grit. Cut them into slices.

2 - Heat the olive oil in a skillet and add the parsley, anchovy, garlic, and chili. Cook for 1 minute or so, stirring frequently. When the mixture is sizzling, add the mushrooms and turn them over and over to coat with oil. Season with salt and continue to cook over high heat to evaporate any liquid.

3 - When the liquid has evaporated, the mushrooms are ready. Taste to check the seasoning. Spoon a quarter of the mixture into each radicchio leaf.

4 - You can either serve the dish warm or at room temperature. Before you bring it to the table, drizzle lemon juice over each portion, and truffle oil, if you have any. Serve with warm crusty bread.

ALTERNATIVELY USE

HORSE MUSHROOMS p.143
PARASOLS pp.138, 238

FIELD MUSHROOM FRITTATA

*This is a perfect omelet for a light supper or a picnic, when it is delicious served
cold, cut into diamond shapes for easy eating. Serves 1 as a main course.*

INGREDIENTS

½ CUP/10G DRIED CEPES
1 SLICE/15G WHITE BREAD, CRUST REMOVED
½ CUP MILK
½LB/120G FIELD MUSHROOMS
4 TBSP EXTRA VIRGIN OLIVE OIL
1 GARLIC CLOVE, VERY FINELY CHOPPED
SALT AND FRESHLY GROUND BLACK PEPPER
2 LARGE EGGS
1 TSP DRIED OREGANO
PINCH OF GRATED NUTMEG

PREPARATION

1 - Soak the dried cèpes in hot water for 30 minutes. Lift
them out with a slotted spoon, then rinse and dry them.

2 - Meanwhile, soak the bread in milk. Wipe the field
mushrooms and finely slice them. Heat 3 tablespoons
of the olive oil in a skillet. Toss in the garlic and
mushrooms and cook over low heat until the mushrooms
begin to release their liquid. Season with salt and pepper
and turn up the heat. Cook until some of the liquid has
evaporated, for 2–3 minutes.

3 - Squeeze the milk out of the soaking bread, and
crumble the bread with your fingers into the pan with
the mushrooms. Cook, stirring, for 1 minute, and then
transfer the mixture to a bowl. Let cool a little.

4 - Beat the eggs lightly to break them up and add to
the mushroom mixture. Sprinkle with oregano and
nutmeg and mix thoroughly.

5 - Heat the remaining oil in a skillet. Pour
the mushroom mixture into the pan and
cook over low heat for about 15–20
minutes, until all but the top surface
of the frittata sets. Turn on the
broiler, place the pan
underneath, and cook until
golden on top.

6 - Allow to cool a
little in the pan and
then gently loosen the
frittata at the edges of
the pan with a spatula.
Turn the frittata out,
upside down, onto a
board, then transfer
to a serving dish, right
side up. Serve warm or
at room temperature.

SAFFRON MILK CAP

The subtle nutty flavor of this popular edible species is best appreciated when the fungi are blanched just before cooking. This removes any trace of bitterness, which is especially common in older specimens. The superb salmon-pink coloring of saffron milk caps makes them an attractive ingredient in many savory dishes.

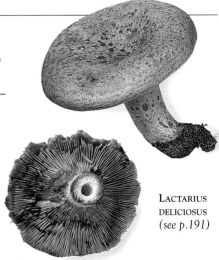

LACTARIUS
DELICIOSUS
(see p.191)

SAFFRON MILK CAPS WITH CREAM

This is a recipe given to me by a friend who lives in the northeastern part of Tuscany. I think it is one of the best recipes for saffron milk caps. It makes a good accompaniment to meat or an excellent sauce for pasta. Try also as a delicious topping for a toasted slice of country bread. Serves 2 as a light meal.

INGREDIENTS

½LB/225G SAFFRON MILK CAPS
2 TBSP EXTRA VIRGIN OLIVE OIL
1 GARLIC CLOVE, VERY THINLY SLICED
SALT AND FRESHLY GROUND BLACK PEPPER
½ CUP HEAVY CREAM
2 TBSP CHOPPED FLAT-LEAF PARSLEY

PREPARATION

1 - Blanch the saffron milk caps in boiling water. Drain and dry them, then cut into small pieces. Put in a pan and heat gently until the liquid has evaporated.

2 - Heat the olive oil with the garlic and add the fungi and seasoning. Cook gently for 30 minutes, then add the cream and cook for 15 minutes longer. Taste to check the seasoning. Mix in the parsley and serve. If serving on toasted bread, garnish with cherry tomatoes.

ALTERNATIVELY USE

CHANTERELLES pp.48, 244
HEDGEHOG FUNGI pp.53, 245

HORN OF PLENTY

Although a tasty fungus with a flavor similar to that of its prettier cousin, the chanterelle, the flesh of horn of plenty tends to be a bit tough. To counteract this, allow time for the fungus to simmer slowly in wine and stock, and, if necessary, slice the trumpet shapes into more manageable pieces.

CRATERELLUS CORNUCOPIOIDES
(see p.48)

SHRIMP, SCALLOP, AND FUNGI SAUCE

To make this sophisticated seafood sauce for pasta, let the fungi cook for at least 20 minutes until there is only a little liquor left in the pan. This will allow time for the tough flesh to soften and to release its full flavor. Serves 4 as a main course.

INGREDIENTS

½LB/225G HORN OF PLENTY
4 TBSP/60G UNSALTED BUTTER
2 TBSP EXTRA VIRGIN OLIVE OIL
3 TBSP CHOPPED PARSLEY
2 GARLIC CLOVES, BRUISED
SALT AND FRESHLY GROUND BLACK PEPPER
6 TBSP DRY WHITE WINE
½ CUP/120ML VEGETABLE STOCK
12OZ/350G PENNE
4 SCALLOPS
½LB/250G LARGE SHRIMP, SHELLED

PREPARATION

1 - Clean the horn of plenty and slice the larger trumpets in half. Put the butter, olive oil, half the parsley, and the garlic in a large skillet. When the garlic aroma begins to rise, remove and discard the garlic.

2 - Add the horn of plenty to the pan and cook gently for 5 minutes. Season with salt and black pepper and add a couple of tablespoons of wine. Continue to add the wine and then the vegetable stock gradually, over the heat, for 20 minutes or so. Remove from the heat.

3 - Cook the pasta until al dente in a large pan of salted boiling water. Meanwhile, wash the scallops and pat them dry. Cut into quarters.

4 - When the pasta is ready, drain and pour it into the skillet with the fungi. Add the scallops and the shrimp, and cook for 2 minutes, stirring constantly. Sprinkle with the remainder of the parsley and serve at once, straight from the pan.

ALTERNATIVELY USE

CHANTERELLES pp.48, 244
BOLETES pp.202, 204, 236

Chanterelles

The beautiful golden-yellow color of the chanterelle, which is retained in cooking, makes this one of the best fungi for decorative dishes. It can be eaten raw, but gentle cooking does its peppery flavor greater justice: chanterelles cooked in butter and served simply with scrambled eggs, pasta, rice, or meat dishes are mouthwatering.

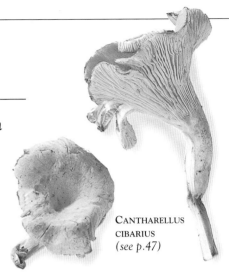

CANTHARELLUS
CIBARIUS
(see p.47)

Chanterelle and Mascarpone Sauce

The smoked flavor of the bacon in this recipe works well with chanterelles, and the mascarpone cheese brings sweetness and creaminess to this sauce, which goes particularly well with fresh tagliatelle. Serves 2 as a main course.

Ingredients

1 TBSP/15G UNSALTED BUTTER
1 SLICE SMOKED BACON,
CUT INTO MATCHSTICKS
2 TBSP CHOPPED SAGE
1 GARLIC CLOVE, FINELY CHOPPED
3½OZ/100G CHANTERELLES, ROUGHLY SLICED
SALT, TO TASTE
4 LEVEL TBSP MASCARPONE CHEESE
FRESHLY GROUND BLACK PEPPER

Preparation

1 - Melt the butter in a small skillet. Add the bacon and fry until it starts to crisp. Add the sage and garlic to the pan and sauté for 2 minutes.

2 - Mix in the chanterelles, season with salt, and sauté for 10 minutes, stirring frequently. Add the mascarpone and a grinding of black pepper and let it heat for a minute or so. Taste and check the seasoning before serving with tagliatelle. Serve immediately.

SCRAMBLED CHANTERELLES

6oz/175g chanterelles ◆ 3 tbsp/40g unsalted butter ◆ 1 tbsp olive oil ◆ 1 garlic clove, cut into 2 or 3 pieces ◆ 4 eggs ◆ salt ◆ 2 tbsp heavy cream ◆ 2 tbsp grated Parmesan ◆ freshly ground black pepper.

Clean the chanterelles thoroughly. Heat half the butter, oil, and garlic in a pan. Add the fungi and cook for 2 minutes, stirring often. Remove the garlic. Melt the remaining butter in another pan. Beat the eggs, season with salt, and add to the butter. Cook the eggs over low heat for 2 minutes, turning often. Add the cream and chanterelles. Continue cooking gently for a couple of minutes. Add the Parmesan and plenty of pepper. Serve on toast. Serves 2 as a light meal.

HEDGEHOG FUNGI

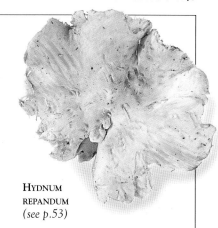

Easy to identify in the wild, hedgehog fungi have firm creamy white flesh that is best cooked slowly in casseroles and soups. Before cooking, it is a good idea to scrape off the spines on the underside of the cap, which taste bitter, and to blanch old specimens. When cooked, this species tastes similar to chanterelles, but it needs help to bring out its delicate flavor.

HYDNUM
REPANDUM
(see p.53)

HEDGEHOG BUNDLES
~

Anchovy, chili, and tomato paste enhance the subtle taste of the hedgehog fungi with superb results. Serves 2 as a main course.

INGREDIENTS

½ CUP/60ML EXTRA VIRGIN OLIVE OIL
1 TBSP CHOPPED FLAT-LEAF PARSLEY
½ DRIED CHILI, CHOPPED
1 GARLIC CLOVE, FINELY CHOPPED
2 ANCHOVY FILLETS, CHOPPED OR
1 SALTED ANCHOVY, CLEANED, RINSED, AND CHOPPED
1 TSP TOMATO PASTE
1 TBSP CHOPPED TOMATOES
9OZ/250G HEDGEHOG FUNGI, CHOPPED
SALT, TO TASTE
3½–5OZ/100–150G PHYLLO PASTRY

PREPARATION

1 - Preheat the oven to 375°F/190°C. Heat half the olive oil with the parsley, chili, and garlic in a pan for 2 minutes. Turn the heat to low and add the anchovy. Squash to a paste against the bottom of the pan and then mix in the tomato paste and the chopped tomatoes and cook for 1 minute. Add the fungi and salt to taste. Cook for 10 minutes. Taste and adjust the seasoning, then let cool.

2 - Cut the phyllo pastry into 16 rectangles 4 x 6in (10 x 15cm). Lay one rectangle on the board. Brush it with oil and then lay three more rectangles on top, brushing each one generously with oil. Repeat with the remaining pastry squares to make 4 piles.

3 - Divide the fungi mixture into 4 portions and spread over the top layer of each pile of phyllo pastry. Roll them up – jelly-roll fashion – tucking in the ends. Brush the top of each bundle with olive oil. Bake in the oven for 20 minutes. Serve at once garnished with parsley. Fennel braised in stock makes a good accompaniment.

ALTERNATIVELY USE
SAFFRON MILK CAPS pp.191, 242
CHANTERELLES pp.48, 244

MIXED FUNGI

More often than not, you will come home from your foray with an assortment of edible fungi rather than a basketful of one particular species. Here, I've devised some wild mushroom recipes to make the most of this mixed bag. The variety of tastes and textures adds greatly to the flavor of soups and stews.

ARMILLARIA
MELLEA
(see p.98)

BOLETUS EDULI
(see p.202)

BAKED MUSHROOM POLENTA

This rich warming winter dish is cleverly transformed into a gourmet delight by the addition of truffle paste. Serves 4–6 as a main course.

MACROLEPIOTA
PROCERA *(see p.138)*

INGREDIENTS

3 CUPS/400G COARSE-GROUND YELLOW CORNMEAL
SALT AND FRESHLY GROUND BLACK PEPPER
4 TBSP/60G UNSALTED BUTTER, PLUS EXTRA FOR GREASING
1LB/450G MIXED FUNGI, CLEANED AND SLICED
¼ CUP/60G FLOUR, PREFERABLY ITALIAN
3⅓ CUPS/750ML WHOLE MILK
1 TBSP TRUFFLE PASTE
¼LB/120G ITALIAN FONTINA, CUT INTO THIN SLICES
¼LB/120G GRUYERE, CUT INTO THIN SLICES
½ CUP/60G FRESHLY GRATED PARMESAN

PREPARATION

1 - Preheat the oven to 400°F/200°C. Put 1½ quarts (1½ liters) of hot water in a large saucepan. Add the ground cornmeal and 1 teaspoon of salt, stirring constantly. Bring to a boil, stirring. Cook for 5 minutes, then spoon the mixture into a buttered shallow oven dish. Cover with buttered foil and bake for 1 hour. Let the polenta cool for at least 2 hours before cutting it lengthwise with a sharp knife into ½in (1.25cm) wide slices.

2 - Meanwhile, prepare the fungi sauce. Melt the butter in a heavy pan, add the cleaned, sliced fungi, and sauté for 10 minutes, reserving a few sautéed slices for the top. Stir in the flour and cook for about 1 minute, stirring continuously. Remove from the heat and then gradually incorporate the milk. Add salt and pepper. Return to the heat and simmer.

3 - Place the saucepan in a larger pan half filled with hot water and continue cooking the sauce gently for 15 minutes. Mix in the truffle paste and check the seasoning.

4 - Lightly butter a 10 in (25cm) long rectangular ovenproof dish. Spread 2 tablespoons of the sauce over the bottom. Cover with slices of cold polenta followed by slices of Fontina and Gruyère cheese. Sprinkle with Parmesan and freshly ground black pepper. Repeat these layers, finishing with the sauce. Scatter the dish with the remaining sautéed fungi. Preheat oven again, and bake for about 30 minutes. Remove from the oven at least 5 minutes before serving.

Filets Mignons in a Fungi Sauce

Use all kinds of fungi for this sauce and, if necessary, buy some cultivated ones. Serves 4 as a main course.

Ingredients

2 tbsp olive oil

2 tbsp/30g unsalted butter

2 shallots, very finely chopped

3 tsp Dijon mustard

2 tsp tomato paste

½lb/225g mixed fungi, coarsely chopped

salt and freshly ground black pepper

1 tbsp lemon juice

2 tbsp dry Marsala or Sherry

6 tbsp red wine

4 filets mignons weighing 5oz/150g each

4 slices smoked bacon

1½ cups/300ml meat stock

3 tbsp flat-leaf parsley, chopped

Mushroom Risotto Sauce

2 shallots, finely sliced ◆ 4 tbsp extra virgin olive oil ◆ 1 tbsp/15g butter ◆ 1 garlic clove, finely chopped ◆ salt and freshly ground black pepper ◆ 1lb/450g mixed wild mushrooms, sliced ◆ 2 tbsp chopped parsley

Sauté the shallots in a large sauté pan in olive oil and butter until soft. Add the garlic, a pinch of salt, and plenty of freshly ground black pepper. Cook, stirring constantly, for 1 minute, then add the mixed fungi and half the parsley. Cook over high heat for 5 minutes, turning the mushrooms over until only a little liquid remains. Sprinkle with the remaining parsley and serve the fungi on risotto (see p.250 for a risotto recipe) instead of the white truffle.

Preparation

1 - Preheat the oven to 400°F/200°C. Heat the olive oil, butter, and shallots in a sauté pan, large enough to hold the steaks in a single layer. When the shallots are soft and golden, stir in the mustard and the tomato paste. Cook for 1 minute, then add and mix in the fungi, the lemon juice, and the seasoning. Cook for 2 minutes, stirring frequently.

2 - Add the Marsala and wine to the pan, then pour in the meat stock. Simmer for about 20 minutes. While the sauce is cooking, season the steaks well and wrap a slice of bacon around each piece of meat. Place the prepared steaks in a roasting pan and bake in the oven for 8 minutes.

3 - When the sauce is ready, add the steaks and cook the meat – 2 minutes for rare, longer for medium – turning twice. Taste and adjust the seasoning, sprinkle with flat-leaf parsley, and serve at once.

MIXED FUNGI SOUP

5 tbsp/75g unsalted butter ◆ 1 medium onion, finely
chopped ◆ 1 garlic clove, finely chopped ◆ ½ cup flat-leaf
parsley chopped ◆ 8oz/225g wild fungi, diced
◆ 4 tbsp milk ◆ salt ◆ grated nutmeg ◆ ⅓ cup/40g flour
◆ 3⅓ cups/1.2 liters vegetable or chicken stock ◆ freshly
ground black pepper ◆ 4 tbsp sour cream

Heat half the butter with the onion, garlic, and parsley
in a sauté pan and sauté for
3 minutes. Add the fungi and
sauté for 5 minutes more.
Add the milk and season
with salt and nutmeg.
Cook for a few more
minutes, then set the
pan to one side. In
another saucepan, melt
the remaining butter.
Remove the pan from the
heat and beat in the flour.
Return the pan to low heat and
cook until the mixture turns a darker color. Remove the
pan from the heat once more and add the stock gradually
by the ladleful. Stir constantly to avoid lumps forming,
and return the pan to low heat. When all the stock has
been added, add the fungi and their juices. Bring to a boil
and boil for 20 minutes. Season with salt and pepper to
taste. Pour into bowls and top with a tablespoon of sour
cream. Serves 4 as
an appetizer.

CHICKEN IN A MIXED FUNGI SAUCE

Supplement this wonderfully creamy sauce for chicken
with cultivated mushrooms mixed with about 30g/
½ cup of dried cèpes to strengthen the flavor.
Serves 2 as a main course.

INGREDIENTS

2 CHICKEN BREASTS, SKINNED AND BONED
SALT AND FRESHLY GROUND BLACK PEPPER
2 TBSP OLIVE OIL
3 TBSP/40G UNSALTED BUTTER
2 SHALLOTS, FINELY CHOPPED
5 TBSP DRY WHITE WINE
7OZ/200G MIXED FUNGI
1 GARLIC CLOVE, VERY FINELY CHOPPED
VEGETABLE STOCK
⅔ CUP/150ML HEAVY CREAM

PREPARATION

1 - Cut the chicken breasts in half and season with salt
and pepper. Heat 1 tablespoon of olive oil and half the
butter in a sauté pan, add the chicken halves, and
brown on both sides. Add the shallots and continue
cooking until soft. Add the wine, boil briskly, then turn
the heat down and cover the pan. Cook for 15
minutes, turning the chicken pieces once.

2 - While the chicken is cooking, clean
and coarsely chop the fungi. Heat the rest
of the butter and oil with the garlic in
a skillet. Add the fungi and cook the
mixture for 5 minutes, stirring
frequently. Season with salt and
pepper and continue cooking for
15 minutes over low heat. Add a
small amount of vegetable stock
to the pan to prevent the fungi
from cooking dry. Pour in the
cream, mixing well, and gently
bring the sauce to a boil.

3 - Transfer the sauce to the pan
with the chicken, scraping up all the
juices. Taste, adjust the seasoning,
and cook for 5 minutes to blend the
flavors. Transfer to a heated dish and
serve. Zucchini is a good vegetable
accompaniment for this dish.

BAKED RED MULLET AND MIXED FUNGI

Red mullet is one of the most delicious and attractive fish. The flesh is white, delicate, and yet full of flavor, complementing the deep earthy taste of wild fungi. Serves 2 as a main course.

INGREDIENTS

4 TBSP CHOPPED FLAT-LEAF PARSLEY

2 GARLIC CLOVES, FINELY CHOPPED

4 ANCHOVY FILLETS, CHOPPED

½–1 DRIED CHILI, SEEDED AND CHOPPED

2 TBSP CAPERS

SALT AND FRESHLY GROUND BLACK PEPPER

½ CUP/100ML EXTRA VIRGIN OLIVE OIL

9OZ/250G MIXED FUNGI, SLICED OR WHOLE

1 CUP/40G FRESH WHITE BREAD CRUMBS

2 RED MULLET

JUICE OF 1 LEMON

PREPARATION

1 - Preheat the oven to 375°F/190°C. Mix together the parsley, garlic, anchovy, chili, and capers in a bowl. Season with salt and pepper.

2 - Stir in about half the olive oil. Mix in the cleaned fungi, coating them with the mixture.

3 - Choose a shallow oven dish large enough for both fish to lie flat, surrounded by fungi. Grease the dish with some of the remaining oil.

4 - Pile the fungi into the dish and sprinkle all over with bread crumbs. Drizzle with a little olive oil and bake in the oven for about 20 minutes.

5 - While the fungi are cooking, wipe the red mullet and season inside and out with salt and freshly ground black pepper. Coat with some of the remaining olive oil and pour a little oil inside each fish.

6 - Take the fungi out of the oven. Push the fungi to the sides of the dish and lay the fish in the center. Drizzle any remaining olive oil over them. Bake for 10–15 minutes, or until the flesh comes away easily from the bone. Sprinkle with lemon juice and serve.

TRUFFLES

The peculiarly distinct flavor of these strictly seasonal fungi is considered a great delicacy, because they are difficult to cultivate and preserve. The white truffle from Alba is best eaten raw and thinly sliced on risotto, a plate of tagliatelle, or cooked eggs. The black Périgord truffle from France, however, is cooked gently to enrich its flavor. The other well-known species, the summer truffle, is also white but has a much milder taste.

TUBER MELANOSPORUM
(see p.34)

TUBER MAGNATUM
(see p.34)

RISOTTO WITH WHITE TRUFFLE

In my opinion, this simple dish is perfection. The subtle delicacy of a plain risotto is the ideal foil to the indescribable flavor of finely sliced Italian white truffle. Serves 4–6 as a main course.

INGREDIENTS

3 CUPS/1.2 LITERS LIGHT MEAT STOCK
2 SHALLOTS OR 1 SMALL ONION
4 TBSP/60G UNSALTED BUTTER
2½ CUPS/300G ITALIAN RICE, PREFERABLY CARNAROLI
1 WHITE TRUFFLE, ABOUT 2OZ/50G
⅓ CUP/40G FRESHLY GRATED PARMESAN

PREPARATION

1 - Bring the stock to a gentle simmer. Meanwhile, chop the shallots or onion fine and put them in a heavy pan with half the butter. Sauté until translucent and soft.

2 - Add the rice to the shallots and stir until it is well coated with butter. Sauté, stirring constantly with a wooden spoon, until the outside of the grains become translucent and the rice begins to stick to the bottom of the pan.

3 - Pour over about 1 cup/200ml of stock. Let the rice absorb the liquid and then add another ladleful of stock. Continue to add stock gradually, in small quantities, so that the rice always cooks in liquid. Stir frequently. The heat should be moderate to keep the rice at a lively simmer. If you run out of stock before the rice is cooked, add boiling water.

4 - While the rice is cooking, brush the truffle free of any surface grit and dirt. When the rice is cooked – Carnaroli rice takes about 18 minutes from when you add the stock – remove the pan from the heat. Add the remaining butter cut into small pieces and the grated Parmesan. Put the lid firmly on the pan. Leave for 1 minute, until the butter and the Parmesan have melted, and then stir the risotto vigorously.

5 - Transfer the risotto to a heated dish and bring to the table with the cleaned truffle. Cut the truffle into thin slices directly onto the rice. If you don't have a truffle slicer, use any other vegetable slicer or peeler.

SPAGHETTI WITH BLACK TRUFFLES

A recipe from Umbria in central Italy where black truffles, similar to the Périgord truffle, are found. In this robust pasta dish, garlic and chili enhance the flavor of the truffle. Serves 4 as a main course.

INGREDIENTS

2OZ/60G BLACK TRUFFLES
4 TBSP EXTRA VIRGIN OLIVE OIL
3 GARLIC CLOVES, PEELED AND BRUISED
1 DRIED CHILI
2 TBSP CHOPPED FLAT-LEAF PARSLEY
12OZ/340G ITALIAN SPAGHETTI
SALT, TO TASTE

PREPARATION

1 - Gently scrub the fresh truffles, then wipe them clean with a damp cloth. Grate the truffles on the fine blade of a grater or slice them into tiny slivers.

2 - Put the olive oil, garlic, chili, and parsley in a large heavy skillet. Heat slowly, stirring frequently, until the garlic begins to color. Remove and discard the garlic and chili.

3 - Turn the heat down to low and add the truffle slivers to the skillet. Heat very gently for 1 minute, stirring constantly. The truffles should only become hot; they should not cook.

4 - Meanwhile, cook the pasta in plenty of salted boiling water. Drain, then turn the pasta into the skillet. Cook over low heat for about 1 minute, turning the spaghetti over and over to coat with the olive oil. Serve immediately, straight from the pan.

TRUFFLE PRESERVES

Truffles cannot be preserved satisfactorily in their natural state. However, if you wish to add their distinct flavor to dishes out of season, there are two good products available at delicatessens. Truffle paste is a concentrated mix of minced truffles and cèpes in butter or vegetable fat. It is well-suited to pasta sauces and risottos. Truffle oil is olive oil flavored with truffle. Perfect for dressing salads, it can also be used for broiling meat.

TRUFFLE
PASTE

TRUFFLE
OIL

INDEX

ACKNOWLEDGMENTS

All photographs by Neil Fletcher except Peter Anderson p1, p4t, p230tl, p230tr, p231tl, p231tc, p231b; Harley Barnhart p49tr, p121br, p145bl; KS Barnhart p131bl, p140bl, p145bc, p156tr, p205bc; The Anthony Blake Photo Library p226–227; Biofotos (Heather Angel) p6bl, p58bl, p229tr, p229bl, p229br; Peter Chadwick p229tl; Francisco Calonge p78br; Bruce Coleman Picture Agency (Hans Reinhard) p2; Gordon Dickson p126bl, p206bc, p209br; Phillip Dowell p6cr; S Elborne p114tr, p225tr; Ernest E Emmett p118bl; Emily J Johnson p206bl, p214bl; Nick Legon p123bl; Thomas Læssøe p27br, p35tr, p54l, p63br, p65r, p72br, p76bl, p92tr, p93bl, p94br, p98bc, p125tr, p135bl, p135br, p138tl, p148br, p153br, p167br, p173bl, p186bl, p221bl, p229cr; Gary Lincoff p139bl, p157tr; Diana Miller p5br, p228, p230br, p235bl, p235br, p236, p237, p238, p239, p240, p241, p242, p243, p244, p245, p246, p247, p248, p249, p250, p251; Jens H. Petersen p52tr, p182rl, p196bl; Alan R Outen p47bl, p98br, p124br, p202bl, p215br;

Erik Rald p137br, 205br; Tim Ridley p6tcl; Joy Spurr p229cl; The Science Photo Library p6c (Andrew McClenaghan); Jan Vesterholt p50tr, p70bl, p83br, p98bl, p122tl, p141bl, p149br, p165bl, p166tr, p170tr, p175tl, p185bl, p188tr, p203br, p204tr, p205bl, p206br, 211bl, p214bc; Matthew Ward p12tl, p12tr, p13b, p222t, p232, p233t, p233cl, p233cr, p234

Illustrations by Pauline Bayne, Evelyn Binns, Angela Hargreaves, Christine Hart-Davies, Sarah Kensington, Vanessa Luff, David More, Leighton Moses, Sue Oldfield, Liz Pepperell, Valerie Price, Sallie Reason, Elizabeth Rice, Michelle Ross, Helen Senior, Gill Tomblin, Barbara Walker, Debra Woodward. Illustrations on p7, p8, p26 and p43 by Liz Pepperell.

The author would like to thank collectors, photographers, illustrators and editors for all their hard work and a very special thanks to former colleagues at the Royal Botanic Gardens, Kew, and especially to Alick

Henrici for all the hard work he put into constructive criticism.

Dorling Kindersley would like to thank: Jenny Speller for additional illustration research; Peter Holland for mycological books; Hilary Bird for the index; Ann Kay for editorial assistance; Fiona Wild for proofreading; Mark Bracey for computer support. Special thanks to: Caroline Liddel; Martin Lewy of Mycologue, Richmond Antiques, and The Kitchenware Company.

Neil Fletcher would like to extend warm thanks to Joyce Pitt and Jo Weightman for their tireless labors in locating and identifying specimens, and to his assistant Paul Copsey for his stocism under duress.

DK Publishing, Inc. would like to thank Nancy Cole, Otis Cole, Joan Whitman, and Michael T. Wise for their many hours of hard work. Special thanks to Miss Phoebe Todd-Naylor for her enduring patience.